Daytrips
SWITZERLAND

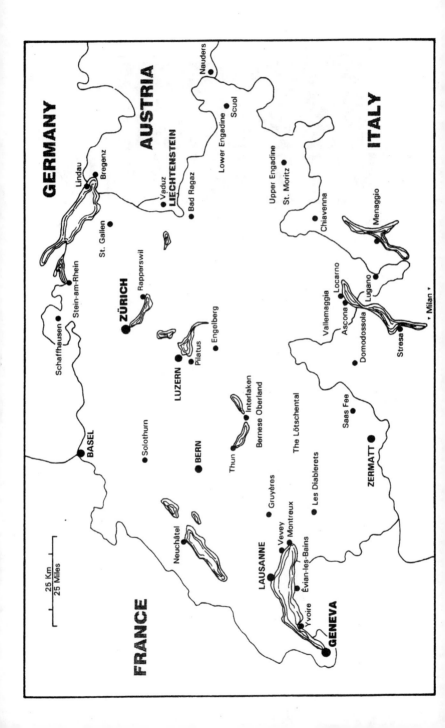

Daytrips
SWITZERLAND

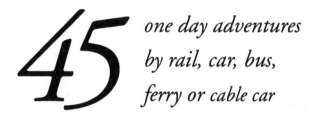

*one day adventures
by rail, car, bus,
ferry or cable car*

NORMAN P.T. RENOUF

HASTINGS HOUSE
Book Publishers
Norwalk, Connecticut

For Kathy:
Without who neither this, or anything else would be possible;
ALWAYS.
And for Carrie and Phil:
Dedicated, loving parents, whose friendship becomes stronger with each passing year.

While every effort has been made to insure accuracy, neither the author nor the publisher assume legal responsibility for any consequences arising from the use of this book or the information it contains.

Edited by Earl Steinbicker, creator of the DAYTRIPS series.

ISBN: 0-8038-9414-7

Printed in the United States of America

10 9 8 7 6 5 4 3 2 1

COMMENTS? IDEAS?

We'd love to hear from you. Ideas from our readers have resulted in many improvements in the past, and will continue to do so. And, if your suggestions are used, we'll gladly send you a complimentary copy of any book in the series. Please send your thoughts on to Hastings House, Book Publishers, 9 Mott Ave., Norwalk CT 06050, or fax us at (203) 838–4084, or E-mail to info@upub.com.

Contents

6   CONTENTS

Introduction

Those tourists not going to Switzerland for the skiing are almost certainly enticed there by its unparalleled Alpine scenery and the anticipation of ascending those peaks by way of dramatic cable car rides. In fact, cable cars make up only a portion of what visitors will find to be an innovative and fascinating array of transportation used to reach the heights. They will also discover numerous beautiful lakes that may be traversed by old-fashioned steamers; one of which may be explored by submarine.

The cities hold a wealth of pleasant surprises, as well. Even the largest of these would not be considered big by international standards, but they are diverse in character, with many built around an historically interesting and charming medieval core. Though some have described Switzerland as being dull, that is a matter of perspective. Certainly, you will not find the rowdy night life prevalent in places such as London or Barcelona. But, even Zürich—a city with a worldwide reputation as a conservative banking center, is, in fact, a bustling cosmopolitan city whose streets come alive on weekends and holidays. In the countryside, though, things are much quieter. The evening meal is taken fairly early, and most retire to bed not much later. But, after a day out in the fresh air exploring the mountains, you will be ready for a hearty meal and a good night's sleep.

The standards of cuisine and wine in Switzerland may come as a surprise to first-time visitors. An array of outstanding restaurants serve an unusually wide selection of gourmet cuisine presented in a most beautiful manner. Don't be hesitant in ordering Swiss wine either. Although not widely known outside of the country, it is very enjoyable indeed.

Switzerland is renowned for its cleanliness—a reputation that is well deserved. Everywhere you go you will find things spotless. In fact, unlike most countries, the public toilets (almost without exception) are impeccably clean—even in the middle of the mountains!

Switzerland also has a reputation as an extremely expensive country, and it would be unfair not to confirm this. There really is no viable way to have an inexpensive vacation in this country. But you get what you pay for. And what you get in Switzerland is a combination of hotels and restaurants, and a public transportation system, that are of the highest standards in the world, with service to match.

Daytrips have many advantages over the usual point-to-point touring, especially for short-term visitors. You can sample a far greater range in the same time by seeing only those places that really interest you instead of "doing" the region town by town. This approach facilitates taking in a more varied diet of sights, and allows you to reexamine your options on a day-by-day basis. Daytrips are also ideal for business travelers with a free day or so interspersed between meetings.

The benefits of staying in one hotel for a while are obvious. Longer-term rates are often more economical than overnight stays, especially in conjunction with airline package plans. You also gain a sense of place, of having established a temporary home-away-from-home in a city where you can get to know the restaurants and enjoy the nightlife. Your luggage remains in one place while you go out on carefree daytrips. There is no need to preplan every moment of your vacation since with daytrips you are always free to venture wherever you please. The operative word here is flexibility, the freedom of not being tied to a schedule or route.

Information for travel by train, bus or car is given in the "Getting There" section of each chapter. A suggested do-it-yourself walking tour is outlined wherever feasible. Because of the unique topography and character of Switzerland, however, many of the daytrip destinations are to tiny villages where a formal tour would be superfluous, or to places where the attractions are the outdoor activities. In those cases I have detailed the options available at each destination.

Visitors taking daytrips in Switzerland are more likely to be touring in the warmer months as those going for winter sports generally opt to stay in one place. I have, however, outlined the basic details of winter sports facilities wherever applicable.

Practical considerations such as time and weather are included, along with price-keyed hotel and restaurant suggestions and historical and background information. Destinations were chosen to appeal to a wide variety of interests, and include a combination of fresh discoveries and proven favorites.

Finally, a gentle disclaimer. Places have a way of changing without warning, and errors do creep into print. If your heart is absolutely set on visiting a particular sight, you should check before going to make sure that the opening times are still valid. Phone numbers of the local tourist information offices are included for this purpose.

One last thought—it isn't really necessary to see, or do, everything at a given destination. Be selective. Your one-day adventures in and around Switzerland should be fun, not an endurance test. If it starts becoming that, just stroll to the nearest café and relax. There will always be another day.

Happy Daytripping!

DAYTRIP
STRATEGIES

The word "Daytrip" may not have made it into dictionaries yet, but for experienced independent travelers it represents the easiest, most natural, and often the least expensive approach to exploring European countries. The strategy is to base yourself in or near a central city, and explore the surrounding areas on a series of one-day excursions from there.

ADVANTAGES:

While not the answer to every travel situation, daytrips offer significant advantages over point-to point touring following a set plan. The following are some reasons for considering the daytrip approach:

1. Freedom from the constraints of a fixed itinerary. You can go wherever you feel like going whenever the mood strikes.
2. Freedom from the burden of luggage. Your bags remain in your hotel room while you run around with only a guidebook and camera.
3. Freedom from the anxiety of reservation foul-ups. You don't have to worry each day about whether that night's lodging will actually materialize.
4. The flexibility of making last-minute changes to allow for unexpected weather, serendipitous discoveries, changing interests, new-found passions, etc.
5. The flexibility to take breaks from sightseeing whenever you feel tired or bored, without upsetting a planned itinerary. Why not sleep late in your base city for a change?
6. The opportunity to sample different travel experiences without committing more than a day to them.
7. The opportunity to become a "temporary resident" of your base city. By staying there for a few days, or more, you can get to know it in depth, becoming familiar with the local restaurants, shops, theaters, nightlife and other attractions etc.—enjoying them as a native would.

8. The convenience of not having to hunt for a hotel each day, along with the peace of mind that comes from knowing that a familiar room is waiting back in your base city.

9. The convenience of not having to pack and unpack your bags each day. Your clothes can straighten themselves out hanging in a closet or even be sent out for cleaning.

10. The convenience, and security, of having a fixed address in your base city, where friends, relatives, or business associates can reach you in an emergency.

11. The economy of staying in one hotel on a discounted longer-term basis, especially with airline package plans. You can make reservations for your base city without sacrificing any flexibility at all.

12. Above all, daytrips ease the transition from tourist to accomplished traveler. Even if this is your first trip abroad, you can probably handle an uncomplicated one-day excursion on your own. The confidence thus gained will help immensely when you tackle more complex destinations, freeing you from the limitation of guided tours and putting you in complete control of your own trip.

DISADVANTAGES:

For all of its attractions, the daytrip concept does have certain restrictions—one of which is that travelers forgo the pleasures of staying in different, usually smaller, towns. To accommodate those who may wish to deviate from this system for a day or so, I have recommended hotels in every town, which allows travelers the option of using daytrips part of the time and touring the rest.

ABOUT SWITZERLAND

Switzerland, a relatively small, landlocked country in central Europe, shares land boundaries totaling 1,881 kilometers (1,168 miles) with Austria, France, Italy, Liechtenstein and Germany. It has an area of 41,293 square kilometers (15,936 square miles)—making it just more than twice the size of New Jersey. The lowest point in the country is Lake Maggiore, at 195 meters (640 feet), and the highest is Dufourspitze, at 4,634 meters (15,203 feet). As of July 1996 the estimated population of Switzerland was just over 7,200,000, the population growth rate was 0.59%, and the life expectancy was 74.5 years for men and 80.8 years for women.

Politically, Switzerland is a Federal Republic, operating under a constitution instituted in 1874. Its citizens celebrate, annually on August 1, the founding of the Swiss Confederation and the country attaining its independence, which took place on that date in 1291. Its seemingly erroneous international country code, CH, is an abbreviation for *Confœderatio Helvetica*, its Latin appellation referring to the origins of the Swiss Confederation. Administratively, the country is divided into the following 26 cantons: Aargau, Ausser-Rhoden, Basel-Landschaft, Basel-Stadt, Bern, Fribourg, Genève, Glarus, Graubünden, Inner-Rhoden, Jura, Luzern, Neuchâtel, Nidwalden, Odwalden, Sankt Gallen, Schaffhausen, Schwyz, Solothurn, Thurgau, Ticino, Uri, Valais, Vaud, Zug and Zürich.

GETTING THERE

Any number of airlines fly across the North Atlantic to Switzerland, offering fares, schedules and package deals that constantly change to meet the competition. As seasoned travelers know, there are certain advantages to flying the national airline of the country you're visiting. For one thing, they are more familiar with your destination and can supply reliable advice and information about it. For another, despite a certain sameness of all aircraft, national airlines do provide a touch of in-flight ambiance that eases the passage from one culture to another. Another, not inconsiderable advantage, is that they also tend to get the most favorable landing slots and airport facilities. **SWISSAIR**, ☎ (800) 221-4750 in the USA, or www.swissair.com, is the national airline of Switzerland, and has direct flights to Switzerland from Atlanta, Boston, Chicago, Cincinnati, Los Angeles, New York, Newark, Philadelphia, San Francisco and Washington D.C., and flights from Montreal to Zürich on Wednesday and Saturday. **SWISSAIR** is noted for its extraordinary comfort and service, and its fleet is one of the youngest in the skies with its aircraft having an average age of just five years. In 1997 the airline introduced Naturalgourmet, which incorporates organically-grown products into the food and beverage service on all flights departing Switzerland, and soon it will expand to include all flights in the network. Passengers in all levels of service enjoy their own personal, interactive touch-screen inflight entertainment system which offers up to 20 different films, 60 hours of music and video games.

Those traveling from Canada will, most probably, want to consider **AIR CANADA**, which has a daily, year round, nonstop wide-body service from Toronto to Zürich. And a seasonal service in the summer peak including one weekly nonstop Calgary-Zürich and one weekly Vancouver-Calgary-Zürich flight.

GETTING AROUND

BY CAR:

North American driver's licenses are valid in Switzerland for 90 days, however the minimum driver's age in the country is 18 years.

The speed limit on freeways is 120 km/h (75 mph), highways 80 km/h (50 mph) and in cities and towns 50 km/h (31 mph).

- Even in daylight, headlights must be turned on while driving through road tunnels.
- Passing on the right side is strictly prohibited, even on superhighways.
- Seat belts must be worn in both front and back seats, if the belts are provided.
- Children under 12 must be seated in the back seats.
- Children under the age of 7 must be seated in a child-seat.

Gas Stations are typically open from 8 a.m. to 10 p.m., and stations located away from major cities/towns are often closed on Sunday. Outside of these hours, look for one of the many self-service stations, some of which accept credit cards but most of which take CHF 10 or CHF 20 bills.

An annual **road toll**, called the *vignette,* of CHF 40 is levied on all cars and motorcycles for use of the freeways (superhighways). Cars hired in Switzerland come with the vignette; those hired abroad must purchase a vignette either at the border, any Swiss Post Office or a participating gas station.

There are any number of **car rental** companies, both international and national, throughout Switzerland, so there is no problem with availability. It is much wiser, and cheaper, to decide on your requirements before leaving home and pre-book through a reputable company. One that I would certainly recommend is **auto europe**, ☎ (800) 223 5555 or fax (800) 235 6321 from the USA and Canada, and at www.wrld.com on the internet. All weekly rates are in U.S. dollars and include unlimited mileage; they guarantee to give you the best rate, and if you find a better one they'll beat it; they have no cancellation charges and have hotel delivery available and free drop-off throughout the country. They also offer an extremely wide range of automobiles, from the smallest mini up to a Ferrari sports car.

CAR TRAINS THROUGH ALPINE TUNNELS:

Albula: Thusis to Samedan, or vice versa, costs CHF 135 per car and CHF 24 per person.

Furka: Oberwald to Realp, or vice versa, costs CHF 34 in summer and CHF 36 in winter.

Lotschberg: Kandersteg to Goppenstein, or vice versa, costs CHF 25 for the car and all passengers. Kandersteg departures leave every 30 minutes from 5:05 a.m. until midnight. Goppenstein departures leave every 30 minutes from 5:35 a.m. until midnight. The travel time is 15 minutes.

Oberalp: Andermatt to Sedrun, or vice versa, costs CHF 73 per car and driver, and CHF 11 for each additional person. This service operates in winter only. At other times the road between Andermatt and Sedrun is open to all traffic.

CITY TRANSPORTATION SYSTEM:

Swiss cities and towns have excellent transportation networks, with a combination of buses and streetcars (trams), that are both clean and frequent. Tickets are not sold on board and, in the event of an inspection—which happens often—those traveling without a valid ticket are charged a considerable fine in addition to the fare. Visitors holding a **Swiss Pass, Swiss Flexi Pass** or **Swiss Card** need not worry, however, as these passes are valid throughout the urban transportation networks. Others should keep some coins handy for use in the ticket machines, which are located at every streetcar or bus stop. When in the larger cities, consider purchasing a pass for a day or longer. It works out considerably cheaper.

PUBLIC TRANSPORTATION:

Switzerland, small in size but challenged by its mountainous terrain, has developed—and is rightly proud of—an innovative and efficient public transportation service that ranks among the finest in the world.

Working in concert under the umbrella of the **Swiss Travel System** (STS), trains, buses, lake steamers, cable cars and city transportation companies offer fast, clean and highly efficient service to all parts of the country. The railway network, which celebrated its 150th anniversary in 1997, is run by **Swiss Federal Railways (SBB)** and numerous private companies. It operates trains on over 5,700 kilometers (3,542 miles) of standard, narrow or other gauge track. At one time, STS had a motto—A train every hour on the hour—and, amazingly, this concept has been applied in nearly all areas of Switzerland's public transportation service. Where the trains do not or cannot go, the omnipresent yellow postal buses, run by the **Swiss Postal Service (PTT)** do. In fact, their services encompass 8,288 kilometers (5,150 miles).

The **Official Swiss Timetable**, valid for one year, is published annually at the beginning of June. It lists arrival and departure times for the entire Swiss Travel System. In most instances, the timetable is uniform for weekdays, weekends and holidays. Excerpts of the timetable are available, free of charge, at any Swiss train station. But you don't have to go that far to access it—check it out on the internet at http://hafas.sbb.ch/hafasle/.

If you do not fancy the idea of lugging your heavy luggage from train to train, take advantage of SBB's **check-in service**. At a cost of CHF 10 to CHF 24 per item holders of either a train ticket or a train pass may have their bags forwarded on to their final destination. If you opt for this service, you may want to take a few essentials with you in a small carry-on bag, as your luggage may arrive at its destination a little later than you do.

Finally, just to prove the Swiss think of everything, over 4,000 **bicycles** are waiting for hire at over 200 Swiss railway stations. These cost from CHF 21 a day to CHF 116 a week, depending upon the type of bike you choose.

SPECIAL TRAINS:

Switzerland offers a variety of special train excursions affording visitors the opportunity to view some of the more scenic parts of the country while comfortably seated in a train. And, often you can have lunch along the way. I will cover these separately here as they really do not fall into the "daytrip" category—the journeys are, typically, too long to accommodate a same-day return to your base city. They should, however, be given serious consideration when planning your itinerary, especially as a novel and elucidating way of getting to your next destination.

The **Glacier Express**, perhaps the most famous of these, runs between Zermatt and St. Moritz, operates year-round, and takes approximately 8 hours in each direction. This is truly an unforgettable trip. From the comfort of a panorama car, you will watch in wonder as you pass over 291 bridges, through 91 tunnels and over the Oberalp Pass at 2,033 meters (6,670 feet). Passengers may also feast on the culinary delights served up in the attractive dining car.

The **Bernina Express** offers spectacular scenery and a change of country. It departs, year-round, from Chur and passes through St. Moritz before beginning its ascent—on gradients of 1 in 14.25 without the aid of rack-and-pinion tracks—up to the Bernina Pass at 2,323 meters (7,621 feet). It then descends through the Poschiavo Valley to Tirano, Italy. From June to October, passengers have the interesting option of continuing on, by postal bus, to Lugano. Services operate daily in both directions, with the trip to Tirano taking four and a half hours each way, and the trip from Chur to Lugano taking nine hours.

The **Palm Express** is a lengthy trip through fascinating terrain, offered during the summer months only and accomplished by a combination of train and postal bus. The first leg involves going from St. Moritz to Ascona/Locarno by postal bus, followed by a marvelous railway journey through the wild and beautiful Centovalli to Domodossola, Italy. From that point, a postal bus shuttles you over the Simplon Pass to Brig, where you may travel either by rail to Zermatt or by postal bus to Saas Fee. The one-way 5-hour trip from St. Moritz to Ascona/Locarno and 11-hour trip to Zermatt/Saas Fee can be accomplished in a single 24-hour period—although it makes for a very long day.

The **Panoramic Express** takes you past lovely lakes and majestic mountains on its way from Montreux on Lake Geneva to Luzern on Lake Luzern. Along the way, it passes through Interlaken where, if the weather is cooperative, you may get breathtaking views of the highest peaks in the Bernese Oberland. Again, the trip may be taken either direction, with the Montreux to Interlaken leg taking three and a quarter hours, and the Interlaken to Luzern leg taking about the same.

The **William Tell Express**, also operates only in the summer. It consists, uniquely, of a turn-of-the-century paddlewheel steamer voyage from Luzern to Fluelen, followed by a train excursion through the high St. Gotthard peaks and down to the lush garden city of Lugano, Ticino.

TRAVEL PASSES:

It is highly advisable to purchase, before you leave North America, one of the following passes. These may be obtained through **Rail Europe** by calling 1-800-4EURAIL (1-800-438-7245) from the USA or 1-800-361-RAIL (1-800-361-7245) from Canada. Alternatively, you may consult **Rail Europe's** website at www.raileurope.com.

The Swiss Pass—This pass allows unlimited travel (with 1st- or 2nd-class options), for periods of 4, 8, 15, or 21 days or 1 month, on the entire network of the Swiss Travel System. It also entitles the holder to a 25% discount on excursions to most mountain tops.

The Swiss Flexipass—This pass allows unlimited travel (with 1st- or 2nd-class options), for any three days in a 1 month period, on the entire network of the Swiss Travel System. It also offers the option of purchasing up to 6 extra days of train travel.

* When traveling with a companion, the companion receives a 40% discount off the price of a **Swiss Pass** and **Swiss Flexipass**.

The Swiss Card—is an ideal choice if you plan on spending your time in Switzerland, basically, at one destination. This includes two trips—each must be completed in a single day—to and from your arrival point in Switzerland and eventual destination. In addition, it entitles the holder to a 50% discount on fares (1st or 2nd class) within the entire network of the Swiss Travel System, and discounts of between 25% and 50% on excursions to most mountain tops, for a period of 1 month.

The Swiss Family Card—Request this free card from Rail Europe. It is valid in conjunction with the **Swiss Pass**, **Swiss Flexipass** or **Swiss Card**, and allows children under 16 to travel free when accompanied by a parent.

General Notes:

Holders of the **Swiss Pass** and **Swiss Flexipass** may travel on the following special trips by paying only the supplemental charges indicated:

The **Glacier Express**—seat supplement US$9/CAN$13, seat and luncheon supplement (I highly recommend this option) US$44/CAN$63.

The **William Tell Express**—seat supplement US$47/CAN$65.

The **Bernina Express**—seat supplement train only US$12/CAN$17, seat supplement train and bus from Tirano-Lugano US$29/CAN$41.

For more details of these, and other, trips see SPECIAL TRAINS, above.

ACCOMMODATIONS

A selection of accommodations has been included for each destination, most of which are known to the author. It must be reiterated, though, that Switzerland is not an inexpensive country, a fact that is certainly reflected in the prices of hotel rooms. It is quite difficult, to say the least, especially in the major cities and the more well-known resort areas, to find any range of accommodation at the bottom end of the price scale. And unlike other countries—particularly those in southern Europe, do not expect to find a plethora of cheap hostels and pensions. In fact, I came across really inexpensive accommodation only in the remotest of places. The bottom line is that, in most places, you will not find a double room for less than $100 a night—take heart, however: that will almost certainly include breakfast. Throughout the country as a whole, the preponderance of hotels fall into the middle and upper categories of the market. In the latter, rates can range from a low of around $400 a night for a double room to a deluxe suite that goes for as much as CHF 2,000 (at the then current rate of exchange that translated to over $1,400) a night! It must be said, though, that you certainly get what you pay for. The standards of decor, facilities and service are so high as to be exemplary. Absolutely nothing is overlooked. It is not unusual, either, for many hotels to offer, in addition to the expected pool and fitness room, complete spa facilities. Seriously, while the prices may well be more than you are used to, a stay in this caliber of accommodation is an experience in and of itself; and it certainly enhances a vacation to be treat yourself to such luxury—once in a while.

The price scale used in this guide is as follows:

$$$ = Over CHF 400
$$ = Between CHF 140 and CHF 400
$ = Under CHF 140

The few hotels that I have recommended in adjacent countries also use this CHF scale.

The following hotels are recommended in this guide: the Grand Hotel Quellenhof, in Bad Ragaz; the Hotel Drei Könige am Rhein, in Basel; the Hotel Bellevue Palace, in Bern; the Hotel des Bergues and Hotel du Rhône, in Geneva; the Grand Hotel Regina, in Grindelwald; the Victoria Jungfrau

Grand Hotel, in Interlaken; the Beau-Rivage Palace and Lausanne Palace, in Lausanne; the Le Mirador Resort and Spa, in Mont-Pèlerin (Vevey); the Le Montreux Palace, in Montreux; the Seiler Hotel Monte Rosa, in Zermatt; the Dolder Grand, in Zürich; the Hotel Palace, in Milan, Italy; and the Domaine du Royal Club Evian—Hôtel Royal, in Évian, France are all members of the **Leading Hotels of the World** organization. You may make reservations by calling, toll free, from the USA, Canada, Puerto Rico or the U.S. Virgin Islands 1-800-223-6800. In New York City the number is (212) 838-3110.

CULTURE

Switzerland is an ethnically diverse country, with 65% of the population being of German origin, 18% French, 10% Italian and 1% Romansch. Relative to language, the country is split along the same lines, although most Swiss are multi-lingual (not necessarily in all three languages) and many speak English as well. This combination of cultures, however, does give rise to some rather strange dialects—unintelligible for many Swiss, let alone foreigners.

Such a multiplicity of languages can be confusing for travelers. And, who wants to carry around three pocket dictionaries? Those with an Internet connection can get a head start even before leaving home. To learn something and have some fun at the same time, log into www.tte.com/Switzerland, scroll down some, and you will find that they offer a very helpful tourist translation service for French, German and Italian. They even have on-line tests so you can measure how much you have learned!

FOOD AND DRINK

As with places of accommodation, a selection of restaurants has been included for each destination. An approximate price range, based on the least expensive complete meal on offer, is indicated as follows:

$ = Inexpensive
$$ = Reasonable
$$$ = Luxurious and expensive

An outgrowth of Switzerland's cultural diversity, the country's restaurants offer an unusually wide range of gastronomical delights, with the French, German and Italian regions offering their own specialties. It is not widely known, as exports are very limited, that Swiss wines are of excellent quality, and especially tasty when ordered in their region of origin.

Breakfast is usually continental in style. Many restaurants offer a special of the day—typically priced between CHF 15 to CHF 25 and served at lunch time—which is known as the *Tagesteller* or *Plat du Jour*. Expect to pay around CHF 30 to CHF 40 for a three-course meal, without drinks of course.

Tourists generally go to Switzerland for the scenery and leave extolling the virtues of its cuisine. Throughout the country, a multitude of beautifully appointed and elegant restaurants, many based within the finer hotels, serve up mouthwatering, creatively prepared cuisine, presented in such an exquisite manner that you may be hesitant to disturb the chef's artistry. The best of these establishments maintain a membership in the **Les Grandes Tables de Suisse** organization and are listed in a lavishly illustrated guide which is updated annually. This is freely available, free of charge, throughout Switzerland. Alternatively, check it out on the Internet at www.tourismus.ch. Really, to fully appreciate this significant component of the Swiss culture, I urge you to sample this kind of dining experience at least once—and once may be all you can afford. Expect this culinary delight to cost, per person and without drinks, a minimum of about CHF 90. I have seen, and had the pleasure of trying, menus costing well in excess of CHF 150!

PRACTICALITIES

ALPINE PASSES:

Name	Altitude		From/ To	Maximum Gradient	Open
	Meters	Feet			
Albula	2,312	7,585	Tiefencastel/ La Punt	12%	June October
Bernina	2,323	7,621	Pontresina/ Poschiavo	11%	All year
Brunig	1,007	3,304	Meiringen/ Sachsein	8%	All year
Fluela	2,383	7,818	Davos/ Susch	11%	All year
Forclaz	1,526	5,007	Martigny/ Chamonix	8%	All year
Furka	2,431	7,976	Gletsch/ Andermatt	10%	June October
Great St. Bernard	2,469	8,100	Martigny/ Aosta	11%	June October*
Grimsel	2,165	7,103	Meiringen/ Gletsch	9%	June October

Julier	2,284	7,493	Tiefencastel/ Silvaplana	12%	All year
Klausen	1,948	6,391	Altdorf/ Linthal	9%	June October
Lukmanier	1,916	6,286	Disentis/ Biasca	9%	May October
Maloja	1,815	5,955	Chiavenna/ Silvaplana	12%	All year
Mosses	1,445	4,741	Aigl/ Chateaux-d'Oex	8%	All year
Nufenen	2,478	8,130	Airolo/ Ulrichen	10%	June September
Oberalp	2,044	6,706	Andermatt/ Disentis	10%	June October
Ofen (Il Fuorn)	2,149	7,051	Zernez/ Santa Maria	12%	All year
Pillon	1,546	5,072	Aigle/ Gsteig	9%	All year
St. Gotthard	2,108	6,916	Andermatt/ Airolo	10%	May October*
San Bernardino	2,065	6,775	Thusis/ Bellinzona	10%	June October*
Simplon	2,005	6,578	Brig/ Domodossola	10%	All year October
Splugen	2,113	6,932	Thusis/ Chiavenna	9%	May October
Susten	2,224	7,297	Innertkirchen/ Wassen	9%	June October
Umbrail	2,501	8,205	Santa Maria/ Stelvio	10%	June October

Opening and closing dates vary according to the prevailing weather conditions. * Tunnel passage open all year.

BANKS:

Banks are usually open Monday to Friday from 8:30 a.m. to 4:30 p.m. Once a week they extend their hours, but this varies by region. They are closed Saturday, Sunday and on public holidays.

CLOTHING:

Good walking shoes, sweaters and a light, plastic poncho are necessities in Switzerland. And remember to pack something formal if you are staying in deluxe or first class hotels, otherwise you may not be permitted in the dining room.

COMPUTERS:
If your laptop computer is not equipped with a built in transformer, you will need to travel with a converter. E-mail users should travel with a RJ-45 adapter.

COST OF LIVING:
It's only fair to warn you that Switzerland is a very expensive country. From hotel rates to soft drinks, prices will be higher than you are accustomed to paying. Of course, the scenery is free, but transport to and from optimum vantage points—the summits of the higher mountains—can be almost prohibitively costly. For example, the regular fare to Jungfraujoch, Europe's highest railway station, was CHF 137 in 1997. Holders of a Swiss Pass, as explained above, are entitled to a reduction, but their discounted fare is still a substantial CHF 104. The railway itself offers a savings in the form of a Good Morning Ticket (allowing you to take the first train up and requiring a return by midday), but that will save you only CHF 5. The bottom line is that there is no bottom line. So, be advised, Switzerland is not the country to choose if you are in the market for a low-budget vacation. Take lots of cash and have the plastic near at hand.

CURRENCY:
The currency of Switzerland is the Swiss Franc (CHF), which is divided into 100 centimes.
Coins: 5, 10, 20 and 50 centimes and 1,2 and 5 Francs.
Bank notes: 10, 20, 50, 100, 500 and 1,000 Francs.

ELECTRICITY:
The current used throughout Switzerland is 220 Volts (AC), 50 cycles. Prongs for outlets differ from those in North America, with most small appliances using the standard Continental two-round-pin plug. Converter packs are readily available from electrical stores through North America.

HOLIDAYS:
Legal holidays in Switzerland are: New Year's Day, Good Friday, Easter Monday, Ascension Day (May 8), Whit Monday, August 1, Christmas Day and Boxing Day (December 26).
Regional and local holidays such as January 2, May 1 (Labor Day) and Corpus Christi among others, are observed in many parts of the country.

PASSPORT AND VISA REGULATIONS:
Each traveler to Switzerland is required to present a valid passport. Visas, for citizens of the American Continent (Belize, Dominican Republic, Haiti and Peru excepted), Europe, Japan, Australia and New Zealand, are required only for a continuous stay of more than three months.

POST OFFICES:

Post offices in large cities are open Monday through Friday from 8:30 a.m. to midday and 1:30–6:30 p.m., and Saturday from 7:30–11 a.m.

TAX-FREE SHOPPING:

In Switzerland a 6.5% tax, called Value Added Tax (VAT), is levied on all goods and included in the sales price. Foreign visitors are entitled to a refund of VAT paid on purchases of over CHF 500. As in other European countries, there is a system in place to facilitate the swift and safe cash refund of the VAT. When purchasing items, look out for the blue, black and white **Europe Tax-free Shopping** logo on the store front, and request the Tax-free Shopping Cheque. You will need this in order to claim a refund, which can be obtained, for example, at either the Geneva or Zürich airports.

Go shopping with the 1-2-3 money back guarantee:

1. Ask the salesperson for a fully completed Tax-free Shopping Cheque, the Tax-free envelope as well as the information leaflet containing a list of the most important cash refund points.
2. When leaving Switzerland **make sure that your Tax-free Shopping Cheque is stamped by the Swiss Customs authorities** after showing the goods to them.
3. Thereafter, you will get your money back, in cash, from any Europe Tax-free Shopping Refund Office.

TELEPHONES:

Switzerland is divided into area codes, and these codes are always shown in the PRACTICALITIES section of each chapter. Remember, though, when making International calls to Switzerland the initial number of the code (0) is dropped.

Care needs to be taken when making **international calls** from Switzerland. Be aware that placing a call from your hotel room is, no matter how convenient, by far the most costly way. Almost every hotel places a very heavy surcharge on any call made from the room, let alone an international one. And using a calling card from your regular long-distance service back home isn't too much cheaper either. A recent innovation are pre-paid cards that can be bought at home and used abroad. These appear to be the cheapest and most convenient way of making calls home. Providing, of course, they work in the country you're going to.

THE WORLD WIDE WEB:

There are numerous sites on the WWW containing information about Switzerland The following ones will more than get you started:

Switzerland Tourism, the government tourist office, sponsors **www. switzerlandtourism.ch**, which will lead you to many other cities and towns in the country.

www.tte.ch/Switzerland is particularly interesting, and offers you many transfers to other relevant sites and two others.

www.tourismus.ch and **http://city.net/countries/switzerland** also have a wealth of information.

Throughout this guide, various other sites, e.g., for particular cities, are shown when relevant.

TIPPING:

Gratuities are automatically included in hotel and restaurant bills, and in most taxi fares. Tipping is customary for special services as well. For luggage handling, it is customary to tip CHF 2 per bag.

SUGGESTED TOURS

The do-it-yourself **walking tours** in this guide are relatively short and easy to follow. Suggested **routes** are designated by heavy lines on the maps. Circled numbers indicate major attractions or points of reference along the way and correspond to numbers in the text. Keep in mind that tour routes are only suggestions—you may prefer to wander off on your own using the maps as guides. You can estimate the amount of time that any segment of a walking tour will take by looking at the scaled map, and figuring that the average person covers about 100 yards per minute.

Trying to see everything in any given place could easily become an exhausting marathon. You will certainly enjoy yourself more by being selective and passing up anything that doesn't catch your fancy—in favor of a friendly café, perhaps. And, sometimes those stops are the ones where you learn the most—about a country's most unique, important and distinctive attributes, its people and its culture. It is a sure bet that not all museums will interest you, and forgiveness will be granted if you don't visit *every* church.

Practical information, such as the opening times of various attractions, is as accurate as was possible at the time of writing, but everything is subject to change. You should always check with the local tourist information office if seeing a particular sight is crucially important.

*OUTSTANDING ATTRACTIONS:

An * asterisk before any attraction denotes a special treat that, in the author's opinion, should not be missed.

SHOPPING

BUCHERER:

Even before visiting Switzerland, most people will be aware its great watchmaking traditions. If not, once in the country they will, very quickly, be enlightened. Wherever you go, whatever publication you read, you will be bombarded with advertisements enticing you to purchase this or that watch. And, as one store may not carry the same brands as another it can, in fact, be quite bewildering.

Let me point you in the right direction. **Bucherer Ltd.,** founded in 1888, is the largest watch and jewelry retailer in Switzerland today, and an official partner of Switzerland Tourism. Every major brand of watch, such as Rolex, Audemars Piguet, Baume & Mercier, Chopard, Gucci, IWC, Michel Jordi, Piaget, Piguet, Rado, TAG Heuer, Tudor and Swatch, is offered here. Bucherer's relationship with the ever-popular Rolex dates from 1925. It is the largest Rolex retailer in the world, selling a variety of over 1,000 models. And, Bucherer manufactures, under its own name, a celebrated line of watches with a range of nearly 1,000 designs. What does this mean to you? It means that when you visit a Bucherer store you will be able to choose from among more than 4,000 different watch models, priced anywhere between CHF 50 to CHF 300,000!

If, this time around, you are in the market for more than a watch, you will find here an equally glittering array of jewelry—either creations of their own award-winning collection or fashion jewelry from such famous names as Christian Dior, Grossé, Lanvin and others. Bucherer are also specialists in unset diamonds of all sizes, cuts and qualities. On offer, also, are a fine selection of clocks and cuckoo clocks; Gucci, Lancel and Dunhill handbags (or leather goods); Mont Blanc and Caran d'Arche writing accessories; Reuge, music boxes—which come with a two-hundred-year tradition; Hummel and Goebel figurines, Swarovski crystal; Victorinox original Swiss Army Knives; Zwilling J. A. Henckels and Twinstar kitchen knives and scissors; Fisba embroidery; and other traditional souvenirs such as tankards, key rings, dolls, handkerchiefs, purses, miniature cowbells and pencil sets. In other words, you are likely to find at a Bucherer store a gift to delight anyone and everyone, no matter their age—even you.

Bucherer stores are conveniently located throughout Switzerland in the cities of Basel, Bern, Geneva, Interlaken, Lausanne, Locarno, Lugano, Luzern, St. Gallen, St. Moritz, Zermatt and Zürich—the addresses of which are detailed in the respective chapters in this guide, as well as in Davos; Berlin, Germany; and Vienna, Austria. The company's headquarters are based in Luzern, home, since 1930, of the main Bucherer store. This, one of the largest watch and jewelry stores in the western world, carries an inventory of in excess of 40,000 items.

Bucherer has a multi-national staff of over 1,000 employees, including highly qualified watchmakers, goldsmiths, designers, gemologists and sales personnel. In addition to offering courteous, proficient service, the sales staff, in combination, are able to converse in over twenty-one different languages—an important service given to the international nature of the clientele.

Bucherer prices, posted in Swiss Francs, are fixed in every Swiss store. All major credit cards and most major currencies are accepted, however, with the exact price, in the currency of choice, calculated using the official bank exchange rate on the day of sale. Be advised, also, that tourists are entitled to a 6% Export reduction on purchases above CHF 500. And, Bucherer does not forget about you after the sale, offering an International one-year guarantee and a worldwide service network manned by more than 200 agents in 55 countries.

If you just can't wait to get to Switzerland to do your shopping or if you find, when you get home, that you want to add to your purchases, never fear. Contact them at Bucherer Ltd., Head Office, CH-6002 Luzern, ☎ (41) 369 70 00 or Fax (41) 369 73 69 to request a catalogue, or check out www.bucherer.ch, make your selection, and arrange for payment either by check or credit card.

VICTORINOX—THE ORIGINAL SWISS ARMY KNIFE:

Victorinox—the Original Swiss Army Knife—is as synonymous with Switzerland as Alpine panoramas, cable cars and skiing. Indeed, it is impossible to miss the red-and-white logo and the knife displays prominently exhibited in nearly every tourist shop, and many other retail stores as well, throughout Switzerland. You, like me, may be attracted time and time again, intrigued to see which of the many pocket knives and other products are on show. And, without doubt, their classic pocket knife is the souvenir of choice, and a good choice it is—useful, durable, unique and, in the overall scheme of things, relatively affordable.

What is now a world-renowned institution began a little over a century ago when a cutler, Carl Elsener, grandfather of the present proprietor, had a vision to create jobs. Then, when Switzerland was a very poor country, he had the very sharp idea of forming a consortium, the Swiss Cutler's Association, which would consist of about twenty-five cutlers and produce knives for the soldiers of the Swiss Army. The first batch of knives was delivered in 1891. Throughout the ensuing years, however, one by one, his partners withdrew as it was found that a German plant could mass produce the knives more cheaply than Swiss craftsmen. Undaunted, Elsener soldiered on, losing his entire fortune in the process and saved from bankruptcy only through the generosity of his relatives. Determined to repay his creditors—with full interest, he developed a lighter and more elegant knife, with more features, for use by officers. With only two springs controlling six tools, the "Officers' and Sports Knife" was legally registered on June 12, 1897. Even though it was not officially included among regulation Swiss Army equipment, army officers purchased the knives personally from cutlery outlets and, very soon, this versatile tool became a tremendous success.

In 1909, following the death of his mother, Carl Elsener chose her name, Victoria, as the name for his company. Twelve years later, in 1921, stainless steel was invented and incorporated into the manufacture of the knives. "Inox," the international designation for stainless steel, was appended to the name, and VICTORINOX as the present name of the company and the factory was born.

Following the Second World War the PX stores of the U.S. Army, Marines and Air Force all sold large quantities of the VICTORINOX "Swiss Army Knife" to U.S. officers and soldiers. Throughout the years since, the "Swiss Army Knife" has been continuously redesigned, adding new features to meet the evolving needs and preferences of consumers in both military and private markets. Today, it is available in over 100 different models, with the most versatile among these being the "SwissChamp," which consists of 64 individual parts, weighs only 185 grams (6.5 ounces) and has 33 different features. In excess of 450 steps are required to complete the manufacture of this intriguing tool, which fits in the palm of your hand!

VICTORINOX, with a full 90% of its production exported to over 100 countries, is renowned the world over for the quality of its products. Only the finest raw materials are used. A special blade steel, made of stainless chromium-and-molybdenum-alloys, is used for both the cutting blades. After hardening at 1,040 degrees and tempering at 160 degrees, the blades have a hardness of RC 56 (RC = Rockwell C, unit of hardness). The wood saws, scissors and nail files have a hardness of RC 53; the screwdrivers, tin openers and spikes have a hardness of RC 52; and the corkscrews and springs measure a hardness of RC 49. The metal saw and file is case-hardened and hard-chrome plated, to accommodate the sawing/filing of even iron and steel. To re-sharpen the knife blades, VICTORINOX recommends using a honing stone, as the alloy from which the blades are manufactured is too hard for honing steel.

The spring pressure is impressive, as well. The spring presses onto the large blade with a force of approximately 12 kilograms (over 26 pounds), and on the smaller one at 8 kilogram (17.6 pounds). This combined force of 20 kilograms (44 pounds), presses backwards onto the corkscrew. These two springs have 6 pressure points, which result in a combined total spring pressure of 70 kilogram (154 pounds). In the SwissChamp, with 8 springs and 24 pressure points, the combined spring pressure is nearly 300 kilogram (661 pounds)! Of course, the success of VICTORINOX has spawned many imitators, but none have come close to achieving the same quality standards, a fact most immediately evident when testing the spring action. With a genuine VICTORINOX knife, the typical clicking noise you hear when the blade is opened and engaged is an audible indication of the high spring pressure which, even after years of intensive use, is guaranteed to remain constant.

In a final quality check 90 people ensure that only those pocket knives which meet the company's exacting and very high standards are sent on for dispatch. Each individual knife blade and function which leaves the production line is submitted to a manual check to ensure a perfect finish. And, the VICTORINOX guarantee covers all material defects or manufacturing faults for an unlimited period.

The VICTORINOX "Swiss Army Knife" has become a celebrity in its own right. The New York Museum of Modern Art and the State Museum for Applied Art, in Munich, Germany, have selected the VICTORINOX "Swiss-Champ" for exhibit in their collections on excellence in design. Since the term of Lyndon B. Johnson, U.S. presidents have presented guests to the White House with VICTORINOX pocket knives, and many major international companies use the VICTORINOX "Swiss Army Knife" as a part of their advertising campaigns. The knives have proved themselves in the most modern of military actions, also. They are a part of the official equipment for the Space Shuttle Crew, and have been on expeditions to the North Pole, Mount Everest and the tropical rain forests of the Amazon.

But there is much more to VICTORINOX than just pocket knives. The company also produces fine cutlery, scissors, manicuring and hairdressing equipment, kitchen knives, professional butchers tools, watches, compasses and even sunglasses and writing tools. Among their latest innovations is the amazing VICTORINOX "SwissTool" with no less than 23 features, including pliers, 5 screwdrivers, a variety of blades, saws, a wire bender, a scrapper, and a stripper—to name a few.

If this intrigues you, but a trip to Switzerland is not imminent in your plans, don't despair. Swiss Army Brands Inc., exclusive distributor of VICTORINOX ORIGINAL SWISS ARMY KNIVES in the U.S., Canada and the Caribbean, One Research Drive, P.O. Box 874, Shelton, Connecticut, 06484-0874, ☎ 800-243-4045 or Fax 800-243-4006, will be more than pleased to send you their latest catalog. I find, however, that it is more fun to log into their web site, www.swissarmy.com, where you can even "Design A Knife" of your own. And, whether shopping by catalogue or by web site, the legendary marketing prowess of VICTORINOX will be readily apparent. What boy (or, perhaps, girl), of any age, wouldn't be thrilled to receive a "Swiss Army Knife" embellished with the name and colors of their favorite NFL, NHL or Major League Baseball teams name and colors on it? As of this writing, NFL knives come in special collectors tins, which will also soon be available for the NHL and MLB teams.

GENUINE SWISS HANDICRAFT:

Everyone traveling through Switzerland will be enticed by typical Swiss Folk Art, and as well as having a typical souvenir for themselves many, surely, will want to surprise someone back home with a really special gift. Obviously, there are many, many souvenir shops as well as department stores that can offer you an array of goods to choose from. But are they the genuine article? Probably not. Don't despair—help is at hand in the form of the **HEIMATWERK** stores, the best places for typical Swiss Folk Art and traditional and contemporary **Genuine Swiss Handicraft**. There you will find up-to-date souvenirs made by Swiss designers or created by craftsmen in the Folk Art tradition of Switzerland. Expect to find pottery, glass, wood-carvings, embroideries, hand woven fabrics, music boxes, toys, dolls, tin, copper, jewelry, scissor cuttings, Ethno watches, knives and much more. And who wouldn't want one of those famous cowbells to take home? At HEIMATWERK you can choose from ones valued between CHF 30 to CHF 1,500! You can be sure, too, that these are souvenirs that will last a lifetime, and bring with them a lifetime's worth of memories.

There is another very practical advantage in shopping at HEIMATWERK as most travelers will be able to do their gift buying at the last moment, and consequently not have to carry everything around Switzerland with them. Not only are there four stores in Zürich: Rudolf Brun-Brücke, ☎ 211 57 80; Bahnhofstrasse 2, ☎ 221 08 37; Galerie, Renweig 14, ☎ 221 35 73 and in the main railway station, Hauptbahnhof, ☎ 212 27 97 but, very conveniently, there are also stores in Transit A and B of Zürich's Kloten Airport, ☎ 816 40 85 and one at Geneva's Cointrin airport, ☎ 816 40 85.

TOURIST INFORMATION

For each daytrip destination, local **tourist office** information is listed in the PRACTICALITIES section, and the location marked on the corresponding map with the word "**info**" or the symbol ❶.

ADVANCE PLANNING INFORMATION:

Switzerland Tourism has established branch offices throughout the world and the staff there will be pleased to help plan your trip. In North America these are:

Swiss Center
608 Fifth Avenue
New York, NY 10020-2303
☎ (212) 757 5944, FAX (212) 262 6116

150 North Michigan Avenue, Suite 2930
Chicago, IL 60601-7525
☎ (312) 332 9900, FAX (312) 630 5848

222 North Sepulveda Avenue, Suite 1570
El Segundo, CA 90245-4300
☎ (310) 640 8900, FAX (310) 335 5982

926 The East Mall
Etobicoke, Ontario, M9B6KI, Canada
☎ (416) 695 2020, FAX (416) 695 2774

Zürich

Although the Romans built a customs post at Lindenhof as early as 15 BC, thereby founding *Turicum,* Zürich was first recorded as a town in official documents in AD 929. It later acquired the status of a Free Imperial Town in 1218. A little over a century later, in 1336, local artisans, organized in guilds and led by Rudolf Brun, successfully conspired to overthrow the city council, instituting a new constitution that, naturally, gave domination to the guilds. These days, however, things have changed. The guilds appear in public only once a year, on the third Monday in April, during the Zürich Spring Festival *(Sechseläuten).* During those festivities, members don traditional guild costume and march throughout the city before reaching their destination, Sechseläuten Square, in early evening.

In 1351, Zürich joined the Swiss Confederation. That same century saw the construction of the walls to fortify the city center. And strong they were, lasting well into the 19th century and standing preserved and intact in the Old Town to this day. During the early 16th century, in 1519 to be exact, Huldrych Zwingli brought the Reformation to Zürich.

In the 19th Century Zürich metamorphosed into the financial and economic center of Switzerland. With the opening of the Zürich Stock Exchange in 1877, it became a major player in international financial and trade markets as well. In fact, today Zürich is home to what is considered the world's fourth most important stock exchange, is the world's largest gold trading center and hosts a variety of thriving industries providing a total of over 350,000 jobs.

You might expect such a business-minded city to be constrained and bland, but culturally-conscious Zürich is neither. It enjoys an international reputation as an art dealing center, with many notable auction houses based in the city, and offers excellent upscale shopping in the numerous boutiques and houses of haute couture on and around the famous Bahnhofstrasse. The charming Old Town is home to a variety of art galleries, antique dealers and book shops while, on the opposite side of the Limmat river, the pedestrian area known as Dörfli offers an array of bars, nightclubs and discos. Whatever part of town you find yourself in, there will be a profusion of restaurants, of whatever standard or flavor you choose. Zürich also boasts a marvelous location at the edge of the lake with the Alps, visible on a clear day, sitting magnificently in the background. Such a cosmopolitan ambiance, and obvious prosperity, is sure to enchant.

GETTING THERE:

By air, international flights from around the world arrive at Zürich's Kloten Airport, located a convenient ten minutes by train from the main railway station.

Trains arrive at Zürich's main railway station *(Hauptbahnhof)* from all other cities in Switzerland, as well as from France and Germany.

By car, Zürich, in the northcentral part of Switzerland, is easily reached by road from all other parts of the country.

PRACTICALITIES:

The **Dialing Code** for Zürich is 1. The **Zürich Tourism** office, ☎ 215 40 00 or Fax 215 40 44, is located on the ground floor concourse at the main railway station. It is open November to March, Monday to Friday, from 8:30 a.m. to 7:30 p.m. and Saturday and Sunday from 8:30 a.m. to 6:30 p.m. From April to October it is open Monday to Friday, from 8:30 a.m. to 9:30 p.m. and Saturday and Sunday from 8:30 a.m. to 8:30 p.m. Zürich hotel reservation service may be reached at ☎ 215 40 00 or Fax 215 40 44. A wealth of information about Zürich can be found on the **Internet** at www.zurichtourism.ch.

Personal computers are not as common in Europe as they are in the USA and, generally, Internet connections are rather expensive. Consequently, market forces have given rise to places where the public may rent the use of a computer with Internet access for a given amount of time. In an effort to make the experience more enjoyable—and profitable—the ever-innovative Swiss have established such places in cafés or small bars. So, at least in this city, the postcard is passé. Surprise your family or friends with an e-mail greeting while you enjoy the experience of the **Internet Café GmbH**, ☎ 210 33 11, Fax 210 33 13 or E-mail sbuesss@café.ch, 3, Urani-astrasse. Hours are Monday from 10 a.m. to 6 p.m., Tuesday to Thursday from 10 a.m. to 11 p.m., Friday and Saturday from 10 a.m. to midnight and Sunday from 10 a.m. to 11 p.m.

Bucherer has three stores in the Zürich area, but it is the one on the most famous street in the city that most people will want to head for. **Bucherer Zürich** is located at Bahnhofstrasse 50, CH-8001 Zürich, ☎ 211 26 35 or Fax 211 39 82. The best stores for buying **Swiss Army Knives** are those owned by Messer Dolmetsch at five convenient locations; Bahnhofstrasse 92, Limmatquai 126, the main train station and, if you have really put your shopping off until the last minute, Terminals A and B at Zürich airport. Expect to find, also, a wide array of other impressive souvenirs such as Swatch watches, kitchen knives, scissors and much, much more. **Shops** in Zürich are open, typically, Monday to Friday from 9 a.m. to 6:30 p.m.—with department stores and many other shops open until 9 p.m. on Thursday and on Saturday from 8 a.m. to 4 p.m. Outside of these hours the only place you are likely to find a store open is the railway station, where you may shop Monday through Sunday from 8 a.m. to 8 p.m. For more pressing needs, the railway station pharmacy is open daily from 7 a.m. to 10 p.m.

Sightseeing can be a tiring exercise, and many upscale hotels offer clients a health club with massage facilities. If you do not have access to this, you might consider contacting Hermann A. Brechbüler at **Body Care**, ☎ 242 41 57, Köchlistrasse 25, CH-8004 Zürich, who offers an enticing array of massages and other body care treatments. Relaxation is reached by taking a Number 3 tram from the Hauptbahnhof, and he accepts major credit cards.

Public transport in and around Zürich on any combination of tramcars, buses, cable cars, boats, the S-Bahn (a rapid suburban train) and some railways is fast, clean and efficient. Tickets must be purchased from ticket vending machines, ticket offices or the tourist office, before each trip and are available for single trips or, more advantageously, as an Unlimited Day Pass. The latter, for 2nd class, cost CHF 6.80 for the City of Zürich and CHF 27.20 for the expanded traffic area.

Lost Property may be reclaimed from the **City Police and Public Transportation** office, ☎ 216 51 11, Werdmühlestrasse 10, Monday to Friday, from 7:30 a.m. to 5:30 p.m. and on weekends from the City Police, ☎ 216 71 11, Bahnhofquai 3. The **Railway (SBB)** Lost Property office, ☎ 157 22 22, is at the main station and is open daily from 6 a.m. to 10 p.m.

ACCOMMODATION:

The **Dolder Grand Hotel** *****, ☎ 251 88 29, Fax 251 88 29 or www.forum.ch/go.exe?662, Kurhausstrasse 65, CH-8032 Zürich, is a member of the Leading Hotels of the World organization. It is found in an absolutely wonderful, romantically-styled building overlooking the city, Lake Zürich and the Alps from its delightfully wooded park-like setting. Just 10 minutes from the city center, and easily accessed by tramcar and the Dolder funicular—at no charge for hotel guests—this is certainly the place to indulge yourself. The Dolder Grand also offers comprehensive sporting opportunities, including a nine-hole golf course and five clay tennis courts. $$$

The **Savoy Baur en Ville Zürich** *****, ☎ 211 53 60 or Fax 221 14 67, Am Paradeplatz, CH-8022 Zürich, is housed in a traditional building at the junction of the famous Banhofstrasse and Paradeplatz in the very center of the city. This luxurious hotel, which fits like a glove into its elegant, stylish surroundings, offers a high level of comfort and service. $$$

The **Splügenschloss** ****, ☎ 289 99 99, Fax 289 99 98, E-mail resarc@calvacom.fr or www.integra.fr/relaischateaux/splugenscloss, Splügenstrasse2/Genferstrasse, CH-8002 Zürich, a particularly charming hotel within a classic turn-of-the-century building, is in quiet suburb near the lake, yet just a few minutes from the center of town. The rooms are decorated in a variety of styles, but each offers all the modern conveniences, including fax and computer connections and voice mail. Non-smoker and air-conditioned rooms available upon request and rates include applicable taxes and a buffet breakfast. $$$

The **Zum Storchen ****, ☎ 211 55 10 or Fax 211 64 51, Am Weinplatz 2, CH-8001 Zürich, offers an appealing combination of history and location. Established more 600 years ago, it sits on bank of the Limmat river encompassed by a maze of narrow lanes lined with numerous historic buildings and churches, intriguing specialty shops, bars and restaurants. A recent and extensive renovation has achieved its stated aim, a healthy balance between the traditional and the modern. Buffet breakfast and taxes are included in the rate. $$

The **Haus Zum Kindli ***, ☎ 211 59 17 or Fax 211 65 28, Pfalzgasse 1, CH-8001 Zürich, occupies an enchanting 16th-century townhouse in the old historic district of Zürich. Each of the 21 distinctive rooms is decorated using the floral patterns and classic color combinations reflective of the warmth of the Laura Ashley style. Each has private bath, toilet, telephone, TV and mini-bar. Breakfast, service charges and taxes are included in the tariff. $$

The **Alexander ***, ☎ 251 82 03 or Fax 252 74 25, Niederdorfstrasse 40, CH-8001, Zürich, is found just five minutes from the railway station in the middle of Zürich's lively old-quarter. All rooms feature soundproofing, individually controlled air-conditioning, private bath/shower and toilet, telephone, color TV and mini-bar. The owners also run a guest house just around the corner where the rooms are simpler and rates are about CHF 50 less. Continental breakfast and service charges are included in the rate. $

The **Leoneck ***, ☎ 261 60 70 or Fax 261 64 92, Leonhardstrasse 1, CH-8001 Zürich, is located less than a 10-minute walk from the train station, at the tramcar stop "Haldenegg," on lines 6, 7, 10 and 15. Its 65 very clean, comfortable and well equipped rooms each have one very distinguishing feature. Behind every bed is an interesting, and often amusing, Swiss ethno-style mural depicting a traditional Swiss scene. Continuing in this unique style guests may take breakfast, though the price is not included in the room rate, in the highly whimsical "Crazy Cow" restaurant. $

The **Limmathof **, ☎ 261 42 20 or Fax 262 02 17, Limmatquai 142, CH-8023 Zürich, is centrally located directly across the Limmat river from the railway station. The comfortable, well equipped rooms are within an historic home in the old part of town. Breakfast and taxes are included in the rate. $

The **Krone **, ☎ 251 42 2 or Fax 251 47 63, Limmatquai 88, CH-8001 Zürich, is located on a busy street and overlooks the Limmat river. Its 25 rooms are clean, comfortable, and reasonably priced. A twin-bedded room with use of a shower down the hall was just over CHF 90 in 1997. The rate for a similar room with private bath and toilet was CHF 132. Breakfast may be included for CHF 8 per person extra. $

The **Swiss Youth Hostels**, ☎ 482 35 44, Mutscellenstrasse 114, Ch-8038 Zürich, are simple and basic, but clean, with rates between CHF 18 and CHF 32 per person, inclusive of breakfast and sheets. $

FOOD AND DRINK:

It really is quite difficult to get a reasonably inexpensive meal in Zürich. Most of the restaurants listed below are not considered expensive by this city's standards, but it would still be difficult to dine for less, including beverages, than CHF 40 per person. If your budget dictates a more restrictive price range, it will most likely be necessary to locate a fast-food outlet. In addition to the ever-present McDonalds, of which there are several, other establishments of this type are found along the narrow Niederdorfstrasse, just across the Limmat from the railroad station, and along the adjoining lanes. Be prepared, though, to eat standing up.

La Rotonde Restaurant (Kurhausstrasse 65) is a classical and formal restaurant associated with the magnificent Dolder Grand Hotel. Exquisitely prepared dishes and marvelous wines may be enjoyed in an elegant atmosphere enhanced by panoramic views over the lake and the distant mountains. Gentlemen are advised that a jacket is required for dinner. ☎ 251 88 29, Fax 251 88 29. $$$

Bodega Española (Münstergasse 15), as the name implies, is a Spanish restaurant. You may be surprised to learn that these are really quite common in Switzerland. This one, housed in a circa 1874 building of much character, is as good, and as authentic, as you will find. The formal restaurant, for which reservations are strongly suggested, is located upstairs. Before or after your meal, though, be sure to stop by the bodega style bar located on the ground floor level, where mouthwatering tapas and robust wine served at bench tables evoke happy memories of Spain. It is open for meals from 11.00 a.m. to 2 p.m. and 6 to 11 p.m. ☎ 251 23 10. $$

Turm, Tony Navarro Restaurant (Obere Zäune 19), located in one of the narrow lanes not far removed from the Cathedral, is a bit challenging to find, but well worth the effort. Tony Navarro has let his imagination run wild with both the decor and the menu, and absolutely nothing about this place is dull. Dishes are based upon Mexican/Spanish cuisine—with a touch of Caribbean thrown in for good measure, and include such unusual, and debatable, delicacies as Kangaroo and Alligator filets. Opening hours are seven days a week from 11:30 a.m. to 11:30 p.m., and reservations only guarantee priority, not an immediate table. ☎ 262 52 00. $$

Raclette Stube (Zähringerstrasse 16) is a delightfully typical Swiss restaurant, of the style found more often in the countryside than in the city. Smallish, with a traditional wooden decor and a unique front window that swings open, it is located just across the Limmat from the railway station. Cheese specialties such as fondue and raclette, at reasonable prices, are the order of the day. Dine each evening from 5 p.m. to 11 p.m. ☎ 251 41 30. $$

Restaurant Zeughauskeller (Bahnhofstrasse 28a). Built in 1487 as the ancient arsenal of Zürich, this enormous restaurant, in which the original wooden beams and walls have been retained, abounds with character. Enjoy hearty traditional Swiss dishes, many featuring pork and sausage, served on huge bench tables in an authentic ambiance. Do not overindulge, however; you will want to save room for one of the chef's famous homemade desserts. Open daily from 11:30 a.m. to 11 p.m., but the kitchen closes at 10 p.m. ☎ 211 26 90. $$

Jules Verne Panorama Bar (Uraniastrasse 9) is not a restaurant in the strict sense of the word, but it should not be overlooked; if only for its spectacular views of the city and the Alps. The entrance is through the Brasserie Lipp, where an elevator will whisk you up to the 12th floor bar. Once there, treat yourself to one, or more, of an enticing selection of tapas and pâtisseries, and wash them down with champagne or a cocktail. It is open Monday to Thursday from 11 a.m. to midnight; Friday and Saturday from 11 a.m. to 1 a.m.; and Sunday from 3 to 11:30 p.m. X: Sun. during July and August. $

Restaurant Rheinfelder Bierhaus (Niederdorfstrasse 15) is exactly what its name says it is—half restaurant, half beer hall—very informal, no privacy, but as cheap as you'll get. It is open daily from 11 a.m. to 11 p.m. $

SUGGESTED TOUR:

This tour begins at the **Main Railroad Station** *(Hauptbahnhof)* (1), a place virtually every visitor to Zürich will pass through at one time or another. Opened in 1872, this station, on the surface at least, looks very much like what it is. But don't be deceived. Delve deeper and you will find, beneath the station, a huge shopping complex of over 170 stores. And, this is important, because this is about the only place in Zürich—and the country for that matter—where you will find shops open on a Sunday. Do not expect this across the board, however, even down under. That would be too simple. Half of the area is owned by the city, and shops in that section are prohibited from opening on the Sabbath.

Exit by way of the main façade of the station, which actually faces the river and away from the main street in Zürich. Looking to the left, it is impossible to miss the large, castle-like structure across the road that houses the **Swiss National Museum** *(Schweiz Landesmuseum)* (2), ☎ 218 65 65, Museumstrasse 1. Enter through a huge courtyard, passing cannons and a small cafeteria, to investigate three floors and a basement filled with exhibits that, together, form the most important collection of items documenting Swiss cultural history. Visit Tuesday through Sunday from 10:30 a.m. to 5 p.m.

The next leg of the tour will pick up on the other side of the station. Because the area between the main façade and the museum serves as an important tram junction it is easier to avoid the congestion by taking the pedestrian walkway under the road. This will also give some perspective of the size of the shopping area, before taking the escalators up to the main concourse. You will find kiosks here—the best place to find the latest editions of foreign newspapers. It is also interesting, besides observing the architectural style, to take note of the arrivals and departures boards above you. The cities mentioned are not just Swiss, and there is an impressive array of train services, including both German and Italian high-speed trains. Outside the south side of the station is a statue of Alfred Escher (1819–82), the founder of the Swiss railway. It would be interesting to hear his comments on the progress made in the century since his death.

Immediately behind Escher, past another important tram junction and stop, is the most famous street in Switzerland. **Bahnhofstrasse**, home to an eclectic variety of fine stores, hotels and restaurants, is a mile long and one square meter of property here is worth an astounding CHF 250,000. The third square block to your right, though, is quite different from the others. The charming park filling this space today gives no clue to its sinister past when it was the public execution site. Hence its present use; no one was overly anxious to build on it. The statue standing guard in the park's center is of **Jo Heinrich Pestalozzi** (3), who acted on his opposition to private education by founding the city's public school system.

Zürich is renowned for its fountains, more than 1,200 of them in all shapes and sizes. What's more, the water flowing from them is considered to be of better quality than that running from the taps in local residences. One fountain of particular note is the small one found at the end of the park on Bahnhofstrasse. Elegant and interesting, it was donated to Zürich by Paris in 1870 to initiate the World Convention of Water Experts. The four nymphs on each corner personify simplicity, purity, sobriety and charity, and are meant to symbolize international cooperation.

Those planning to shop at some time during this trip should note that this is the street to come back to. For the moment, however, continue the tour by crossing Bahnhofstrasse and taking the side street to Werdmühleplatz. On the 12th floor of the unusual octagonal tower across the street is the Jules Verne bar, which offers an impressive panoramic view of the city and the surrounding countryside. Continue, next, left along Uraniastrasse, climbing the rather elaborate steps, passing the Internet Café, and taking a left at the top before turning into **Kaminfegergasse** (4), a most interesting tiny cobblestoned street. Lining the way are ancient houses, one of which dates from

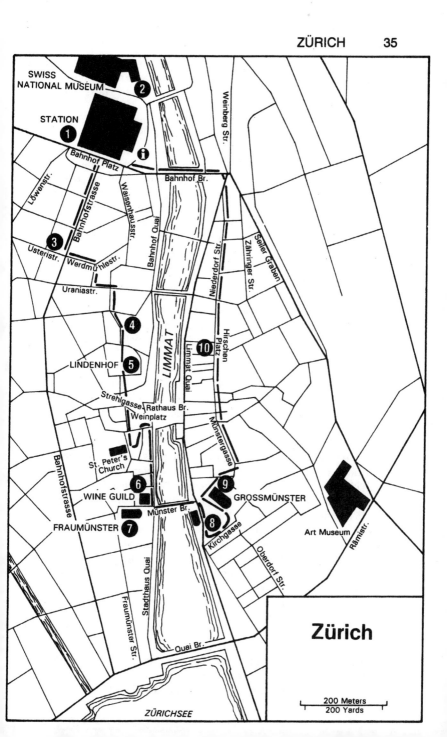

Zürich

200 Meters
200 Yards

1401 and is thought to be the oldest brick home in Zürich. Note, also, the pulleys in the gables which are ingenuously used, as in many houses in Amsterdam, to haul furniture and other unwieldy objects by crane to the upper floors.

A left at the end followed by a right will bring you to **Lindenhof** (5) which, though it may look insignificant, has a story to tell. Your clue is the statue, dating from 1292, of a woman dressed in military uniform. On one occasion, the Hapsburgs were attacking the city from below, while the men of Zürich were away battling at Winterthur. The women of the city, determined to defend their homes, devised a clever plan which foiled the advancing troops. Dressing in military uniforms, they stood in lines along the walls of Lindenhof. The Hapsburgs, convinced the city was formidably protected, retreated. These days it is a more peaceful place. Besides offering wonderful views over the Limmat river, with the old Town Hall in the foreground and the two towers of the Cathedral on the hill behind, it is a place people simply come to relax.

As you leave Lindenhof, opposite where you entered by way of another cobbled street, you are confronted with a very unusual perspective. Directly ahead, with one almost directly behind the other, are two contrasting spires, both embellished with striking clocks. The first, belonging to St. Peter's Church, has (at 28½ feet) the largest clock face in Europe—beating Big Ben in London by just an inch or so. The latter is the Fraumünster, home of Chagall's famous stained-glass windows—which we will explore later.

Continuing on you will see that St. Peter's Church has quite a charming small plaza outside and, as you draw nearer, it becomes increasingly obvious that the shops here are rather upscale. The overhanging windows are of interest, also, especially one with a lion on it, found above the Naomi store. Pay close attention now because, even though its easy to miss, you really will want to descend down through the narrow **Thermengasse** (5), the name of which offers a clue as to what is to be seen. Metal grille steps allow a view of the ruins that lie beneath, and diagrams and other documentation verify that, in Roman times, this was a thermal spring. What you see is only a part of what once was, and quite impressive it must have been!

Following around brings you out to Weinplatz, an attractive little square with a wonderfully ornate wrought-metal fountain, right next to the Limmat river. It is also home to Zum Storchen, the hotel with the finest river views in Zürich. Pass its entrance and turn right, following a footpath alongside the Limmat towards the next bridge. Stop for a moment, though, to admire the view of the ancient Town Hall, across the crystalline, swift-flowing waters of the Limmat. The closer you get to the bridge the more aware you will become of the elegant building to the right, most especially its ornate, gold wrought-iron balcony. This merits further investigation and, as you turn the corner it will become apparent just what a fine house this is. As previously explained, guilds have played an important part in Zürich's history, and the

Wine Guild (6) is one of the grandest of them all. Obviously not wishing to skimp on any luxury for themselves, they constructed this as their head-quarters in 1757. It now houses the Ceramics Museum, and the exhibits are fine indeed. Note, also, the memorial in honor of Sir Winston Churchill (1874–1965), who made his famous "Europe Arise" speech from here on September 19, 1946.

Churches abound in Zürich. There are over 100 in the city—60% Protes-tant and 30% Catholic, but the ***Fraumünster** (7), with its magnificent spire, is special. As the name denotes, this is the women's cathedral, and it has a truly ancient history. Legend, of course, plays its part, but it is documented that as far back as AD 853 the German king, Ludwig, donated an existing convent to Hildegard, his daughter. Soon after, it was she who commis-sioned the construction of a new church that has been perpetually enlarged, renovated or reconstructed over the ensuing centuries. Those curious to learn more about this interesting story would do well to purchase the small booklet available there, a part of the *Guides to Swiss Monuments* series. As intriguing as this history is, it is not the primary reason people from around the world come to the Fraumünster. That honor goes to its innovatively in-terpretive stained-glass windows. The most famous of these are by the Russian emigré, Marc Chagall (1887–1985), who was commissioned by the church in the 1960s and whose works were installed in 1970. Not to be overlooked, either, is the work of the Swiss artist Augusto Giacometti (1877–1947), whose "Heavenly Paradise" was installed following the Second World War. Open daily May 1 to September 30 from 9 a.m. to 12:30 p.m. and 2–6 p.m.; October from 10 a.m. to midday and 2–5 p.m.; November 1 to the end of February from 10 a.m. to midday and 2–p.m.; and March 1 to April 30 from 10 a.m. to midday and 2–5 p.m.

Time to cross the Limmat now, by way of the Münsterbrücke. The eques-trian statue guarding the bridge is of a past mayor. Before crossing, though, take a peek to the right, where you will see the women's swimming pool, some fortifications, and the first bridge over the Limmat. Just past that is where the steamers embark on tours around the lake, and you are certain to see, gliding past you, some of the swans and ducks so common here. Also, on a clear day, the distant Alps will glimmer. A right, once on the other bank, will lead you to the picturesque **Kirchgasse** (8), which dates from the 11th and 12th centuries. The different styled houses that line it, a bit younger, were built during the 13th to 18th centuries.

The twin towers, and they were not always round, of your next destina-tion, the ***Grossmünster** (9) now beckon. Walking around the plaza to the main entrance, you will note on the exterior the representation of a horse and rider, and a figure of Charlemagne. The former dates from around 1180 and is considered the earliest portrayal of a horseman in the northern Alps. The latter is just a copy. The 15th-century original was being damaged by exposure to the weather and can now be seen in the crypt. Legend says that the Grossmünster was founded by Charlemagne, and he is a story in himself. He was crowned three times, married four times, and of his seventeen children fourteen were girls. Apparently, he never allowed the girls to marry, but made their boyfriends princes and, by the time he died it was too late for them to wed. Back to the church. Construction commenced on this Romanesque type structure at the beginning of the 12th century, though it was not completed for another one hundred years. The interior, with the exception, perhaps, of the stained-glass windows by Augusto Giacometti, is rather austere, and that is not without reason. This, the parish church of Zürich, was at the epicenter of the Swiss Reformation movement, led by Huldrych Zwingli (1484–1531) and Heinrich Bullinger (1504–75). One of the first initiatives of these leaders was to remove, in 1519, all artwork, altars and other physical embellishments—even the organ. It is open April to October, Monday to Saturday from 9 a.m. to 6 p.m. and November to March, on the same days from 10 a.m. to 4 p.m. Throughout the year, it is open after Sunday services until 4 p.m.

Time, now, to leave all thoughts of austerity behind. Exiting the Grossmünster by way of Münstergasse you will be struck by just how cosmopolitan Zürich can be, especially here in the Dörfli, Zürich's pedestrian zone. Among the trendy shops, art galleries and the interesting restaurants, there are two places that merit special attention. The Bodega Española, housed in a colorful building dating from 1874, presents the ultimate in authenticity both in its delightful upper level dining room and in the typical bodega located on the street level. A few yards away is a place entirely different in character, but no less authentic. The Chocolate Café Conditorei is as delightful as delightful can be, with several floors and a small outdoor plaza where you may sample some of the most delicious chocolates, and other candies, you have ever tasted. If you will be returning home soon, why not take some back as gifts? Besides being beautifully presented, these confections are definitely tastier than our domestic sweets.

Back outside and farther along, you will come upon a warrior—standing at a safe distance—atop another fountain. This, the **Stüssihofstatt Fountain** *(Brunnen auf der Stüssihofstatt)* (10), dates from 1574, although the failing water receptacle was replaced in 1811. From here Niederdorfstrasse slopes gently down to Central, just across the Limmat from the Hauptbahnhof, the end of the tour. Expect it to get somewhat seedier along the way. Sex shows and stand-up restaurants—not much more than shop fronts really—and, of course, the irrepressible McDonalds predominate. But it is by no means threatening. You may even find the craft market near the Hotel Biba open and enjoy the entertainment of street artists along your way.

Schaffhausen and Stein-am-Rhein

Schaffhausen owes its existence to the Rhine *(Rhein)* Falls, the largest in Europe. These rapids, formerly known as the upper and lower Laufen, interrupted the transport of goods by water so that all commodities not sold locally were, of necessity, moved by horse-drawn carriages around the falls. Count Eberhard III of Nellenburg, anticipating the importance of this site to river merchants of the Rhine, Danube and Aare, founded a town here. His cousin, Heinrich III, who was the German Emperor, in a document dated July 10, 1045 granted Eberhard the right to mint coins for the new town, *Scafusun*. Four years later, in 1049, Eberhard founded the All Saints Abbey. And, in 1080, Eberhard's son, Burkhart, gave the town to the abbey. The needs of the abbey soon outgrew its structure, however and, in 1104, the Bishop of Constance inaugurated a much larger replacement, which stands today as a magnificent example of the Romanesque style of architecture.

During the early 13th century Schaffhausen became a free town and expanded rapidly over the next century and a half. Surprisingly, though, the size of the population changed little between 1370 and the 19th century. In 1330 Schaffhausen again lost its freedom when the Duke of Austria loaned money to the German Emperor who pledged Schaffhausen in return. This did not inhibit economic expansion, though, and the town flourished as goods from Germany and the Tyrol were also traded there.

Schaffhausen received a guild constitution in 1411, which allowed each of the twelve guilds formed to send a proportionate number of guildsmen to the government. A few decades later, in 1454, it entered into a 25-year alliance with eight Swiss cantons, which was renewed in 1479 for a further quarter of a century. In 1501, it joined the Swiss Confederation, becoming the most northerly of the cantons.

The early 16th century brought the Reformation. In turn, the religious wars that ensued between 1564 and 1585 caused the need for improved fortifications; hence the construction of the Munot. Schaffhausen enjoyed the fruits of prosperity for two centuries longer, especially during the 18th century when a flurry of construction saw, among other things, approximately 150 beautiful, and now famous, bay windows (oriels), added to its houses. Gradually, though, changes in the customs association, the discovery of new salt deposits in Schweizerhalle and, perhaps more importantly, the coming of the railroad, altered the economic balance.

All was not lost. In 1866, Heinrich Moser constructed a large dam across the Rhine, and the power generated from its hydroelectric works provided Schaffhausen with the spark it needed to play a prominent role in the Industrial Revolution. Unfortunately, this later attracted the attention of the Allied Forces, and Schaffhausen was bombed by American aircraft on April 1, 1944.

Today, this town of 34,000 people has the ambiance of one that time has passed by. On nearly every street, all of which are dominated by the massive Munot fortress towering above, you will find picture-perfect houses with elaborately decorated, painted and sculptured façades. Squares, large and small, are graced by fountains and guarded by statues of the likes of William Tell. This town is a real delight that has, thankfully, escaped the ravages of tourism.

GETTING THERE:

Trains arrive at Schaffhausen directly from Zürich, on a regular basis. On the return from Stein-am-Rhein, trains travel directly to Zürich but, depending upon the schedules, you may find it more time efficient to return to Schaffhausen and continue from there to Zürich.

Boats offer transport up the Rhine between Schaffhausen and Stein-am-Rhein.

By car: Because the enjoyment of this trip relies upon a combination of train and boat transportation, cars are not recommended.

PRACTICALITIES:

The **Dialing Code** for Schaffhausen and Stein-am-Rhein is 52. The **Tourist Office** (Schaffhausen Tourist-Service), ☎ 625 51 41 or Fax 625 51 43, Fronwagturm, CH-8201 Schaffhausen, opens Monday to Friday from 10 a.m. to midday and 2–5 p.m.

The **Tourist Office** (Verkehrsbüro) in Stein-am-Rhein, ☎ 741 28 35 or Fax 741 51 46, is at Oberstadt 9, CH-8260 Stein-am-Rhein.

ACCOMMODATION:

Neuhausen:

The **Hotel-Restaurant Bellevue über dem Rheinfall ***, ☎ 672 21 21 or Fax 672 83 50, Bahnhofstrasse 17, CH-8212 Neuhausen, has a very unusual location—just above the Rheinfalls. A convenient few minutes by bus from Schaffhausen, it has spacious, modern rooms and a restaurant that specializes in fish dishes. $$

Schaffhausen:

The **Rheinhotel Fischerzunft *******, ☎ 625 32 81, Fax 624 32 85, E-mail fischerzunft@relaischateaux.fr or www.integra.fr/relaischateaux/fischerzunft, Rheinquai 8, CH-8202 Schaffhausen, captivated my interest long before I experienced it for myself. Standing within a few feet of the majestic Rhine river, the 19th-century building is home to just ten rooms, classified Standard, Superior or Superior-Deluxe. Each is appointed to the highest standards and decorated in a contemporary style that makes for a comfortable, warm, ambiance. Though some would point out that it is rather incongruous with the town's medieval flavor, that is a part of its charm. Combine these attributes with the chance to savor owner/chef André Jaeger's simply astounding culinary creations, and it is enough to tempt the most discerning traveler to break their journey in Schaffhausen overnight. Be forewarned, it is closed on Tuesday and from January 25 to February 16. **$$$**

Stein-am-Rhein:

The Hotel **Chlosterhof ******, ☎ 742 42 42 or Fax 741 13 37, Oehningerstrasse 2, CH-8260 Stein-am-Rhein, situated upon the banks of the Rhine, offers rooms and suites—many with balconies, that blend modern facilities with a romantic atmosphere. Restaurants, bars and a Rhine Terrace add to the ambiance. **$$$**

FOOD AND DRINK:

Rheinhotel Fischerzunft (Rheinquai 8 in Schaffhausen) is truly a unique restaurant. André Jaeger, the owner/chef, has combined the best of Oriental and French cuisine to create dishes that are not only delectable to the palate, but beautiful to the eye. He also utilizes the design of *Yin et Yang* (symbolic of the opposite attractions of male and female) in his presentation. Perhaps the best example is his Bento Box dish—well, two dishes actually. The top dish is the "Box," black and divided into four sections which each hold a Chinese delicacy. The "Box," in turn, sits upon a round plate with roses and other flowers arranged around the exposed edges. Some would say it looks too good to eat and you may concur; but that would, surely, be a waste—as you will agree when you taste! And, the dining room is an experience in itself. Its decor, accentuated by wooden beams, antiques and even a collection of modern art; and its lovely tables, set to perfection right down to the fine crystal, are a fitting a complement for these unique dishes. You will have surmised by now that Switzerland has an abundance of fine restaurants, many of which are also creative. The Fischerzunft, though, is extraordinary even among such distinguished company and, if there is one place on your itinerary that is worthy of splashing out, this is it. So go ahead; indulge. You will not be disappointed, it is a dining experience of a lifetime. It is closed on Tuesday and from January 25 to February 16. ☎ 625 32-81, Fax 624 32 85. $$$

Restaurant Sonne (Rathausplatz 13, Stein-am-Rhein) is found in a delightful old house dating from 1463. Philippe Combe, the chef/proprietor specializes in poultry, lake or river fish and terrines. His restaurant is a member of Les Grandes Tables de Suisse organization. It is closed on both Tuesday and Wednesday. ☎ 741 21 28 or Fax 741 50 86. $$$

SUGGESTED TOUR:

This tour demands an early start from Zürich; it is best to arrive at Schaffhausen around 8:30 a.m. Outside the station keep your eye out for a Number 1 or Number 9 bus, with **Rheinfalls** as its designated destination. These run a continual loop service between Schaffhausen and Neuhausen, but the driver will be happy to advise you where to disembark in Schaffhausen, about fifteen minutes later. The falls will be a very short walk away, but you will hear them before you see them and, most probably, you will see an upwards rush of foam and spray before you arrive. No, it is not the Niagara Falls but, with a width of 164 yards, a height of 25 yards, and a volume of over 24,720 cubic feet of water passing over the falls each second, it is impressive enough. Like Niagara Falls, however, you can either walk out onto a platform that extends into the falls themselves, or take a somewhat precarious ride in a small boat that travels very close to the bottom of the falls. If you prefer not to get so up close and personal, take the easy way—enjoy the view from the Hotel Bellevue. And, if you are in the area on August 1, Swiss National Day, you are in for a treat indeed. In the evening a glorious fireworks display will explosively add a rainbow of illumination to this already magnificent sight.

By the time you get back into town, the **Schaffhausen Tourist Office** (1), will most probably be open. Unusually for such places, the work day does not begin until 10 a.m. and, in truth, this one does not have a great deal to offer—at least in English. The office is, however, housed in the **Fronwagturm** tower, which is adorned with an astronomical clock that dates from 1564 and shows no less than ten different features.

Immediately in front of the tourist office is **Fronwagplatz** (2), the traditional market place, and at its end is the colorful **Moor's Fountain** (Mohrenbrunnen) (3). In 1535 this, named after Kaspar, the youngest of the Three Holy Kings, replaced a wooden statue that earlier stood on this spot. Continuing on just a bit you will find, at Vorstadt 17, a particularly beautiful house, the **House of the Golden Ox** (Haus zum Goldenen Ochsen) (4). One of the grandest houses in Schaffhausen, this functioned as an inn prior to 1608, at which time it was renovated for use as a townhouse. Notable among its features are a late Gothic façade decorated with frescoes showing a golden ox and symbols from Babylonian and ancient Greek history.

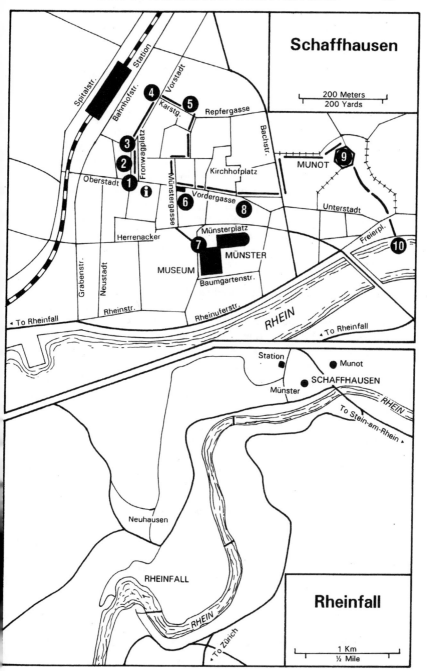

Next, make a right into Karstgasse and, at Platz 7, note another of these elaborately decorated houses. The house of the **Three Kings** (Zu den Drei Königen) (5), dates from 1746 and, in addition to its Rococo façade, is known for the statues of the Three Kings sitting above the second-floor windows. By this time you will have become aware of the proliferation of picturesque bay windows, over 150 in all, that are the signature feature of Schaffhausen.

Press on, crossing the plaza, parallel to the way you came along Vorstadt, until you come to Vordergasse, just down from the tourist office. There, near its corner with Münstergasse, is the **Knight's House** (Haus zum Ritter) (6), considered to be the most beautiful home in town. Knight Hans von Waldkirch rebuilt it in 1566, commissioning a local artist, Tobias Stimmer, to decorate the exterior. Stimmer worked his magic here between 1568 and 1570 with such mastery that his fresco has been acclaimed the most significant north of the Alps! Of course, the centuries have taken their toll but, in 1943, the fresco got a face lift when it was brilliantly restored by Carl Roesch.

Time, now, for a short but inspiring diversion. Go down Münstergasse, where the street name alone gives a clue to the destination—well, destinations, really. Originally founded by Eberhard von Nellenburg in 1049, and rebuilt shortly afterwards, the **Cathedral of All Saints** (Münster zu Allerheiligen) (7) is one of the finest examples of pure Romanesque architecture in Switzerland. Its tower, constructed around 1200, is thought to be among the most beautiful in the country. Surprisingly simple in style, this is a haven of peacefulness; with a serene silence broken only occasionally—perhaps by the song of a bird, perhaps by dulcet strains from the music school located in the complex. And, this aura of tranquillity extends itself into the adjoining cloister and herb garden. The former, part 12th-century Romanesque and part 13th-century Gothic, is the largest in the country. It includes a delightful garden and the **Noblemen's Cemetery** (Junkernfriedhof), in which civic dignitaries and other important townspeople were laid to rest between 1582 and 1874. The garden, easily distinguished by the its alluring perfumes and fragrances, is a re-creation of that which the monks are thought to have cultivated during the medieval times, and all the herbs are identified individually. Before retracing your steps back to Vordergasse you may be interested in visiting the **Museum of All Saints** (Museum zu Allerheiligen), which is open Tuesday to Sunday from 10 a.m. to midday and 2–5 p.m.

Continue down Vordergasse, away from the tourist office, passing the early 13th-century Gothic church of St. Johann. At numbers 26 and 28 you will come upon yet another attractive house, actually a double house, that was built in 1738. This is fronted by an octagonal pool, dated 1632, which surrounds the statue and water fountain of **William Tell** (Tellenbrunnen) (8). The original of this work was erected in 1522; the one you see today is a copy.

A little farther on is the larger, and busier, Bachstrasse, from which you get your first real look at the imposing, and unusual, ***Munot** (9), the symbol of Schaffhausen. Surely you will want to pay this formidable fortress a visit—which entails crossing the road and negotiating a considerable flight of steps before you reach the walkway. This highly unusual defensive battlement was constructed between 1564 and 1585 in a prominent defensive position with views over the town, Rhine and surrounding countryside. Its circular keep, unique in itself, is protected by thick walls and a ceiling supported by round, very thick, columns and arches. The watchman and his family still reside in the solitary, but pleasing, tower. Every evening, at 9 p.m. on the dot, he rings a bell that in days gone by was the signal to close the town gates and public houses. Visit between May and September from 8 a.m. to 8 p.m. and the rest of the year from 9 a.m. to 5 p.m.

There is one more surprise, though, as you exit. Steep, covered steps lead you down through a vineyard and, finally, deposit you very close to the landing from which the **boat to Stein-am-Rhein** departs. It is, fortuitously, next door to the Rheinhotel Fischerzunft. If you have timed it right you might just have time, and time you will need, to have the lunch of a lifetime in its restaurant before a boat sets sail at either 1:30 or 3:30 p.m. Please note that these departure times vary according to the season, so contact Schweizerische Schiffahrtsgesellschaft Untersee und Rhein, ☎ 625 42 82 or Fax 625 59 93, to confirm the schedules before making your plans. Really, the experience of lunch and/or dinner here, if you prefer to stay the night, just should not be missed. Do not expect the bill to be inexpensive, but do expect a meal and an experience that you will savor long after the flavor is gone.

Sit back now and relax for the penultimate leg of this tour, as the boat slowly takes you, against the current, on a pleasant two-hour sailing to Stein-am-Rhein. Few stretches of the Rhine river, no matter which country it is flowing through, have not been industrialized; but this is one of them. Green hills, in places overlaid with woods, slope gently down to river banks scattered with quaint houses, often with private docks, and dotted with sleepy, picturesque, little towns. There are also a few surprises along the way— lovely reminders of the past. At Diessenhoffen, for example, you will float under a medieval covered wooden bridge.

*Stein-am-Rhein, at a strategic spot where the Rhine leaves the Untersee—one of the three sections of Lake Constance, will be immediately recognized by a large castle set on the hilltop behind it. As the boat pulls slowly into the dock, you will see at once that this pretty town, with its 1,000-year history and a population of just 3,000, has much to offer. It will be equally obvious that its charms are well known. Tourists, milling around everywhere, often arrive and depart on buses that await their return in the many public car parks. This is, to most minds, the consummate medieval town, where wooden-beamed houses predominate, many decorated with intricate frescoes and oriels. The **Rathausplatz** is the social center, and the Town hall, although renovated twice since, was built between 1529 and 1542. Another building that is a "must see" is the 1,000-year-old **St. Georgen Cloister**, a couple of hundred yards away. Make a point to see, also, the outbuildings around the courtyard, where the huge wooden press and barrels are sure to be of interest. The complex is open March to October from 10 a.m. to 5 p.m.

When you are ready to return to the railroad station, cross the bridge, turn right at the intersection with Wagenhauserstrasse and left into Bahnhofstrasse. The way the schedules are structured it is more time efficient, if you have narrowly missed the hourly service to Zürich, to catch the next train to Schaffhausen, and return to Zürich from there.

St. Gallen

Local legend weaves a fascinating tale of the founding of St. Gallen. It goes something like this: In 612, a roving Irish monk, by the name of Gallo, from Lake Constance was passing through the Steinach river valley when he fell into a briar patch. On that very spot, Gallo decided to build a hermitage, which he did with the assistance of a friendly bear. The legend goes on to tell how an abbey was later constructed around that site.

In 719, Otmar assumed leadership of that Benedictine Abbey and, as the original abbot, oversaw the construction of the first stone buildings to be erected there. Art and culture thrived within this complex, and during the 9th and 10th centuries it was considered one of the foremost centers of learning in the Western World. The foundation of the world-renowned library housed there today was laid during that period as well, although many of its more famous literary treasures and artifacts originate from the Middle Ages.

The increased attention and growing numbers of visitors to St. Gallen, in turn, attracted tradesmen and others who lived in Villa Sancti Galli just outside the monastery. A 926 invasion by the Magyars brought an increased awareness of the need for defensive fortifications and, hence, the first wall was constructed around the abbey shortly thereafter. The first mention of St. Gallen in official documentation was made in 1170.

In the middle of the 14th century a guild constitution was instituted, with the effect of giving power over the city to the six trade guilds and the association of powerful businessmen (zum Notenstein). The manufacture of textiles has played an important role in the history of St. Gallen since the Middle Ages, with linen production being predominant until the 18th century, when it was superseded by cotton and embroidery.

The early 16th century brought the Reformation in a movement led by Joachim von Watt, better known as Vadian. The city's first independent library was built in 1551.

Among the noteworthy events of the 18th century was the demolition and reconstruction of the ancient monastery. The Helvetian Revolution of 1798 shifted the balance of power away from the abbey, the city and the

47

republic of St. Gallen, and it became capital of the canton of the same name in 1803. In 1824, the establishment of the dual diocese of St. Gallen and Chur gave rise to the elevation of the abbey to the status of cathedral.

Today, you will find St. Gallen, the seventh-largest city in Switzerland, a thoroughly charming town whose medieval center co-exists in easy harmony with 20th-century demands.

GETTING THERE:

Trains arrive at St. Gallen's station on a frequent service from Zürich.

By car, St. Gallen, just 53 miles east of Zürich, is reached by taking the N 1/E-60 Autoroute from that city.

PRACTICALITIES:

The **Dialing Code** for St. Gallen is 71. The **Tourist Office**, ☎ 227 37 37, Fax 227 37 67, E-mail tisg@dial.eunet.ch or www.bodan.net/tourism/tisg, Bahnhofplatz 1a, CH-9001 St. Gallen, is located directly across from the railway station. It is open Monday to Friday from 9 a.m. to midday and 1–6 p.m.; and Saturday from 9 a.m. to midday.

Hotel reservations may be made in advance by calling ☎ 227 37 47.

Stores are typically open in St. Gallen on Monday, Tuesday, Wednesday and Friday from 9 a.m. to 6:30 p.m.—although some do not open until 1 p.m. on Monday; Thursday from 9 a.m. to 9 p.m. and Saturday from 9 a.m. to 5 p.m.

ACCOMMODATION:

The **Hotel Walhalla ******, ☎ 222 29 22 or Fax 222 29 66, Bahnhofplatz, CH-9001 St. Gallen, is a modern hotel, refurbished in 1994 and conveniently located outside the station and very close to the Old Town. The rooms are comfortable and quiet, and the on-site restaurant serves Japanese Sushi-Bar cuisine. $$

The **Hotel Gallo *****, ☎ 245 27 27 or Fax 245 45 93, St. Jacobstrasse 62, CH-9000 St. Gallen, easily recognizable by its second-floor oriel, is a refined and stylish hotel situated in close proximity to the exhibition grounds, theater and concert hall and near the city center. Affiliated with it is an Italian restaurant named, appropriately enough, Galletto. $$

The **Im Portner *****, ☎ 222 97 44 or Fax 222 98 56, Bankgasse 12, CH-9000 St. Gallen, is typical of the half-timbered medieval buildings so common throughout the Old Town. You will find clean rooms with much character in a superb location just seconds away from the Cathedral. $

FOOD AND DRINK:

One of the more esoteric pleasures of St. Gallen is a visit to one of the "1. Stock-biezlie." These quaint first-story taverns serve tasty local specialties such as St. Gallen sausage—made using a singular recipe dating from

1438, and *Biber*—a spicy honeycake filled with marzipan. You will find the perfect accompaniment to be a glass, or two, of *Rheintaler* wine. Typical examples of *1. Stock-biezlie* are: **Anker**, ☎ 222 06 96, Schmiedgasse 20; **Schlössli am Spisertor**, ☎ 222 12 56, Zeughausgasse 17; and **Schwarzer Adler**, ☎ 22 75 07, Marktplatz 12.

SUGGESTED TOUR:

This tour begins at the **Railway Station** *(Bahnhof)* (1), a rather unconventional mixture of old and new. The first stop is the **Tourist Office** (2), directly across the road. From there walk through the alley and make a left onto the busy St. Leonardstrasse where, almost immediately, you will come upon an interesting Art-Nouveau building that now houses the Austrian Consulate. Although not exactly up to the standard of Gaudi's intricate irrelevancies it is nonetheless striking and, surprisingly, it is not alone in St. Gallen. Constructed during the beginning of the 20th century, these outlandish structures are attributable to the wealth generated by the lucrative textile industry that was based here. Farther down the street, at its junction with Oberergraben and the beginning of the Old Town, is the **Broderbrunnen** (3), a water fountain embellished with a bronze statue, fish and turtles—the striking and intricate design of which is right at home with its eccentric neighbors.

Press on, turning next into Multergasse. While this quaint street has now been incorporated into the pedestrian shopping area, the buildings tell you a different story altogether. The narrow streets and alleys of the Old Town essentially remain the same today as they were in the street plan laid out following the Great Fire of 1418—and rarely will you find a shopping area of such charm. Look, especially, for the oriels—extended upper-level windows, a unique architectural feature—of which over 100 of have been preserved—found on the façades of the houses here. These were once considered an indication of the wealth of the owner, and the affluent cloth merchants would compete among themselves to design the most ornamental and intricate beau ideal. Two of the more notable examples along Multergasse are found on the Gothic edifice of the Zum Schiff (the Ship), on which the oriel dates from circa 1600; and on the Zum Rebstock (the Vine), a structure first mentioned in 1422, renovated in 1793 and embellished with a wooden oriel from 1783. These, and others like them, provide a strange, yet pleasing, contrast with others exhibiting more Art-Nouveau ornamentation.

The junction with Marktgasse presents an array of contrasting options. Down the hill, where the tour will take you later, sits the Vadian Memorial. To the right, the towers of the Cathedral inspire. And, to the left, with a lengthy and interesting history, is the **St. Laurence Church** (4)—your next destination.

Indications are that the first building on this site, a tiny 27 by 20 feet,

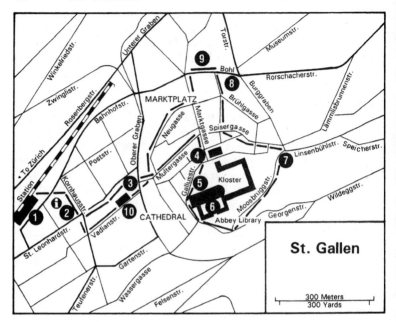

St. Gallen

300 Meters
300 Yards

was a cemetery chapel erected around AD 850. Another, larger one, replaced it sometime in the 11th century, and it is this structure that was likely dedicated to St. Laurence. It is widely held that, at this particular time, the church was associated in some way with the monastery. In the 13th century, however, it became the parish church, giving the people who worshiped there some degree of autonomy from the monastery. Unfortunately, the fire of 1314 destroyed the church and it was a full century later, in 1413, that work commenced on a new, Gothic style, building. During the Reformation, in 1527, Holy Communion was celebrated in St. Laurence's according to Protestant rites, and it emerged as the town's Protestant church. The parishioners consented to the removal of the traditional Catholic artwork and statues. Over the course of the next 300 years, until a major renovation in the mid-19th century, the church fell into a state of disrepair. It underwent a series of subsequent modifications until, in 1977, St. Laurence's was completely restored and modernized, at which time a massive 45-stop organ was installed. Visit Monday to Saturday from 9:30–11:30 a.m. and 2–4 p.m.

As you turn your attention to the **Monastery Courtyard** *(Klosterhof)*— where the size and splendor of the Cathedral complex will become increasingly apparent, pause for a moment or two to glance down Schmiedgasse at the splendid medieval houses and oriels in residence there. Back to the courtyard, you will note that this consists of three wings which, in addition to forming the Bishop's residence, house the cantonal offices.

The **Cathedral** *(Kathedrale)* (5) itself, dominated by two immense spires, was constructed by Peter Thumb between 1755 and 1767 as a replacement for the previous medieval structures. The interior design was a collaborative effort by Josef Wannemacher, artist; the Gigel Bros., stucco work; and J. A. Feuchtmayer, wood carving. An extensive restoration undertaken between 1961 and 1967 restored the building to its original condition, most notably uncovering the most marvelous ceiling frescos of the chancel and restoring that entire room to its original colors. Opening hours of the cathedral are, generally, Monday to Saturday from 9 a.m. to 6 p.m. and Sunday from 12:15–5:30 p.m.

As imposing a sight as this is, however, it is not considered the main attraction here. That honor is reserved for the world-famous **Abbey Library of St. Gallen** *(Stiftsbibliothek St. Gallen)* (6), the entrance to which is found at the rear of the Cathedral. On your way around, take a few moments to investigate the buildings in Gallusstrasse and Gallusplatz as these are some of the finest examples of wooden-framed buildings and oriels in St. Gallen. The Abbey Library is one of the oldest in the world, and houses a collection of over 100,000 books and manuscripts, 2,000 of which date from the earlier and late Middle Ages. Included among these are many magnificent examples of handwritten books and a collection of 1,650 incunabulum. I think you will concur that a library as fine as this is deserving of equally resplendent quarters; and its present abode—constructed in 1758, with a highly elaborate interior completed nearly a decade later in 1767—fulfills this challenge with glorious elegance. Two tiers of incredible glassed-in bookcases stand beneath intricate ceiling frescoes depicting the first four Ecumenical Councils (Nicaea in 325, Constantinople in 381, Ephesus in 431 and Chalcedon in 451); between side lunettes portraying the Fathers of the Church; and above a lovely inlaid parquet floor. Really, this is an extraordinary room. In all of my travels, I have come across only one other library that can compare—the King John Library in the University of Coimbra, Portugal. It will come as no surprise, then, that the Abbey complex was added to the UNESCO world cultural treasures list in 1983. Be advised, however, that it has unusual opening hours: January to March and December, Monday to Saturday, from 9 a.m. to midday and 1:30–4 p.m.; April to November, Monday to Saturday, from 9 a.m. to midday and 1:30–5 p.m., and Sunday from 10 a.m. to midday and 1:30–4 p.m. ☎ 227 34 15. Oh, one other curious note: Prior to entering the library you will be obliged to slip your shoes into huge slippers. The official reason given is that this minimizes damage to those marvelous wooden floors, but I surmise there is an ulterior motive—it sure helps to keep the floors polished!

Exit the Cathedral complex, turning left along the outside of the walls and passing **Karl's Gate** *(Karlstor)* (7). This originates from 1570 and is the only fully preserved gate of the former city walls. Tradition has it that the gate was named in honor of the first person to pass through it, Cardinal Karl

Borromäus of Milan. Continuing around, stroll through Spisergasse and Kugeigasse, taking time along the way to more fully appreciate the charms of Old Town on your way to the statue of Vadian in Marktgasse.

Just down a slight hill is **Marktplatz** and, yes, it still keeps alive the tradition inherent in its name—there is a vegetable, fruit and food market here every Saturday. Walking away past the modern bus and tram station, you will surely be intrigued by a building directly ahead adorned by an intricate clock. This, the **Waaghus am Bohl** or **Kaufhaus** (8), is where, beginning in the Middle Ages and through the 19th century, merchants took their goods to be weighed. Since its restoration in 1963 it has served as a meeting place for the Greater District Council.

Crossing the road and turning left into Katherinegasse will take you, after a hundred yards or so, to the former **Convent of St. Catherine** (St. Katharinen) (9). Now designated an historic monument, this was originally founded in 1228 but closed three centuries later. Pride of place here belongs to the **Gothic Cloister**, a veritable oasis in this bustling part of St. Gallen. Concerts are given here during the summer months and it is also used as a lending library for toys (Ludothek).

Museum lovers will be particularly fascinated by St. Gallen's institutions, mostly grouped together on one street—you've guessed it; Museumstrasse. It is here that you will find the Historical, Ethnology, Art, Natural History and Kirchhofer museums, as well as the Puppet Theater and Concert Hall—all within a short walk from the St. Catherine convent. If time is limited and you must restrict your museum visitation to just one, I would strongly recommend the **Textile Museum** (Textilmuseum) (10), Vadianstrasse 2, which is located just around the corner from the Broderbrunnen and, conveniently, on the way back to the station. The history of St. Gallen and its affluence are inextricably linked to the textile industry, and the exhibits found here will heighten your appreciation of the quality and intricacy of the goods produced in this city. Expect to find, among other things, historical embroidery from the 14th to 20th centuries and European lace from the 16th through 20th centuries. Visit year round Monday to Friday, 10 a.m. to midday and 2–5 p.m. From April to October it is open for the corresponding hours on Saturday as well. ☎ 222 17 44.

The tour comes to a close as you retrace your steps along St. Leonardstrasse back to the railway station.

Lindau (Germany) and Bregenz (Austria)

When starting out to research this daytrip, on an overcast and rather miserable Saturday morning, my destination was Bregenz, Austria, where, I knew, there was a most unusual theater located right on the lake. I had never even heard of Lindau. As is often the case, however, curiosity foiled my plans and I decided to continue on the train, rather than alight at Bregenz. That, in retrospect, was a very intuitive decision. I discovered the charms of Lindau, a medieval town situated on a small island on the Bodensee, a genuine step back into the past and a real gem. I did, eventually, return to Bregenz. And, a visit there does have its merits, notably a chance to observe the cultural differences between Switzerland and Austria, but it is, in all honesty, much larger and not as attractive, or unusual, as Lindau.

Lindau has a fascinating history. The Romans, around 15 BC, conquered the Celts who lived around Lake Constance. They in turn were set upon by the invading Alemanni and driven from the area in the 3rd century AD. Five hundred years later, Count Adalbert von Rätien established a convent in Lindau, which was subsequently converted into the Foundation for Ladies.

It wasn't until late 9th century, 882 to be exact, that the name Lindau was recorded in an official document. Two centuries later, in 1079, the market was relocated from its original site on the mainland lakeside to the island itself, thus allowing for the development of commerce. This venture enjoyed such success that a financial document prepared in 1241 names Lindau as the second most prosperous city on Lake Constance.

At some time between 1274 and 1275, King Rudolf I confirmed the rights of Lindau to be a "Free Imperial City." Local unrest led to a revolt in 1345 in which the guilds prevailed, winning for themselves representation on the City Council. Later that century, Lindau's autonomy was expanded when, in 1396, King Wenzel granted the city the power of "High Jurisdiction," empowering the city to sentence and effect capital punishment.

As an interesting aside, during the 15th century, a new job position was instituted—the "Lindau Messenger." It was his responsibility to carry merchandise, mail and sometimes even travelers between Milan and Lindau, thus linking Lindau to Italy. This practice was terminated as recently as 1822.

In 1496, Lindau was honored when it was chosen to host a full meeting of the Reichstag in the city. Reformation was introduced in 1528, and the populace converted to Protestantism. In 1647, during the Thirty Years War, Lindau's freedom was jeopardized by advancing Swedish forces. It was successful, nevertheless, in defending itself against their advances. A period of relative calm ensued with the only notable event in the 18th century being the great fire of 1728 that destroyed more than forty prominent buildings around the Market Square.

The early 19th century brought with it many upheavals, however. In 1802 its status of "Free Imperial City" was revoked, and Lindau was placed under the rule of the Prince of Bretzenheim. Two years later it was annexed by Austria, and a year after that, in 1805, Bavaria wrested control of the city. In the midst of these troubled times, progress brought the railway, in 1853, to bridge the small channel that had separated the island from the mainland.

Following the Second World War Lindau was occupied by French troops, an occupation that continued until 1955 when, with the bestowing of the special status of autonomous district, it was returned to Bavaria.

The wealth and diversity of this small island's history is evident wherever you roam throughout its ancient streets. It is also, however, modern thinking and outward looking. With a population of 24,500, the city, building upon its natural and historical appeal, has become very much a holiday resort. In fact, up to 4,200 visitors can be accommodated simultaneously in a variety of establishments. When planning your itinerary try, if you can, to take this trip on a Saturday when the Market Square comes alive with a colorful and kaleidoscopic array of people and produce.

GETTING THERE:

Train is the best choice of transportation for this trip. In 1997, the EC 99 Bavaria departed Zürich at 7:41 a.m., with its final destination being Munich *(München)* a little over four hours later. The first three stops were in Switzerland, before its arrival in Bregenz, Austria, at 9:21 a.m., and Lindau, Germany sixteen minutes later. The equivalent return train, the EC 94 Gottfried Keller, departed from Lindau at 2:29 p.m. and Bregenz at 2:40 p.m. on its way to Zürich. If that timing is not convenient, you may take a local train or, perhaps, a lake steamer, between Lindau and Bregenz. This would be followed by another local train to the first station in Switzerland, St. Margrethen, and a connection to Zürich, via St. Gallen.

PRACTICALITIES:

The **Dialing Code** for Lindau is (International Code 011 49) 83 82. The **Dialing Code** for Bregenz is (International Code 011 43) 55 74.

The **Lindau Tourist Office**, ☎ 26 00 30 or Fax 26 00 26, Ludwigstrasse 68, D-88131 Lindau, is located directly in front of the railway station and opens Monday to Friday from 9 a.m. to midday and 2–5 p.m.; between April to October it also opens on Saturday from 9 a.m. to midday.

The **Bregenz Tourist Office** *(Bregenz Tourismus)*, ☎ 43391-0 or Fax 43391-10, is located at Anton Schneiderstrasse 4a, A-6900 Bregenz.

ACCOMMODATION:

The **Hotel Bayerischer Hof**, ☎ 50 55 or Fax 50 54, Seepromenade, D-88131 Lindau, is rather a large hotel situated on the promenade overlooking the lake. Traditional in style and decor, it has an outdoor pool with a lake view. $$

The **Hotel Weisses Kreuz ******, ☎ 4988-0 or Fax 4988-67, Römerstrasse 5, Bregenz, located in the center of the city, is a member of the Best Western organization. Expect modern, comfortable rooms, on-site restaurant and bar, and a pleasant terrace. $$

FOOD AND DRINK:

There are any number of delightful outdoor restaurants overlooking the harbor and lake in Lindau. Which you choose is simply a matter of personal preference as to style and menu.

SUGGESTED TOUR:

The tour begins at the **Railway Station** *(Hauptbahnhof)* (1) in Lindau. Although this traditional railway terminal was once rather grand, it must be said that today it is a little drab and dreary. Consequently, it suffers by comparison with the cleaner, and tidier, stations you will have become accustomed to finding in Switzerland. Directly across from the exit is the tourist office, where you can pick up a brochure/city plan in English. Before setting out to explore Lindau, though, practicalities must be taken care of. A change of country necessitates a change of currency, although, strangely, this is not of major concern when traveling between Germany and Austria. In any event, you will find a bank at the end of the station forecourt.

Retrace your steps back past the tourist office to the Seepromenade, and the spectacular **Harbor** *(Seehafen)* (2), from which, on a fine day, you can see the Alps in the background. On such a day Bregenz, also, can be seen clearly just around the lake, a sight which may tempt you to consider taking a steamer, as opposed to the train, for a return there later. For now, however, there is plenty to occupy you in and around the harbor. At the end and to the left of the promenade, past a host of delightful restaurants and open-air bars, is the distinctive rectangular tower of the **Mangturm** (3)—the name of which is derived from the Mangel, a tool used in the local cloth trade. It was built in the 13th century, with its upper floor and colorful, tiled roof added in the 19th century; it stands 121 feet tall. The Mangturm functioned

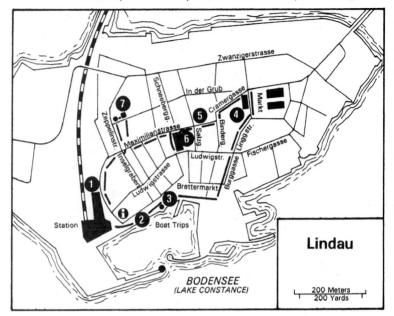

as the harbor lighthouse, until the new one was constructed, in 1856, at one side of the lake entrance to the harbor. It was also during that year that a magnificent 20-foot lion, the heraldic animal of Bavaria, came to sit proudly on a plinth at the other side of the entrance.

Continue along the promenade now, past the Mangturm and on around the harbor, before taking a left down Burggasse and Linggstrasse to the **Marktplatz** (4), home to a number of interesting sights. When planning your schedule, you will want to know that the Marktplatz is seen at its best on Wednesday and Saturday, traditional market days for over 900 years, when this square comes alive with a myriad of colorful stalls attended by people wearing traditional *Lederhosen* and Tyrolean hats—with a feather added of course. At the center of this bustling display stands a fountain with Neptune, his Trident and a fish at the top. This particular fountain dates from 1840 and was installed as a replacement for an earlier one dating from the Middle Ages.

The dominant structure in the square is the **Cavazzen House** *(zum Cavazzen)*, built shortly after the great fire of 1728. Named after the original owners, the von Kawatz, or da Cavazzo, family, it features a huge Mansard roof and a beautifully frescoed façade, and is considered one of the finest residences on Lake Constance. Presently, it houses the City Museum where the exhibits consist primarily of furniture, arts and crafts and an antique mechanical musical instrument collection. It is open Tuesday through Sunday from 10 a.m. to midday and 2–5 p.m.

Next door, and dating from the same period, is the classical **Baumgarten House**, so named after the fruit orchard of the convent that once stood on this site. Nearby is the **Holy Spirit Hospital** *(Heilig-Geist Hospital)*, which dates from the early 13th century, though the façade you see today dates from the early 19th century. One of the oldest social assistance institutions in this part of Germany, this hospital has, since its inception, served as a home for the poor and aged. Today it is a retirement home. And, its charities have not been confined solely to the medical field; uniquely, during the 15th century it offered to the citizens of Lindau the opportunity to borrow money at the unusually low interest rate of 5%.

Directly behind the square, with a façade dating from a 16th-century renovation of the original 1180 structure, is the parish church of Lindau. Its guardian angel must work overtime as this, the **St. Stephen's Church** *(Stephanskirche)*, was the only building overlooking the Market Square to survive the fire of 1728.

Pressing on, you will come, just around the corner, to the most significant street in Lindau, the **Maximilianstrasse** (5). Named after a Bavarian king, this pedestrians-only thoroughfare is one of the most enchanting shopping areas you could hope to find. Interspersed with the shops, which advertise by quaint overhanging signs the wares they sell (or sold), are a collection of graceful patrician houses, often frescoed and/or wooden-beamed and with gabled roofs and cheery doors—colorfully painted after the local tradition. At the ground level numerous arcades *(Brodlaube)* have been constructed to protect people from inclement weather.

Definitely the most dramatic and splendid of the buildings here is the ***Old Town Hall** *(Altes Rathaus)* (6). Set back a bit from the street, it has a highly unusual façade. Constructed between 1422 and 1436 on land that was once a vineyard, the building has wonderful frescoes and a spectacular frieze depicting the meeting of the Reichstag at Lindau in 1496. Notable on the lower section is a covered, wooden staircase—a 16th-century addition—which rises diagonally to a covered Proclamation Oriel from where laws and rules were proclaimed. The triangular-shaped upper portion has a stepped and decorated roof that culminates in a bell tower, also added during the 16th century. The ground-floor hall, which now houses the town's archives and the library of the former Imperial City, also contains over 23,000 works of art. Prominent among these is what is considered to be the most important collection of Bibles in southern Germany. In the small square is the **Lindavia Fountain**. Erected in 1884, it is composed of bronze figures, set between four marble basins, which symbolize the main activities of Lindau: vineyards and gardening, fishing, agriculture and navigation.

On the way back to the station, at the bottom of Maximilianstrasse, take a short detour along Zeppelinstrasse to take a look at the 14th-century

Thieves' Tower *(Diebsturm)* (7). Small watchtowers around the bottom of the spire give evidence of the role it once played in the defense of Lindau. Less evident, unless you have seen the cells still preserved inside, is its tenure as the city jail.

As this part of the tour is at an end, it is time for the first phase of the journey back to Zürich. If time, and sailing schedules, are on your side, the most pleasant journey to Bregenz is by Lake Steamer. If not, then take the train. Either way, you will arrive, at the dock or the railway station, in very close proximity to the extensive park that follows the lakeside. In looking around, you will quickly surmise that **Bregenz** is much larger than Lindau and, with the exception of the Old Town, much newer. The reality is, given the time constraints of this particular tour, that visitors will have very little time to see the town. And, if you have chosen Saturday to visit, another problem presents itself—all the shops will be closed by the time you arrive.

It is unlikely, also, that many will opt to stay the night. Notwithstanding its other attractions, Bregenz's chief claim to fame is the **festival** it hosts annually for one month during the summer. What makes this event even more eventful is the stage upon which it is performed—the world's largest stage on a lake under open skies and a theater which seats 4,000. As if the natural setting, with the lake and Alps as its backdrop, is not spectacular enough, the theater sets will most certainly amaze. The are renowned for their sheer enormity, their innovative design and their vibrant colors. A constellation of international stars and famous artists perform in a variety of spectacular opera productions, plays and concerts for the pleasure of hundreds of thousands of spectators. More information about this season can be found on the Internet at www.vol.at/bregenzerfestspiele, or by contacting the organizers via E-mail at bregenzer@festspiele.vol.at. If you can't arrange to be in Bregenz during that time—when you will, indeed, need to stay overnight—then, at least, take a look at the theater. It will astound you! Afterwards, if you still have time, wander around to get the flavor of Bregenz, and maybe purchase a souvenir from one of the kiosks, before returning to the station.

As it is highly unlikely that you will find a direct service back to Zürich, be prepared to take the slow Austrian train to St. Margrethen, the first station in Switzerland. From there you will find a fairly frequent connections on to Zürich.

Rapperswil

The first recorded documentation relative to this area dates back to 1229, when Rapperswil was settled by people who moved across from the other side of the lake. Very shortly thereafter, in 1233, an earldom was awarded to the first lords, though the dynasty lasted only another 60 years. During the next century, in 1350, the town was ravaged by the forces of Rudolf Brun, Bürgermeister of Zürich, and it was subsequently taken over by Austrian forces four years later. In 1415, officials granted permission for Rapperswil to hold a market, a tradition still adhered to every Friday morning from March to December. The city joined the Swiss Confederation later that century, in 1458. And although its freedom was threatened, it withstood the siege by the forces of Zürich in 1656. In 1803, it was incorporated into the canton of St. Gallen. Later that century, between 1830 and 1836, the town walls were demolished, and that is how you will find it today—an open town.

GETTING THERE:

Trains arrive at Rapperswil's station on a frequent basis from Zürich.

Lake Steamers, operated by Zürichsee, ☎ 482 10 33 or Fax 482 84 00, run a regular schedule of sailings between Zürich and Rapperswil.

PRACTICALITIES:

The **Dialing Code** for Rapperswil is 55. The **Tourist Office** *(Verkehrsbüro Rapperswil)*, ☎ 210 70 00 or Fax 210 43 61, is located directly outside of the railway station at Fischmarktplatz 1, CH-8640 Rapperswil. It opens Monday to Friday from 8 a.m. to midday and 1–5 p.m., and Saturday from 8 a.m. to midday.

ACCOMMODATION:

In reality Rapperswil is very near Zürich and most visitors will not consider an overnight stay. If, however, that is your choice, I suggest:

The **Hotel Schwanen ******, ☎ 220 85 00 or Fax 210 77 77, Seequai 1, CH-8640 Rapperswil, has an attractive façade and a delightful location on the lake side. Expect traditional style and decor, attentive service and a fine restaurant. $$

FOOD AND DRINK:

A major attraction of this daytrip is the return cruise to Zürich aboard one of Zürichsee's lake steamers. The restaurants found on board are very nice and, certainly, the place to eat on this trip. To avoid disappointment, be sure to secure a table reservation by calling ☎ 482 68 30 or Fax 483 01 61.

SUGGESTED TOUR:

This tour begins at the **Train Station** *(Bahnhof)* (1), connected by frequent trains from Zürich, some 31 miles away at the other end of Lake Zürich. Conveniently, the **Tourist Office** (2) is located just outside of the station. Less fortunately, though, you will not find a great deal of their information to be in English, besides a rather sparse brochure on both Rapperswil and the neighboring town of Jona.

The city plan in the brochure will confirm what you will have already observed—Rapperswil is rather small. In fact, its population numbers just 7,400, half of that of its neighbor. It is not, however, small on charms, and these are found mostly on the hill up by the castle.

To reach the castle, you will need to wind through the lower part of town, passing the Town Hall, on your way to the sloping **Hauptplatz** (3). The street pattern in this area was, in large part, laid out in the 13th century. The original houses, however, were constructed of wood and, age having taken its toll, these were replaced by stone homes over the course of the 16th and 17th centuries. The architectural harmony you see today is no accident as the construction, renovation and maintenance of all buildings is subject to strict local regulations.

This part of town, the social center of Rapperswil, is also the access point to the Castle, by way of an impressive double stairway, easily recognizable by the elegant water fountain set between the flights at its base. Believed to date from the early 13th century, this formidable **Castle** *(Schloss)* (4) sits at the highest point of a narrow promontory. Inside you will find what would best be described as a miscellany. A restaurant and banqueting hall occupy the lower floor and a museum, opened in 1975 and dedicated to Poland's contribution to western civilization, occupies the top floor. In fact, from 1870 to 1927, the castle housed the Polish National Museum. Equally as curious as the idea that Rapperswil should be the site for a Polish museum are its opening hours. From April to the end of October it opens daily from 1 p.m. to 5 p.m.; in November, December and March it opens only on Saturday and Sunday from 1–5 p.m., and it closes entirely during January and February.

Immediately to the left, which is the town side, of the castle is another

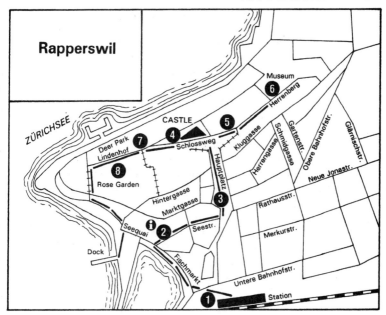

domineering structure, the Catholic Church. The first church on this site, built in 1253, succumbed to fire in 1882, with this new one consecrated shortly thereafter in 1885. Be sure to investigate, also, the **Cemetery Chapel** *(Liebfrauenkapelle)* (5) found just behind the church. It dates from 1489.

Not very far away, and within another interesting building, is the **Museum of Local History** *(Heimatmuseum)*(6), where you will find some interesting exhibits, including a model of the town as it appeared around 1800. This, believe it or not, has even weirder hours than the castle; Saturday from 2–5 p.m., Sunday and public holidays from 10 a.m. to midday and 2–5 p.m., and during the busiest months of the year, July and August, it opens on Wednesday as well from 2–5 p.m. It closes entirely from November to Easter Monday—definitely the most unusual hours of any museum I've ever seen and hardly solicitous of patronage!

Retrace your steps back past the castle and follow Lindenhof along the promontory, where you will find a host of surprises. From this vantage point, the views are spectacular indeed. The vast expanses of Lake Zürich unfold on either side, and the Alps stand majestically in the distance. It also offers the finest perspective of the Seedamm causeway connecting Rapperswil with Hurden at the other side of the lake. The predecessor to the current bridge was constructed on the orders of Archduke Rudolf IV, in 1358, and withstood the rigors of time and travel for over a half a millennium—until 1878. At that time a road/rail link was opened, which was subsequently modernized in 1939 and 1951. Today this is among the busiest stretches of roadway in Switzerland.

Continuing on, upon the slopes to the right-hand side of the promontory is a **deer park** (7), established in 1871. Today it houses between 10 and 15 of the dear animals. These are held in special reverence by locals due to their legendary role in the founding of the village.

To the left side is an expansive **rose garden** (8) where, between June to October, 6,000 rose bushes—of 180 varieties—bathe the horizon in a breathtaking display of kaleidoscopic blooms. This, too has a distinctive connection to the town; upon Rapperswil's coat of arms you will find displayed two rose blossoms.

The Capuchin monastery, built around 1606, and other fortifications occupy the tip of the promontory, and steep steps running between the monastery and the Rose garden descend back to the lake side. From there it is a pleasant walk back around to the small harbor, across from the Hotel Schwanen. This is the docking point for the **lake steamer** that will carry you back to Zürich. In 1997 a vessel departed at 1:45 p.m., perfect timing for you to enjoy a leisurely lunch as the boat slowly crisscrosses Lake Zürich on a relaxing and scenic two-hour voyage.

Vaduz (Liechtenstein)

Liechtenstein, a tiny landlocked country in the center of Europe—between Austria and Switzerland—is the fourth-smallest country in Europe with a land area of just 62 square miles and a population, as of December 31, 1995, of a mere 30,923. It does, though, have a long and interesting history. Permanently inhabited since 3000 BC, it was colonized by the Celts and later, around 800 BC, by the Rhaetians. In 15 BC it was conquered by the Romans, who built a north/south road that traversed the narrow country. Other evidence of their occupation here can be found in Roman villas that have been excavated in Schaanwald and Nendeln.

The 5th century saw a mass migration of Germanic peoples from the north, who forced the Romans out. Centuries later the area came under the rule of a German dukedom, becoming part of the country of Lower Rhaetia. Historically, Liechtenstein was divided into two parts; the Lordship of Schellenberg and the County of Vaduz, each owned over the years by various dynasties of counts. Prince Johann Adam Andreas von Liechtenstein's purchase of first Schellenberg in 1699 and, subsequently, Vaduz in 1712 earned him a seat in the Diet of the Princes, which was under the dominion of the German Empire. On January 23, 1719 Kaiser Karl VI decreed that Schellenburg and Vaduz be elevated to the status of the Imperial Principality of Liechtenstein. Today it has the distinction of being the only country in the world to still carry the name of its original dynasty.

In 1806 Napoleon formed the Rhine Confederacy under which 16 regions, including Liechtenstein, were granted sovereignty in return for a pledge of loyalty to him. Following Napoleon's defeat, the Vienna Congress of 1815 determined that Liechtenstein would be incorporated into the German Confederation, to which the country remained subjugated until the Confederation's dissolution in 1866.

From that time forward, Liechtenstein has remained a fully sovereign, neutral country, which has not kept an army since 1868. Between 1852 and 1919 it operated within a customs union with the Austro-Hungarian Dual Monarchy. Since 1924 it has maintained a customs treaty with Switzerland which, effectively, has formed a common economic region between the two small countries in which Swiss customs officers patrol the border with Austria and the Swiss Franc (CHF) is the legal currency. In 1978, Liechtenstein joined the Council of Europe, followed by memberships in the United Nations in 1990, the European Free Trade Association (EFTA) in 1991, and the European Economic Area (EEA) in 1995.

Liechtenstein is presently governed under the Constitution of 1921, which established "a constitutional hereditary monarchy upon a democratic and parliamentary basis." The Prince, as head of state, represents Liechtenstein in its relationships with other countries, while the rights and interests of the citizens are protected by a Parliament *(Landtag)*, which consists of 25 deputies. Incidentally, the right to vote was extended to women as recently as 1984.

Liechtenstein is divided into two regions, corresponding to the two historical domains, *Oberland* (Upper Country) and *Unterland* (Lower Country). Between them they encompass 11 communes which retain substantial traditional autonomy. High German is taught in the schools and used as the official language, but the majority of the natives speak a dialect similar to the Swiss-German *Schwiizertütsch*—a derivative that is difficult even for other German-speaking peoples to understand. Eighty percent of the population is Roman Catholic, while the remainder belong either to one of a variety of Christian churches, or none at all. The first prince to make his permanent residence in Liechtenstein, rather than Vienna, was Franz-Josef II who reigned from 1938 until his death on November 13, 1989. He was succeeded by his oldest son, Prince Hans-Adam II, the current reigning monarch.

Just as a point of interest, a curious aspect of the government of Liechtenstein presents itself in the judicial system. The courts are presided over by judges from Austria and Switzerland as well as those from Liechtenstein. This oddity can be attributed to the country's size, and the fact that the laws of Liechtenstein are an amalgam of Austrian and Swiss legal principles.

Liechtenstein enjoys the privilege of an Alpine landscape dominated by the Rhaetikon Massif and the Rhine River. The latter, however, lovely as it is, was labeled one of the three "National Plagues." At one time prone to massive flooding that endangered the country—the last one was the *Rheinnot* flood in 1927—the river has now been restrained by high embankments. Debris slides from the mountains *(Rüfen)*, the second of the "plagues," have now also been controlled. Third in the league of destruction was a natural phenomenon, the warm southerly wind known as the *Föhn*, that brings Liechtenstein its temperate climate. On more than one occasion the mostly wooden houses of Liechtenstein succumbed to extensive fires fanned by Föhn's pestilent breezes. Today, however, most buildings are constructed of brick and concrete, and each village maintains a well-equipped voluntary fire brigade.

GETTING THERE:

Trains from Zürich arrive at Sargans, from where buses depart to Liechtenstein, just 12 miles away.

By car, Liechtenstein, 68 miles east of Zürich, is reached by taking the N-3 to Sargans and then the N-13/E-43 north to Liechtenstein.

PRACTICALITIES:

The **Dialing Code** for Liechtenstein is 75. The **Vaduz Tourist Office**, ☎ 232 14 43 or Fax 392 16 18, is located at Städtle 37, FL-9490 Vaduz. Opening hours are Monday to Friday from 8 a.m. to midday and 1.30–5.30 p.m.; Saturday, May to October, from 9 a.m. to midday and 1–4 p.m.; and Sunday, June to October, from 10 a.m. to midday and 1–4 p.m.

The best place for buying Swiss Army Knives, and just about any other souvenir you can possibly think of, is Thönys Schuhgeschäft, ☎ 232 23 18 or Fax 233 26 18, Städtle 17. Shops in Liechtenstein are open Monday to Friday from 8 a.m. to midday and 1.30–6.30 p.m.; and on Saturday from 8 a.m. to 4 p.m. In Vaduz, though, from April to October souvenir shops also open on Sundays and holidays. Peculiar to Liechtenstein is an absence of supermarkets. Food and other consumer goods are purchased from a variety of small stores.

You will soon notice, and wonder at the significance of, the recurrent appearance of the initials FL—especially in street addresses and on stickers on the back of cars. In Europe these stickers, displaying letters representing their country of origin, are mandatory for vehicles crossing international borders. While the initials used by most countries are self-evident—F for France, I for Italy and so on—the derivation of Liechtenstein's are more obscure. FL stands for *Fürstentum Liechtenstein*, the Principality of Liechtenstein. The city of Vaduz, with a population of around 5,000, is the capital of Liechtenstein.

ACCOMMODATION:

The **Park-Hotel Sonnenhof** ****, ☎ 232 11 92, Fax 232 00 53, E-mail sonnenhof@relaischateaux.fr and www.integra.fr/relaischateaux/sonnenhof, Mareestrasse 29, FL-9490 Vaduz, is a particularly comfortable hotel located just a short distance from, and overlooking, Vaduz. Situated in a parklike setting it offers a traditional ambiance, every modern facility, on-site pool and health club, and marvelous views of the Rhine river and Swiss Alps in the distance. It will not be an option, however, if your vacation coincides with their vacation—annually from December 22 to February 15. $$$

The **Hotel Le Real** ***, ☎ 232 22 22, Fax 232 08 91, E-mail real@relaischateaux.fr and www.integra.fr/relaischateaux/real, Städtle 21, FL-9490 Vaduz, is, like the Park-Hotel Sonnenhof, owned and run by a members of the Real family. This small hotel, comprised of just ten rooms and 2 suites, is extremely comfortable and centrally located on the one really main street in Vaduz. It closes, annually, for the Christmas holiday from December 24 to December 26. $$

FOOD AND DRINK:

Park-Hotel Sonnenhof (Mareestrasse 29, Vaduz) features a delightful restaurant specializing in International and French cuisine. It serves a wide range of Sonnenhof Classics, caviar specialties, and vegetarian dishes as well as an innovative array of meat, poultry and fish entrées. It is open daily from midday to 2 p.m. and 7–10 p.m., except for the period December 22 to February 15 when it is closed. Reservations are required for those not staying in the hotel. ☎ 232 11 92, Fax 232 00 53. $$$

Restaurant Au Premier (Städtle 21, Vaduz), a member of the *Les Grandes Tables De Suisse* is found within the Hotel Real. A rustic-style dining room on the ground floor is augmented by a traditional one on the first where International and French cuisine, from a menu built upon seasonal market produce, is the order of the day. Particularly interesting are the home-grown asparagus festival held from May to June, and a five-day fish-and-seafood feast which begins on Ash Wednesday. Dine Saturday through Thursday from 9 a.m. to 11 p.m. and Friday and Saturday from 9 a.m. to midnight. It is closed December 24 through December 26. ☎ 232 22 22, Fax 232 08 91. $$

Gasthof Löwen (Herrengasse 35, Vaduz), Liechtenstein's first inn, dates from 1380. Nestled within scenic vineyards with views back to the castle and recently renovated, it serves regional and International specialties, with an emphasis on a short menu and snacks. Its food festivals are contrived around asparagus, game and flambé. Opening hours are daily from 7 a.m. to 11 p.m. They are closed for the winter holiday from Christmas day through January 6. ☎ 232 00 66 or Fax 232 04 58. $$

SUGGESTED TOUR:

Though Liechtenstein is a country of many rural delights, it is most probably fair to say that most visitors, and particularly those on daytrips from Zürich, will head for Vaduz. And, as there is not a great deal to see or do in Vaduz, the allure in most cases is curiosity. That isn't to say, though, that a daytrip to Vaduz is without merit; it certainly is.

Physically, Vaduz is dominated by the very grand castle, home of the prince and, unfortunately, not open to the public. Best guess is that the original, which was destroyed by troops of the Swiss Confederacy during the Swabian War of 1499, was constructed in the Middle Ages. The present structure dates from the 16th and 17th centuries.

Three hundred or so feet below the castle is the main street of Städtle,

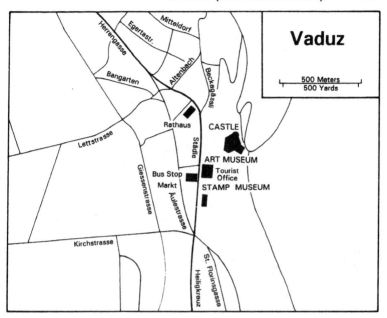

along which you will find the places of most interest and, of course, numerous tourist shops, hotels, restaurants and bars. There is one interest in Liechtenstein, however, that receives the stamp of approval from many visitors—philately, and two buildings on Städtle are of particular interest to collectors. The **Postage Stamp Museum** *(Briefmarkmuseum)*, Städtle 37, established in 1930, houses a large collection of stamps issued by Liechtenstein from 1912 forward, and of swapped stamps from other countries in the International Philatelic Society which date from 1921 forward. In addition to the above, many of which are not on public display, there are numerous other exhibits of items relevant to the design and printing of stamps, the Liechtenstein postal service, and other documents and instruments from postal history. Appropriately, the museum is run by a department in Liechtenstein responsible for the production of stamps—from the choice of subject to the final printing. In addition to managing the resident collection, they dispatch collections for temporary exhibition to locations throughout the world, thus arousing the interest of international philatelists and other curious parties. Again to build interest, stamps are issued four times a year in Liechtenstein, at the beginnings of March, June, September and December. Typically, approximately 25 stamps are issued with a face value of around CHF 35. These can be purchased in any post office. The main one in Vaduz just across the road is open, Monday to Friday, from 7:45 a.m. to 6 p.m. and Saturday from 8–11 a.m. Alternatively, you may place a standing order for the new issues, either for yourself or a philatelist friend, by following the instructions in a leaflet available from *Postwertzeichenstelle der Regierung*, ☎ 236 64 44 or Fax 236 66 55, FL-9490 Vaduz.

Liechtenstein's wine-making tradition also has a long and distinguished history, with nearly all of the production vinified and sold within the country's borders. Though this industry is relatively small, with only 43 acres under vine, the naturally conducive conditions—ideal south-western orientated hillside locations, calcareous soil and a climate that gives out about 1,500 hours of annual sunshine—bring in a harvest that can reach around 98,500 liters (just over 26,000 gallons) each year. The most famous of the wines are the dry reds of Süssdruck and Beerli. Those wishing to imbibe of this delicacy should make their way to the **Wine Cellars of the Prince of Liechtenstein** *(Hofkellerie des Fürsten von Liechtenstein)*, ☎ 232 10 18 or Fax 233 11 45, at Fürstliche Domäne, Feldstrasse 4, just a short distance from the center of Vaduz. Although formal tastings for groups of ten or more can be arranged, they were more than happy to offer me samples of wines from both of the Prince's vineyards, this one in Vaduz and another, more extensive holding in Wilfersdorf, Austria. Of course, they will be extremely gratified if you buy a few bottles to be savored later during your trip, or once you return home. Visit Monday to Friday from 8 a.m. to midday or 1:30–6 p.m. and Saturday 8 a.m. to midday.

Obviously, with its Alpine features—the highest peak, Grauspitz, is 8,525 feet—winter sports are an important feature of the locals' life. Although daytrippers from Zürich are unlikely to come for the skiing, they may well be interested in the **Ski Museum**, ☎ 232 15 02, Bangarten 10. Founded by former ski racer and ski expert Noldi Beck, its exhibits trace the evolution of skiing from its inception as a necessity for farmers and hunters to what it is today, almost exclusively a leisure pursuit. And, in their diversity they represent a comprehensive documentation of European skiing history. It is open Monday to Friday from 2–6 p.m.

Another curiosity that you will unlikely not escape is the volume of visitors flocking to the tourist office. At first thought, this must not seem unusual but, after a while, you may begin to wonder what the urgency is. I'd suggest you stop by the tourist office and, once there, I'll wager you will want what everyone else does. It is not tourist information, although most everyone needs that as well. It is a stamp, but of a different kind than that found at the Stamp Museum or the Post Office. Capitalizing on the fact that there are no border controls and that visitors are always in the market for a permanent reminder of their visit, the tourist office staff will quite happily, and for a fee of only CHF 2, impress upon your passport the official **Fürstentum Liechtenstein** stamp.

Bad Ragaz

The name Ragaz was officially recorded in conjunction with this area in AD 831—specifically as *Curtis Ragazes*. Its climb to international fame did not begin, however, until the warm springs at Tamina Gorge, for which Bad Ragaz is renowned, were accidentally but fortuitously discovered in 1242 by hunters from the Benedictine Monastery at Pfäfers. The operation of the baths began shortly thereafter. Just over a three centuries later, in 1535, Theophrastus von Hohenheim, better recognized by the name Paracelsus, stayed as a guest and as a physician at Bad Pfäfers.

It was another three hundred years before Bad Ragaz acted upon the commercial advantage intrinsic in its natural endowments. It was then, in 1840, that a nearly two-and-a-half-mile-long wooden pipe was installed, allowing the thermal waters to flow, at a temperature of 97.7 degrees Fahrenheit, between the Tamina Gorge and the Hof Ragaz hotel. This innovation gained marketable momentum 28 years later in 1868, when the architect Bernhard Simon purchased the estate of Ragaz and was granted a concession by the canton of St. Gallen for use of the thermal waters over a period to span one hundred years. This, inevitably, led to the opening of the Grand Hotel Quellenhof and the Kursaal. Since that time, the Grand Hotels Bad Ragaz Spa and Golf Resort have never looked back, committing to the ongoing renovation and enhancement of its facilities, at a cost of many millions of dollars, and creating, through the process, a facility that really is one of Switzerland's most unique and luxurious spas.

GETTING THERE:

Trains leave Zürich on a frequent basis throughout the day for Sargans, where a change is necessary prior to the very short trip to Bad Ragaz.

By Car, Bad Ragaz is reached from Zürich by taking the N-3 eastward to its junction with the N-13, and following the latter southward for the last few miles.

PRACTICALITIES:

The **Dialing Code** for Bad Ragaz is 81. The **Tourist Office** *(Verkehrsbüro*

Bad Ragaz), ☎ 302 10 61 or Fax 302 62 90, Haus Schweizerhof, CH-7310 Bad Ragaz, is open in the summer, between the end of April and end of October, Monday to Friday, from 9 a.m. to 6 p.m., Saturday from 9 a.m. to midday and 1–4 p.m., and Sunday from 10 a.m. to 2 p.m. During the remainder of the year it opens Monday to Friday from 9 a.m. to 6 p.m., Saturday from 9 a.m. to midday, and Sunday from 10 a.m. to midday. Desirous of fostering a reputation as exemplary hosts, they also hold, once or twice a month, a **Visitors' Cocktail Party** *(Gäste-Apéro)*. Information on and times of these are available through the office.

ACCOMMODATION:

The **Grand Hotel Quellenhof *****, ☎ 303 20 20 or Fax 303 20 22, CH-7310 Bad Ragaz, a member of the Leading Hotels of the World organization, certainly lives up to its grand name. Established in 1869, it was re-opened on November 2, 1996 following the completion of an extensive renovation spanning a period of 20 months and costing an estimated CHF 70 million. The exterior owes much to the original design, while the interior now provides the latest in modern comfort and technology. Guests may choose from among 97 spacious Junior suites—with an area of 60 square yards, eight full suites—with an area of 96 square yards, or the majestic Royal suite that, within its 239 square yards, pampers its guests with a private whirlpool, a fireplace and a concert piano. And let me not fail to mention the elegant Restaurant Bel-Air, where lovely pictures of the old Quellenhof adorn the ceiling and innovative gourmet dishes are both delicious and beautifully presented. $$$

The **Grand Hotel Hof Ragaz ****, ☎ 303 30 30 or Fax 303 30 33, CH-7310 Bad Ragaz, connected to both the Spa and the Quellenhof by way of an underground shopping plaza, underwent a renovation a few years earlier during the late 1980s. Its 133 commodious rooms and suites are each decorated to the highest standard and offer every convenience. On site for your dining pleasure are the gastronomic Äbtestube restaurant, an Inn, a piano bar and the Wintergarten café which is located on the terrace. $$$

The **Hotel Tamina ****, ☎ 302 81 51, Fax 302 23 08 or www.digi-tech nik.com/tamina.ch, Am Platz, CH-7310 Bad Ragaz, offers an interesting and appealing alternative to the Grand Hotels Bad Ragaz Resort. Situated in the heart of town, it has a charming Art-Nouveau style, spacious and well-appointed rooms and a very pleasant garden. Look, also, for an enticing gourmet restaurant and bar. Alternative, as well, in its approach to health issues, it is home to a traditional Chinese medicine center. $$

FOOD AND DRINK:

Rates quoted for the above hotels are demi-pension, and, as such, include the evening meal—and what a treat it is! I do not, therefore, feel it is necessary to include details on many restaurants in this section. If, however,

if you find yourself wandering around Bad Ragaz at lunch time, the following restaurant deserves your serious consideration:

> **Restaurant Rustico** (Fläscherstrasse 71) offers an interesting menu
> which, in addition to a variety of regional dishes, features numer-
> ous specialties—most of which have unusual names. It is open from
> 11:30 a.m. to 1:45 p.m. and 6-9:30 p.m. ☎ 302 36 37. $

SUGGESTED TOUR:

As you will find with many places in this guide, this section does not outline a formal tour. Neither is it a description of the activities available in and
around Bad Ragaz. While it must be said that these are numerous and interesting they are, generally, overshadowed by similar offerings in other
parts of Switzerland—which are detailed in other chapters of this guide.

Far and away, the majority of visitors to Bad Ragaz will come here because of its international prominence as a spa town. From the outset, those
contemplating a daytrip—a perfectly feasible plan logistically—should be
advised that only a limited number of the spa facilities here are open to the
public. Visitors who wish to take the waters and/or pamper themselves with
any number of the health and beauty treatments available should plan,
therefore, a minimum stay of one night. Also, while a number of hotels offer on-site health treatments and physiotherapists—one even has a center
for traditional Chinese medicine, just two afford their guests the privilege of
exclusive entry to a magnificent, wonderful world of health, beauty, exercise, golf, and tennis as well as free entry to the extensive public pools.

In truth, inclusive of the services provided guests at many upscale hotels
in Switzerland are the use of any number of combinations of indoor swimming pools, health club facilities, saunas, steam baths, exercise areas and
massage opportunities. No other establishment, though, brings these amenities together in total, under one roof and in such innovative fashion as the
Grand Hotels Bad Ragaz Resort. In fact, the Bogn Engiadina Scuol, at Scuol
in the Lower Engadine offers facilities and treatments that are similar; and
the many and impressive merits of that spa are discussed in detail in the
Lower Engadine chapter. The Bogn Engiadina Scuol, however, is situated in
a remote corner of Switzerland—certainly not possible as a daytrip from a
major city such as Zürich and really not conducive to an overnight trip either. In addition, being a public facility, it lacks the exclusivity of the posh
Bad Ragaz Resort.

When planning your budget, be sure to factor in that a stay at the Grand
Hotels Bad Ragaz Resort is not inexpensive. During 1997 the most economical choice at the Quellenhof was a Double Junior suite which was CHF
671 in winter and CHF 730 in summer. A double room at the Hof Ragaz was
priced at CHF 496 in winter and CHF 545 in summer. Keep in mind, however, that, in addition to accommodation in an ultra luxurious room, included in the tariff are a delicious buffet breakfast, a marvelous evening

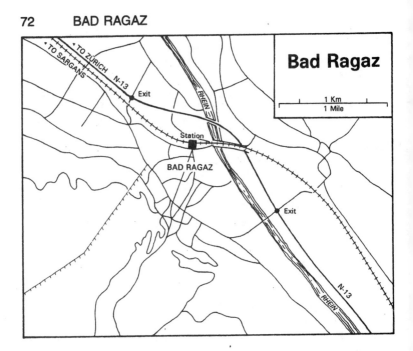

meal, and unlimited access to the TO B HEALTH CLUB. If you are driving, you will incur an additional charge. The management, understandably, wishes to keep the park area outside of both hotels car free and, to accomplish that goal, they have constructed an underground car park. This is not included in the rate however, the cost is CHF 14 a night. Also, if you take a dog with you, as many Europeans do when they travel, add another CHF 40 per night to your tab. So, total this up and make a determination whether this package is affordable for you—remembering that other options in Switzerland are generally not inexpensive either and taking into account what you would spend on meals and entertainment, if not included in the rates, elsewhere. If you can manage it financially, this represents a rare opportunity to indulge yourself in the utmost luxury—as they say, to stroke your soul and immerse yourself in the soft world of water, scents and temperatures, floating somewhere between the charms of Roman bathing culture and the playful lightness of our own times.

To tempt you further, here is a preview of what you will find at the Grand Hotels Bad Ragaz Spa and Golf Resort:

The **TO B The Leading Health Club** is a 2,511-square-yard harmoniously-designed wellness island, exclusively reserved for hotel guests, where the entire range of services— with the exception of performance-diagnostic tests, fitness checks, massages and beauty programs—are included in the price of the hotel room. Look for, in alphabetical order: the **Aroma Steam Bath** *(Aroma Dampfbad)*—a classical steam bath with aromatherapy (hayseed, chamomile, conifers and balm); **Aurarium**—a double whirlpool at 100 degrees Fahrenheit, with automatic freshwater refills; **Freshwater Whirlpools** *(Friscwasser Whirlpools)*—four individual whirlpools at 100 degrees Fahrenheit, with automatic freshwater refills; **Helena Bath** *(Helena Bad)*—a Roman thermal bathing temple, at 93 degrees Fahrenheit, with either sitting or laying massage jets and whirlpool and an adjacent Roman-Irish cycle of alternating steam and water baths; **Kneipp Room** *(Kneipp Raum)*—alternating baths for arm and foot as well as body affusion, under expert supervision; **Massage** *(Massagen)*—classical whole-body and back massage, sport massage, neck massage, foot reflex zone massage and relaxation massage; **Relaxarium**—two single rooms for deep relaxation augmented by music, light, water and aromas; **Sauna Landscape** *(Sauna Landschaft)*—mixed sauna (private sauna on request), a cold water open-air pool in the central atrium and a shower sensation; **Solaria** *(Solarien)*—an ergonomically-shaped Colani solarium and intensive tanner with massage bed—after all, the sun doesn't shine every day in Bad Ragaz; **Swimming Pool** *(Sportbad)*—a 55.7-foot pool with a water temperature of 82 degrees Fahrenheit; **Tamina Gorge** *(Tamina Schlucht)*—a reconstruction of the Tamina Gorge with its granite cliffs and waterfalls for Kneipp therapy; and the **Thermarium**—a classical steam bath with fine temperature regulation between *Tepidarium* 102 degrees Fahrenheit and *Laconium* 131 degrees Fahrenheit.

At the TO B BODY: **Cardio Station**—sets individual training programs, based on your optimal pulse rate, on bicycle ergometers, stepping and rowing machines, upper arm ergometer, running machines and a skywalker; **Fitness and Gymnastics**—offers daily lessons (private upon request), with qualified instructors overseeing yoga, body forming, Tai Chi, fitball, step, stretching, Qi Gong, water and spinal gymnastics, autogenics and much more; **Power Station**—features 14 training machines that incorporate the latest in ergonometric know how; and the **Super Circuit**—offers group dynamic stamina training with music, colors and movement.

The TO B The Leading Health Club and TO B BODY are open from 7 a.m. to 7 p.m., and information is available by calling ☎ 303 30 50.

Staying at the Resort also qualifies you for admission, at no extra charge, to the **Tamina Thermals** *(Tamina Therme)*—the modern, public, thermal bath with two indoor pools and one open air pool—in all of which the water temperature hovers between 95 and 96.8 degrees Fahrenheit. Features of these pools include bubble jets, massage and pearl jets; a waterfall; a bubble grotto; and a water current canal—similar to a "lazy river." Pamper yourself here daily from 7 a.m. to 8:30 p.m.

And let me not fail to mention the TO B BEAUTY, a beauty oasis for both ladies and gentlemen that opens Monday to Saturday from 9 a.m. to 6:30 p.m. Treatments/services here range from a single massage to a complete beauty program which covers a period of six days. Your choices include: **Exclusive Face and Body Care** *(Exklusive Gesichts und Körperpflege)*—treatments using products by Kanebo, Sisley, Carita, Thalgo, Boucheron and Escada; **Medical Pedicure and Massage** *(Medizinische Fusspflege und Massagen)*—a regimen whereby qualified staff take extra special care your feet; **Prevention of Skin Aging** *(Prävention Gegen Vorzeitige Hautalterung)*— Myo lifting and energy treatment for tired skin, ionotherapy with ampoules of active substances and face lymph drainage; **Slimming and Cellulite Treatments** *(Schlankheits und Cellulite Treatments)*—treatments designed to prevent fat accumulations and tissue change which include partial and whole body packs, Thalasso therapies, purging baths with underwater massage, body modeling and special low-temperature leg treatments; **Thalasso Therapy** *(Thalassotherapien)*— highly effective algae concentrate (comprised of vitamins, trace elements and marine ions drawn from the ocean) is applied to improve the circulation, refine and tone the figure, alleviate cellulite and purge and purify the entire body—truly the elixir of life for both body and soul. While this is, indeed, an enticing mélange, you may have to be selective in your selection—the treatments here will be charged in addition to your tariff.

Also on site is the **Bad Ragaz Medical Center**, which was created originally for hotel guests, but now enjoys an outstanding international reputation in its fields of specialty: rhumatology, neurology, orthopaedics and internal medicine. Combining the very latest advances in medicines, diagnosis and therapy with the natural healing power of thermal water, the center now fulfills an important role in the regional health service. Hopefully, though, not too many readers will be in need of its services.

Other, more traditional options for hotel guests include golf, tennis or mountain bike riding. Adjacent to the hotels is the Resort's private 18-hole par-70 **golf course** which, with a length of 6,288 yards, is considered to be one of the most beautiful in Switzerland. It is playable between March and November and hotel guests enjoy a 50% reduction in green fees and the benefit of reserved teeing-off times. Also supervised by the four resident pros are a two-story outdoor driving range and an indoor driving range with a Mastergolf Swing-Analyser. Teeing-off times may be reserved up to three days in advance by calling the Golf Club Office during its opening hours, daily from 7:15 a.m. to 7 p.m. The direct line from the Grand Hotels is 3717.

Tennis is available on five outdoor courts, open from April to October. Guests also have privileges at the St. Leonhard Tennis and Squash Center in Bad Ragaz.

The Resort makes ten **mountain bikes** available to guests for rental at CHF 25 for a half-day and CHF 30 for a full day, inclusive of helmet. Either afford yourself of the opportunity to join a complimentary, organized, tour which explores the Rhine Valley, or pedal off on your own to discover the local wine-producing region of the Bünder Herrschaft.

So there you have the Grand Hotels Bad Ragaz Resort, a place guaranteed to provide for the regeneration of your body, soul and mind. Contact them at ☎ 303 20 60 or Fax 303 20 66 for details of their special weekend and other packages and/or to make reservations.

Basel:Tour #1

Basel's strategic location, in the center of Europe at the point where the mighty Rhine *(Rhein)* river takes a dramatic ninety-degree turn to the north, ensured from the outset that this city would play no small role in the history of Europe and, indeed, the world. Although the origins of the city can be traced back to Celtic times, it was in 44 BC that a Roman general, Lucius Munatius Plancus, founded the settlement of *Augusta Raurica* (Augst), on the hill where the cathedral stands today. And, it was in AD 374 that the name of *Basilea* was first documented, during a visit by Emperor Valentinian I to the city. In the 7th century the Bishop's seat was transferred from Augst to Basel. Three hundred years later Basel was overrun by the Hungarians, who destroyed the settlement. In 1006, the civil power of the bishop was established by decree of Emperor Henry II who, thirteen years later, inaugurated the Münster. The same century saw the first fortifications of the city which, in 1185, was burned down by a great fire. Early the next century, in 1226, the city's recovery continued as Bishop Henry of Thoune organized the construction of the first bridge across the Rhine. The 14th century wasn't so kind to Basel. During the period around 1340 the "Black Death" plague raged throughout Basel and, just sixteen years later—on October 18, 1356—a substantial part of the city was destroyed by an earthquake. During the reconstruction, the second town wall was completed; parts of which and some of the gates are preserved to this day. Yet another fire struck Basel in 1417 and, in the 1444, the city once again felt the scourge of war, when the battle of St. Jacob, between the Swiss Confederates and French dauphin and his allies, took place close to Basel.

It was Basel's geographic position that encouraged leaders of the Church to hold their council in the city between 1431 and 1448, during which Amadeus VIII of Savoy was elected Pope—taking the name Felix V, an event that would have far-reaching cultural and intellectual consequences. Aaneas Silvius Piccolomini, later to become Pope Pius II, familiar with the city from his attendance at the Ecumenical Council, the last Church Council of the Middle Ages, thereafter founded the University of Basel, which was the first university of the Swiss Confederation. Basel, in turn, became an educational base and a center for humanism and the arts. Many great scholars such as Erasmus of Rotterdam—who published the first edition of the

New Testament in the original Greek text in 1416, the physician Paracelsus, mathematicians Euler and Bernoullis, philosopher Friedrich Nietzsche and the historian Jakob Burckhardt were attracted to the city. Trade blossomed and, in 1471, Basel obtained permission to hold two fairs annually. Monuments to the resulting wealth are still visible in the array of elaborate medieval buildings, most notably the highly decorative and very unusual Town Hall, which dates from 1504; the equally impressive, but rather more austere, Romanesque/Gothic Cathedral and the imposing Spalentor, which dates from when Basel was last walled in during the 14th century.

In 1501, Basel was accepted into the Swiss Confederation, and 1529 saw the Reformation accepted by the city. Since 1833, the canton of Basel has been divided into two half-cantons, Basel Town and Basel Country. Travel between Basel and other parts of Switzerland was made considerably easier when the first railway reached the city in 1844, and maritime connections were enhanced by the opening of the port of Basel in 1906.

Today, Basel, Switzerland's second largest city, is a lively and progressive place with a population of some 200,000. Situated at the border of three countries—France, Germany and Switzerland, it is home port to more than 500 river-going vessels, serves as one of Europe's largest railroad junctions and is recognized as a great financial and industrial center. It is also headquarters for some of the world's major pharmaceutical companies, and is the base for the Bank of International Settlements (BIZ), where representatives of all industrialized countries routinely meet to discuss the world economy. The church council held there five centuries ago was only the start of Basel's vocation as a center for worldwide conventions and trade fairs. In 1917, the first Swiss Industries Fair took place here, and it is now the largest fair and congress organizer in the country, responsible, in its own right, for over one million visitors to the city.

Art and culture also play a major role in the life of Basel. Approximately thirty museums, ranging from the more traditional and world-renowned Fine Arts Museum to the less conventional Paper and Cinema museums, not to mention numerous other galleries, concern halls and theaters, call the city their home. The most popular cultural event, however, is the colorful and wild *Basel Fasnacht* carnival. The festivities begin in January with the appearance of three mythological figures who appear to chase winter away. The Monday after Ash Wednesday, at the ungodly hour of 4 a.m., the Carnival breaks loose with a morning parade. What follows are three days of unbroken revelry complete with traditional feasts and a procession of elaborate floats, brass bands and a motley collection of followers in outrageous costumes that have to be seen to be believed.

Basel is an absolutely charming place to visit; the medieval flavor—enhanced by the sight of more than one hundred and fifty fountains, the attractions of the Rhine and the progressiveness of its people together create a truly unique and enticing ambiance.

GETTING THERE:

By air, transatlantic flights arrive in Switzerland at Zurich's Kloten International airport, from where there are connections on to Basel-Mulhouse EuroAirport. Direct flight service is available from numerous other Continental cities.

Trains arrive at Basel's railway station *(Bahnhof SBB)* from all other cities in Switzerland, and from France and Germany. This station is unusual in that it serves as the railway border between France and Switzerland and, accordingly, half the station is operated by the French National Railway *(SNCF)*.

By car, Basel, in the far northwestern corner of Switzerland, is easily reached by road from all parts of the country, as well as from bordering France and Germany.

PRACTICALITIES:

The **telephone code** for Basel is 61. The **Tourist Office** *(Basel Tourismus)*, ☎ 268 68 68, Fax 268 68 70 or E-mail office@baseltourismus.ch, Schifflände 5, CH-4001 Basel, located between the Drei Könige Hotel and the central bridge, is open Monday to Friday from 8:30 am. to 6 p.m. and Saturday from 8:30 a.m. to 4 p.m. A **Basel City Information** office, ☎ 271 56 84, Fax 272 93 42 or E-mail hotel@messebasel.ch, is found in the train station. October to May hours are Monday to Friday from 8:30 a.m. to 6 p.m. and Saturday from 8:30 a.m. to midday. June to September it opens Monday to Friday from 8:30 a.m. to 7 p.m., Saturday from 8:30 a.m. to 12:30 p.m. and 1:30 p.m. to 6 p.m. and Sunday from 10 a.m. to 2 p.m. **Basel Hotel Reservation** service, ☎ 686 26 30, Fax 686 21 84 or E-mail hotel@messebasel.ch., is also located in the station and is open Monday to Friday from 8 a.m. to midday and 1–5 p.m. A wealth of information about Basel may be accessed via the Internet at www.baseltourismus.ch.

The most economical way to make long-distance phone calls is from the Telecom office at the train station. It is open Monday to Friday from 7 a.m. to 10 p.m. and Saturday and Sunday from 7:30 a.m. to 10 p.m.

Bucherer has had a family presence in Basel since the 19th century, first with a toy store and today with its fashionable watch and jewelry store in the heart of the city at Freie Strasse 40, ☎ 261 40 00 or Fax 261 73 40. It is open Monday, Tuesday, Wednesday and Friday from 8:30 a.m. to 6:30 p.m., Thursday from 8:30 a.m. to 8 p.m. and Saturday 8:30 a.m. to 5:30 p.m. Typical shop hours in Basel are Monday to Friday from 8:30 a.m. to 6:30 p.m., with many open until 8 p.m. on Thursday, and Saturday from 8:30 a.m. to 5 p.m. Most are closed on Sunday, and many are also closed on Monday morning. If you are in need of basic supplies on a Sunday, there are a couple of small grocery stores open in the concourse under the railway station. A supermarket directly across from the station is open as well. The latter presents an interesting social phenomenon; so many people want to get in that security guards regulate the store traffic, only allowing a certain number of shoppers in at any given time.

Public transport in and around Basel, on any combination of tramcars and buses, is fast clean and efficient. Tickets must be purchased, from ticket vending machines, ticket offices or the tourist office, prior to each trip and are available for a singe trip or, more advantageously, for an Unlimited Day Pass. The latter, for 2nd class, costs CHF 7.40 for the City of Basel and CHF 23.40 for the expanded metropolitan traffic area.

ACCOMMODATION:

The **Hotel Drei Könige am Rhein *******, ☎ 261 52 52 or Fax 261 21 53, 8 Blumenrain, CH-4001 Basel, is considered to be the oldest hotel in Europe and, justifiably, is a member of the Leading Hotels of the World group. Generations of travelers have found rest here for nearly ten centuries. In fact, an inn, called "The Flower," stood on this site in 1026. The present name dates from 1032, when fate decreed that a royal delegation, scheduled to convene at Muttenz, should meet instead at "The Flower." This meeting was of tremendous import, settling questions over the succession of the royal line among three kings and ensuring that Switzerland would become a part of the Holy Roman Empire. Hence, the inn became known as the "Three Kings," the name it bears to this day. Throughout its illustrious history, this establishment has played host to all manner of kings and royalty, politicians, artists and entertainers, from the likes of Bonaparte to Picasso. The "Three Kings" sits on a fantastic riverside site, very near to the city center, the tourist office and the important middle bridge. No effort has been spared here to ensure first-class service, an elegantly traditional ambiance, and all modern comforts. Needless to say, it is not inexpensive, but the special "Weekend des rois" rate of CHF 263 per night per person, inclusive of both breakfast buffet and gala dinner, is well worth consideration. $$$

The **Hotel International Basel *******, ☎ 227 27 27 or Fax 227 28 28, Steinentorstrasse 25, CH-4001 Basel, is a large, 200-room, superior first-class hotel in a prime, quiet, downtown location. Guests are near to the theater, business and banking district and a convenient five minutes walk from the main railway station. All of the generally spacious rooms are furnished in an elegant International style with every modern facility. Special rooms are available for ladies, non-smokers and the handicapped, and there is an indoor leisure center featuring a pool, fitness machines, sauna, steam bath, massage services and a solarium. Rates include service charge, taxes, VAT and a breakfast buffet. $$$

The **Hotel Drachen ******, ☎ 272 90 90 or Fax 272 90 02, Aeschen-vorstadt 24, Ch-4010 Basel, with an interesting and quiet location between the theater and the Fine Arts Museum—and just a few minutes walk from the railway station—will appeal to those seeking the intimacy of a smaller hotel. Each of its 40 rooms is elegantly decorated and offer the expected amenities. Its restaurant, the walls of which are embellished with wonderful murals, specializes in health food cuisine. $$

The **Hotel Merian ****, ☎ 681 00 00 or Fax 681 11 01, Rheingasse 2, Ch-4005 Basel, is a charming, medium-sized hotel with a fine riverside location just across the central bridge from the city center. $$

The **Swiss Youth Hostels**, ☎ 272 05 72, St. Alban-Kirchrain 10, CH-4052 Basel, are simple, basic and clean with rates between CHF 18 and CHF 32 per person, inclusive of breakfast and sheets. $

FOOD AND DRINK:

Rôtisserie des Rois (8 Blumenrain), located in the inimitable Drei Könige hotel, is one of the finest gourmet restaurants in Basel. In September 1997, the chef, Eric Cizeron, and the restaurant received yet another star from Gault Millau, giving them 14 in total. Expect classic French cuisine served, in summer, on the terrace overlooking the Rhine, where you will find a bar as well. A magical combination of delectable cuisine and unparalleled views is sure to delight the most discerning of patrons. Opening hours are daily from 11 a.m. to 3 p.m. and 6–11:30 p.m. ☎ 261 52 52 or Fax 261 21 53. $$$

Stucki Bruderholz (Bruderholzalle 42) is located above the city and ranks high above most other restaurants in Basel. Hans Stucki manages this Relais Gourmand restaurant, with its spacious dining room and beautiful garden. His gourmet creations have earned for him two Michelin stars and, like those served in the restaurants of this genre throughout Switzerland, are nearly too beautiful to be eaten. Indulge yourself, though, in a culinary delight that will long be remembered. ☎ 361 82 22 or Fax 361 82 03. $$$

Rôtisserie Charolaise (Steinentorstrasse 25) is a very elegant restaurant located within the Hotel International. A gastronomic menu, dictated by produce fresh from the market, is complemented by a fine wine list. ☎ 227 27 27 or Fax 227 28 28, X: Sunday. $$$

Café Spitz (Rheingasse 2), found in the Hotel Merian, is famous for its sea and freshwater fish specialties. ☎ 681 00 00 or Fax 681 11 01. $$

Steinenpick (Steinentorstrasse 25) is the city restaurant of the Hotel International. Open daily, it is informal and offers various specialties in an agreeable ambiance. ☎ 227 27 27 or Fax 227 28 28. $$

King's Brasserie (8, Blumernrain), located in the incomparable Drei Könige hotel, offers an elegant ambiance and reasonably-priced set meals. It is open daily from 6:30 a.m. to 11:30 p.m. ☎ 261 52 52 or Fax 261 21 53. $

Churrasco Grill & Restaurant (Schifflände 1) is one in a national chain of restaurants that feature steaks and meat dishes. Their lunch special is certainly worth consideration. ☎ 269 91 91. $

Brasserie zum Braunen Mutz (Barfüsserplatz 10) has a traditional beer saloon on the ground floor, with the brassiere offering a special business lunch. It is open daily from 8 a.m. to midnight, until 1 a.m. on Friday and Saturday and until just 10 p.m. on Sunday. ☎ 261 33 69 or Fax 261 13 23. $

Bodega zum Strasse (Barfüsserplatz 16) is a neat little Italian restaurant. Its small dining room, decorated with modern paintings and photographs, does not offer a great deal of privacy, but the menu is enticing. Dine Monday to Saturday from 11:30 a.m. to 2:30 p.m. and 17:45 p.m. to midnight, and Sunday from 6 p.m. to midnight. ☎ 261 22 72. $

Hasenburg Château Lapin (Schneidergasse 20) is a small, delightfully quaint, family run restaurant in a tiny street just behind the Marktplatz. A typical beer hall type place, it has a varied cuisine and a very reasonable set meal. It opens until 10 p.m., but is closed on Sunday. ☎ 261 32 58. $

SUGGESTED TOUR:

This tour begins, conveniently, at the **tourist office** (1). Pass the Schifflände boat landing and an equestrian statue of Karl Burckhardt (1878–1923), then cross the famous **Middle Bridge** *(Mittlere Brücke)* (2). Once on the other side of this usually flag-bedecked bridge, pause a moment to look back. Directly across the mighty Rhine, 870 feet wide, stands the inimitable façade of the ancient Three Kings Hotel, and high on the hill to the left sits the imposing Cathedral *(Münster)*. Pass in front of the Merian Spitz Hotel, and walk along the wonderful embankment. Really delightful tall houses, no two the same, line the river front and are embellished by all manner of trees and plants sprouting from their window boxes. Cafés, too, add to the atmosphere. In the warm summer months you will come across a surprising phenomenon. The sloping quay side will be literally covered with almost totally uncovered sun bathers.

For centuries the cheapest and most efficient way of crossing the Rhine has been by way of one of four ferry boats, and these are quite unusual indeed. Small, wooden and only half covered, they would have no hope whatsoever of succeeding against the swift flowing currents under their power alone. Innovation, therefore, caused a strong cable to be stretched from bank to bank, with a much smaller one attached from that to the ferry itself. Still, the undertow keeps the smaller cable stretched to its limit, and it is this that determines the position of the landing pier. Watch closely and you will notice how the ferryman skillfully holds the boat to the pier solely by the pressure of his wooden pole. Three-quarters of the way along the embank-

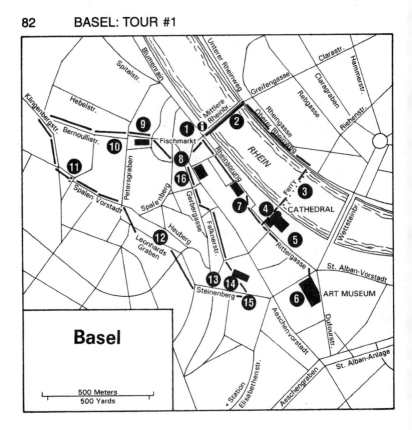

ment towards the new bridge is the **Münster "Leu"** ferry (3), and it is this that you should board for the short trip across the Rhine. This is quite an experience, as well as an unparalleled opportunity to see a parade of diverse vessels plying their trade on the river. And the price is just CHF 1.20. After disembarking comes the strenuous part of the journey. The bank on this side of the river is much steeper, and seemingly endless rows of steps lead up to the red-brick Münster towering above you. Before you get there, though, a plaza—which actually winds around the Cathedral—gives a perfect opportunity for a rest and a review of Basel from a different perspective. The Rhine, below you, is flanked on both sides by rows of gorgeous houses and, in the background, loom the mountains of southern Germany.

Begin your exploration of the ***Cathedral** (Münster) (4) from the exterior grounds, noting the tall spires and colored tiled roof. It appears that the forecourt was, at one time, gated in and this space, Müsterplatz, is now rather charming. There are *boules* courts, a French passion akin to Lawn Bowling in the UK, and also the intriguing Café/bar Zum Isaak. The modern photographs inside provide an interesting contrast with the old tree-shaded garden on the outside and, if you fancy some entertainment later, there is a theater in the basement. Turning your attention to the façade of the Münster, you will find it adorned with various statues, prominent among them St. George slaying a dragon. Impressive though it is, it is just a copy of the 14th-century original. This area of Basel has been inhabited for two thousand years, and a variety of churches and cathedrals have existed on this site. It is recorded that, in 1019, a cathedral was consecrated here in the presence of Emperor Henry II, heir of the last Burgundian king. Construction of the present structure was begun at the end of the 12th century, in the late Romanesque style. But by the time it had been completed, it had gained Gothic additions. Of course, it has seen many more additions and renovations throughout the centuries.

The comparatively plain interior is highlighted by stained-glass windows, a simple altar, elaborately-carved choir stalls and, particularly, a dragon sculpted into the floor of the nave, that is thought to date from around 1170. The very ambitious may want to consider climbing to the top of the **St. George Tower**. The reward for such an endeavor is a splendid birds-eye panoramic view over this fascinating city. It is open Monday to Friday from 10 a.m. to 5 p.m., Saturday from 10 a.m. to midday and 2–4 p.m., and Sunday and holidays from 1–5 p.m. Outside again, the **Cloister** is worthy of investigation. And, don't overlook the small garden where, incongruously, modern sculpture—including one of a metal market stall with different kinds of produce and another, more ghoulishly, of a skeleton covered in a black cape—stand in restless harmony with the ancient gravestones and sepulchers.

A little diversion is in order now. Outside the cloister and about one hundred yards down Rittergasse is a most charming **house and garden** (5), protected by beautifully-crafted wrought-iron railings. If you walk down the road along its side you will see a courtyard of smaller, but no less interesting, houses. Almost directly across from the larger house is a reminder of just how long ago this area was settled—ancient walls, and even some bones, encased in glass to protect them from the elements.

Basel is famous, also, for its museums, and visitors are certainly spoiled for choice. In fact, there are approximately thirty of them, catering to most any conceivable taste. For more information you may investigate these further by visiting their web site, www.unibas.ch/museum although, at the time of writing, most of the text was in German only. If you must make a choice of one, though, you certainly would want to visit the **Fine Arts Museum** *(Kunstmuseum)* (6). To get there, simply follow Rittergasse to its junction with St. Alban-Graben and then turn right. Opened in 1661, this claims to be the world's first public art collection, and it is still considered one of major importance. In addition to works by Old Masters, such as Holbein and

Grünewald, it also houses an impressive collection of 20th-century paintings, including "degenerate art" from the 1930s, when Basel served as a refuge from those fleeing from Nazi Germany. ☎ *271 08 28 or Fax 271 08 45, St. Alban-Graben 16.*

Retrace your steps to the Cathedral and follow through the Münsterplatz and out to Augustinergasse. There, at Number 2, is the **National History Museum** *(Museum der Kulturen)* (7), which often holds special exhibitions. Opening hours are Tuesday to Sunday from 10 a.m. to 5 p.m. ☎ *266 56 04 or Fax 266 56 05, Augustinergasse 2.* From this vantage point, too, there is a particularly fine perspective back to the spires of the cathedral. You are also sure to notice the elaborate water fountain, red with faces and angels and a rather weird dragon atop it. From their prevalence, one must assume that dragons have always been in vogue in Basel. Following on down the hill the lane changes its name to Rheinspring, and here you will find a series of delightful half-timbered houses; two of which date from 1438 and 1573, respectively.

At the bottom of the hill, by the Middle Bridge, make a quick left and then a right which will bring you out into **Fischmarkt** (8). This is actually a traffic circle dominated by a very elaborate, tall column standing in the middle of a large pond with statues, flowers and three fountains. The original dated from around 1390; this is a replica. Immediately behind are a series of steep steps whose walls are covered with the unfortunately all-too-common scourge of graffiti. If you are tall enough to manage a peep over the walls, you will see a lovely garden. Approaching the top, expect to see an array of fine medieval houses and, at the top, find the rather austere **Peterskirche** (9), behind which public gardens lead to a pleasant surprise. Even non-gardeners will be impressed with the **Botanical Gardens** (10), but green-fingered visitors will be positively envious. The gardens themselves, open from 9 a.m. to 6 p.m., are pleasing enough, and the huge glass houses, often with a central pond, are home to tremendous cacti and a variety of other flora. Note, though, that these close an hour earlier than the gardens.

Leave by what appears to be the rear but is, actually, the main entrance and, upon turning left, you will be faced with one of Basel's splendors from the past. Dating from the 14th century, when the city was last walled in, the **Spalentor** gate (11) is magnificent indeed. Twin turrets, joined by fortifications topped by another colorful tiled tower, protect a portcullis and an obviously ancient wooden gate. There is, also, the obligatory moat—well, so it was in bygone centuries. Time to head back down to the center of town. First, follow Spalenvorstadt, quite an interesting street that is lined by antique and other specialty stores. At Number 9, Restaurant Casanova specializes in vegetarian dishes. There is another elaborate fountain at its junction with Schützenmattstrasse. A dog-leg right and left, at the end, leads into Leonhards Graben, a street with quite a different character. Pretty ivy-covered houses, some with private rose-filled gardens, are tucked in among cafés, antique shops and chapels. Here, also, find the very unusual hotel/restaurant Teufelhof and, typical of Basel, a dragon statue. As you near the end, take a little detour into **Leonardskirchplatz** (12), a quiet square where you will find a very old wooden house with an attractive balcony, just across from the church.

Out into the main road again, Kohlenberg winds steeply down the hill and curves sharply round into the busy **Barfüsserplatz** (13). This is one of the transportation hubs of Basel, a most important tram station, and almost always busy. There are some old houses, dating from the late 17th century, but the ambiance these might otherwise evoke is surely spoiled by the omnipresent McDonalds on the corner. Other, more interesting, restaurants have their home in the plaza and, across the road, the Stadt Casino features many restaurants and bars of its own. And, just to the left of that is an imposing church. Constructed in the mid-13th century, the **Barfüsserkirche** now functions as the **Basel History Museum** (*Historiches Museum Basel*) (14), which may be visited Wednesday through Monday from 10 a.m. to 5 p.m. Incidentally, the name *Barfüsser* originates from the barefooted Franciscan monks who once occupied the church and, if you take a moment to look around the back, you will discover traces of its past—burial and other stones protected by a wooden shelter.

Another short diversion is definitely in order here. Turn left out of Barfüsserplatz, passing the Stadt Casino along the way, and make another left into Steinenberg. Your destination is about one hundred yards up on the right-hand side, and you certainly will not be disappointed. A combination of different level plazas here, just outside the Municipal Theater, provide a popular gathering place for young and old alike. The favorite attraction by far, though, and set in the midst of a large pond, is the **Jean Tinguely Fountain** (15). Tinguely, who lived from 1925 to 1991, had, to understate the obvious, quite a creative mind. Any attempt to describe this unbelievably outlandish fountain, opened in 1977, would never do it justice. Suffice it to say that the numerous components are made from parts of old machines, etc. connected by other pieces of metal—and you never know where to look next for the fine sprays of water they emit. In truth, I have never seen anything like it before. The best comparison that can be made, I believe, is with the wondrous inventions of Salvador Dalí, an analogy that will be reinforced if you are curious enough to visit the recently-opened Museum Jean Tinguely. Unfortunately, this is located some distance out of the center of Basel, and is not too easily reached. It is found in the Solitude Park, and can be seen from the boat cruise detailed in the following tour. More information may be obtained by calling 681 93 20, faxing 681 93 21 or checking them out on the Internet at www.tinguely.ch.

Retrace your steps back, now, to Barfüsserplatz and, on the way through to Falknerstrasse, note the tram station and the jumble of houses with uneven roofs and a church in the background. At the end of this shopping street, bear left around the huge post office and follow Gregergasse to this tour's ultimate destination. **Marktplatz** (16) is not just, as the name implies, the past and present site of Basel's open air market. It is also home to the city's magnificent **Town Hall** *(Rathaus)*. This red, frescoed façade, recently restored but dating from the early 16th century, dominates the plaza as its impressive tower, added retroactively earlier this century, does the façade. Both are roofed with the colorful tiles so popular in Basel. These days it is occupied by the government of the canton of Basel City.

Basel goes to extreme efforts to assist its visitors. You will find evidence of this on the side of the plaza opposite the Town Hall, where the authorities have erected a metal signpost directing you to five different strolls throughout the city. These all begin here, last between 30 and 90 minutes, and are named after a prominent personality of Basel—Erasmus, Thomas Platter, Jakob Burckhardt, Paracelsus or Holbein. To keep you on course, signs are posted along each route displaying a portrait of the respective person. An information book to accompany the strolls is available from the tourist office in either a tourist edition at CHF 22 or a gift edition at CHF 45.

Basel: Tour #2

Continue your exploration of Basel with this little excursion:

GETTING THERE:

PRACTICALITIES:

FOOD AND DRINK:
See pages 80–81 for the above.

SUGGESTED TOUR:
Once again, begin at the **tourist office** (1) and follow the route of the first tour until you reach the end of the **Middle Bridge** *(Mittlere Brücke)* (2). This time, though, continue straight along from the bridge to the junction of Greifengasse and Rebgasse, where you will wait for a number 14 tram. Take this to the end of the line. Alighting, follow the signs directing you towards your destination, **Three Countries Corner** *(Dreiländereck).* This journey winds you through the docks, passing a small transport museum along the way. No need to go inside, though; there is not too much of interest and all descriptions are in German. Within a short distance you will reach the banks of the Rhine and a river side walk, which snakes around to the right. Small marinas are on one side, docks on the other and, across the Rhine, it will be immediately apparent from the architectural styles where Switzerland and France meet. After a few hundred yards the land narrows, and you come to the **Three Countries Corner** *(Dreiländereck)* itself, with Germany and its rolling hills forming a backdrop straight ahead. Of course, some entrepreneur could not resist the temptation to open the futuristic Dreiländereck bar/restaurant here in February 1996, and it is innovative as well. The waiters dress in sailor's outfits, and they move around on in-line skates!

Return back to town by tram, cross the river to Schifflände, and prepare to see the Three Countries Corner from a different perspective. **Basler Personenschiffahrt,** ☎ 639 95 00 or Fax 639 95 06, operates a variety of Rhine cruises but, for the purposes of this tour, I recommend their "Cruise round the city and port with lunch." This sails between May 1 and October 12, with additional trips on Sunday until the end of October. Casting off at 12:15

p.m., it cruises up the river then turns around, allowing the swift currents to carry it speedily to Three Countries Corner, before finally docking again at Schifflände. You will alight with a clearer understanding of just how closely intertwined Basel and the Rhine are. It is especially interesting to note the bathing stages on the left bank, which are not just used by sunbathers. In fact, some ardent swimmers leave their clothes at a down-river stage, cadge a ride to one up the river, and then, daringly, dive in and let the free flowing Rhine carry them speedily back down river. Not something, though, the uninitiated should not attempt!

*Luzern
(Lucerne)

The first mention of Luzern, Luciaria as it was known at the time, was made in AD 840. Early on it was christened the "city of lights," reference to a miracle in which, legend has it, an angel guided its early citizens with a heavenly light to the place where they were to erect a chapel in honor of St. Nicklaus, patron saint of sailors and fishermen. Around 1220, a little over a century and a half after its founding, this small fishing and monastery village was catapulted to international importance when the opening of the nearby Gotthard Pass facilitated a lucrative trade between the north and south. From that time on, rich merchants, pilgrims, diplomats and messengers either prepared for their journeys or started one from the city of Luzern which, by 1450, was home to over 400 inns and restaurants. It was the resulting exposure to a wealth of international influences that endowed this city with its adventurous and outward-looking character, and in the 18th century led to a great emphasis not only on trade, but on a keen educational awareness of foreign cultures. The 19th-century completion of the European rail network was the key that finally opened the door for travelers from all over the world to discover the charms of Luzern—and many they are.

Late-14th-century walls, with their nine defensive towers, stand defiantly behind a town chock-full of wonderfully decorated, frescoed old houses adorning a maze of small streets, lanes and squares. Among the more prominent of Luzern's monuments are the Baroque Jesuit Church, dating from 1666, and standing as a reminder of the profound influence over the city the Jesuits had from 1574 until their demise in the Sonderbund War of 1847. The Italian Renaissance Old Town Hall was built between 1602 and 1606. The City's main focal points, though, are two medieval covered bridges that link the old and new areas of town. Best known is the stunning 14th-century wooden-covered Chapel Bridge *(Kapellbrücke)*, the roof supports of which were embellished during the 17th century with triangular paintings of scenes depicting Swiss history and illustrating the legends of St. Leodegar and St. Mauritius. At its side is the distinctive 13th-century octagonal water tower—the city's signature landmark. Below the city walls stands the Spreuerbrücke, built in 1408. Its roof is similarly decorated with a series of paintings known as the "Dance of Death."

Also famed for arts and culture, Luzern boasts many fascinating museums, an International Festival of Music that was begun in 1938 and today attracts music lovers from all over the world, and two curious places of interest—the Lion Monument and Glacier Garden. The arcades and cafés of the Reuss river promenades are a lively meeting place, and visitors can browse or shop to their hearts' content in the Old Town's assortment of shops. In fact, both the city government and private donors spent large sums to renovate Luzern on the occasion of its 800th birthday in 1978. If all this was not enough, Luzern is blessed with a lovely location—in the heart of Switzerland on the northern end of the beautiful Lake of Luzern *(Vierwaldstätter See)* and with panoramic views of the surrounding Alps.

Without doubt, Luzern is among Switzerland's most beautiful cities and, although large numbers of tourists flock to the many luxury hotels built away from the city center, Luzern has developed the ability to accommodate them without letting their demands detract from its charm.

GETTING THERE:

By air, international flights arrive either at Zürich's Kloten or Geneva's Cointrin airport. From the former there are hourly train services to Luzern; from the latter they run every two hours.

Trains arrive at Luzern's main railway station from all other cities in Switzerland.

By car, Luzern, in the central part of Switzerland, is easily reached by road from all parts of the country.

PRACTICALITIES:

The **Dialing Code** for Luzern is 41. The **Tourist Information** office, ☎ 410 71 71, Fax 410 73 74 or E-mail Information.cent@CentralSwitzerland.ch, located at Frankenstrasse 1, CH-6002 Luzern, is open from November to March, Monday to Friday from 8:30 a.m. to midday and 2–6 p.m., and Saturday from 9 a.m. to 1 p.m. April to October hours are Monday to Friday from 8:30 a.m. to 6 p.m., Saturday from 9 a.m. to 5 p.m., and Sunday from 10 a.m. to 1 p.m. Information about Central Switzerland, including Luzern, can be found on the **Internet** at www.CentralSwitzerland.ch.

An institution in Swiss shopping, **Bucherer**, has its main store in Luzern, and this is one of the largest European stores of its genre. Under one roof you will find watches of every major brand, jewelry, gems, leather goods and other high quality souvenirs. The sales staff can answer any question you might have regarding the merchandise—in up to 21 languages. It is located at Schwanenplatz 5, ☎ 369 77 00 or Fax 369 77 78.

An ideal store for purchasing **Swiss Army Knives**, kitchen knives, knife block sets, scissors, cork screws and similar souvenirs is **Riethmüller AG**, ☎ 410 82 24 or Fax 410 86 10, Kapellgasse 7. On the subject of souvenirs, there are two other stores you should put on your agenda. **CG Collectors Gallery**, ☎ 412 06 66 or Fax 412 06 65, at Hertensteinstrasse 35, has a most incredible collection, in fact the world's largest, of **Swatch** watches, including a display with a sample of each style made between 1983 and 1997. You will also want to check out their Christmas specials, selection of musical watches, and museum boutique articles (for which this store has exclusive sale rights in Switzerland). Whether shopper or browser, you will most certainly be impressed by the displays of **pewter articles** at **Schwyer's Zinn-Zentrum**, ☎ 210 20 07 or Fax 210 20 48, at Seidenhofstrasse 3. Easily found, just off Bahnhofstrasse a block from the famous Kapellbrücke bridge, this store stocks most anything you can imagine that is made of pewter—including wine jugs and goblets, coffee sets, plates, mirrors and candelabras—as well as a wide array of other souvenirs. In the summer season many shops open on Sunday at 11 a.m. The shops under the railway station are generally open until 8 p.m.

ACCOMMODATION:

The **Château Gütsch ****,** ☎ 249 41 00, Fax 249 41 91 or Internet www.chateau-guetsch.ch, at Kanonenstrasse, CH-6003 Luzern, is a white castle-like structure that would be at home in the most romantic of fairy tales. Sitting majestically on a hilltop overlooking the city and reached by its private funicular, this is a "must see." You shouldn't pass up the opportunity to experience its charms in a more personal and practical way. The small tower built on the site in 1590 remained unchanged until the late 19th century when a hotel was constructed there. Following a tragic fire in 1888, the present structure was built and endured a series of ups and downs until the present owners undertook an extensive renovation in 1992. The results are spectacular indeed. The most selective couples, especially those celebrating a special occasion or seeking a particularly romantic experience, will opt to stay in the very grand and imposing Arturo Toscanini Suite. Reached by a private spiral staircase, this boasts a spacious private terrace and a jacuzzi bath tucked in one of the turrets with glorious views over the city, lake and mountains. Inquire about the "Perfectly Pampered" package for newlyweds, honeymooners or the incurably romantic. $$$

The **Hotel Des Balances ****,** ☎ 410 30 10 or Fax 410 64 51, Weinmarkt, CH-6000 Luzern, is located in the former Guildhall, in a most distinguished position in the Old Town. With an attractively painted façade, it has 57 rooms decorated and equipped to the highest standards, many of which—and the terrace—overlook the Reuss river, Kapellbrücke and the Jesuit Church. You will find, also, an elegant bar and a restaurant famed for its Swiss cuisine. $$

The **Seehotel Kastanienbaum ****,** ☎ 340 03 40, Fax 340 10 15, E-mail Kastanienbaum@dial.centralnet.ch or Internet www.forum.ch/kastanien baum, at St. Niklausenstrasse 105, CH-6047 Kastanienbaum-Luzern, is conveniently located just ten minutes from Luzern when traveling by car. It is also on the bus route to town or can be reached by Lake Steamer which, as the hotel has an enviable lakeside position, even docks there. The rooms are contemporary in ambiance, offering every modern convenience. Those fronting the lake afford beautiful views of the surrounding mountains. Enjoy, also, the well-appointed health club. $$$

The **Hotel Krone *****, ☎ 419 44 00 or Fax 419 44 90, at Weinmarkt 12, CH-6004 Luzern, is a charming hotel located in a pedestrian shopping zone just a few minutes walk from the train station. Entirely rebuilt in 1994, this small, 24 room, hotel has two restaurants, and offers a high degree of comfort at reasonable rates. $$

The **Tourist Hotel Luzern**, ☎ 410 24 74 or Fax 410 84 14, at St. Karliquai 12, CH-6004 Luzern, is located alongside the river, a short distance behind the town center and about ten minutes walk from the train station. In this fairly basic hotel many of the 100 rooms do not have a private bath/shower. But, to compensate, the rates are quite reasonable, and guest have the use of on-site laundry facilities. $

FOOD AND DRINK:

Luzern's international character is well reflected in its varied cuisine. A local specialty to look for is *Kügelipastete*. This creamed meat-filled shell is made from a recipe imported by mercenary soldiers who fought in Spain.

Restaurant St. Martin, at Kanonenstrasse, is found in, and is reflective of the style of, the Château Gütsch hotel. Candlelight, live music, a dance floor, terrace dining and an upstairs balcony combine with beautifully prepared and unusual dishes for an evening to remember. After dinner, enjoy a house cocktail in the Oyster Bar. ☎ 249 41 00. $$$

Li Tai Pe, at Furrengasse 14, a particularly fine Chinese restaurant, has established for itself a great reputation in Luzern. The dishes, well prepared and plentiful, can be ordered à-la-carte or through a selection of menus. Some specialties, including Peking Duck and Braised Whole Carp, must be ordered in advance and reservations are definitely recommended. ☎ 410 10 23. $$

Restaurant Walliser Kanne, Burgerstrasse 3, is a delightful restaurant with an interesting façade, that specializes in dishes and wines from the Valais region of Switzerland. $$

Churrasco Grill & Restaurant, Rössligasse 2, is one in a national chain that features steaks and meat dishes. Their lunch special is certainly worth considering at CHF 13.90 for the main course. ☎ 410 74 00. $

SUGGESTED TOUR:

Start the tour at the **Schwanenplatz** (1), the main plaza connecting the Old Town with the lake, and walk towards the bridge over the Reuss river, the main thoroughfare joining the two halves of the city. Do not cross by that bridge, however. Instead, turn right by the notable Saint Pierre Chapel and tower of the Zurgilgen into Rathausquai. Immediately, you will see the Kapellbrücke and Wasserturm, Luzern's internationally renowned landmarks. Delay investigating these further, though, and first spend a little time exploring the Old Town itself.

Continue down the very pleasant Rathausquai, where the most prominent structure is that of the Italian Renaissance-style **Town Hall** *(Rathaus)* (2). Built between 1602 and 1606, this has a Bern farm house roof, and the open façade facing the Reuss serves, still today, as a weekly marketplace. Right next door is the **Picasso Museum** (3) Furrengasse 21, ☎ 410 35 33, which holds important works created by the artist in his last twenty years, and an exhibition of over 200 photos of Picasso by David Douglas Duncan. It is open daily, April to October from 10 a.m. to 6 p.m., and the rest of the year from 11 a.m. to 1 p.m. and 2–4 p.m. The Old Town itself is not very large, but there is still plenty to see. And although I have not included it as part of the formal tour I suggest that, at a later time, you admire the compact plazas and brilliantly painted façades at your leisure. Double back now to the entrance of the wooden, covered ***Chapel Bridge** *(Kapellbrücke)* (4). Named after the nearby St. Peter's Chapel, it was built in the early 14th century as part of the city's fortifications. Take time to admire the unusual paintings adorning its gabled roof. Dating from the 17th century, they are representations of Swiss and local history, including Luzern's two patron saints, Mauritius and Leodegar. The **Water Tower** *(Wasserturm)* (5), dating from the beginning of the 14th century and situated about two-thirds of the way across the bridge, is a formidable 112-foot-tall octagonal stone tower that was originally part of the city wall. Subsequently utilized as an archive, treasury, prison and torture chamber, these days the base—as might be expected—houses a tourist shop. The water tower and the bridge have long been the most photographed monuments in Switzerland. However, being made of wood, the bridge is always susceptible to the danger of fire. Tragically, that danger materialized in the early hours of August 18, 1993, when a fire destroyed two-thirds of the bridge and 65 of the 111 gable paintings. Only 30 of the paintings could be restored, though facsimiles supplied by Ilford, the camera/film maker, and made on fadeless Ilfachrome Classic Deluxe materials, have temporarily replaced the originals. The substructure of the bridge was undamaged, however, enabling it to be rebuilt and reopened to the public on April 14, 1994.

Across the other bank you will come out on Bahnhofstrasse and, strangely, the railway station is not so close at all. It isn't even actually on the street. The modern terminal is back to the left across the main road. What you will notice, a little to the right, is the tall, elegant but rather somber, façade of the **Jesuit Church** *(Jesuitenkirche)* (6). Constructed in 1666 and considered to be the first sacred Baroque structure in Switzerland, it has a

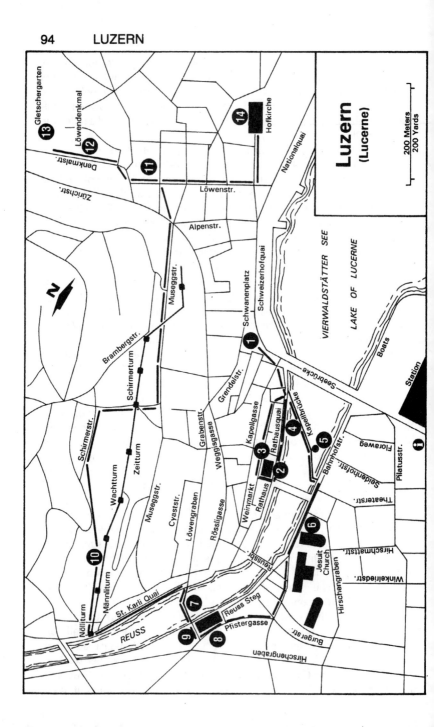

rather complex interior design with a beautiful central ceiling painting of St. Francis Xavier.

Leaving here, take the left fork and then a right into Pfistergasse, a small street with many interesting stores. At the end you again come upon the roaring river, and another wooden covered bridge, the **Spreuer Bridge** *(Spreuerbrücke)* (7). Before crossing it you may want to check out either one, or both, of the two museums in the immediate vicinity. The **Museum of National History** *(Historiches Museum)* (8), Pfistergasse 24, ☎ 228 54 24, located in the old arsenal, has exhibits that are interesting, well displayed and varied, detailing the history of both Luzern and Switzerland. It is open Tuesday to Friday from 10 a.m. to midday and 2–5 p.m., and on Saturday and Sunday from 10 a.m. to 5 p.m. The **Museum of Natural History** *(Natur Museum)* (9), Kasernplatz 6, ☎ 228 54 11, designated the "European Museum of the Year" in 1987, is a lively, hands-on museum with a variety of live animals and interactive displays. Opening hours are Tuesday to Saturday from 10 a.m. to midday and 2–5 p.m., and Saturday and Sunday from 10 a.m. to 5 p.m.

Turning your attention back to the bridge, you will find that the **Mill Bridge** *(Spreurbrücke)* is altogether less pristine than the Kapellbrücke. Completed in 1408 as part of the city's fortifications, it came by its name for the ruling that only chaffs of wheat were to be thrown into the river from this bridge. It is embellished by 67 paintings depicting the "Dance of Death," which are the work, between 1626 and 1635, of Kaspar Meglinger. As the rear portion is presently undergoing reconstruction, a modern adjunct takes you across to the right bank. Along the way, note the shrine standing in the middle of the bridge, and the unusual forts of water spikes—in the direction of the lake—that regulate the water flow. Interestingly, neither this nor the Chapel Bridge were built to service pedestrian traffic but, rather, to close the gap over the water in the city's walled fortifications.

The impressive, and remarkably well preserved, city walls now tower above you—and their formidability is awesome. To get a closer perspective, walk away from the city, along the rather drab St. Karliquai, and then ascend the steep steps by the closest, quite small, tower. These take you behind the **Musegg Wall** *(Museggmauer)* (10) where you will note, perhaps with some surprise, that the steep adjacent fields leading up to them are occupied by grazing cows. Maybe it should not be surprising; after all this is Switzerland! These walls were completed in 1408, as part of Luzern's medieval fortifications and, of the nine remaining towers *(turme)*, six are quite different from each other. One of these towers, the Zytturme, is the proud host of the oldest clock in Luzern, which is visible from a great distance. The respect endowed upon it by the city is such that it is this clock's privilege to chime one minute before all others. Three other towers, Männli, Zeit and Schirmer, and some battlements are open to the public, but only in the summer between 8 a.m. and 7 p.m.

Continue now along the path, up and around following the curvature of the walls until, at the top, the lake and distant mountains come into view behind the ramparts. Then, as if materializing out of nowhere, a memorial chapel and a fountain with a strange water-emitting head, greet you before a pathway, Schirmertoweg, leads under an archway, decorated with two lions and a shield, to the city side of the walls. Walk along the Museggstrasse, a rather distinguished street, to its junction with Museumplatz. The area to the left, Löwenplatz, a strange traffic junction with a combination of old and new structures, is home to the **Bourbaki Panorama** (11), Löwenstrasse 18, ☎ 410 99 42. This, at 1,316 square yards the largest round mural in the world, depicts the retreat and internment of the French Eastern Army at Les Verrières in Switzerland during the Franco/German War of 1870/71.

The predominance of tourist shops in what is, in all honesty, a less than inspiring area of Luzern, will alert you that something else here beckons. In fact, there are two places fully deserving of your attention, and they are both unusual indeed. The **Lion Monument** (Löwendenkmal) (12) was designed by the classicist Danish sculptor, Thorvaldsen, and was carved, between 1820 and 1821, from natural sandstone indigenous to this area by a stonemason from Constance, Ahorn, who lived between 1789 and 1856. In addition to agriculture and town crafts, mercenary military service was an important and gainful trade during the era of the old Confederation and, at the beginning of the French Revolution in 1789, about 40,000 Swiss were serving under foreign banners. The Lion Monument is dedicated to the Swiss mercenaries who were either killed during the invasion of the Tuilleries in Paris, seat of Louis XVI, on August 10, 1792 or executed by guillotine on September 2 and 3, 1792 for their part in that heroic, but unsuccessful, revolt. The inscription helvitorium fidei ac virtuiti means, "to the loyalty and bravery of the Swiss." Measuring 6.6 yards high by 10.9 yards long, it was dedicated on August 10, 1821 and purchased by the town of Luzern in 1882.

Almost next door, the **Glacier Garden** (Gletschergarten) (13), Denkmalstrasse 4, ☎ 410 43 40, exhibits a most unique and contrasting combination. Discovered in 1872, it is one of the oldest of natural wonders. Gigantic potholes and rocks carved in the strangest of shapes by the ice age 10,000 years ago co-exist with fossilized remains from over 20,000,000 years ago when Luzern was a subtropical palm beach. Also found here are the oldest relief map of Switzerland, a historical model of Luzern, a variety of other geological exhibits and, very incongruously, a Hall of Mirrors based on a juxtaposition of aspects of the Alhambra in Granada, Spain. Visit daily, March and April from 9 a.m. to 5 p.m., May to October 15, from 8 a.m. to 8 p.m., October 16 to November 15 from 9 a.m. to 5 p.m. and November 15 to the end of February on Tuesday to Saturday from 10:30 a.m. to 5 p.m.

On the way back to the Schwanenplatz, on the lake front, retrace your steps to the Löwenplatz, continue down Löwenstrasse, a street of no particular distinction, and turn right at St. Leodegarstrasse, which soon changes to Schweizerhofquai, where you will find the final attraction of the tour. It is impossible to miss, on the left, the imposing façade of the **Collegiate Church of St. Leger** *(Hofkirche)* (14). A Benedictine monastery was founded her in the 8th century and, although a fire destroyed the church in 1633, it was rebuilt twelve years later. The result is considered the finest Renaissance church in Switzerland.

Engelberg

The Engelberg valley was civilized as far back as the early 12th century, when a Benedictine monastery was founded, in 1120, by Baron Konrad von Sellenbüren of Zürich. This gained distinction quickly, being renowned for its scientific and artistic activity. The history of the valley and the monastery remained inexorably entwined, with Engelberg retaining its status as a "state in miniature," under spiritual auspices, up to the time of the French Revolution. Suitably, two brothers from the monastery were the first to climb Mount Titlis in 1744, a full forty years before Mont Blanc was conquered.

It was not until the middle of the 19th century, however, that Engelberg was commercially developed as the summer tourist resort we find today. Realizing the wider potential, the enterprising citizens at the beginning of the 20th century determined to expand the facilities to include winter sports. Initially, in 1913, a funicular was opened between Engelberg and Gerschnialp, and fourteen years later the first aerial cable car in Switzerland, connecting Gerschnialp and Trübsee, began operation. In the mid-1960s this was extended from Trübsee to the top of Titlis itself. Engelberg's main claim to international fame, though, originates from 1992, when the Rotair, the world's first revolving cable car, was installed between Stand and Titlis.

GETTING THERE:

Trains of the Luzern-Stans-Engelberg (LSE) take just one hour to cover the journey between Luzern and Engelberg, via Hergiswil and Stans.

By car, travel the N-2, Basel to Gotthard, motorway south, and take the Stans-Süd exit to Engelberg.

PRACTICALITIES:

The **Dialing Code** for Engelberg is 41. The **Tourist Office** (*Engelberg Tourism*), ☎ 637 37 37, Fax 637 41 56 or www.englebergtourism.ch, found at Klosterstrasse 3, CH-6390 Engelberg, has complicated opening hours. In the summer and winter seasons it opens Monday to Saturday from 8 a.m. to 6:30 p.m. and Sunday from 4–7 p.m. At other times of the year, basically between mid-April to mid-June and mid-October to mid-December, it is open Monday to Friday from 8 a.m. to 12:15 p.m. and 2–6:30 p.m., and Saturday from 8 a.m. to 6:30 p.m.

ACCOMMODATION:

The **Hotel Hess ****, ☎ 637 13 66 or Fax 637 35 38, CH-6390 Engelberg, has been managed by the founding family, Hess naturally, since 1884. It features 80 recently renovated rooms offering every modern convenience, as well as a variety of communal activities including a sauna, solarium, small fitness center, and the gourmet Tudor Stübli restaurant. $$

The **Hotel Engelberg ***, ☎ 637 11 68 or Fax 637 32 35, Dorfstrasse 14, CH-6390 Engelberg, is a small, 20-room hotel located on the main, pedestrian only, street in Engelberg. It is quiet, comfortable and has a restaurant on site. $

FOOD AND DRINK:

Most everyone visiting Engelberg for the day will plan to take a trip to the top of Titlis, and it would be a mistake not to savor the occasion by having a meal up there. After all, how often do you get an opportunity to dine in the company of such stunning views? And, you have a choice as well. The **Panorama Restaurant**, a self-service restaurant seating 140, has views out over the Alps to the Black Forest. The more intimate **Titlis Stübli**, seats 50 and has vistas of the Bernese Alps. And then there are the **Pizzeria** and a bar, the **Stove Bar**, named in honor of the antique stove used as a decoration. Incidentally, you may be higher in this bar than you thought; it is considered to be at a greater altitude than any other in Europe.

SUGGESTED TOUR:

As is generally the case when describing a place as small as Engelberg, this narrative will not be as much an organized tour as a description of activities and places or interest in and around the village. Either in summer or in winter, there are a wide variety of things here to attract visitors. Among these, though, one in particular is responsible for attracting the most interest.

The ***Luzern Engelberg TITLIS ROTAIR**, ☎ 639 50 50, Fax 639 50 60 or www.titlis.ch, P. O. Box 88, CH-6391 Engelberg, not only provides the highest viewpoint in Central Switzerland but, much more innovatively, is the first revolving cable car in the world. It is open year round, except during annual maintenance—usually during November, from 8:30 a.m. until the last ascent at 3:40 p.m. What's more, the Titlis is also accessible to the handicapped in wheelchairs.

The trip begins on the valley floor at an altitude of 3,280 feet, from where a six-passenger **gondola car** will glide across the lower pastures and rise up to the first stage Gerschnialp, at 4,265 feet. Here it is your choice whether you disembark to admire the scenery or continue directly up another 1,600

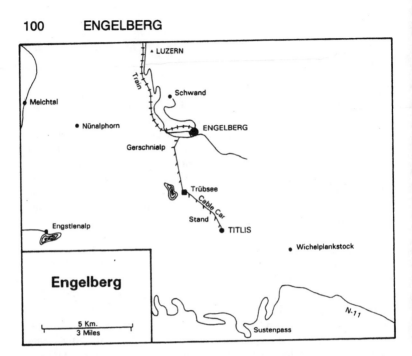

feet to Trübsee, at 5,905 feet. This was opened in 1983, has an hourly capacity of 2,400 people and a journey time of just 15 minutes. Here you must make a change, and the ascent gets much steeper after you board the cable car, with its capacity of 80 people, that whisks you up to **Stand**, 8,038 feet, in just five minutes. This Trübsee to Stand cable car was opened in 1965 and, two years later, the final leg from Stand to Titlis, 9,908 feet, was inaugurated.

Coming to the conclusion, however, that a spectacular ride over glacier falls and ice crevices among craggy mountain peaks was not sufficiently exciting, the authorities decided to add another thrilling aspect to the last five minutes of the trip. In 1993 the installation of two revolving ***Rotair cable cars** was completed, and these were—and still are—a world-wide innovation. Actually, "revolving" is a bit of a misnomer in this instance, and can be confusing. Like me, you may envision the whole cable revolves, but that is not what you will find. Rather, the mechanism used is similar to that of the revolving restaurants in Leysin, Saas Fee and Schilthorn. Shortly after the trip begins, the cabin floor, which accommodates 75 travelers, begins to revolve, leaving only a central podium—with room for 5 more—and the walls fixed. Thus, the spectacular Alpine scenery all around you may be viewed from an unparalleled variety of angles. Certainly, this is quite an experience, but a vertiginous one for those not blessed with a head for heights. Seriously, this can be disconcerting for some people, and my suggestion is that those with a propensity towards any form of vertigo get to the front of the line and head for the central podium.

The summit holds a wealth of things to do. In addition to the ever-captivating views that reach out over the Alps and, on a clear day, to the Black Forest in Germany, there are numerous restaurants and a traditional bar which, as described above, is advertised as the highest in Europe. Learn about your surroundings from a ten-minute movie about Mount Titlis, aptly named the **Toporama**. Maybe, relax on the sun terrace or, for something really different, take a stroll out onto the glacier. Along the way you may even be entertained by a gentleman dressed in typical Alpine costume, with a St. Bernard by his side (of course) who will, with a little financial encouragement, treat you to a burst or two on an Alpine Horn. If you are taken with the Alpine costume, then you may want to consider having a photo taken of yourself in such a traditional outfit. And, you can. On the second floor, look for **Nostalgic Photos**. Their helpful staff will dress you accordingly, click the shutter and deliver the photos in just five minutes. Also not to be overlooked is the Glacier Grotto, which traverses 164 yards into the highest point of the Titlis Glacier. As a note of interest, you will find that the temperature inside the grotto varies only between 30.2 and 29.3 degrees Fahrenheit, regardless of the outside conditions.

During your visit here you may, on a fine day, see paragliders cavorting in the air currents around the valley. Well, you don't just have to look and admire. Why not have a go yourself? **Impuls Sport and Flugschule Engelberg AG**, ☎ 637 07 07 or Fax 637 34 07, Wasserfallstrasse 135, CH-6390 Engelberg, is open every day, weather—global or local—permitting. Experienced paragliders can pilot themselves or, if you are a novice, you can enjoy the same exhilarating experience as a passenger on a flight. You will travel to your take-off point by cable car and, after preparing your paraglider for flight, then soar like a bird around the valley, with the rushing wind, clean mountain air and the panoramic view as your companions.

Time now to head back. On the descent to the valley some may be tempted to stop for a rest at Stand, but a better option is **Trübsee**. You will, most likely, have noticed the small lake here on the way up and, between July 5 and October—providing the weather conditions are favorable—you can take an enchanting horse-drawn carriage ride around idyllic Lake Trübsee.

Most visitors will finish their trip to Titlis the easy way, by taking the gentle gondola ride back down to Engelberg. The more adventurous have other options, either up on the mountainside and/or getting back down. **Mountain bikes** may be rented, CHF 25 for a half-day and CHF 35 for a full day, from the Bike'n Roll sports shop, located across from the tourist office. You can then take them up to Trübsee and, from there, on to the Jochpass if you want to go higher, then bike down. You will, however, have to plan ahead if you choose this option. On the first stage transportation up is possible between 8:30 a.m. to 5 p.m., but if you fail to get a reservation—by calling 639 50 61 between 8 a.m. to 5 p.m.—a maximum wait time of 25 minutes can arise. Similarly, on the second stage, transportation is available between 8:45 a.m. and noon and between 1:15 p.m. and 4:30 p.m. Reservations for that leg may be made by calling 637 21 52.

Consider, also, renting a gentler, and more unusual form of bike, the **Trotti bike**, actually more like an old-fashioned scooter, which can be used on the descent from Gerschnialp to Engelberg. Purchase your ticket for the ascent at the Titlis aerial cable car main station in Engelberg. Travel up, alighting at Gerschnialp. Pick up your Trotti bike and the scoot off for the 984-foot, 15-minute descent to Engelberg. Please note, though, that neither the transportation operator or the landowner will take any responsibility for your safety, and remember cows have the right of way!

There is a way, but this is really for those with both a strong stomach and a head for heights, of getting down quickly and then going straight back up. Puzzled? Read on. Each weekend between May and October **Bungy Jumping** is offered from the cable car that operates between Trübsee and Stand. And you can even choose the height, either 70 or 120 meters (76.5 and 131.2 yards).

The journey up to Titlis is an exciting trip, and certainly will be the highlight of a visit to Engelberg. Truthfully, those coming for a daytrip, or even staying overnight, will be satisfied with going up Titlis, and then spending some time in the pleasant village. It would be unfair, however, not to add that Engelberg, the largest summer and winter resort in Central Switzerland, really does have much more to offer in either season. In summer, you can explore over 224 miles of marked walking and hiking paths, and enjoy any variety of outdoor activities. Some of the more unusual of these are mountain glacier hikes, the Flying Fox experience and canyoning; all of which are arranged by the **Mountain Guide Office**, ☎ 637 46 91, Dorfstrasse 31, CH-6390 Engelberg. In winter, downhill and cross-country skiers have the run of over 45 kilometers (28 miles) of marked ski pistes and 40 kilometers (24.9 miles) of cross-country tracks. Hikers and walkers can choose from among 36 kilometers (22.4 miles) of pathways. Other facilities include a sledge and toboggan run, and indoor pool.

In either season some visitors may even want to spend a little time understanding more about the history and life of the high Alpine valleys at the **Engelberg Museum** *(Tal Museum Engelberg)*, ☎ 637 04 14, and also, perhaps, visiting the monastery and its famed library.

*Pilatus

One of the easiest, and yet most enjoyable, daytrips that can be made in the Luzern area is the classic round-trip excursion to nearby Mount Pilatus.

GETTING THERE:

As this is a round-trip, it may be taken in either direction. My recommendation, though, is to do it this way:

By bus, Bus Number 1 from Luzern to Kriens.

By gondola car, from Kriens to Fräkmüntegg, via Krienseregg.

By cable car, from Fräkmüntegg to Pilatus.

By cogwheel railway, from Pilatus to Alpnachstad.

By boat or train, from Alpnachstad to Luzern.

PRACTICALITIES:

The **Dialing Code** for Pilatus is 41. Information on virtually any aspect of Pilatus may be obtained from **Mount Pilatus Railways** *(Pilatus-Bahnen)*, ☎ 329 11 11, Fax 329 11 12, E-mail pilatus@pilatus.com or www.pilatus.com/. Alternatively, the tourist office in Luzern will be happy to assist you.

Information regarding weather conditions is available by calling ☎ 329 11 29.

ACCOMMODATION:

The **Hotel Bellevue**, ☎ 670 12 55 or Fax 670 26 35, CH-6011 Kriens-Pilatus, built in the shape of a circle, sits perched precariously on the ridge of the mountain. Each of the 27 comfortably furnished double rooms has private bath or shower, toilet and TV. There is a small supplemental charge for a single room. $

The **Hotel Pilatus Kulm**, ☎ 670 12 55 or Fax 670 26 35, CH-6011 Kriens-Pilatus, the smaller of the two hotels here, has a less dramatic location. It is also more basic. The 20 double rooms have hot and cold running water, but showers and toilets are located within separate rooms on each floor. $

FOOD AND DRINK:

Between them, the Hotels Bellevue and Pilatus Kulm offer a choice of six restaurants, with a combined seating capacity of 560.

SUGGESTED TOUR:

You should not be surprised to learn that this excursion, which encompasses a famous, mythical mountain and the most eclectic array of transportation on any singular tour in this guide, is known as the **Golden Roundtrip** (Goldene Rundfahrt). And, although the distances covered are not particularly great, you should plan to dedicate the better part of a day to enjoy this journey to its fullest. Obviously, being a round trip it may be executed in either direction—that is provided you visit between May and mid-December as, during the winter months, the cog wheel railway is closed. In any event, no matter the time of year, I would suggest that it is far more pleasant to leave the more relaxing leg of the trip until the last—and this is the tact I shall take when continuing below.

Depart Luzern on the Number 1 bus for the 15-minute, 3.1 kilometer (1.9 mile) trip to **Kriens** (1). Here you should proceed to the gondola station, originally opened in 1954, but re-opened on May 10, 1996 after a thorough reconstruction. From this point, one of 132 gondola cabins will silently whisk you from Kriens, at 516 meters (1,692 feet), through the middle station of Krienseregg at 1,026 meters (3,366 feet), and on to the upper station of Fräkmüntegg, at an altitude of 1,415 meters (4,642 feet). Traveling at 4.5 meters (14.76 feet) per second, it will take just 18 minutes to traverse the 4,900 meters (16,076 feet) that raises you, in total from your beginning point in Kriens, 899 meters (2,949 feet) in altitude.

Fräkmüntegg (2) is, itself, the starting point for numerous hikes, as well as being the origination point for the longest **toboggan run** in Switzerland—which winds back down to the valley. This run is normally open between April and October/November, and tickets may be purchased at the gondola car ticket office. Depending upon the weather and your interest, you may check further details relating to this attraction by calling ☎ 329 11 29.

The ultimate stage of the ascent is made via a cable car inaugurated in 1956. The distance of 1,389 meters (4,557 feet), traveled at 6.5 meters (21 feet) a second and covered in just five minutes, raises you to your destination, the **Pilatus Kulm** (3) station, at an altitude of 2,070 meters (6,791 feet).

Although far from being the highest mountain peak in Switzerland, Mount Pilatus, the dominant natural landmark of Luzern, appears much taller than it is as it stands isolated from the main ranges of the Alps. It is most definitely not the prettiest peak either—in fact, it is rather forbidding, both physically and mythically. Nevertheless, more has been written about this mountain—the first in Switzerland to be given a name, than any other in the country.

Legend has it that, within the lake on this "mountain of dragons," are in-

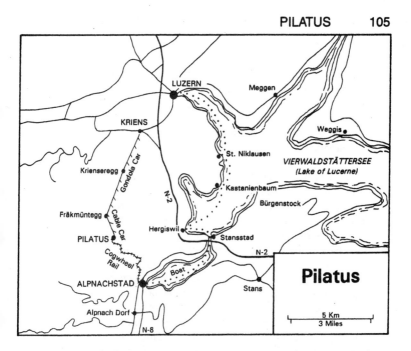

terred the remains of the Roman Governor Pontius Pilate—hence, its name. The legend goes on to tell that his anguished spirit surfaced annually, on Good Friday, in an unsuccessful attempt to cleanse his bloodied hands. Long before Pilate lived, however, this mountain, then known as *fraactus mons* (the Broken Mountain), was believed to be inhabited by dragons, which could be, at various times, either benevolent or terrifying. Numerous stories have long been told of these flame-spitting, flying creatures, and of a dragon-stone, said to be endowed with miraculous healing powers—which, in fact, is presently on display in Luzern. There is also the legend of the moon milk *(modmilchloch)*, which was considered a universal cure for the infirmities of mankind.

The sum total of these myths led the government of Luzern to declare Pilatus a "forbidden" mountain, with even the local shepherds placed under oath that they would not approach the waters of the lake there. In 1585, however, a determined parish priest of Luzern and some brave citizens ascended Pilatus. The goal was the exorcism of the spirits domiciled there. In continuation of the purgation begun by their mission, the lake, believed to be a home of spirit beings, was completely drained in 1594. This remained a dry bed for a full 400 years, until it was dammed again in 1980.

Pilatus today is the starting point for numerous hikes, and you may, if you are very fortunate, catch a glimpse of an elusive chamois perched precariously on a cliff face, or come vis-à-vis with a shy marmot. Do not be concerned, however. You will not have to confront any angry dragons, and the spirits of Pilatus now reside peacefully in this mountain respite. What you will find are absolutely *magnificent views; a horizon bedecked with glorious mountain peaks and glaciers, Lake Luzern and its tributary rivers glistening below, and the frost-clad hills giving way to a kaleidoscopic mix of farmhouses dotting the slopes and towns and villages scattered around the lakeside. This scene is enchanting enough at any time of day, but is especially remarkable at sunset and sunrise—for those who decide to spend the night on the mountain.

The journey back to Luzern is not without its attractions, either. As long ago as June 4, 1889, a remarkable cog wheel railway opened between Pilatus Kulm and Alpnachstad on the shores of Lake Luzern. It operates by toothed racks of a rack- and-pinion system, with two horizontally-moving pinions that mesh each side of the rack with a series of teeth milled throughout the 4,618 meter-(2.9 miles)-length of the rack. To prevent the vehicles from derailing, or raising up, two guide pulleys rotate beneath the pinions. In its early days, steam engines were used on this 80-centimeter (2 foot, 7½ inch)-gauge track. But in 1937 these were replaced by electrically motorized cars of the type used here today. This dramatic trip along the mountainside, which takes 30 minutes when ascending and forty minutes when descending, still retains the distinction of being the steepest rack railway in the world—with an average gradient of 42%, and a maximum of 48%.

Down at **Alpnachstad** (4) those opting for the quick, 20-minute, return to Luzern will take the Brünig railway. Others, with a little more time to spare or, perhaps, a bit more discernment, will chose the pleasurable 70-minute *cruise back across the enchanting Lake Luzern. And, if your choice of accommodation is the Seehotel Kastanienbaum, the vessel will dock right at the hotel.

*The Bernese Oberland: Seven Daytrips

Among the many places in Switzerland that have drawn to themselves the attention of the world, there is none more internationally acclaimed than the Bernese Oberland. Although there are records of the ancient Romans passing through the area and even though it was known in medieval times, it has only been since the middle of the last century that these often remote valleys and mountains have been opened up to tourism. And, since the enterprising locals realized the wealth that lay at their doorstep, they have not stopped developing, in the most careful and controlled of ways, the tourist market.

Not content to rely upon the natural splendor of the Eiger, Mönch and Jungfrau, and the lovely serenity of the lakes of Brienz and Thun, they have developed what must be the most eclectic array of transportation possible to link together the towns, villages and mountains. Regular trains and buses leading to rack railways that take you to the highest station in Europe; cable cars, one of which deposits you at a world-famous revolving restaurant 10,000 feet in the sky; a steep funicular; the longest gondola cableway in Europe; the quaint steam railway between Brienz and Rothorn; old-fashioned steamer voyages on either lake and, of course, any number of ski and chair lifts highlight the myriad of options. Going one step further, and being not just clever but wise, they decided that the villages of Wengen and Mürren would best retain their character if they were "car free." Following the same line of thinking, some of the roads that transverse the valleys have been reserved for post buses only. Is it any wonder, then, that tourists from all over the world converge on the truly unique Bernese Oberland?

In fact, there are no end of daytrips, and other activities, to be undertaken here. In the normal format of the "Daytrips" series these would be described using each of the towns and villages as separate bases. However, in this instance, as all of these places are so close to each other and so well connected by both public transportation and pathways, attractions for each base would overlap and this approach would become somewhat redundant. To head this problem off at the pass, and present the options as clearly as possible, I will add into this chapter two extra sections, TRANSPORTATION and TOWNS AND VILLAGES that will work in tandem. The former will detail how the latter, and other scenic destinations, can be reached, and the latter will give a brief overview of the principal towns and villages. The map shows the relationship between mountains, lakes, towns and villages as well as the different means of transportation that connect them. One final new section, found after the SUGGESTED TOURS, called OTHER ACTIVITIES, details activities not included in a SUGGESTED TOURS that may be of interest to readers.

Although the Bernese Oberland is divided into seven sub-regions, this guide will concentrate upon only the Eiger, Mönch & Jungfrau, Brienzersee and Thunersee regions.

GETTING THERE:

The following information will get you to Interlaken, the gateway to this area of the Bernese Oberland. Advice on getting to destinations beyond Interlaken is detailed in the TRANSPORTATION section.

By air, most international flights arrive at either Zürich's Kloten or Geneva's Cointrin airport, although a limited number of flights from other European countries use Basel-Mulhouse or Bern-Belp airports. In any event there are regular train connections from all of the above, some with changes needed, to Interlaken West station.

Trains arrive at Interlaken West, with most continuing on to Interlaken Ost (East), from throughout Switzerland. Direct services arrive from Berlin and Amsterdam via Cologne, while other services (that require a connection) arrive from Hamburg, Milan, Prague, Paris, Vienna and Brussels.

By car, Interlaken, surrounded by mountain ranges to the north and south, can be accessed by car only from the east or west. The topography is such that it is not so difficult to reach Interlaken from those directions. To avoid a long, and not always easy, roundabout trip from the Valais it is highly advisable to take the car-rail link from Goppenstein to Kandersteg.

PRACTICALITIES:

The **Dialing Code** for this region is 33.

The **Brienz Tourist Office** *(Tourismusverein Brienz-Axalp)*, ☎ 952 80 80 or Fax 952 80 88, Hauptstrasse 143, CH-3855 Brienz am See, is open Monday to Friday from 8 a.m. to midday and 2–6 p.m., and between May 1 to October 31 it opens on Saturday from 8 a.m. to midday.

The **Grindelwald Tourist Office** *(Verkehrsbüro Grindelwald)*, ☎ 854 12 12 or Fax 854 12 10, CH-3818 Grindelwald, is open Monday to Friday from 8 a.m. to midday and 2–6 p.m., and Saturday from 8 a.m. to 5 p.m. Grindelwald offers further assistance to travelers through a special number, 853 25 55, which provides information on holiday apartments and mountaineering on the Eiger.

The **Interlaken Tourist Office** *(Interlaken Tourism)*, ☎ 822 21 21, Fax

822 52 21, E-mail mail@InterlakenTourism.ch or on the world wide web at www.InterlakenTourism.ch, is located at Höheweg 37 (the Metropole Hotel building), CH-3800 Interlaken. It is open during July and August, Monday to Friday from 8 a.m. to 6:30 p.m., Saturday 8 a.m. to 5 p.m., and Sunday 5 p.m. to 7 p.m. At all other times it opens Monday to Friday from 8 a.m. to midday and 2–6 p.m., and Saturday from 8 a.m. to midday.

The **Mürren Tourist Office** *(Verkehrsbüro Mürren),* ☎ 856 86 66 or Fax 856 86 96, CH-3825 Mürren, is open Monday to Saturday, excluding Thursday, from 9 a.m. to midday and 1–6:30 p.m., Thursday from 9 a.m. to midday and 1-8:30 p.m., and Sunday from 1–5:30 p.m.

The **Wengen Tourist Office** *(Verkehrsbüro Wengen),* ☎ 855 14 14 or Fax 855 30 60, CH-3823 Wengen is open year round, Monday to Friday from 8 a.m. to midday and 2–6 p.m., and from June 14 to September 20 offers extended hours on Saturday from 8:30 a.m. to 11:30 a.m. and 4–6 p.m., and on Sunday from 4–6 p.m.

Bucherer has one store in the Bernese Oberland, next door to the celebrated Victoria-Jungfrau Grand Hotel at Höheweg 43, Interlaken. ☎ 822 26 26 or Fax 822 26 30.

The best places for purchasing **Swiss Army Knives** in Interlaken, Grindelwald, and Wengen are: The **Swiss Knife Center**, ☎ 822 32 20, is located in a very attractive pavilion at Höheweg 125, Interlaken—quite incongruously, as it is in the middle of town, directly in front of a field of grazing cows. In addition to a full range of the Victorinox Swiss Army Knives—with complimentary engraving, it offers a wide and varied selection of other wonderful souvenirs, including kitchen knives, stuffed animals, and cowbells etc. Look, especially, at the T-shirts. Those with the Victorinox logo are, far and away, the best value at just CHF 10. The quality is good, and the price is so low only because the Victorinox owners realize the value of advertising and subsidize their production. And they always are a topic of conversation back home. In **Wengen,** the shop to head for is **Photohaus Fritz Lauener,** ☎ 855 11 54. Besides, as the name implies, offering a full range of photographic equipment, this is the shop in the village that carries Victorinox Swiss Army Knives—with complimentary engraving, watches and an array of sunglasses. They are also particularly proud of their selection of 1,000 different postcards.

Shops in this area are generally open—with some variations, most notably in Interlaken where many are open during the lunch hour in summer, Monday to Friday from 8 a.m. to midday and 1:30–6:30 p.m., and on Saturday from 8 a.m. to 4 p.m. Keep in mind when making your plans that, outside of these hours and especially in the villages, it will be nearly impossible to find even a grocery store open.

TRANSPORTATION:

BY CABLE CAR:

To **Männlichen** (Luftseilbahn Wengen-Männlichen—LWM): Wengen to Männlichen.

To **Pfingstegg** (Pfingsteggbahn): Grindelwald to Pfingstegg.

To **Schilthorn** (Schilthornbahn): Stetchelberg, Gimmelwald, Mürren, Birg to Schilthorn.

BY COG RAILWAY:

To **Jungfraujoch:**

1) Berner Oberland Bahnen (BOB): Interlaken Ost (East) to Grindelwald or Lauterbrunnen.

2) Wengeralpenbahn (WAB): Grindelwald or Lauterbrunnen (via Wengen) to Kleine Scheidegg.

3) Jungfraubahn (JF): Kleine Scheidegg to Jungfraujoch.

To **Schynige Platte** (Schynige Platte Railway—SPB): Wilderswil to Schynige Platte.

BY FUNICULAR:

To **Allmendhubel** (Mürren-Allmendhubel—SMA): Mürren to Allmendhubel.

To **Grütschalp** (Lauterbrunnen-Mürren—BLM): Lauterbrunnen to Grütschalp.

BY GONDOLA CABLEWAY:

To **First** (FIRSTBAHNEN): Grindelwald, Bort, Grindel to First.

To **Männlichen** (Gondelbahn Grindelwald-Männlichen—GGM): Grindelwald (Grund), Mittelstation Holenstein, to Männlichen.

BY LAKE STEAMER:

To **Brienz** (Thuner und Brienzersee Schiffsbetreib der Lötschbergbahn—BLS): Interlaken Ost (East), Ringenberg, Bönigen, Iseltwald, Giessbach See to Brienz.

To **Thun** (Thuner und Brienzersee Schiffsbetreib der Lötschbergbahn—BLS): Interlaken West, Sundlauenen, Beatenbucht, Spiez, Oberhofen, Hünibach to Thun.

BY NARROW GAUGE NON-COG RAILWAY:

To **Mürren** (Lauterbrunnen-Mürren—BLM): Grütschalp to Mürren.

BY POSTAL BUS:

To **Meiringen** and **Brienz**: Grindelwald, Meiringen to Brienz.

To **Stechelberg**: Lauterbrunnen, Trümmelbach to Stechelberg.

BY STEAM LOCOMOTIVE RACK RAILWAY:

To **Rothorn**: Brienz to Rothorn.

BY TRAIN:

To **Brienz**: Interlaken Ost (East), Niederried, Oberied to Brienz.

To **Thun**: Interlaken West, Spiez to Thun.

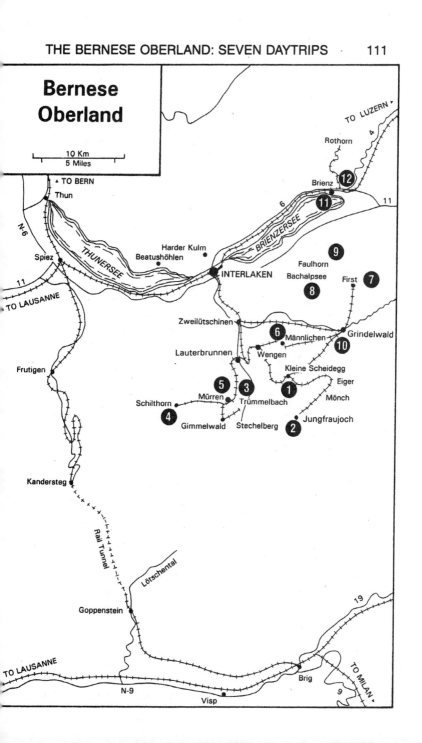

TOWNS AND VILLAGES:
Grindelwald:

For such a small village Grindelwald certainly has an intriguing history. It is believed that mountain Celts were the first inhabitants of the Grindelwald valley, presumably in the early centuries of the Chris-tian era. The village name is thought to originate from an old German-Celtic word *Grindel*, which is defined as a block of wood used as a barrier. As *Wald* translates to forest, scholars have reasoned that *Grindelwald* could, therefore, have been descriptive of a forest valley that was blocked off from the outside world. This would certainly accurately describe the topography of that era. As time passed the Celts migrated down from the rough hills to the milder climate of the lower pastures, thus forming the scattered community of Grindelwald.

The first written mention of Grindelwald is found on a document dating from 1146. At that time, King Konrad promised his protection to the Augustine monastery in Interlaken, which also owned property in Grindelwald. The monks' greed for more and more land occasioned periodic revolts by the citizens of Grindelwald, a conflict that continued until the Reformation in 1528, when the Interlaken monastery was abolished. Thinking that it would augment their independence, the people of Grindelwald allied themselves with the Bernese government—but only on condition that they would not be taxed. The Bernese were cognizant about the wealth of the monastery however, and very quickly found the idea of relinquishing this source of revenue too taxing. The population of Grindelwald rebelled against this breach of faith, dismissed their Protestant pastor and, in October of 1528, re-instituted the old faith. Enraged, the Bernese dispatched an expedition to Grindelwald that devastated the town.

Over the centuries Grindelwald has also battled numerous attacks of the plague, with over 788 people dying in the outbreak of 1669 alone.

Relations with the Bernese improved during the 18th and 19th centuries, when both sides became aware that a cooperative effort could be mutually beneficial. The late 19th century brought the steam train to Grindelwald, opening the area to convenient travel and bringing in its wake an ever-increasing number of tourists from all over the world. As early as 1900, visitors were accommodated by 18 hotels with 1,250 beds, and six years later the number of hotels had grown to 30. This trend has continued until today so that, in little over a century, Grindelwald has gone from a cattle-breeding economy to one where 92% of its total income is derived from tourism. The allure of Grindelwald is not limited to the summer season; it is also a favorite for skiers and other winter sports enthusiasts. There is an impressive choice of ski runs, inclusive of beginner through expert levels, covering 200 kilometers (124.3 miles) and descending from altitudes as high as 2,971 meters (9,747 feet). These are accessed via a combination of no less than 43 mountain railways, ski-lifts, etc.

In 1962, when I first visited Grindelwald, it was still little more than an overgrown farming village. That, now, has changed, but as most of the new development has been spread out across this fairly wide valley, progress certainly has not spoiled its ambiance. Unlike some of its neighboring villages, Grindelwald is too large to ban the use of cars, but that does not mean they have the freedom of the valley. They do not. Many of the roads outside the village are reserved for residents and farm vehicles, and only postal buses are allowed on the valley road to Meiringen.

Interlaken:

As the name implies Interlaken lies between two lakes, Brienz and Thun, at an altitude of 570 meters (1,870 feet) above sea level. As the natural gateway to the famous mountain trio of the Eiger, Mönch and Jungfrau, the town grew rapidly during the last century to meet the demands of tourists awakening to the splendor of these peaks. The luxury accommodation of large and gracious hotels and the diversion of the casino and other attractions have transformed Interlaken into a celebrated resort. Today, this small town—though still far and away the largest in the area with a population of less than 15,000, has a capacity of over 5,300 beds. You can imagine, therefore, that Interlaken gets somewhat crowded at times, although never enough to spoil its natural charms.

Wengen:

A bill of sale, dated 1268, contains the first mention of Wengen, *Dorf auf der Wange*, the village on the slopes. The Augustine monastery at Interlaken, which also controlled Grindelwald, in the mid-14th century extended its power through the Lauterbrunnen valley, including in its sphere of influence Wengen and Wengernalp, farther up the mountain. Following the Reformation, the entire area came under the domination of the Bernese and then, notwithstanding that it is the largest village, Wengen became a part of the community of Lauterbrunnen, and not autonomous.

And so, this dramatically beautiful village clinging to the slopes of the mountain, with its stupendous views of the Eiger, Jungfrau and the glorious waterfalls that cascade hundreds of feet into the valley below, passed its days in relative obscurity until the middle of the 19th century. It was during that period, 1834 and 1835, that the first licenses were issued for the operation of inns over the pass at Kleine Scheidegg, to Wengernalp and Kleine Scheidegg, respectively. A few years later the first inn was opened in Wengen, and tourism grew at such a rapid rate over the ensuing decades that, by 1880, the Pension Wengen, with a capacity of 100 beds, was opened. The opening of the railways, Berner Oberland in 1890 and Wengernalp in 1893, brought even more visitors and by 1890 the area supported 21 hotels with a total capacity of 1084 beds. Prior to 1909, Wengen's tourist season was confined to the summer months but, during the following year, the rail link to Kleine Scheidegg opened up the higher peaks to winter sports.

Today, all year round, visitors leave their cars in the huge car park in Lauterbrunnen to board trains that transport them to this charming village—an absolutely ideal base for daytrips around this part of the Bernese Oberland.

ACCOMMODATION:

Bönigen:

The **Hotel Seiler au Lac ★★★★**, ☎ 822 30 21 or Fax 822 30 01, CH-3806 Bönigen-Interlaken, a delightful family-run hotel with a rather modern ambiance, is located just a few feet from the charming Lake Brienz—a more peaceful alternative to busy Interlaken, just five minutes or so away. The guest rooms are well appointed, especially the mini-suites, and a fine restaurant, a pizzeria and grill are on site. $$

Grindelwald:

The **Grand Hotel Regina ★★★★★**, ☎ 854 54 55 or Fax 853 47 17, CH-3818 Grindelwald, a member of the Leading Hotels of the World group, is the only 5-Star hotel in the village. Located just across from the railway station, it has 100 rooms, including 15 suites, all of which are furnished with bath/shower, direct dial telephone, color TV with satellite programs, mini-bar and radio. The public rooms are decorated with antiques, oil paintings, engravings and clocks from the 18th and 19th centuries—part of the private collection of the Krebs family, owners of the hotel since 1953. You will be entertained in the gourmet restaurant, the La Pendule d'Or, by a pianist, or you can choose the more informal Jägerstube restaurant, which offers Swiss specialties. In either most of the vegetables come from the hotels own organic vegetable garden. Afterwards, retreat to Herbie's Bar, where you can enjoy live music and Herbert's seductive cocktail creations. Look, also, for indoor and outdoor heated pools, sauna, massage and solarium. $$$

The **Hotel Belvedere ★★★★**, ☎ 854 54 54 or Fax 853 53 23, CH-3818 Grindelwald, boasts an enviable location just across the valley from, and almost in the shadow of, the north face of the Eiger. The personality of the Hauşer family, owners and operators for over 90 years, is lovingly imprinted on every aspect of this hotel. A recent comprehensive renovation has yielded tastefully appointed rooms with a modern ambiance. The well equipped spa features both a pool and a large jacuzzi with picture windows allowing superb views of the Eiger. $$$

The **Central Hotel Wolter ★★★**, ☎ 853 22 33 or Fax 853 35 61, CH-3818 Grindelwald, in the center of the village is run by Andreas and Monic Kaufmann. Expect very comfortable rooms with all facilities priced at just CHF 110 a person for a double room. Add an extra CHF 30 per person for half-pension, and enjoy delightful specialties homegrown on their farm. $

The **Pension Gydisdorf**, ☎ 853 13 03, CH-3818 Grindelwald, a typically Swiss chalet set in its own verdant gardens, is in close proximity to the

Firstbahn cableway. All rooms, with a typical Alpine decor, have hot and cold running water. Some have views of the Eiger. $

The **Mountain Hostel**, ☎ 853 39 00 or Fax 853 47 30, CH-3818 Grindelwald, is the ideal place for those looking for basic, and very inexpensive, accommodation. Found down by the Männlichenbahn gondola station, it has bunk bedrooms which sleep from four to six people. Prices range from basic, where you bring your own sheets or sleeping bag; to deluxe—they supply bed linens and a Nordic duvet. This comes with a breakfast buffet, and half-board is available for a minimal amount extra. $

The **Swiss Youth Hostels**, ☎ 853 10 09, Terrassenweg, CH-3818 Grindelwald, are simple, basic and clean with rates between CHF 18 and CHF 32 per person, and that includes breakfast and sheets. $

Interlaken:

The **Victoria-Jungfrau Grand Hotel & Spa** *****, ☎ 828 28 28, Fax 828 28 80, E-mail victoria@bluewin.ch or www.victoria-jungfrau.ch, built in 1864 and located in the very center of Interlaken, is a very grand, traditional hotel that, quite rightly, is a member of the Leading Hotels of the World group. The 228 rooms, junior suites and suites have every modern facility and a classically elegance decor. Look for the La Terrasse—the gourmet restaurant, the Jungfrau-Stube—an informal restaurant where you can find typical Swiss dishes, a selection of bars and an intimate night club. And then there is the Victoria-Jungfrau Spa. There, you will find a fully equipped health, fitness and beauty center with whirlpools, steam bath, saunas, massage, gymnastic center and a wonderful Art-Deco pool area. During 1997/98 there were any number of special packages, and guests were even given the unparalleled opportunity of test driving for a whole day, free of charge, a Jaguar, Land Rover or BMW—depending upon availability, of course. $$$

The **Metropole Hotel** ****, ☎ 828 66 66 or Fax 828 66 33, Höheweg 37, CH-3800 Interlaken, is a large, 100-room, tower block hotel in the center of town. It may look a little incongruous but the rooms lack for no modern facility, and some even have a south facing balcony with views of the Jungfrau. Guests enjoy the use of an indoor swimming pool, sauna, solarium, car park, indoor shopping arcade, bank and tourist information office. Look also for the Italian specialty IL Bellini restaurant and, on the 18th floor, the "Top O' MET" restaurant with panoramic views of the lakes and Alps. $$

The **Restaurant Hotel Bären** *, ☎ 822 76 76, is a tiny unassuming place with clean, simple, rooms—many without a private bathroom. It is close to the West railroad station in the shopping district part of town. $

The **Happy Inn Lodge**, ☎ Kleine-Scheidegg:

The **Scheidegg Hotels** **, ☎ 855 12 12 or Fax 855 12 94, c/o Röstizzeria-Bahnhof, CH-3801 Kleine Scheidegg, has a most unusual location, and a clue is in the address. It is, also, at this isolated railway junction, right across from the towering north face of the Eiger, where the lines from Grindelwald and Lauterbrunnen/Wengen meet, and passengers change for the last leg of the journey to the Jungfraujoch. $

Mürren:

The **Hotel Eiger ******, ☎ 855 13 31, Fax 855 39 31, E-mail hoteleigerK-ibm.net or www.murren.ch/eiger, CH-3825 Mürren, established in 1886 and run by the same family ever since, offers magnificent views of the Eiger, Mönch and Jungfrau from most of the 4 rooms, 4 luxury suites and 4 apartment suites. All guest and public rooms are well appointed and have an elegant, yet comfortable, ambiance. The hotel is run with a relaxed personal touch and features an indoor pool, sauna, solarium, a terrace with wonderful views and the Eiger Stübli, an exquisite gourmet restaurant. $$

The **Hotel Jungfrau & Jungfrau Lodge *****, ☎ 855 45 45, Fax 855 45 49 or WWW.forum.ch/go.exe?1484, CH-3825 Mürren. These are located in the middle of the village, and the rooms in the hotel have bath/shower, radio, TV, telephone, and some have a balcony with views over the Eiger, Mönch and Jungfrau, while those in the Lodge are somewhat simpler. It is located next to the ski run, and offers free admission to the ice rink. $$

The **Belmont Hotel Bar/Restaurant,** ☎ 855 35 35 or Fax 855 35 31, Mürren, directly opposite the main station, offers very inexpensive, yet clean and comfortable, accommodation and reasonably priced meals. A basic room went for CHF 30 per person in 1997. $

Wengen:

The **Hotel Regina ******, ☎ 855 15 12 or Fax 855 15 74, CH-3823 Wengen, dating from 1894, is the consummate luxurious, traditional, mountain hotel. Renovated rooms include modern facilities without sacrificing character. Guests may relax, alongside the family dog, on comfortable furniture in antique-laden, wood-paneled public rooms glowing in the warmth of cozy fireplaces. Talking of the family, Ariane and Guido Meyer — and their charming daughter — have a hand in all aspects of the hotel, and encourage a family ambiance. It also offers unhindered views of Jungfrau. $$

The **Victoria-Lauberhorn ******, ☎ 856 51 51 or Fax 855 33 77, Dorfstrasse, CH-3823 Wengen, just a few moments from the railway station, has a most interesting façade and traditional style public areas. Many of the comfortably furnished guest rooms have private balconies. $$

The **Hotel Belvedere *****, ☎ 855 24 12 or Fax 855 37 30, CH-3823 Wengen, was built in 1912, is now a magnificent Art-Nouveau hotel with all modern comforts. It features a specialty restaurant, La Marjolaine, and the Paradise nightclub. Be sure to investigate their special romantic packages. $$

The **Hotel Falken *****, ☎ 856 51 21, Fax 855 33 39, E-mail falken.wengen@spectraweb.ch and WWW.spectraweb.ch/~pfalken, CH-3823 Wengen, is situated in a park with lovely views of the Jungfrau. The current management continues a 102-year tradition of friendly, family run, ambiance. $$

The **Hotel Edelweiss ****, ☎ 855 23 88 or Fax 855 42 88, CH-3823 Wengen, wears a suitable name for such a traditional style chalet. Just five minutes from the train station in a very peaceful area, it has been recently renovated. $

FOOD AND DRINK:

Here, as in other parts of in Switzerland, the most expedient decision is to take demi-pension. This ensures a good quality evening meal at a reasonable price. For those not choosing this option, for whatever reason, the restaurants listed below come highly recommended from my personal experience, or are either mountain restaurants ideally used for lunch or snacks or, like the Piz Gloria, one that just shouldn't be missed.

Bönigen:

Hotel Seiler au Lac has a charming restaurant with calming views of Lake Brienz. For each delightful dish he prepares, the chef carefully selects the ingredients from those that are "in season." Fresh fish from the surrounding lakes and rivers, meats raised on organic feed and locally-grown fruit and vegetables top the list. And, every plate is beautifully presented. ☎ 822 30 21 or Fax 822 30 01. $$

Grindelwald:

Hotel Belvedere is worth choosing for the view alone—the north face of the Eiger virtually looms over the dining room. And the cuisine isn't to be overlooked either. A typical dinner might consist of asparagus salad with duck breast, soup or juice, salad bar, goulash or poached fillet of fera—a local fish, cheese platter and dessert. As a bonus, a bottle of Swiss wine will only cost about CHF 35. ☎ 854 54 54 or Fax 853 53 23. $$

Bergrestaurant Schreckfeld is, as the name indicates is a mountain restaurant found near the penultimate stop, Grindel/Schreckfeld, of the Firstbahn. This is an ideal resting place following a hike across from, or to, Grosse Scheidegg. The menu offers a variety of choices—from soup, salads, pasta, cold meats and local specialties. And, although it seems rather incongruous, the fact that the menu is also in Japanese speaks for itself. ☎ 853 54 30 or Fax 853 54 32, $

Interlaken:

Top O' MET is found on the 18th floor of the Metropole Hotel. The lunch buffet, served between 11 a.m. and 2 p.m., at just CHF 31, is a bargain in itself, but when complimented by the stupendous views it's incomparable. ☎ 828 66 66 or Fax 828 66 33, Höheweg 37. $

Mürren:

Piz Gloria has the distinction of being the world's first mountaintop revolving restaurant. Situated at the peak of the Schilthorn, 10,000 feet high, it came to the attention of the world when it was used for a location shoot in the James Bond movie "On Her Majesty's Secret

Service." Solar energy powers the mechanism that rotates the dining room once every 55 minutes, offering visitors an unparalleled 360-degree panoramic view that takes in over 200 mountain peaks and stretches as far as the Black Forest in Germany. One of three of its genre in Switzerland, Piz Gloria is far and away the most dramatic. ☎ 856 21 41 or Fax 856 21 31. $$

Wengen:

Restaurant **Chez Meyer's** is the à-la-carte restaurant of the Hotel Regina. The dining room is small and intimate, and the menu includes such deliciously prepared and beautifully presented dishes as consomme of game with fresh truffles; feuillete with spinach and crayfish with fresh coriander; filet of sea bass flamed with Pernod and served with artichokes and wild rice; or grilled pigeon with sautéed potatoes and wild mushrooms. Or opt, instead, for the Menu Dégustation at CHF 92. ☎ 855 15 12 or Fax 855 15 74. $$$

Le **Grand Restaurant**, also found in the Hotel Regina, offers a set-price dinner that includes a hot and cold first-course buffet, a salad buffet, a daily choice of four main courses—including a fish and vegetarian dish, and a buffet of fresh fruits and cheese. ☎ 855 15 12 or Fax 855 15 74. $$

SUGGESTED TOUR NUMBER 1:

*Jungfraujoch

See map on page 111.

This tour will, undoubtedly, be the highlight—quite literally the highest and brightest—of your visit to the Bernese Oberland.

Most everyone is familiar with the concept of taking a cable car to the summit of a mountain, and they are a highly visible form of transport. Even today, however, it would take a knowledgeable eye to see a way, other than climbing, to reach the top of the Jungfrau. And that is exactly how it was back in 1893 when Adolf Guyer-Zeller, a prominent Swiss industrialist captivated by the towering peaks of the Eiger, Mönch and Jungfrau, had the idea of constructing a railroad to the top. Utilizing his notes and sketches, work on this project began from Kleine Scheidegg on July 27, 1896. It took two full years just to complete the first section of the track, which ran over open ground, to the **Eigergletscher** station, which stands at an altitude of 2,320 meters (7,612 feet). This became then, and remains today, the operative headquarters of the Jungfrau Railway *(Jungfraubahn)*. The staff quarters of the railway, as well as the kennels for their famous Husky dogs, have this as their base and, because of the gauge difference between the Jungfrau and Wengernalp railways, all Jungfrau trains must also be serviced here. Back to the tracks themselves, where the really difficult work was about to begin.

From the point of the station onward, the track had to be tunneled through the mountain. This, as you might imagine, was not undertaken without problems. In 1899, a blasting accident claimed six lives. In a subsequent accident, over 29 tons of dynamite exploded. Fortunately no human lives were lost in this mishap, but it is said that the blast was heard in Germany! Work continued, albeit much slower than expected, and two other intermediate stations, **Eigerwand** at 2,865 meters (9,400 feet) and **Eismeer** at 3,160 meters (10, 368 feet), were completed before the final breakthrough out of the rock at **Jungfraujoch** in February of 1912. Europe's highest railway station, at 3,454 meters (11,333 feet), was finally opened on August 1, 1912.

To get to Jungfraujoch, begin from either Grindelwald or Lauterbrunnen/Wengen, taking a Wengernalpbahn (WAB) train to **Kleine Scheidegg** (1), a line that was inaugurated in 1893. At Kleine Scheidegg listen for the familiar refrain, "Change for the Jungfraujoch," signaling that a brown, beige and red train of the Jungfraubahn (JB) waits to carry you upwards. A word of advice, here. This trip is by no means inexpensive, even taking into account the discounts available for holders of a Swiss or Eurail Pass. A bargain to consider is JB's "Good Morning Ticket," which offers 40% off the regular fare. There is a catch, of course—you can only take the 8 a.m. or 9 a.m. train from Kleine Scheidegg and you must leave the Jungfraujoch by midday.

During the first stage of the trip, that across open land to the entrance to the **Grosser Tunnel**, two hundred meters (219 yards) past the Eigergletscher station, you will be bombarded by a proliferation of ***Alpine vistas** so wondrous that, literally, you will not know which way to look first. The peaks loom above you, and it will be your first opportunity for a close-up look at those awesome glaciers. At certain times, there are tremendous views back across the Lauterbrunnen valley to Mürren and the Schilthorn.

Once inside the 7,122 meter-(4.4 mile)-tunnel, you won't leave it for the remainder of the journey. If you think that means there are no more views, however, you will be pleasantly surprised. There are two five-minute stops along the way at the intermediate stations of Eigerwand and Eismeer, each of which offer contrasting panoramas viewed from glassed-in platforms. The first, built into the fearsome north wall of the Eiger, allows you a bird's-eye view of Grindelwald, in the valley far below, out over smaller mountains to northern Switzerland and, on occasion, even to the Black Forest in Germany. The second, at Eismeer, is quite different. Looking out eastwards, behind the Eiger and Mönch, the surreal and chilling specter of eternal ice unfolds before you in the forms of the Grindelwald and Fiescher glaciers. And on closer look, as amazing as it might seem, you may see climbers out there as well.

A word of warning here. When you disembark at either station, but most especially at Jungfraujoch, proceed at a reasonable pace. If you rushing or climb the steps too quickly, you will very quickly find yourself out of breath.

This rarefied atmosphere, with 16% less oxygen, affects most everyone—especially those with respiratory problems. Those suffering from any form of heart trouble should certainly seek their doctor's approval before contemplating this trip. I recall, on my first trip here, getting off the first train and rushing to be first at the viewing platform. After a couple of hundred feet and one staircase, I was more than happy, obliged in fact, to find a seat quickly. The message is simple; take it easy, and do things much slower than usual.

Once at **Jungfraujoch** (2) itself the attractions are numerous. Notwithstanding that, for many years there was no overnight accommodation. In 1924 a hotel was opened at the summit but, unfortunately, it succumbed to flames on October 21, 1972 and, surprisingly, has not been replaced. The growing popularity of Jungfraujoch—the number of visitors in agreeable weather numbers in excess of 4,000 a day—requires the continual improvement and expansion of its facilities. The byproducts of this demand are numerous. On Friday, June 28, 1996 Europe's highest observation terrace, at an altitude of 3,571 meters (11,716 feet) was opened. Visitors are transported up 108 meters (354 feet) in an astounding 25 seconds, to the new Sphinx building by way of Switzerland's highest-speed lift. From here, you can not fail to be entranced by the 360-degree panoramic *vista over the Alps. Immediately below you, the vast Aletsch Glacier (Europe's largest) totally fills the wide valley between the towering peaks. It is impossible not to wonder, watching as it serenely takes its course, what secrets lay beneath that impenetrable ice.

Once you enter the Top of Europe **Berghaus** complex, you will find a number of attractions that are imposing in their own right. Within the newly renovated **Ice Palace**, inside of the glacier, the ice has been sculpted into beautiful patterns and models that certainly should not be missed. On a more lively note, no one could fail to be captivated by the resident Husky dogs, and on a fine summer's day you may take a **dog sleigh ride** across the ice. Additionally, for those who want some refreshment and a leisurely view of the scenery, there are no less than five restaurants, with a combined seating capacity of 700. Before departing, take this opportunity to send a postcard home, franked—excuse the pun—by Europe's highest post office. Not only does it have a special postmark, it has its own postal code as well—CH-3801.

Finally, a suggestion. A favorite combination of mine is to immediately follow this tour with a train journey down to Lauterbrunnen and Suggested Tour Number 2. This is certainly practical, time wise, if you take advantage of the "Good Morning Ticket." Also, it gives an interesting perspective of where you have just been—viewed from across the valley from the Piz Gloria revolving restaurant at Schilthorn.

Trümmelbach, *Schilthorn and Mürren

This tour begins at Lauterbrunnen, and the first leg is to take the postal bus service to Trümmelbach. Be sure to get a seat on the right-hand side of the bus because, soon after passing through the village, there are views on that side of the magnificent Staubbach waterfall cascading and plunging 288 meters (945 feet) from the rock face above. So steep is it that much of the water dissipates into fine spray before reaching the valley floor. The water that eventually reaches there combines with that of the 70-plus other falls in the valley, and the mountain streams, to feed the eternally fast-flowing Weisse Lütshcine river.

Waterfalls are, again, the focus of attention at the first stop, **Trümmelbach** (3), just 3 kilometers (1.9 miles) from Lauterbrunnen. Crossing the road from the bus stop, go around the restaurant/bar and follow the pathway for a sight—the memory of which will forever remind you of the intrinsic strength, ferocity and power of water. The ***Trümmelbach Falls** are open daily between mid-April and the end of October. Hours are either 8 a.m. to 5 p.m. or 9 a.m. to 6 p.m., depending upon the time of year. While these may well be one of the lesser acclaimed spectacles in this area of spectacular places, they are certainly one of the more fascinating. Trümmelbach, alone, drains the mighty glaciers of the Eiger, Mönch and Jungfrau. Its drainage area of 24 square kilometers, half of which is covered by glaciers and snow, carries off up to 5,283 gallons of water transporting as much as 20,200 tons of rock and other debris per year through the only glacial waterfalls in Europe that lie inside a mountain, yet are still visible. A lift actually carries you up inside the mountain and footpaths, though sometimes a little precarious in nature, lead you back past through ten different waterfalls, weaving both inside and out of the mountain. The endless current of water can be both visibly and audibly mesmerizing, and falls' corkscrew paths down the mountain, and the patterns they have carved into the rock, will leave you well advised of their power.

Back outside, you have a choice to make. If it will be a while before for the next bus departs for Stechelberg—usually they run once an hour—either refresh yourself at the restaurant or, if you prefer, take a pleasant riverside stroll. The walk is a total of two kilometers (1.2 miles) but, long before you reach the end, you will see the purpose for this diversion, the first leg of the **Schilthorn cableway** (Schilthornbahn), soaring into the sky. The cableway is comprised of four sections: Stechelberg to Gimmelwald, to Mürren, to Birg and finally to the summit of the **Schilthorn** (4), which in total rise from an elevation of 867 meters (2,844 feet) to 2,970 meters (9,744 feet) over their course of 7 kilometers (4.3 miles). This is the longest cableway in the Bernese Oberland. The first three sections, including one stretch between Mürren and Birg where the 40mm-(1.6 inch)-thick track cables hang free for nearly two kilometers (1.2 miles), were completed in 1965. The last leg, ascending to the summit, took two more years to complete. The total journey time up is just over 30 minutes. The 80- or 100-person cars depart every half an hour, although this can be increased to every 15 minutes if the demand dictates. As you soar skywards, passing an ever-changing array of green pastures, Alpine farms, chalets, forests, bare rock face, snow and ice, you will be forever mindful of the feat of engineering which has enabled such a journey. Obviously, such technology requires careful maintenance, so the Schilthornbahn is closed for a handful of days each spring and fall for scheduled inspection and repairs. An example, most would gratefully agree, of prevention before decension!

The ingenious wonder that resides at the top was recognized very early in its development by the producers of the James Bond film "On Her Majesty's Secret Service." They were persuaded that this was just the type of unique setting to showcase the daring and debonair 007, and did some location filming here for that movie. The film brought well-deserved international acclaim to the Schilthorn, making it one of Europe's most popular destinations—which it remains to the present day. The idea of a revolving restaurant at the summit of a mountain is not unique to the Schilthorn. Although it was the first there are, in fact, two others in Switzerland—in Saas Fee and Leysin. What is unique, however, is that the isolation of the Schilthorn affords visitors an unobstructed 360° **panoramic vista** of the surrounding Alps. In excess of 200 peaks, including the Eiger, Mönch and Jungfrau just across the valley, vie among themselves and with forty-plus glaciers, deep valleys, mountain lakes and views, which can range as far as the Black Forest in Germany, for your attention. And your only exertion is to relax in the Piz Gloria restaurant and enjoy a leisurely meal and drink while solar power drives you slowly to one complete rotation every hour.

Of course, the weather will have a say in what you see and, to ensure that your trip is not a wasted journey, cameras are installed at each stage to show the conditions at the top. In reality, though, while conditions may appear to be poor, swirling winds can change matters very quickly. I once ascended as far as the cable car stop at Schilthorn through thick cloud, but the few extra feet up to Piz Gloria brought me out to glorious sunshine. And, this made for some surreal scenes indeed as the numerous mountain peaks seemed to appear from nowhere out of the clouds. This scenario can also give a somewhat false sense of security for those with an aversion to heights; when you venture out on to the viewing platform the vertiginous slopes are, obviously, invisible. Other attractions include the James Bond Bar—well, it would be, wouldn't it?—serving an array of lighter snacks and, beneath the viewing platform, a multivision show comprised of 17 different projectors showing highlights of the surrounding Alpine panorama and, yes, you've guessed it, excerpts from "On Her Majesty's Secret Service."

On the way down, you have options on how to arrive at Mürren. The easiest, of course, is to take the Schilthornbahn directly there. Alternatively, and weather and fitness providing, you can hike directly from Shilthorn, which will take approximately five hours or, much easier, take the cable car to Birg and then track down, via Blumental—the Valley of the Flowers—to Mürren, which is about a two-and-a-half-hour walk.

Whichever route you take you are sure to be enchanted by **Mürren** (5). Traffic-free, like Wengen, but much smaller and more rural, it sits on a ledge with simply stunning, and more unfamiliar, views across this steep valley to the Eiger, Mönch and Jungrau. Mürren is famous for its winter sports. Switzerland's first ski school opened there in 1930, 1937 marked the opening of the first ski lift service in the Bernese Oberland, and today there are around 50 kilometers (31 miles) of piste and more than 16 downhill ski runs. The most famous of these is the "Inferno Run," first raced in 1928, which covers a distance of 15.8 kilometers (9.8 miles) from the summit of Schilthorn and descends 2,150 meters (7,054 feet) down the valley to Lauterbrunnen. Hot air ballooning is also popular in Mürren. Eduard Spelterini made the first Alpine balloon crossing from here on August 12, 1910, eventually landing in Turin, Italy. One of the most important summer events is the annual International High Alpine Ballooning Competition, which was inaugurated in 1957.

A particularly interesting side trip from Mürren, when it is open—usually between mid-June to mid-September and mid-December to mid-April—is the Mürren-to-Allmendhubel funicular. Opened in December 1912, its original purpose was to service the Allmendhubel toboggan run. Now, however, it raises passengers 258 meters (846 feet) in four minutes, through a tunnel and over arched bridges, to a delightful spot which serves as an origination point for a series of mountain hikes. Alternatively, at this altitude of 1,912 meters (6,273 feet) take life a little easier and enjoy a fondue, perhaps at the mountain restaurant, while admiring the mountain scenery.

There are choices, too, for the final leg of this tour, from Mürren back to Lauterbrunnen. Those with any energy in reserve—and remember ascending and descending mountain peaks is more tiring than one might think—may elect to walk back. It takes a couple of hours and, even though the journey is downhill all the way, is more difficult than it might, at first, appear. Without doubt, your calves will be screaming for a rest long before, and for a long while after, you reach Lauterbrunnen. Given the magnitude of the design and ingenious construction of the Jungfraujoch railway and the Schilthornbahn, visitors taking the train and funicular back to Lauterbrunnen may not have reason to give a thought to what went into making this journey possible, and may be surprised to learn that this endeavor had its problems also. The topography of the mountainside behind Lauterbrunnen, a nearly 700 meter (2,297 feet) high cliff face, made the use of a cog wheel train to and from Mürren impractical. But that did not dissuade the indomitable Swiss, and their solution to the problem was twofold. They first constructed a funicular, at the time the steepest in Switzerland, straight up the cliff face to Grütschalp. Then, to connect Grütschalp with Mürren, a distance of four and a quarter kilometers (2.6 miles), they built a 1-meter (3.3 feet) narrow-gauge non-cog wheel railway that progresses along a slight gradient, sometimes through meadows and, at other times, precariously alongside the cliff's edge.

SUGGESTED TOUR NUMBER 3:

Männlichen and Kleine Scheidegg

The beautiful, and totally unobstructed, views of the Eiger, Mönch, Jungfrau and numerous other peaks in the range are reason enough to take this tour. What makes it even more interesting is the option of leaving and returning, from either Grindelwald or Wengen/Lauterbrunnen, by different methods of transportation.

The initial destination, Männlichen, is reached from Grindelwald via the **Gondelbahn Grindelwald-Männlichen** (GGM) Gondola Cableway opened in December of 1978. From its departure point at the Grindelwald Grund station, it takes 30 minutes to travel the 6.2 kilometers (3.4 miles)—which earn it the distinction of being the longest gondola cableway in Europe— elevating you the 1,280 meters (4,199 feet) up to Männlichen. The ride is taken in comfortable four-car cabins. Two gondolas, equipped to accommodate the special needs of the handicapped, each hold a single wheelchair and have seats for two companions. Beginning from the other side of the mountain, travelers can either embark at Lauterbrunnen and take the train to Wengen, or leave directly from Wengen and ascend up to Männlichen on the **Luftseilbahn Wengen-Männlichen** (LWM) cable car. Opened in 1954 but completely renovated in 1992 with a new ropeway and a cabin capacity of eighty, it whisks you up 930 meters (3,051 feet) in just five minutes. Both the GGM and LWM are only open daily June to October and December to April, and open only on weekends at other periods.

Männlichen (6), at an altitude of 2,222 meters (7,290 feet), forms a natural balcony between the valleys of the Weisse Lütschine river of Lauterbrunnen and the Schwarze Lütschine of Grindelwald. Before continuing on, refresh yourself at the Bergrestaurant and take a few moments to contemplate your surroundings. You will note that the valleys form a contrast in themselves. The Weisse Lütschine, the narrower of the two, can boast little of its unprepossessing peaks. The other valley is longer, much broader and is surrounded by an array of highly impressive mountains, including the north face of the Eiger—3,970 meters (13,025 feet), which forms its south wall. But it is the scene directly to the south, that holds the greatest fascination. There, alongside the Eiger, tower the summits of the Mönch—4,099 meters (13,448 feet) and the Jungfrau—4,158 meters (13,642 feet) with their respective glaciers *(Gletscher)*; Eigergletscher, Guggigletscher and Giessengletscher. The sheer power these evoke will compel you to draw nearer, and they seem to loom ever larger as you move towards them on the none-too-strenuous, and relatively flat, one-and-a-quarter-hour hike to Kleine Scheidegg.

By now, the mountain air will certainly have brought on an appetite, and the station at **Kleine Scheidegg** (1) is an ideal place to sample a regional specialty. Pizzerias everyone is familiar with, but who will have heard off a Röstizzeria? *Rosti* is a belly-warming deep-fried potato dish, often embellished with fried egg, and you can try it inside or at the outdoor terrace.

Close by, and near the tourist kiosks, a strange activity may come to your attention. Kleine Scheidegg is the junction for trips to the Jungfraujoch, and don't be surprised to see parties of Japanese rushing to have a group photograph taken with the resident St. Bernard dog. There is nothing coincidental about this either; it is a real cottage industry. The sitting, well at least the St. Bernard might be, will have been pre-planned as a part of the group's itinerary, and they only have a few minutes between trains to fit it in. The photographer makes out like a bandit, too; charging maybe CHF 30 for each copy of the photograph. But he does have more overhead, in this case literally, than just camera, film and developing costs, and you may have guessed it by now. The dog is not his. He rents it from a breeder, who also rents dogs out to photographers at other locations. Certainly not a poor example of entrepreneurship.

The descent back to your choice of Grindelwald or Wengen can be made either by train, or if the Rosti has restored your energy, by walking. In the latter instances, the trek is all downhill, of course, and either hike will take around three and a half hours.

SUGGESTED TOUR NUMBER 4:

Grindelwald, First, Bachalpsee and Faulhorn

The original Grindelwald-First chair lift, at its inception in 1950, was the longest in Europe. Just over 40 years later, a combination of age, poor routing, inability to handle the transport capacity and, last but not least, pas-

senger comfort—especially in the colder months, led to its closing on August 18, 1991. Fortuitously, the planning of a replacement had begun in
1986, when it was decided that a modern 6-passenger gondola cable car
should be the successor. Construction on that system, begun on June 7,
1990, was completed just two months after the closure of the chair lift. The
new system, 5,226 meters (3.25 miles) in length, takes just twenty minutes
to ascend 1,105 meters (3,625 feet) in altitude through three stages; Grindelwald to Bort, Bort to Grindel and Grindel to First.

First (7), at an altitude of 2,168 meters (7,113 feet), sits directly across
the valley from, and offers a different perspective of, four peaks that rise over
13,000 feet—the Schreckhorn, Eiger, Mönch and Jungfrau. As a bonus, it is
also immediately in front of the famous Grindelwald Glacier the size of
which, even from this distance, is staggering. This stage is also a marvelous
spot from which to begin any variety of mountain hikes. And, while you
ponder which one, sit on the terrace of the Berggasthaus First, to savor a favorite drink and the fabulous views around you.

Perhaps the most popular of the hikes, and one that is not too difficult
either, is the trek to **Bachalpsee** (8). Just about an hour away, this mountain
lake is particularly popular with photographers. The topography of the land
here creates an optical illusion that there is no valley between the lake and
the distant mountains. Add to this the verdant foreground which paints a
stark contrast with the distant snow and ice, and a little luck with the
weather, and you have all the ingredients for a stunning photograph. And,
can you imagine, how lovely this scene would be bathed in moonlight?
There is no need just to imagine. The tourist office in Grindelwald arranges
such evening trips—so give them a call.

The more adventurous will want to strongly consider pushing on to **Faulhorn** (9), another hour or so away and at an altitude of 2,681 meters (8,796
feet), where there is a vantage point almost without equal. The views range
from Grindelwald and its majestic mountains to the lakes of Brienz and Thun
and even, in the distance, the Black Forest of Germany. Sunsets and sunrises
are glorious here and you can enjoy both if you plan to stay overnight at the
Berghaus Faulhorn, ☎ 853 27 13 or Fax 853 10 25, the oldest and highest-
altitude hotel in Switzerland. From the time it opened in 1832 until just recently, the owners relied on mules to deliver supplies and mail. Today, they
are airlifted in by helicopter. You, however, will still have to go in on foot!

If, alternatively, you chose to return from Faulhorn immediately after enjoying the scenery, you have two options. Either return the way you came,
or take the path down to Bussalp, where yet another mountain restaurant
awaits your investigation, then continue on to Bort from which you will
make the final descent back on the Firstbahnen.

Weather conditions, obviously, will be a major factor when choosing
your hike. Very low cloud cover spoils the view on all the hikes but often
the cloud cover is quite high. If this is the case you will need to determine

whether it covers the area above First. If so, a hike from that point wil, ally not be very enjoyable. But don't despair; all is not lost if you are determined to get out and about. Stay below the clouds, take the Firstbahnen to the second, and penultimate, station Grindel, where you can take a break at the modern Bergrestaurant Schreckfeld before following the footpath to Gross Scheidegg.

This is an easy undulating walk, of about an hour and a half, along which the altitude changes only by 7 meters (23 feet), from 1,955 to 1,962 meters (6,414 to 6,437 feet). And, even if the peaks across the valley are ensconced in cloud, the ever-changing perspectives, especially of the glacier, will not cease to fascinate. Not far out from Grindel you will come upon a collection of old cow sheds built in the middle of nowhere. While these are of no particular architectural or historical note, you may want to be aware that they serve as public toilets, which you will find, even in such an isolated place, to be spotlessly clean. Where else in the world could you expect to find such thoughtfulness and cleanliness? You must be in Switzerland!

When you finally arrive at Gross Scheidegg don't expect too much of interest. But, the Berghotel Grosse Scheidegg—after all what else would it be called—makes a welcome resting place until the next postal bus, on its way up the car-free valley from Meiringen, arrives to transport you back to Grindelwald. A seat on the left hand side of the bus is favored for this trip. Even before it arrives at the Hotel Wetterhorn, just outside Grindelwald, your attention will have, inevitably, been drawn to the Grindelwald-gletscher.

SUGGESTED TOUR NUMBER 5:

Pfingstegg, Glaciers and the Blue Ice Grotto

This tour will gives a close-up perspective of two glaciers, and even affords you the experience of being inside of one. To begin, take the cable car from the Talstation in Grindelwald for the short five-minute ride up to **Pfingstegg** (10). After disembarking, follow the path around the mountainside to the Restaurant Stieregg, which offers a magnificent panorama of the Eismeer Lower Glacier *(Unterer Gletscher)*. From here experienced mountaineers, and experienced mountaineers only, can attempt to follow the track up to the Schreckhorn hut. Anyone else should, wisely, content themselves with retracing their steps back to Pfingstegg, and continuing on around the other side of the mountain towards the Upper Glacier *(Oberer Gletscher)*. As with the first part of the trip, this will take about one hour and, on the way to your destination, the Restaurant at Milchbach, you will pass through an area known as **Breitlouwina**. The sediments deposited here many millions of years ago have created an amazing variety of strange rock formations that will surely intrigue.

It is the huge mass of the **Upper Grindelwald Glacier**, though, that will captivate the attention of most visitors. Relaxing on the terrace of the Restaurant Milchbach, your gaze will be drawn again and again to the grotesquely beautiful shapes the ice has birthed within itself. It is mind boggling to contemplate that this enormous, solid mass is perpetually, if imperceptibly, in a state of evolution. Although the way is not such an easy one your curiosity will, certainly, compel you to take a closer look at this astounding natural phenomenon. The first step is to take the path down towards the Hotel Wetterhorn where, at the bottom, comes the challenging, but only, way up to the **Blue Ice Grotto**. In fact, you have to climb 890 steps! If this prospect discourages you, and you are not inclined to press on, continue, instead to the hotel and either walk, or take the postal bus, back to Grindelwald. Those making the effort, though, will certainly get their just reward. As you wander along the passageways tunneled through the ice, penetrated by the reflection of the blue skies above, it becomes apparent how this place came by its name. And, for those in need of refreshment, the Glacier Bar beckons.

SUGGESTED TOUR NUMBER 6:

Brienz, Rothhorn and Ballenberg

This tour, which takes in an interesting variety of methods of transportation, an equally interesting array of scenery on and around Lake Brienz, and an unusual museum is also one of my favorites in this area. The first leg is by a steamship of the BLS company, which may be boarded at Interlaken Ost (East) or, if you are staying at the Seiler au Lac in Bönigen, from the dock just outside the hotel. There are several steamers of this type, all with lounges and a restaurant or snack bar. On a warm and sunny day there are few things as relaxing as sitting on the top deck of one of these vessels, sipping your favorite beverage, and drinking in the scenery on the beautiful, tree-covered mountain sides that slide gently into the peaceful waters. The steamer will serenely traverse the lovely lake, **Brienzersee**, which nearly fills this elongated, narrow valley, crisscrossing from one pretty village to another until, an hour and a quarter later, it docks at **Brienz** (11). Pay special attention to the penultimate stop across the lake at Giessbach where you will find the legendary Giessbach Falls and, glimpsing through the forest, the Grandhotel Giessbach.

Across from the dock at Brienz it is impossible to miss the **Brienz Rothorn Bahn**, ☎ 951 44 00, railway station. The passenger carriages, unusual enough, are pulled or pushed by small, squat steam engines that are slightly angled to meet the contours of the line. As many as eight steam engines, and a couple of their diesel companions, operate daily—whenever possible, trains number 5, 7 and 9 are steam operated. The track twists and turns as it meanders up and around for approximately one hour, covering the distance of 7.6 kilometers (4.7 miles) and climbing, at an average gradient of 22%, a total of 1,678 meters (5,505 feet). Along the way, the train dodges in and out of the forests, allowing tantalizing glimpses of the ever-receding lake far below. Once you disembark at the 2,350 meter (7,710 feet) summit, you will have numerous unhampered views of the surrounding countryside. Also at the top, you will find the Hotel Rothorn Kulm, ☎ or Fax 951 12 21, established in 1892—contemporaneously with the opening of the railway. Constructed entirely of timber, the structure has been renovated over the years to ensure guests the convenience of modern amenities in this typical Alpine ambiance. If, however, an overnight stay here is not on your itinerary, you may want to consider indulging in a fondue at the restaurant. Be aware that the railway is open only from the end of May to the end of October, but even during that period heavy snowfall at times prevents the trains from getting farther than the midway station at Planalp. If this happens on the day of your visit here, you needn't worry, there are some delightful hiking paths nearby that implore you to explore them. A word of warning, though; take your own soft drinks if that is what you plan. The nearby mountain bar charges CHF 9 for a one-and-a-half-liter bottle of Coke!

Back in Brienz you will be faced with a decision. Are you interested in and, if so, do you have time to see, the Freilichtmuseum, ☎ 951 11 23 or Fax 951 18 21. Just a short bus ride away, the **Ballenberg Open Air Museum** (12) offers you a look at rural Swiss life as it has been down through the centuries. In a pleasant natural setting you will find cattle, farming exhibitions, country crafts and completely restored buildings. In addition to daily tours and demonstrations there are a number of restaurants within the grounds. The museum is open daily, from mid-April to the end of October, between 10 a.m. and 5 p.m. For those who have their fill, for the moment, of ascending and descending mountains or for those traveling with children, this provides a commendable alternative to the Rothorn trip. No matter what your decision, it is, most likely, too late to return to Interlaken by steamer. So, take the regular train to Interlaken Ost, which is, in any event, much faster.

SUGGESTED TOUR NUMBER 7:

Harder Kulm and St. Beatus Caves

This is an up-and-down tour contrived to appeal to the inquisitive. At an altitude of 1,322 meters (4,337 feet) on the mountain behind Interlaken, in an isolated position surrounded by the forest, you will find the Harder Kulm Restaurant. And, it is not necessary to walk there either. In fact, you are sure to enjoy the brief ten-minute excursion on the rather unusual small red carriage of the Harder Railway. Opened in 1908, this is actually a funicular which, to preserve the integrity of the landscape, was constructed along a mile-long winding route that includes a quarter-mile loop to the summit. There is a human interest story here as well. Two local women, unbeknownst to their husbands, responded when the landlord, Jungfrau Railways, solicited applicants for the restaurant tenancy. What Rosemarie Feuz and Hilde Zurbrügg started as a bit of a joke has now, with much encouragement and support from the railway, become a resounding success. It has become somewhat of a tradition for the locals to meet there for Sunday morning breakfast, but visitors will enjoy it an any time—especially for its breathtaking views across the lakes and over entire Jungfrau region. An added attraction is the Alpine Wildlife Park with its resident Ibex.

Now, back down to Interlaken and it is time to launch off on an delightful trip to an entirely different sort of attraction. From Interlaken West take the steamer along the north side of Lake Thun to either Sundlauenen or Beatenbucht. Your destination, the **St. Beatus Caves**, is in between these two stops, at Beatushöhlen. Thousands of years ago cave-dwellers inhabited this area, and you can gain quite an insight into their lifestyle by visiting this well-presented reconstruction of a prehistoric settlement. To what those first settlers called this place, there is no clue, and so we must content ourselves with the present name, derived more recently—in the 6th century—when, legend has it, an Irish missionary, Beatus, made his home at the entrance to these underground chambers. He reportedly exorcized a dragon from the caves, and preached Christianity to the local heathen population. Between Palm Sunday and the third Sunday in October, guided tours leave on the half-hour between 9:30 a.m. and 5 p.m. daily. Visitors venture to a depth of 1,000 meters (3,609 feet) through just a portion of the 8.1 kilometers (5 miles) of known paths and trails which wind through numerous caverns and grottos, passing lakes, waterfalls and, of course, a staggering array of weirdly wonderful stalactites and stalagmites.

OTHER ACTIVITIES:

There are any number of activities, possibly of interest to readers, that for one reason or another are not suitable for inclusion in a Suggested Tour. These are detailed, in alphabetical order, below.

ADVENTURE PROGRAMS:

Adventure World, CH-3800 Interlaken, ☎ 823 55 23 or Fax 823 41 01, offers an multitude of thrilling adventures such as: **Bridge Jumping** and **Bungy Jumping** from an aerial cable car; **Canyoning**—a new sport combining trekking, swimming, cave exploration and abseiling, which allows you to discover secrets previously hidden in the gorges of the Bernese Oberland; **Flying Fox**—which entails a dizzying descent through the Saxteen Gorge on a zip line; **Fun Yak**—a thrilling trip on the Lütschine river taken with an instructor, in a water craft that is a cross between a kayak and a raft and **Lake Kayaking**—on this region's rapidly flowing, swirling rivers.

ALPINE FLIGHTS:

BOHAG, Berner Oberländer Helikopter AG, CH-3814 Gsteigwiler— between Interlaken and Widerswil, ☎ 828 90 00 or Fax 8289 90 10, offers a trip you will never, ever, forget. Their helicopters will whisk you up to and around either the north or south faces of the Eiger, Mönch and Jungfrau. If this leaves you begging for more, consider taking the longer trip to Zermatt and the Matterhorn. In summer, flights depart from the airport at Gsteigwiler. In winter, they leave from Männlichen. As you might expect, such flights are not inexpensive—CHF 150, 200 and 600 in summer and CHF 80, 110 and 600 in winter; but I can personally assure you that it will be the adventure of a lifetime.

ALPINE ORIENTEERING COURSE—GRINDELWALD:

Your starting point, your route and even your destination are variable at your option, but the aim is the same. You are to locate a number of sign posted checkpoints and, using the punches installed at each, mark a control card to track your progress. Further details are available at the tourist office.

GLACIER EXPERIENCE:

Swiss Alpine Guides, Bergsteigerschule, P.O. Box 29, CH-3800 Matten/Interlaken, ☎ and Fax 822 05 69, offers, in total safety, the chance of a lifetime to trek to and explore glacial formations. You may even try ice climbing! The same organization can arrange for guides to take you mountaineering, sports climbing or, in summer or winter, hiking or walking in the Jungfrau region.

HORSE TREKKING:

Voegli Riding School, Scheidgasse 66, CH-3800 Unterseen, ☎ 822 74 16, offers a one-hour ride for CHF 30, or a three-hour trek along purely natural trails for CHF 75. A guide accompanies riders on either trip.

MOUNTAIN BIKE ARENA—GRINDELWALD:

Information on mountain bike routes, which cover in excess of 100 kilometers (62.1 miles) throughout the Grindelwald valley, is found at the tourist office. Bikes for the journey may be rented through Graf Sport ☎ 853 28 66, Bernet Sport ☎ 853 13 09 or Kaufmann Sport ☎ 853 13 77.

PARAGLIDING:

Flugschule SHV, Grindelwald, ☎ 853 55 53 or Fax 853 56 48, offers tandem flights that take off from First, Lauberhorn or Männlichen.

WILLIAM TELL OPEN AIR THEATRE:

Ticket Sales & Brochures, Bahnhofstrasse 5, CH-3800 Interlaken, ☎ 822 37 2 or Fax 822 57 33. Friedrich Schiller's "William Tell" has been performed in the Rugen Woods, very close to Interlaken, every summer since

1912. Set 700 years ago, in an era during when Switzerland was under the tyrannical rule of Austria, it tells of the Swiss people's hardship and suffering and their heroic struggle for freedom. Over 250 actors, outfitted in national costume, reenact the story against a background of authentic 13th-century wooden houses and towering trees. It is performed primarily on Fridays and Saturdays, between the end of June and beginning of September. And weather conditions need not be a concern; all 2,300 seats are under cover.

Bern
(Berne)

Drawn by Bern's strategic location on a long promontory surrounded by the Aare river, Berchtold V, Duke of Zähringen, founded the first settlement here in 1191. Emperor Lothar III of Upper Burgundy had bestowed this title upon Berchtold, and Bern subsequently became a part of that region. Tradition has it that Bern came by its name in a curious manner. The surrounding areas were covered with forest and the Duke was determined to name his new town after the first animal he killed while hunting there. This happened to be a bear, the German name for which is *Bär*. The legend is somewhat collaborated by the local dialect pronunciation of Bern—*Bärn*. In 1224 the oldest version of the city's well known coat-of-arms, featuring a bear and the name *ob Berne,* first appeared. And, high on the list of the city's main tourist attractions are the Bear Pits *(Bärengraben)* in which bears, known affectionately as *Mutze* by the local population, have been living since 1480.

Berchtold entrusted the construction of the city to Cuno of Bubenberg. Among his achievements was the clearing of the surrounding oak forests, the wood from which was used to construct houses. Around the initial settlement, situated at the end of the promontory, Cuno built a first city wall, which was dominated in the center by the huge Clocktower. This also served as the main gate, giving access to and from the city.

Bern was expanded in the 13th century when, under the protectorate of Count Peter of Savoy, the walls were extended westwards along the promontory. The main gateway then became the prison tower *(Käfigturm)*, which was subsequently reconstructed in the 17th century. The additions that took place during the 14th century, the city walls, dismantled only a hundred years ago, stretched to where the railway station stands today.

Times were not all peaceful, however, and Bern often had to defend itself against attackers. The most significant of the battles occurred in 1339 when Bern fought, successfully, against the combined troops of the nobility of Burgundy and the city of Fribourg, which had been founded by the father of Berchtold V. This victory not only guaranteed the future independence of the city, but initiated an expansion of its powers. Soon after, in 1353, Bern joined the Swiss Confederation, and the succeeding centuries saw its power base widen considerably. Between 1536 and 1798 it gained, mostly at the expense of the House of Savoy, large tracts of territory along Lake Geneva. It is mainly because of these Bernese efforts that much of the French area of Switzerland is a part of the Swiss Confederation today. The French invasion of 1798, and the new Switzerland that emerged like a phoenix in 1815 from the ruins left by Napoleon I, destroyed Bern's dominance. It was forced to cede nearly half its land, which was used to form the new cantons of Aargau and Waadt. The city even lost control of the canton of Bern. By way of compensation, however, it became the cantonal capital and, in 1848, was chosen by the first Swiss Parliament as the capital of the Swiss Confederation.

Another unwelcome change that befell Bern, this one fundamentally altering the city's appearance, occurred in 1405. In that year a great number of the timber buildings were destroyed by a city-wide fire. Most of the houses were rebuilt on the their original foundations, this time using sandstone from local quarries instead of wood. Many of these were rebuilt for a second time in the 16th and 17th centuries, and the consequent harmony of appearance and elaborate detail still delights the visitors of today.

An interesting characteristic, and one relatively unique to Bern, is its extensive labyrinth of arcades, actually six kilometers (3.7 miles) of them. These line the long, comparatively narrow streets, giving Bern one of the longest covered shopping promenades in the world. You could say that they are the medieval equivalent of a late 20th-century American shopping mall.

More romantic, though, are the famous historic fountains that adorn the streets of Bern. Built mostly in the mid-16th century to replace the wooden ones of earlier centuries, these are guarded, more often than not, by an elaborate and vividly colored figure standing proudly atop a column.

It must in fairness be said that the city of Bern, with a population of 133,000, has not managed to escape some of the social problems prevalent in the late 20th century. Because of its small size and physical topography, these are perhaps more discernible here than in many other Swiss cities. To witness open drug use on the streets of this charming town is surprising, if not shocking—as is the sometimes less than discreet policing of the problem.

GETTING THERE:

By air: International flights from certain European destinations arrive directly at the Bern-Belp Airport. Longer distance flights, and those from other European cities, arrive either at Zürich's Kloten airport or Geneva's Cointrin airport. From either there are hourly train services on to Bern.

Trains arrive at Bern's main railway station from all other cities in Switzerland, as well as from France, Germany and Italy.

By car, Bern, in the eastern central part of Switzerland, is easily reached by road from all other parts of the country.

PRACTICALITIES:

The **Dialing code** for Bern is 31. The **Tourist Office** *(Bern Tourismus)*, ☎ 311 66 11, Fax 312 12 33, or E-mail info@bernetourism.ch, CH-3001 Bern, is located in the railway station. Opening hours October to May are Monday to Saturday from 9 a.m. to 6:30 p.m. and Sunday from 10 a.m. to 5 p.m. June to September hours are Monday to Saturday from 9 a.m. to 8:30 p.m. This office also offers a hotel reservation service. A great source of information about Bern can be found on the **Internet** at www.bernetourism.ch.

Bucherer Bern can be found in one of those traditional, arcaded properties at Marktgasse 38, ☎ 328 90 90. The best stores for purchasing **Swiss Army Knives**, kitchen knives, scissors or any other kind of souvenir you could possibly imagine are **Swiss Plaza**, Kramgasse 75; **Edelweiss**, Gerechtigkeitsgasse 21 and **Boutique Regina**, Gerechtigkeitsgasse 75. These all offer a free engraving service and share the same ☎ 311 56 16 number. Typically, shops in Bern are open Monday from 2–6:30 p.m., with department stores and some other shops opening at 9 a.m.; Tuesday to Friday from 8:15 a.m. to 6:30 p.m., with department stores and many other shops open until 9 p.m., and on Thursday and Saturday from 8:15 a.m. to 4 p.m.

Public transport in and around Bern, on any combination of tramcars, buses and some trains, is fast, clean and efficient. Tickets must be purchased from ticket vending machines, ticket offices, hotels or the tourist office before each trip and are available for single trips or, more advantageously, as an Unlimited Day Pass. The latter, for 2nd class, cost CHF 7.50 for access to the entire network of the public transport system within the area of validity.

The **Lost Property Office**, ☎ 321 50 50, Zeughausgasse 18, is open Monday to Friday from 7:30-11:30 a.m. and 1:45-5 p.m. The **SBB** (Railways Lost Property Office), ☎ 680 23 37, is located at Bern railway station and is open Monday to Friday from 8 a.m. to midday and 2–6 p.m.

ACCOMMODATION:

. Bern is constrained by its topography with the central area being quite small. Consequently, many of the more economical hotels, guest houses etc. are located away from the city center. Because of the inconvenience that presents those are not described here.

The **Hotel Bellevue Palace *******, ☎ 320 45 45 or Fax 311 47 43, Kochergasse 3-5, CH-3001 Bern, a member of the Leading Hotels of the World group, is unquestionably the largest and most impressive hotel in Bern. Standing adjacent to the Swiss Parliament building and, as such, used as an official residence of visiting dignitaries, this is close to the city center. The rooms are tastefully decorated, in a variety of styles, and are furnished with every modern facility. The terrace, and some rooms, have marvelous views over the River Aare and panoramic views of the Alps. $$$

The **Hotel Continental—Garni *****, ☎ 311 26 26 or Fax 311 85 24,

Zeughausgasse 27, CH-3011 Bern, is very conveniently located in the center of the city, but still just a few minutes walk from the railway station. Very clean, comfortable and well appointed, the rooms are reasonably priced. $$

The **Hotel Krebs—Garni *****, ☎ 311 49 42, Fax 311 10 35 or E-mail hotel-krebs@thenet.ch, Genfergasse 8, CH-3011 Bern, is a pleasant city center hotel, just a couple of minutes' walk from the railway station, that offers good value. $

The **Hotel Glocke ****, ☎ 311 37 71 or Fax 311 10 08, Rathausgasse 75, CH-3011 Bern, is located in the heart of old Bern, in close proximity to the celebrated clock tower. Each of the 26 rooms is comfortably furnished, and offers excellent value for money. You can even choose from two restaurants on site. $

The **Landhaus Restaurant und Bar**, ☎ 331 41 66 or E-mail landhaus@spectraweb.ch, Altenbergstrasse 6, CH-3013 Bern, advertises itself as a backpackers' paradise, and has rates as low as CHF 30 per person per night. $

The **Swiss Youth Hostels**, ☎ 311 63 16, Weihergasse 4, CH-3005 Bern, are simple, basic and clean with rates between CHF 18 and CHF 32 per person, inclusive of breakfast and sheets. $

Bern à la carte is an accommodation package that merits serious consideration by those planning to stay in Bern for a period of 2 to 4 nights. Basically, charges are based on two seasons. The Low Season, January to April, November and December; and the High Season, May through October. Separate lists are available for each season. Quotes are per person, based on double occupancy. This package also includes a "Bern Pass" voucher booklet with free offers and price reductions, a ticket for a city sightseeing tour in summer, a 24-hour Visitors Card for the city public transport network in winter, an Old Town booklet guide, detailed information on Bern, its surroundings and service and all applicable taxes. Contact the office of Bern Tourismus for further information.

FOOD AND DRINK:

Churrasco Grill & Restaurant (Aarbergergasse 60) One in a national chain of restaurants featuring steaks and meat dishes. Their lunch special is certainly worth consideration. ☎ 311 82 88. $

Swiss Chalet Restaurant (Rathausgasse 75) A very typical Swiss country restaurant right in the middle of Bern, affiliated with the Hotel Glocke. An ambiance of authenticity created by wooden beams, cowbells, horns and a Swiss musical show complement a very Swiss menu that highlights, among its many dishes, a selection of home-made fondues. It is open daily and, conveniently after a long day of sight seeing, much later than many other restaurants: Monday, Tuesday and Wednesday until 1 a.m.; Thursday, Friday and Saturday until 3 a.m. and Sunday until midnight. ☎ 311 10 08. $

Kaiser Garden (Rathausgasse 73) It may seem a rather foreign name for a Chinese restaurant, but the menu features an array of mouth-watering dishes that will be familiar to lovers of Chinese cuisine. ☎ 311 39 22. $

Boomerang's Bar & Bistro (Speichergasse/Sternengässchen 5) Yes, the name really does give this restaurant away. It is Australian—and they certainly do want you to come back. Look for Spicy Crocodile Balls—yes, really; Bush Veggie burgers, Lamb Fillets and even Kangaroo steaks. And, their array of *Aussie cocktails* are, if you are not very careful, sure to send you "Down Under." Closed Sunday. ☎ 311 32 71. $

SUGGESTED TOUR:

Begin at the modern **main train station** *(Hauptbahnhof)* (1), but don't expect to see the trains; they are sequestered away on the lower levels. It is also the home of the **Tourist Office** *(Bern Tourismus)*, and the starting point for some interesting walking tours that they organize. Exit into the ever-busy Bahnhofplatz, dominated by the Church of the Holy Ghost *(Heilig-geistkirche)*. Walk in the direction away from that, along Bollwerk, passing the large Hotel Schweizerhof before turning into Nuengasse. You will not find much of interest along this route until, having taken a left at Genfergasse, you reach the T-junction with Hodlerstrasse. The classical style building, enhanced by statues and engravings, just across the road is the ***Fine Arts Museum** *(Kunstmuseum)* (2), ☎ 312 28 28. In addition to holding the world's largest collection of works by Paul Klee, among its other exhibits are paintings by Swiss and International masters that span the centuries, and an array of Impressionist art. The museum is open Tuesday from 10 a.m. to 9 p.m. and Wednesday to Sunday from 10 a.m. to 5 p.m.

A left out of the museum will soon bring you to Waisenhausplatz and a really attractive old house. Constructed between 1782 and 1786, this once served as the **Boy's Orphanage** *(Knabenwaisenhaus)* (3) but since 1941 it has housed the police headquarters. Isn't it strange, no matter where you go in the world, the police always seem to get the nice places! Across the road is a fountain, and though there is nothing strange about seeing fountains in Bern, this one is most unusual. Generally, they are brightly colored and topped by an historic figure; this one is rather bland with moss growing around and under the water that perpetually runs down it. Somebody's idea of Art Deco, I suppose.

Directly behind this is Waisenhausplatz, which hosts a general **market** on Tuesdays and Saturdays. While worth a look for the cultural interest alone, you can also find a bargain or two if you are attentive. Zeughausgasse, to the left, has some shops and hotels but it is the two buildings near the end that will allure. The first of these, the **French Church** *(Französische Kirche)* (4), is the oldest house of worship in the city. Originally constructed in the late 13th century as the church of the Dominican monastery it has been renovated many times over the succeeding centuries. Next you will come to the **Cornhouse** *(Kornhaus)*. Pass underneath its arches; the impressive **Municipal Theater** *(Stadttheater)* (5) will be to the left, just before the bridge that carries traffic high over the Aare.

Cross the road to Rathausgasse, an interesting street indeed. Running directly to the end of the promontory it is parallel to, but much quieter than, Kramgasse. Arcades line either side, as is typical of many streets in Bern, and these are populated by quaint shops, hotels and restaurants. But make a note to look up. Near the tops of the houses the windows of the small rooms are often adorned with flower boxes, making for a colorful and pretty sight. At the street's end you will find the Catholic Church of St. Peter and Paul, dating from the middle of the 19th century, as well as the building after which the street is named. The **Town Hall** *(Rathaus)* (6), dating from the beginning of the 15th century but completely restored between 1939 and 1942, has a most distinct façade. Directly across the road stands the Venner Fountain *(Vennerbrunnen)*, over which a knight holding the flag of Bern in one hand and brandishing a sword in the other, stands vigil. The street changes names here, as all the streets running towards the end of the promontory do at cross roads, and becomes Postgasse. Though the scenery continues much the same, if a little bit older, pay some attention to the **Antonite House** *(Antonierhaus)* (7), at Number 62. Noticeably different in style, particularly in the curved arches, to its neighbors, it was built at the end of the 15th century as the church of the Order of Antonites. Rebuilt in 1939, it has over its history been used as a granary, coach-house and even an antique hall.

The end of Postgasse brings with it different sights. From here, you will be able to see clearly how the River Aare doubles around on itself, in the process forming the promontory upon which sits the city of Bern. The church in front of you is the **Nydegg** (8), which was originally built in the mid-14th century over the foundations of the old Nydegg fortress destroyed nearly a century before. It was completely renovated in the 1950s. Next, the choice is yours. Either take the scenic route, winding down the hill, crossing the **Untertorbrücke**, the oldest bridge over the Aare, and following the road around to the end of the Nydeggbrücke, or cross the Aare by way of that bridge itself. If you take the former be sure to note, at the end of the older bridge, the strange building on the corner. This, the **Felsenburg**, constructed around the mid- to late-13th century, was the original bridge gate. As you can see, nowadays it is occupied, having been converted into residences around 1860.

Your next destination, and the favorite spot for most visitors to Bern, are the ***Bear Pits** *(Bärengraben)* (9). As described in the introduction, bears have been associated with Bern since its foundation. But it was not until 1513, when Bernese troops returned victoriously home accompanied by a

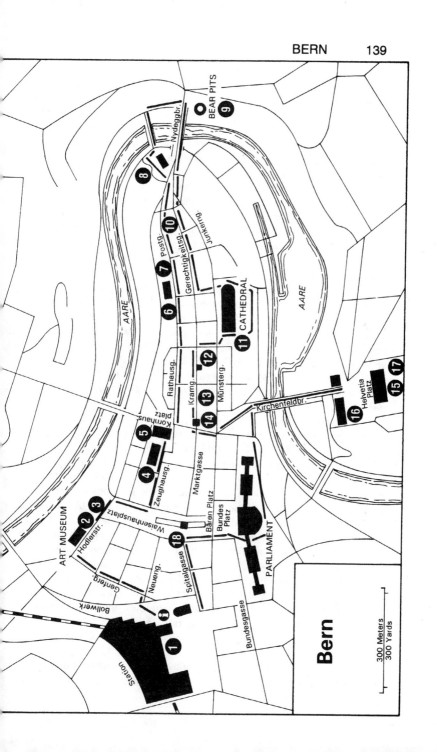

Bern

300 Meters
300 Yards

PARLIAMENT

Bundes Platz

Bundesgasse

Bären Platz

Marktgasse

Spitalgasse

Neueng.

Genferg.

Bollwerk

Station

Hodlerstr.

ART MUSEUM

Waisenhausplatz

Zeughausg.

Kornhaus platz

Rathausg.

Kramg.

Münsterg.

CATHEDRAL

Gerechtigkeitsg.

Junkerng.

Postg.

Nydeggbr.

BEAR PITS

AARE

AARE

Kirchenfeldbr.

Helvetia Platz

bear, that they were formally kept in the city, which they have been ever since. The present pits, there are two, have been a permanent home for the bears since 1857. Recently they have been renovated to improve the facilities—for the bears that is. Limited to five in number they are well cared for, but still perfectly willing to do all sorts of tricks to get you to throw them extra treats. Easter is a particularly popular time at the pits, as it is then that the new cubs make their first public appearances.

There is no choice next; the singular route back into the city is across the Nydeggbrücke. The views, however, are compensation enough; the city directly ahead with the Cathedral spire dominating to the left, the river below and the rolling green hills behind. Pay attention, also, to the row of old buildings on the city side, and to the right of the bridge. The strange one, with no ground floor and steps leading to the river, is the **Ländtetor**. Dating from the late 13th century, it served as the entrance to the landing stage for boats crossing the Aare.

Head, now, for Gerechtigkeitsgasse which, although it is the main street through the center of the narrow promontory, changes its name four times before finally reaching the railway station. Colonnaded and arched along the entirety of its length, it is particularly pretty here where commercialization isn't so predominant. Antique shops, specialty stores, bars, restaurants and even a hotel or two co-exist in complete harmony and peace. And, being Bern, you will not be surprised to find another of those colorful water fountains-cum-statues; this time the **Justice Fountain** *(Gerechtigkeitsbrunnen)* (10) of 1543.

Continue on, turning left at the first intersection and crossing Junkerngasse to go behind the Cathedral into a wonderful plaza. Take a refreshment from the café and then stroll to the edge and enjoy the vistas. Immediately below, the patchwork of picturesque rooftops makes for an uneven sight. The Aare flows forcefully through its locks and the surrounding countryside, wrapping itself around the promontory, and showing clearly what an unusual city Bern is. You can not fail to be enchanted by the immense, snow-capped peaks of the Bernese Oberland in the distance. Although it is believed that a chapel has stood on this site since Bern's very founding, construction of the present **Cathedral** *(Münster)* (11) was not initiated until 1421, with the 100-meter- (328 foot)-high spire not added until 1893. The interior, as the effects of the Reformation dictated more often than not in Switzerland, is rather bland. Look, though, for the sculptured main portal and stained-glass windows, most of which date from the mid-15th century. The adventurous, and fit, may attempt the 344 steps to the second tower platform, where the rewards are unsurpassed **views** of the city.

Leave by the main entrance, passing the **Moses Fountain** *(Mosesbrunnen)*, erected in 1790 on the site of an earlier one dated 1544, on your way through Münstergassen to Kramgasse, an extension of Gerechtigkeitsgasse. Immediately, you will notice the increase in activity; after all it is very near to the epicenter of Bern. It is, in fact, captivating in its vitality, and also far from short of sights. The **Einstein House Museum** (12), ☎ 312 00 91, Kramgasse 49, is housed in the genius's apartment where, in 1904, he developed his revolutionary theory. Visit February to November on Tuesday to Friday from 10 a.m. to 5 p.m. and Saturday from 10 a.m. to 4 p.m. And, if this boggles the mind, then the Einstein bar/restaurant, underneath the apartment, is just the place to recover.

Back outside, you will notice that the museum is sandwiched between two fountains. To the right is the **Samson Fountain** *(Samsonbrunnen)*, but most visitors' sights will, by now, be riveted to the left. Though the **Zähringer Fountain**, *(Zähringerbrunnen)* (13), commemorating the city's founder Berchtold V, is elaborate enough with a Bern bear and Zähringer coat of arms, it is overshadowed in every sense by the ***Clock Tower** *(Zytgloggeturm)* (14) directly behind it. This ranks alongside the bears as the city's emblem. The original 12th-century tower, some parts of which still stand, formed the boundary to the first extension of the city. Following the devastation of a fire in 1405 the structure was rebuilt in stone and a tower bell installed. At that time, when the clock chimes had to be struck by hand each hour, it showed the official time and all other clocks were set from it, a practice that continued until the advent of modern communications. It was not until 1530 that the Astronomical Clock and humorous Figure Play were added. The latter, which commence playing four minutes before the hour, attract so many people these days. Less known is the fact that all road distances in Switzerland are measured from this point. Among the tours organized by Bern Tourismus is one dedicated to the Zytgloggeturm, and well worth taking it is.

It's now time to stray, for only the second time, off the promontory and walk south, on Kirchenfeldbrücke high over the Aare, to **Helvetiaplatz**. If you are fortunate, the day will be clear allowing you an unobstructed view to the mesmerizing peaks of the Eiger, Mönch and Jungfrau, shimmering on the horizon. The opposite bank of the Aare differs dramatically from the city side. Less densely populated and with large houses, some of which are embassies, there are also no less than six museums and the Swiss National Library in the space of a few blocks. Now, don't panic, this isn't a museum guide and I will refrain from treating you to a long entreaty on each one. You will want to be aware, however, that the grand **Berne Historical Museum** (15), ☎ 351 18 11, Helvetiaplatz 5, is the second-largest historical museum in the country, and is open Tuesday to Sunday from 10 a.m. to 5 p.m. Also in the plaza is a museum that may well be of topical interest. The **Swiss Alpine Museum** *(Schweizerisches Alpines Museum)* (16), ☎ 351 04 34, Helvetiaplatz 4, gives you a real insight into those magical mountains that bring people from the world over to Switzerland. Open year round Monday from 2–5 p.m., Tuesday to Sunday from 10 a.m. to midday and 2–5 p.m., but with additional hours between mid-May and mid-October when it does not close during the lunch time. Philatelists, and many others, will be fascinated by one of the world's largest public collections of postage stamps on exhibition at the **Swiss Postal Museum** (Schweizerisches PTT-Museum) (17), ☎ 338 77 77. This is found at Helvetiastrasse 16, and is open Tuesday to Sunday from 10 a.m. to 5 p.m. My guess, though, is that most visitors will be quite content to bypass the attractions of the Swiss Rifle Museum, the Natural History Museum, the Art Gallery and the Library.

Strolling back over the bridge you will see, dominating the left bank, four buildings that form an elongated façade accentuated by a central dome. The building to the far right, and nearest to the bridge, is the very grand Bellevue Palace Hotel. The others, and there are three, form the **Swiss Houses of Parliament**. Erected between 1851 and 1902, there is very little difference in style between the east and west wings, but the central parliament building, home to the Federal Council and Federal Assembly, truly is architecturally impressive. In any event, to get a closer view turn left at the end of the bridge, and then walk along the terrace that runs in front of it. If you feel it is time for a refreshment, head for the open-air terrace of the Bellevue Palace Hotel. There you will find an elegant ambiance, fine service and magnificent vistas to the peaks of the Bernese Oberland in the distance.

Just past the domed section of the Parliament building, climb the steps that bring you out into Bundesplatz. It, in conjunction with Bärenplatz—which leads out of it—and Waisenhausplatz, mentioned earlier, serve as the sites for Bern's famous markets. Every morning after mid-May there is a colorful Geranium market in Bundesplatz. On Tuesday and Saturday mornings the vegetable, fruit and flower market occupy Bundesplatz, Bärenplatz and their surrounding streets. Between May and October it is in Bärenplatz daily. In the middle of Bärenplatz, between Marktgasse and Spitalgasse, is the **Prison Tower** (Käfigturm) (18), which was actually used as such until 1897. This was constructed on the site of the second west gate, circa 1256, in 1690.

Time, now, to bring the tour to a close. Walk down Spitalgasse in the direction of the train station, where your final impressions of Bern will include two more marvelous water fountains-cum-statues. You will see, also, the people of this enchanting city passing their time, as they will on sunny days, just sitting and enjoying each others' company on the steps leading to the arcades.

Although it doesn't really fit in to a tour, there is one other trip that visitors to Bern should give serious consideration to. **Alpar AG**, ☎ 960 21 11 or Fax 960 21 12, operating out of Bern-Belp airport, offers thrilling flights in a light plane over the peaks of the Bernese Oberland and even as far as

Zermatt and the Matterhorn and back. Those who are not too keen on the thoughts of helicopter flights may find this a little easier on the mind. Give them a call to arrange a flight; there are frequent buses to the airport from the forecourt of the railway station. Taxis are the other option, but they aren't cheap.

A Daytrip from Bern

Neuchâtel

The earliest verifiable evidence of human life in this area dates back to the middle Paleolithic period. Indications are that between 3000 to 1000 BC lake dwellers, *lacustrians,* lived in villages built on piles along the lake shore. The Helvetians, who succeeded the lacustrians and lived in huts built on the land, were accomplished in their working with iron. In 58 BC the inhabitants attempted to emigrate to Gaul but, defeated by the forces of Julius Caesar, they were forced to return. The Romans then overcame the Helvetians, incorporated their land into the Roman Empire and ruled for over four hundred years. The Alemanians, early in the 5th century, rampaged through the region destroying everything in their wake. Their withdrawal allowed the Burgundians, in turn, to take control, establishing during their occupation many agricultural settlements. The land was subsequently incorporated into the Empire of Charlemagne and, later, the kingdom of Burgundy.

In the 10th century a fortified township, of which the Prison and Diesse Tower remain as evidence today, were built in Neuchâtel, as was a new castle—from which the name Neuchâtel originated. This was constructed on the instigation of Rudolph III of Burgundy and presented in 1011 to his wife Irmengarde, as a "most Royal seat" *(regalissima sedem).* It is from this century that the first written accounts of the Neuchâtel vineyards originate.

At the beginning of the 12th century the first Counts of Neuchâtel were titled and, in 1214, granted the city burghers their first charger. It was during this era, also, that the Romanesque wing of the present castle and Romanesque apse and apsidioles of the Collegiate Church were constructed. The cenotaph of the Counts of Neuchâtel, dated 1373 and considered a masterpiece of medieval sculpture, can still be admired in the latter.

The early 16th century saw much activity. From 1512 to 1529 the territory was occupied, for strategic reasons, by the Swiss cantons, whose coat of arms painted on the castle wall is much admired today. Neuchâtel adopted the Reformation in 1530 and, soon afterwards, the territory of Neuchâtel was recognized as an indivisible entity, with future rulers required to seek investiture from the populace.

Henry II of Orléans-Longueville, whose family coat-of-arms is emblazoned on the 16th-century Market Hall, became the first Prince of Neuchâtel at the beginning of the 17th century. In 1707 Mary of Orléans died without leaving an heir, and the citizens chose her successor from among fifteen claimants. It appears they were selective, too, wanting their new leader to be Protestant and strong enough to protect them but distant enough not to be meddlesome. Eventually, they settled on Frederick I, King of Prussia, whose entitlement originated through the Houses of Chalon-Orange and Nassau.

Following a fire in 1714, which occasioned reconstruction of the most ancient quarter of the Old Town, changes came in the street and plot patterns that eased crowded living conditions. The 18th century also saw the emergency of industry—especially watchmaking, the manufacture of printed fabrics and lace, commerce, banking and agriculture. The tide of affluence that ensued brought with it many fine houses, most constructed of local yellow stone. Among the most magnificent of these is that built by Du Peyrou, between 1765 and 1770, a friend of Jean-Jacques Rousseau. In 1843, another obstacle to town traffic, the River Seyon, which flowed swiftly through the middle of town, was eliminated when the river was diverted to make way for a commercial thoroughfare, which assumed the river's name. During this period a portion of the lake shore was converted to a promenade.

The Napoleonic era brought more changes. The defeated King of Prussia exchanged Neuchâtel for Hanover, and Napoleon elevated his favorite Marshal, Berthier, to the rank of Prince of Neuchâtel—a place he never actually visited. Napoleon's demise allowed the then King of Prussia, Frederick-William III, to retain control of Hanover and reassert his rights to Neuchâtel. Being too distant from his territory, however, he encouraged its incorporation into the Swiss political system. Accordingly, on September 12, 1814, the Principality of Neuchâtel was admitted to the Swiss Confederation as the twenty-first canton. The paradox of a principality within the confederation was short lived, though, as the French Revolution encouraged the citizens of Neuchâtel to follow suit. Fortunately this revolution was bloodless, and Neuchâtel was proclaimed a republic on March 1, 1848.

The canton is governed by a Council of State, consisting of five Councilors, who sit in the Castle, with municipal matters managed by a Communal Council of five members whose seat is in the Town Hall.

GETTING THERE:

Trains arrive at Neuchâtel station from Bern, a journey of approximately 45 minutes on a frequent schedule throughout the day.

By car, Neuchâtel, almost due west from Bern, is reached by taking the Autoroute to the Kerzers exit, then Route 10 to the lake and around it to Neuchâtel.

PRACTICALITIES:

The **Dialing Code** for Neuchâtel is 32. The **Tourist Office** (*Tourisme neuchâtelois*), ☎ 889 68 90, Fax 889 62 96, E-mail neuchâtel@ tourisme.etatne.ch or www.etatne.ch, at Hôtel des Postes, CH-2001 Neuchâtel, is open Monday to Friday from 9 a.m. to midday and 1:30-5:30 p.m., and Saturday from 9 a.m. to midday.

ACCOMMODATION:

The **Hotel Beau-Rivage *****, ☎ 723 15 15 or Fax 723 16 16, Esplanade du Mont-Blanc 1, CH-2000 Neuchâtel, a member of the Leading Hotels of the World organization, is both on the lake front and in the city center and offers 65 highly luxurious rooms. An elegant restaurant and verandah face the Alps, which rise across the lake on the horizon. $$$

The **La Maison du Prussien**, ☎ 730 54 54 or Fax 730 21 43, Au Gor du Vauseyon, CH-2006 Neuchâtel, a member of the Romantik Hotel chain, is housed within an historical building. It features large, attractively appointed rooms, two junior suites and a gastronomic restaurant. $$

The **Hotel Beaulac ***, ☎ 723 11 11 or Fax 723 60 35, Esplanade Léopold Robert 2, CH-2000 Neuchâtel, boasts a delightful location on the edge of the harbor and overlooking the lake. Expect comfortable, pleasantly furnished rooms at a reasonable price. $$

The **Hotel City ***, ☎ 725 25 77 or Fax 721 38 69, Place A. & M. Pi- aget, CH-2001 Neuchâtel, located near the harbor, has comfortable, ac- ceptable rooms at a reasonable price. $

FOOD AND DRINK:

Restaurant de la Maison des Halles (Rue de Trésor 4/Place du Marché), within a most delightful 15th-century building in the pedestrian old part of town, is actually two restaurants. The brasser- rie *Au Rez-de-Chaussée,* is open seven days a week from 11:30 a.m. to 11 p.m. The more gastronomic *Au Premier,* featuring specialties created by the chef/owner Albert Reichl, is open Tuesday to Friday both lunch time and evening and on Saturday for the latter meal only. ☎ 724 31 41. $$ and $$$

SUGGESTED TOUR:

The **Train Station** (*Gare CFF*) (1), sits high on the hill behind Neuchâtel and, on clear days, affords majestic views over the lake to the Alps. Across the street from the station, a zig-zagging path and steps will take you down past apartments and pretty houses, eventually leading to the Faubourg de l'Hôpital. If the name isn't enough to tip you off, then the architectural styles and signs certainly will—Neuchâtel is in the heart of the French-speaking part of Switzerland. You will also have noticed that Neuchâtel is quite an attractive town. This street, on which you will walk to the right, is lined with

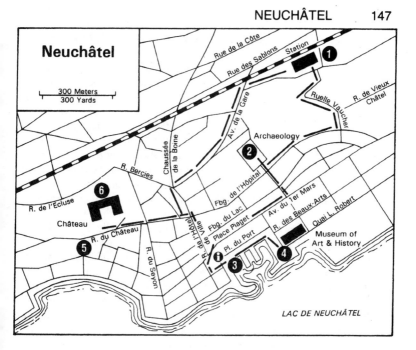

large, beautiful old houses set in spacious private gardens. One of the larger of these, the Hôtel DePeyrou, is home to the **Archeology Museum** *(Musée d'archéologie)* (2), ☎ 889 69 10, which houses exhibits collected from throughout the canton. Visit Tuesday to Sunday from 2–5 p.m.

Take the Rue de l'Orangerie, opposite the museum, and turn right onto the Avenue du Premier Mars to reach the next destination, the **Tourist Office** *(Tourisme neuchâtelois)* (3). This is found in the post office *(Poste principale PTT)*, at the Place du Port, a very impressive structure with the names of the countries of the world sculpted around the top. Directly behind this is the very picturesque port *(Port de la Ville)*, which is the departure point for cruises on the lake, and also a wonderful place just to pass the time of day. Yachts bob gently at their moorings, and swans and ducks glide effortlessly over the waters or waddle around the promenade begging for lunch. With the Alps glistening in the distance, it is an idyllic sight indeed.

There are actually three interconnected lakes here: **Lac de Neuchâtel**, the greatest of them is, in fact, also the largest lake located entirely in Switzerland; **Lac de Bienne**, *Bielersee* in German, to the north, is much smaller; and **Lac de Morat**, or *Murtensee* in German, to the east, is smaller again. Any number of voyages may be made, taking in any combination of the lakes, or just the Lac de Neuchâtel itself. The choice is yours, and the only parameters time and preference. Further information can be obtained from the **Société de Navigation sur les Lacs de Neuchâtel et Moral**, ☎ 725 40 12 or Fax 724 79 61, CH-2001 Neuchâtel.

Stroll around the picturesque port now, and out along the jetty which offers fine views of the town, the lake and the mountains. If you are ready for a break, underneath the Hotel Beaulac you will find the Café de Port; rather nondescript, perhaps, but with a fine location and set lunches at low prices. The steps beside it lead up to the hotel, the bland, modern façade of which contrasts starkly with the classic outline of the building opposite. This is home to the **Museum of Art and History** (Musée d'art et d'histoire) (4) ☎ 717 79 60 or Fax 717 79 69, Quai Léopold-Robert. The exhibits here are both varied and interesting, ranging from paintings—such as the huge one of Christ rising to the Heavens which dominates the lobby, to carriages, household wares and furniture. While these would be an intriguing mix on their own, they are not the main attraction. That honor falls, indubitably, to three 18th-century androids invented by the creative mind of Jaquet-Droz. To see the automatons in action you will either have to time it right, the first Sunday of each month at 2, 3 and 4 p.m.; or by special and prior arrangement pay for a private showing. The museum is open Tuesday to Sunday from 10 a.m. to 5 p.m. Admission is free on Thursday. After exiting and before carrying on the tour in the Old Town, many visitors will want to take a short stroll down the promenade, Quai Léopold-Robert, away from the museum, to admire an array of impressively beautiful houses.

Retrace your steps, passing the post office and taking the right turn leading into Rue de l'Hôtel de Ville. The handsome, classical columns that greet you belong, as the street name verifies, to the Town Hall. The next left, the Rue de l'Hôpital, leads to the Croix du Marché, the most ancient square of the town where the surrounding 18th-century façades provide a suitable backdrop for the brightly-colored fountain of the Standard Bearer (Banneret). The adjacent Hôtel du Banneret, built in 1609, is considered to be the finest example of late Renaissance style architecture in the region, and has been perfectly conserved.

Press on as the Old Town beckons, traveling along the Rue de Château which, in due course, becomes the Rue J. de Hochberg—named in honor of a Countess who reigned here from 1516 to 1543, and soon you will come to the prison. This, more modern, structure built in 1826 was constructed on top of a cliff at the site of the first Château of Neuchâtel, and has become one of the more conspicuous residents of the hill. The nearby **Prison tower** (5) has the distinction of being the most ancient edifice in Neuchâtel. It is fascinating to note how easily-discernible layers chronicle its constructive history; a white limestone base dating from Roman times is topped by uncut blocks of granite from around the beginning of the 11th century and finished off by medium-sized white limestone and yellow stone added by 11th- and 12th-century builders. The entire tower was renovated in 1803. The interior, open between Easter and September, offers glorious views of the lake and Alps and an interesting perspective of the neighboring district. Inside, also, are models of Neuchâtel as it appeared during the 15th and 18th centuries. Be forewarned, though: The entrance is through an automatic turnstile that will demand a 50-centime coin before it allows admission.

Méander back now the way you came, through cobblestoned streets in this fascinating part of Neuchâtel where no two structures are the same. Take a left onto Rue Collegiate, which winds its way around before bringing you up to the two most important structures of this city—which are also buildings of national importance; the ***Château and Collegiate Church** (6).

Construction of the imposing **Château** (castle) was begun near the end of the 12th century. It was enlarged in several stages over the next three centuries, and renovated extensively following the citywide fire of 1450. Initially serving as the principal dwelling for the first Lords of Neuchâtel, it became, after 1405, a residence for the Governors and a series of Councilors. From 1848 to the present it has housed important government offices. In short, in one form or another, the regional authority has made its home in the castle for the past 800 years! The structure is divided into three main sections: the Romanesque, the Main Gate and the Southern Gallery. The highly ornamented Romanesque section, the oldest part of the Château, has an interesting carriage gateway that gave access to the wine cellars—the principal source of income of the counts. The Southern Gallery was built in 1488, and has as its main focal point a wall upon which are emblazoned the coats-of-arms of the first thirteen Swiss cantons. Desirous of leaving a permanent reminder of his service to the French kings, Philippe de Hochberg commissioned the construction, between 1496 and 1498, of the twin-towered Main Gate. Free guided tours start from the entrance at door number one, between April 1 to September 30 from Monday to Friday at 10 and 11 a.m., midday, and 2, 3, and 4 p.m.; on Saturday at 10 and 11 a.m., 2, 3, and 4 p.m.; and on Sunday and Bank Holidays at 2, 3, and 4 p.m.

Alongside is the **Collegiate Church** and, though there is little documentation regarding its early history, it is known that the building was begun prior to 1185 in the Romanesque style. A now-obliterated inscription on the southern portal identified the founders as Ulrich II of Neuchâtel and his wife Bertha. It was consecrated on November 8, 1276, a date which, most likely, marks the completion of the western end, the style of which is largely Gothic. Renovations followed in 1360 and 1428 and, in October of 1530, the Reformation saw the interior stripped of altars and decorative additions. Major alterations were made to the exterior during a general renovation in the mid-19th century, including the destruction of the original church tower in favor of a stone spire. A copy of that tower was grafted onto the northern side of the building, leaving the southern steeple as the only original on the structure. Stained- glass windows were added to the chancel in 1905 and others, most notably a wonderful rose window, were installed between 1930 and 1951. Inside, however, the pride of place rests with the gloriously sculpted funerary monument of the Counts of Neuchâtel, begun on the order of Louis of Neuchâtel in 1372. Before leaving the area, though, most visitors will want to take a walk around the battlements and admire these wonderful buildings from quite a different perspective.

As the tour draws to a close, retrace your steps and pass through the Croix du Marché and along the Rue de l'Hôpital where a left at the junction with Terreaux will bring you face-to-face with modern art work and sculptures that adorn the sandstone façade of the Natural History Museum. From here on the road gets considerably steeper and curves into the Avenue de la Gare. About the only place of interest before you finally return to the station is the marvelous house and gardens at Number 47, which is quite out of place with its immediate surroundings.

Solothurn

Tribes of hunters settled this area, between the Jura mountains and the Aare river, as far back as the Neolithic Age. The name, however, derives from its Celtic heritage, *Saloduron*—meaning the "Stronghold of the Salos." The Romans established a fortress here around AD 370, the remains of which are still visible today.

As the northern corner of the Burgundian kingdom, Solothurn flourished in the 10th century. In 1481 it became the 11th canton to join the Swiss Confederation. Consequently, the number 11 has great significance here and, in fact, is referred to as the "Holy Solothurn Number 11." You will find, as you tour the town, that many, many things here are found in multiples of eleven.

The town's greatest days were between 1530 and 1792. Affluent merchants brought fame and prosperity and, in turn, ambassadors were sent by the French kings; hence, the sobriquet "Ambassadorial Town." These entrepreneurs built luxurious mansions, many of which can be seen today, harmoniously combining French charm, Italian splendor and German-Swiss stability. Quite rightly, Solothurn has acquired the reputation of being Switzerland's best-preserved Baroque town.

Solothurn—also known as Soleure and Soletta, and the capital of the canton of the same name, has a population of just 16,000. Although it is one of the oldest towns north of the Alps, today it must be described as dynamic and outward looking. An interesting array of cultural events are on show throughout the year. Once a year, at carnival time, the town goes wild as citizens, disguised by weird and wonderful masks *(Guggenmusik)*, parade through the streets to celebrate *Chesslete*. During this period, when life is turned upside down, the town is re-christened Honolulu. And as incongruous as this may appear, it has its logic. Honolulu is directly opposite Solothurn—on the other side of the world!

GETTING THERE:

Trains arrive at Solothurn's main railway station on a frequent basis from Bern. Note, though, that the trains leave from their own platform area on the lower concourse at Bern station.

By car, Solothurn, almost due north of Bern, is reached by taking the E-25 autoroute.

PRACTICALITIES:

The **Dialing Code** for Solothurn is 32. The **Tourist Office** *(Solothurn Tourismus)*, ☎ 622 15 15 or Fax 623 16 32, Hauptgasse 69, CH-4500 Solothurn, is open Monday to Friday from 8:30 a.m. to midday and 1:30-6 p.m., and Saturday from 9 a.m. to midday.

ACCOMMODATION:

The **Hotel Krone ★★★★**, ☎ 622 44 12 or Fax 622 37 24, Hauptgasse 64, CH-4500 Solothurn, is a delightfully traditional hotel located in the center of the Old Town. Expect comfortable, well equipped rooms, charming public areas and a fine restaurant. $$

The **Hotel Baseltor**, ☎ 622 34 22 or Fax 622 18 79, Hauptgasse 79, CH-4500 Solothurn, is an absolutely enchanting small hotel housed within a three-hundred-year-old town house. Rooms are neat, clean and well appointed, and a Mediterranean style restaurant is on site. It has been honored as the "Most environmentally friendly town hotel in Switzerland." $$

FOOD AND DRINK:

Asian Food Self-Service Restaurant (am Marktplatz) An ideal place for an inexpensive snack. It is open Monday to Wednesday from 10 a.m. to 8 p.m., Thursday from 10 a.m. to 11 p.m., Friday from 10 a.m. to 9 p.m., Saturday from 8:30 a.m. to 8 p.m. and Sunday from 11 a.m. to 7 p.m. ☎ 623 40 83. $

SUGGESTED TOUR:

The tour begins at the **main railway station** *(Hauptbahnhof)* (1), from where you take the aptly-named Hauptbahnhofstrasse, which runs at a ninety-degree angle away from the station, to the **Kreuzackerbrücke** which crosses over the Aare river to the Old Town. Here you will find an array of fascinating buildings. The first, just to the left of the bridge, is the Besenval Palace and connected to that by a small garden, is the imposing **Landhaus**, which dates from 1722 and is easily recognized by its large sloping roof.

Kroneng leads away from the bridge and soon, to the right and laid back behind a small square, you will come upon the façade of the **Natural History Museum** (2). This, one of the most modern of its kind in Switzerland, operates under the theory that visitors should not just see, but touch also. It does, though, have rather strange opening hours; Tuesday, Wednesday and Friday from 2–5 p.m., Thursday from 2–9 p.m., and Saturday from 10 a.m. to midday and 2–5 p.m.

The most dominant structure in Solothurn sits just up the street, across from the Hotel Krone. Reached by a sweeping stone stairway of eleven steps,

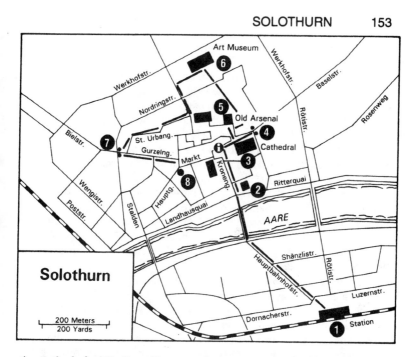

the **Cathedral of St. Ours** (3) towers above every other building, and has a most impressive tower. The inside, somewhat austere, as is the norm for Swiss cathedrals, has eleven bells and eleven altars. It is open from 6 a.m. to midday and 2–7 p.m., but closes at 6 p.m. in winter.

Just across from the Cathedral is the tourist office, but it is worth taking a short detour here along to the **Basel Gate** (4). From the town side it's quite bland, but from the outside impressive. From that vantage point you will see a central tower, with a portcullis of course, dominated by a figure of a knight, rather unusual horizontal arrow slits on the bastions and, on each side, two smaller towers. These days the main doorway is used as a road, so pedestrians are relegated to a minor pathway to the right.

Back inside the Old Town, a right turn will bring you past another of those brightly painted, slightly quixotic, water fountain/statues, one of eleven in Solothurn, and face-to-face with a really fascinating building. Even from the outside its allure is unmistakable. Its massive façade is dominated by a steeply sloping roof, which tapers the levels above the third floor. Two great wooden doors guard the ground-floor level. Formidable it looks, and formidable it was meant to be. In the old days of the Swiss Confederation, power in a city-state was symbolized by two buildings; the Arsenal, of which this is a perfect example, and the Town Hall, which, in Solothurn, is just around the corner. That building, with its elaborate and ornate façade— constructed over a period of time between 1476 and 1711, is not a part of this tour, though you may wish to give it a look if you have a bit of extra time. Back to the armory—although an earlier armory was located on this site in the mid-15th century, this one, unlike others of its genre, was built solely for military purposes between 1609 and 1614. It is now designated an ancient monument of Switzerland and, appropriately, houses the ***Old Arsenal Museum** *(Altes Zeughaus)*(5). Although the subject may not, at first thought, set your blood boiling, it really is one of the more fascinating museums in Switzerland. In addition to a vast collection of weapons—one of Europe's largest, the six floors contain an array of fascinating military exhibits, including uniforms, drums, swords, huge muskets, canons and even an armored personnel carrier. Among those, the Armor Room, where over 400 suits of armor are lined up in battle order beneath a beautiful wooden beamed ceiling, is the most impressive. Exhibits are open May to October on Tuesday to Sunday from 10 a.m. to midday and 2–5 p.m.; and November to April, Tuesday to Friday, from 2–5 p.m., and Saturday and Sunday from 10 a.m. to midday and 2–5 p.m.

Turn left and climb the hill beside the museum, passing delightful old houses along the way. To the right, you cannot miss the round Riedholz Tower—one of eleven in Solothurn, that reinforces one of the corner fortifications of the old walls. Pass through those walls now and, immediately facing you across the Nordringstrasse in a pleasant park area, is the traditional façade of the **Fine Arts Museum** (6). You can barely fail to notice it as several statues of nude women point the way. Once inside, look for a fine collection of post-1850 Swiss art—along with Old Masters including the "Solothurn Madonna" painted in 1522 by Hans Holbein the Younger. It is open Tuesday to Sunday from 10 a.m. to midday and 2–5 p.m., with an extension on Thursday evening to 9 p.m. Also found in the park area are the Concert Hall and a Protestant Church that is dominated by a huge spire.

Cross back over Nordringstrasse and pass through another gate back into the Old Town where you will be greeted by the Franciscan Church, one of eleven in Solothurn, which is just in front of the Town Hall. Turn right here and travel along the tiny St. Urbangasse, which is lined by small, ancient, wooden shuttered houses with irregular roofs. Continue along to another gateway through the walls, the **Biel Gate** (7). This, actually an integral part of a clock tower, dates from the 13th and 14th centuries, and its exterior merits your attention. You will also find an array of houses, each distinctive in style and character, built into the wall and, looking to the right, a monumental round tower with an odd-shaped roof, the Buri Tower, which dates from 1534.

Pass back inside the walls and take a few moments to investigate Gurzelngasse, one of Solothurn's main shopping streets which, if you are visiting on a Wednesday or a Saturday, you will find lined with a colorful display of fresh produce. This street is also home, oddly enough, to the museum honoring the Polish freedom fighter and hero Tadeusz Kociuszko.

Marktplatz (8), at the bottom of Gurzelngasse, is the social hub of Solothurn. Here, standing sentry, is a colossal clock tower, indwelled by enchanting animated figures designed to lie dormant until the toll of the hour would bring them, magically, to life. I must report, however, that, on my last visit, the clock's hands were curiously missing and, therefore, I did not have the opportunity to verify that the characters were still operational. Here, also, is another colorful water fountain, this one topped by a bearded knight proudly holding a shield in his left hand and a flag staff in the other. Obviously, he feels that he is in no danger, as his enormous sword remains sheathed in his belt.

Marktplatz is a timely place to rest for a while, and take stock of your options. My favorite, if the season, timing and weather permit, is the **boat cruise** between Solothurn and Biel/Bienne. In addition to being considered one of Switzerland's most attractive trips, it offers a unique opportunity to disembark at Altreu and visit the country's largest colony of storks. The journey from Biel/Bienne to Bern can then be made by train. If this trip interests you, please be aware that, due to restrictive sailing times, it really does have to be coordinated in advance. It may well be more convenient to travel early to Biel/Bienne, take the boat trip in the opposite direction, and then take your tour of Solothurn.

The other option is a leisurely stroll back over to the Cathedral, from which point you can retrace your steps back to the railway station, and a train that will return you to Bern.

Thun

Tools, weapons and utensils excavated locally, and now on display in the castle museum, indicate that the earliest inhabitants of this area date as far back as the Late Stone Age, around 2500 BC. Although derived from the Celtic name *Dunum*, meaning a fenced hill, the name of Lake Thun and Thun itself was not authenticated until around AD 700.

In the early 12th century the Barons of Thun are first mentioned in historical annals. Very late in the same century Duke Berchtold of Zähringen conquered and expanded the town and also, around 1190, built the castle that still stands today. By 1218 the County of Kyburg had succeeded the House of Zähringen, though they ruled less than fifty years. In 1264, Countess Elisabeth of Kyburg granted Thun a City Charter with special privileges, and these documents are now in safe keeping in the town hall. With the 14th century came a barrage of civic problems so severe that Thun was put under the rule of Bern. Consequently, in 1384, the castle was taken over by the Bernese authorities as the residence for their governors and mayors. Among the highlights of the next century were the construction of the Town Hall and the expansion of the guilds. In the 16th century, Thun joined in the Reformation movement.

Today, Thun has a population of around 40,000 and is, perhaps surprisingly for such a low figure, Switzerland's tenth-largest city. With the castle still dominating the skyline, and the Bernese Oberland as a backdrop, it remains an interesting example of a quaint medieval town, and well worth a visit.

GETTING THERE:

Trains arrive at Thun on a regular basis from Bern. Be careful, though, in your selection. The slow "stopping" train takes nearly twice as long as a non-stopping express.

By car, Thun, less than 30 kilometers (under 20 miles) almost due south of Bern, is reached by the N-6 highway.

PRACTICALITIES:

The **Dialing Code** for Thun is 33. The **Tourist Office** *(Thun Tourismus)*,

☎ 222 23 40 or Fax 222 83 23, Bahnhofplatz, CH-3600 Thun, is located in the railway station. It is open September to June, Monday to Friday from 9 a.m. to midday and 1–6 p.m., and Saturday from 9 a.m. to midday. During July and August hours are Monday to Friday from 9 a.m. to 7 p.m., and Saturday 9 a.m. to midday and 1–4 p.m.

ACCOMMODATION:

The **Schlosshotel Freienhof ✶✶✶✶**, ☎ 227 50 50 or Fax 227 50 55, Freienhofgasse 3, CH-3600 Thun, a member of the Best Western organization, has a marvelous façade, a long history and a privileged position on the peninsula in the Aare river, in a central location in the old part of town. Expect to find 63 traditionally decorated rooms, but with all modern conveniences. The restaurant has an International style cuisine, and specializes in fish. $$

The **Hotel Krone ✶✶✶✶**, ☎ 227 88 88 or Fax 227 88 90, Rathausplatz, CH-3600 Thun, located in the Town Hall square of Thun, has a delightful medieval exterior. Inside, spacious rooms have a contemporary decor, and every modern convenience. It also features, strangely, French and Chinese restaurants. $$

The **Hotel Emmental**, ☎ 222 01 20 or Fax 222 01 30, Bernstrasse 2, CH-3600 Thun, an establishment that has been serving travelers since 1898, has recently undergone a thorough renovation. A pretty chalet-style exterior conceals comfortable, modern rooms, a restaurant, bar and sun terrace. $

FOOD AND DRINK:

Kaffeebar Mühleplatz (Mühleplatz 1) is located right next to the Mühlebrücke bridge and, with its impressive menu of cocktails and other drinks, is a great place to soak up the ambiance of this charming old town. Open daily from 10 a.m. to 11:30 p.m. and until 1:30 a.m. on Friday and Saturday nights.

SUGGESTED TOUR:

Leave from the **station** (1), taking Bahnhofstrasse, which runs at a ninety-degree angle to the left from it. Shortly you will come to the Bahnhofbrücke, which crosses you over the fast-flowing, outer branch of the Aare to the narrow island nestled between the river's channels. Travel now along Freienhofgasse, a charming street lined with interesting shops, which bisects the island, to Sinnebrücke, the bridge across the other channel of the Aare. This takes you into the old part of town.

At this point lovers of pop art and photo realism might want to turn right and follow the road around to the **Museum of Fine Arts** *(Kunstmuseum)* (2). Housed in the former Grand-Hôtel Thunerof is a representative collection of 20th-century, mainly Swiss, works in those media. Visit Tuesday to Sunday from 10 a.m. to 5 p.m., with an extension until 9 p.m. on Wednesday.

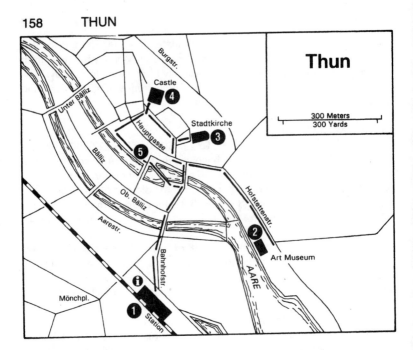

Thun

300 Meters
300 Yards

Castle ④

Stadtkirche ③

⑤

Art Museum ②

ⓘ

① Station

Mönchpl.

Others, and those returning from the museum, will continue on, turning left at Obere Hauptgasse where, to the right and just after a clothes and drug store, you will find a staircase that leads to the castle. This is not an ordinary old staircase. These wooden steps, built with a very low rise, are covered with a wooden roof. At the top you have a choice—the castle or the church? In fact, the latter, **Stadtkirche** (3), which dates from around 1330 and boasts an impressive clock tower, is rarely open, so it may not be worth those extra steps up to it. Carry on, instead, to ***Thun Castle** (*Schloss Thun*) (4). For a basic history of this structure refer to the introduction to this chapter, above. The main attraction here, besides the building itself, is the multi-faceted **Castle Museum** (*Schlossmuseum*), housed in the formidable tower. Located on several floors, the exhibits are impressively varied and, in addition to giving an insight into the region's cultural development, it offers some enlightenment as to how the castle itself evolved throughout the history of Thun. Also from the tower, there are views of the Bernese Oberland in the distance beyond Lake Thun. Opening hours are daily April, May and October from 10 a.m. to 5 p.m.; June through September from 9 a.m. to 6 p.m., and the remainder of the year from 1–4 p.m.

As you exit the castle, note, if you missed it on your arrival, the small, sloping field which is home to miniature goats, geese and an apparently shy horse. Follow the steps down and around to the right of the castle, passing an attractive chalet along the way. Pause here for a moment to admire the views, not only of the Alps but of a delightfully haphazard collection of red-tiled roofs below you. Another of those covered wooden staircases soon presents itself but, as you will note on the descent, this is in less than pristine shape and, unfortunately, is decorated—if that's the descriptive word—with graffiti. Nevertheless, these steps deposit you back into the Old Town and out onto the pretty Rathausplatz, dominated by the Town Hall and Hotel Krone. Follow the inner Aare to the left and soon you will come to a small plaza by the **Mühlebrücke** (5). Stop here for a while, maybe having a drink at the Kaffeebar Mühleplatz, and just enjoy the tranquillity of the surroundings. Swans and ducks move gracefully over the clear water while the typically Swiss, centuries-old houses stand vigil over their comings and goings.

When you are ready to press on, cross the water via the old covered sluice bridge immediately in front of you. Note, as you pass over it, the fascinating machinery that operated the ancient gates. At the end, a narrow passage runs alongside the river and ends at the Sinnebrücke. Near that junction you will find the charming Ponte Restaurante Pizzaria. Its outdoor tables, resting under weeping willow trees and overlooking the river, make a wonderfully relaxing place to stop for a while. Then, continue towards the bridge and a right turn will allow you to retrace the original route back to the railroad station.

Geneva:

(Genève, Genf)

Tour #1

The geographical location of Geneva, set in the far south-western corner of Lake Geneva *(Lac Léman)* where the fast-flowing Rhône River leaves the lake and continues its meandering way to the Mediterranean, has made it a strategically important site for thousands of years. There is evidence of human occupancy around the shores of Lac de Genève, as the locals prefer to call it, dating back to around 3000 BC. It is likely, though, that it wasn't until nearly 500 BC that the Celtic Allobroges clan settled in the area, and built a stockade on the hill that is now the Old Town of Geneva.

Between 122 and 120 BC the Romans defeated the Allobroges, making the settlement a major stronghold. In 58 BC Julius Caesar destroyed its bridge to prevent the Helvetic people, who later gave their name to the country, from escaping the invading Barbarians and fleeing into the Roman Empire. In fact, his account of the event in "Comments on the Gallic Wars," penned six years later, contains the first known written reference to Geneva. The town thrived under Roman rule, and shortly before AD 400 it was awarded the status of a bishopric, at the center of a huge diocese. The Roman influence is still in evidence today. Geneva's oldest square, Bourg-de-Four, was formerly a Roman Forum, and there are extensive, and well restored, remains underneath the Cathedral of St. Pierre.

The Germanic Burgundian tribe displaced the Romans in 443 and, for the next six hundred years, control of the city passed from one faction to another. Beginning in the 11th century through to the Reformation, Geneva was a part of the Holy Roman Empire, yet was governed by its bishops as their own seigneury. Although Geneva didn't gain any real importance until the 15th century, when its trade fairs placed it on the world's map, it was continually under threat from the neighboring House of Savoy. The attacks were particularly strong during the first three decades of the 16th century, when the use of reinforcements from the cantons of Fribourg and Bern was necessary to preserve the city's autonomy.

The year 1535 saw the triumph of the Reformation, and Geneva attained the political status of a republic. A year later Jean Calvin arrived to live in the city and, under his leadership, the Republic was elevated to "Mother of the Protestant Church." From that time forward large numbers of Protestants, many fleeing persecution in neighboring countries, found their way to Geneva, establishing it as a city of faith and learning. These influences led, in 1559, to the founding of the Academy, the predecessor of the current university.

The night of December 11 is the anniversary of an event that is still commemorated in Geneva to this day. On this date in 1602, forces led by Charles-Emmanuel, Duke of Savoy, tried, unsuccessfully, to storm the city. The French term *Escalade* makes reference to this ill-fated attempt to scale Geneva's walls, and is the name given to the three-day festival weekend, held annually in mid-December to celebrate the event.

The 18th and 19th centuries were periods of prosperity for Geneva, as it blossomed into an important center for industry—particularly watchmaking, commerce, banking, arts, medicine and science. Among its more prominent citizens of that era were Jean-Jacques Rousseau, Voltaire and the biologist Charles Bonnet. In 1798 French troops entered, and annexed, Geneva (where Napoleon stopped for one night on May 9, 1800) and it remained a part of France until the defeat of the French forces resulted in its freedom, on December 31, 1813. Determining the time to be right, Geneva joined the Swiss Confederation and became a canton on May 19, 1815. Yet another, and the last to date, revolution took place in 1846, and the new constitution forged from that conflict is still in use today.

Geneva is renowned for its international connections. The first of these to claim the city for its headquarters was the International Committee of the Red Cross, founded in 1864. In 1919, following World War I, it was chosen as the seat for the League of Nations. After the Second World War, in 1945, New York City became the headquarters of the newly-founded United Nations Organization, successor to the League of Nations, but Geneva remained its European base. This trend has continued and, today, many other international organizations, numbering around 200, make Geneva their headquarters. In return, the city has gained affluence and a cosmopolitan ambiance; a fascinating combination considerably enhanced by a decidedly Gallic flair. Art and culture flourish here too; Geneva hosts thirty museums exhibiting a variety of prestigious collections, and is justly proud of its musical conservatories and opera.

With its lakeside location and mountainous backdrop, many beautiful parks, and world-famous towering water fountain, the *Jet d'Eau,* Geneva truly is a delightful place to visit, and no one will leave unimpressed.

GETTING THERE:

By air, international flights arrive at Geneva's Cointrin International Airport, just six minutes by train from the main railway station, from destinations around the world.

Trains arrive at Geneva's main railway station *(Gare de Cornavin)* from all other cities in Switzerland, and from neighboring countries.

By car, Geneva, in the southwestern corner of Switzerland, is easily reached by road from all parts of the country, as well as from neighboring France.

PRACTICALITIES:

The **Dialing Code** for Geneva is 22. The **Tourist Office** *(Genève Tourisme)*, ☎ 909 70 00, Fax 909 70 11 or E-mail info@geneva-tourism.ch, is located at 3, rue du Mont-Blanc, CH-1201 Genève. It is open September to June 14, Monday to Saturday from 9 a.m. to 6 p.m.; June 16 through August, Monday to Friday from 8 a.m. to 7 p.m. and Saturday and Sunday from 9 a.m. to 6 p.m. Additional tourist offices are located at the Gare de Cornavin, ☎ 738 52 00, open September to June 14, Monday to Saturday from 9 a.m. to 6 p.m.; June 16 through August, Monday to Friday from 9 a.m. to 8 p.m. and Saturday and Sunday from 9 a.m. to 6 p.m. At the International Airport, ☎ 788 08 80, an office opens daily, year round, from 9:30 a.m. to 10 p.m. Hotel reservations *(Informations hôtelières)* may be made by calling 909 70 20 or faxing 909 70 21. A wealth of information about Geneva is found on the **Internet** at www.geneva-tourism.ch.

Personal computers are not as common in Europe as they are in the USA and, generally, Internet connection is considerably more expensive. Consequently, market forces have given rise to establishments where the public may rent the use of a computer for a given amount of time. Not bland, as you might expect, these usually take the form of cafés, or small bars. So, when in Geneva, forget the postcard. Send an e-mail "wish you were here" back to family or friends from the **CyberCafé**, ☎ 901 13 13, 7, Rue de Fribourg, CH-1201 Genève, open Monday to Saturday 10 a.m. to 10 p.m.

Bucherer has two stores in Geneva. The one at 45, Rue du Rhône, ☎ 319 62 66 or Fax 319 62 62, has an impressive façade indeed, and is topped by the famous ROLEX symbol and name, and the other is between the tourist office and the railway station, at 22, Rue du Mont-Blanc, ☎ 732 72 16 or Fax 738 45 10.

To purchase **Swiss Army Knives**, watches, kitchen knives, scissors, cork screws, wine stoppers, beautiful cutlery, wooden engraved pen knives, baby sets, frames, rings, key rings, and a whole array of similar souvenirs, the best place to head for is Pastor Frères, ☎ 731 45 19 or Fax 738 82 28, at 7, Rue du Mont-Blanc, which is conveniently located just a few yards from the tourist office. If you fancy, as well, a special gift for that cherished someone in your life, the same brothers operate a very classy jewelry shop adjacent to this store.

As a general rule **shops** in Geneva are open Monday to Friday from 9 a.m. to 6:45 p.m., with department stores and many other shops open until 8 p.m. on Thursday, and on Saturday from 9 a.m. to 5 p.m.

Public transport in and around Geneva on any combination of tramcars, buses, cable cars and ferry boats is clean and efficient. Tickets must be purchased from ticket vending machines, ticket offices or the tourist office, before each trip and are available for single trips or, more advantageously, in the form of an Unlimited Day Pass. The former costs CHF 2.20 for one hour on the city network, and CHF 5 for a day pass.

ACCOMMODATION:

The **Hôtel Du Rhône *****, ☎ 731 98 31, Fax 732 45 58, E-mail mkt@durhone.com or Internet www.durhone.com, Quai Turrettini, CH-1211 Genève 1, the very first hotel opened in Europe after World War II, has a fine city-center location overlooking the fast-flowing Rhône River. A member of the Leading Hotels of the World group it has seven floors that accommodate, in the utmost luxury, 11 suites and 175 rooms all of which have been renovated to include the latest modern facilities. Each includes a desk, two telephone lines—one of which can be used as a fax line, a fax machine with a new private number for each guest, and five telephone handsets. Private bathrooms of fine Greek St. Helena marble, are supplied with fine toiletries, bio-degradable soaps, gels and other accessories by Molton-Brown. $$$

The **Hôtel des Bergues *****, ☎ 731 50 50 or Fax 732 19 89, 33 Quai des Bergues, CH-1201 Genève, a member of the Leading Hotels of the World organization, boasts a prestigious lakeside location only a few minutes away from the commercial and shopping areas of Geneva. Its 99 rooms, including 14 deluxe rooms and 10 suites—graciously individual in character, are appointed with fine fabrics and Louis-Philippe style furnishings. The Bel Etage executive floor offers suites and deluxe accommodations, including the famous Presidential Suite, and one floor is reserved for non-smokers. The L'Amphitryon is an on-site gourmet restaurant specializing in seasonal cuisine and seafood and offering soothing entertainment at its piano bar. No need to forego your fitness routine either, guests have access to a nearby club, equipped with a pool, by arrangement with the concierge. $$$

The **Hôtel Le Warwick ****, ☎ 731 62 50 or Fax 738 99 35, 14, Rue de Lausanne, CH-1201 Genève, is located in the heart of the city, close to both the commercial center and the railway station. It offers 169 rooms recently renovated to the highest standards expected. Look, also, for a fine restaurant, bar and private parking. $$$

The **Hôtel At Home**, ☎ 732 26 93 or Fax 738 44 30, 16, Rue de Fribourg, CH-1201 Genève, is an independent hotel conveniently located just one block across from the railway station. Its single, double and triple rooms, studios and suites are well appointed and modern in style. Studios and apartments may be rented by the month. $$

The **Hôtel Montana ***, ☎ 732 08 40, Fax 738 25 11, E-mail hotel montana@span.ch or Internet http://geneva.yop.ch/hotels/montana, 23, Rue des Alpes, CH-1201 Genève, is found in one of the streets that run at a tangent directly across from the railway station. It has forty well furnished rooms, some with three beds, and all modern facilities including sound proofing. A Continental buffet breakfast is included in the price. $$

The **Hôtel Windsor** ***, ☎ 731 71 30, Fax 731 93 25 or Internet http://geneva.yop.ch/hotels/windsor, 31, Rue de Berne and 12, Rue de Neuchâtel, CH-1201 Genève covers the width of a city block and, thus, the address designates entrances on two streets. Again, just a couple of blocks from the railway station, this has well appointed, comfortable rooms at reasonable rates. $$

The **Hôtel Capitole** ***, ☎ 909 86 26 or Fax 741 22 45, 15 Rue de Berne, CH-1201 Genève, located just a couple of minutes from the railway station, offers 32 rooms furnished in a pleasant, modern style. Guests may enjoy a meal, snack or favorite drink in the on-site pub. $

The **Hôtel Des Tourelles** **, ☎ 732 44 23, Fax 732 76 20 or E-mail 100700.1151@compuserve.com, 2, Boulevard James-Fazy, CH-1201, Genève, is within a charming 19th-century building that overlooks the Rhône river. Its 23 comfortable rooms combine a flavor of the past with modern comforts, at very reasonable rates indeed. They even have a three-bedded room for between CHF 110 to 140. $

The **Hôtel Saint-Gervais** *, ☎ and Fax 732 45 72, 20 Rue des Corps-Saints, Ch-1201 Genève, is a small, rather basic, hotel just one minute by foot from the railway station. $

The **Swiss Youth Hostels**, ☎ 732 62 60, 30, Rue Rothschild, CH-1202 Genève, are simple, basic and clean with low rates that include breakfast and sheets. $

Genève Tourisme operates a **Budget Hôtels** scheme for people visiting any day of the week in January, February, July, August, November or December, and on weekends (Friday to Monday) or bank holidays the rest of the year. They also offer a variety of **packages** throughout the year, of which the weekend plan will appeal to many readers. These cover from one to three nights accommodation. Rates, per person per night, include breakfast, VAT, taxes and service; a 2-hour-long city tour; a voucher book offering an assortment of privileges and discounts and some helpful documentation about Geneva. Those booking for two nights or more also receive two days free travel on the city's transportation system. Further details are available from the tourist office, or hotel reservation office, the numbers for which are listed in the PRACTICALITIES section.

Those wishing to stay at a **Bed and Breakfast** establishment in Geneva may want to call 707 16 64, Fax 707 16 26 or E-mail bvangess@infomaniak.ch.

FOOD AND DRINK:

Geneva is, decidedly, a city with an international flair boasting numerous, sometimes unusual, ethnic restaurants.

Le Café Rafael (Quai Turrettini, in the Hôtel Du Rhône) With seating for 90 indoors and 30 additional on the terrace, Rafael features an Art-Deco design with a relaxed and informal ambiance. Its light, seasonal, menu, based on Nouvelle Cuisine, changes daily, and is supplemented on occasions throughout the year when outstanding chefs visiting from around the world are invited to showcase their skills. Open daily from 7 a.m. to midnight. ☎ 731 98 31. $$$

Aux Halles de l'Ile Café Restaurant Terrasses (1, Place de l'Ile) is worth considering for location alone, set apart on an island in the midst of the fast flowing Rhône. The menu, though fairly small, is innovatively International in selection. ☎ 311 52 21. $$

Hung Wan (7, Quai du Mont Blanc) is prominently positioned alongside the lake. A Chinese restaurant is a must in any International selection and this, serving the highest level of traditional Chinese cuisine, is one of the best. ☎ 731 73 30. $$

Swiss Cottage (6, Rue Barton) is one that, though not international in style, has a flavor that shouldn't be overlooked. On the ground floor there is a bar, a small café and a souvenir boutique, but it is the main dining room on the upper level that is the real attraction. The walls are embellished with the most imaginative murals of typical Swiss scenes that you are ever likely to see, and prove a perfect backdrop to an equally imaginative array of fondues, raclette, fish and meat dishes. ☎ 732 40 00. $$

Restaurant La Péliserrie (Rue de la Péliserrie) is a very neat restaurant and bar that serves traditional French and Italian cuisine. Closed Saturday lunch time and Sunday. ☎ 310 10 39. $$

Shahi Restaurant (2, Place de Cornavin) is located on the first floor of a building diagonally across from the railway station. Open daily, it serves spicy Indian and Pakistani dishes illustrative of these countries' cuisine, and offers an impressive hot buffet at lunchtime. If you decide to dine in your hotel room, place a take-away order by calling 738 44 36. $

Tamaris (6 Place de la Navigation) is a Turkish restaurant serving a wide selection of that country's typical regional dishes. Closed Sunday. ☎ 732 96 25. $

La Marina Tavern (8, Rue du Simplon) is a typical Greek taverna specializing in local cuisine from that country and Cyprus. Open in the afternoon and evenings from Tuesday to Friday, and Saturday evening. ☎ 736 74 02. $

El Faro (5, Rue de Fribourg) is, surprisingly, one of three Spanish restaurants found on this street. These are common in Switzerland

and this one features all of the customary dishes one would expect, as well as an enticing array of tapas. ☎ 732 21 98. $

Chez Uchino (66, Rue de Zürich) is a very small, and very reasonably priced, Japanese restaurant located next door to a Japanese store. ☎ 755 10 32. $

Khmer Angkor Restaurant Cambodgien, (31, Rue du Môle) is a little difficult to find, but well worth the bother. It seems that all the Cambodians resident in, or visiting, Geneva congregate here, and the authentic ambiance is subtly matched by the exotically prepared dishes. Open Monday to Friday from 11 a.m. to 3 p.m. and 7 p.m. to midnight, Saturday from 7 p.m. to midnight, closed Sunday. ☎ 732 38 43. $

El-Halal El-Tayep (44, Rue de Lausanne), found on the main road to the left of the railway station, is a place for the adventurous. This typical Iraqi tea house and small restaurant serves a good couscous dish, but no alcohol. ☎ 738 54 98. $

Restaurant Manora (6, rue Cornavin) has a most unlikely location— the Placette department store, but despite that it shouldn't be missed. The fare is self-served from innovatively arranged stages that each specialize in a different type of food—meat, fish, cheese, vegetables, fruits etc. ☎ 909 44 10. $

SUGGESTED TOUR: THE OLD TOWN AND JET D'EAU

From the **tourist office** (1), on the Rue du Mont-Blanc, walk down to the Rhône river. Then stroll, again to the right, along the Quai des Bergues to the Place St. Gervais where, by the fourth bridge, your attention will be drawn to an equestrian statue featuring a nude woman. Next cross the river, and the island which sits in the middle of it, noting just how swiftly the river flows out of Lac Léman.

The opposite side of the river, initially at least, is rather more modern. Here you will pass a combination of shops, offices and apartments along your way through the Place Bel-Air and Rue Corraterie to the **Place Nueve** (2). This square, new in name but older in character; is surrounded by some memorable buildings. The **Rath Museum** *(Musée Rath)*, housed in a Greek-style colonnaded building opened in 1825, is considered to be the first building in Switzerland dedicated to exhibiting the fine arts. It's open Tuesday, Thursday, Friday, Saturday and Sunday from 10 a.m. to 5 p.m. and Wednesday from midday to 9 p.m. To its right are two other delightful edifices. First is the **Grand Théâtre**, Geneva's opera house, inspired by the Paris Opera and built in 1879. For some unknown reason you can only visit on Thursday, from 12:30–1:30 p.m. Second is the **Conservatoire de musique de Genève**, a delightful Florentine-style building dating from 1856.

To the left are the walls of the Old Town and, in their shadows, a bust of the founder of the Red Cross. In the center of the square stands an eques-

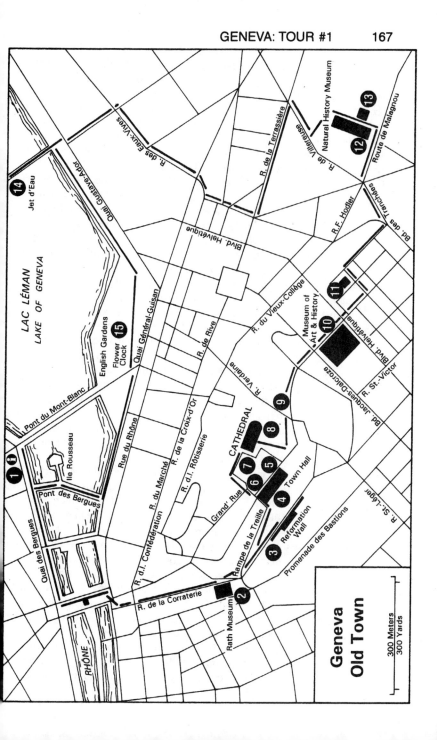

Geneva
Old Town

300 Meters
300 Yards

trian statue of Genèvese **Général Henri Dufour**, a national hero and cartographer of the first geographical map of Switzerland. Take a few moments to explore the park across the road. The **Promenade des Bastions** (3), chosen in 1816 as the site of Geneva's first botanical gardens, is delightful indeed. Although that garden is now officially housed elsewhere, lovely plants and trees remain here as testimony to its former use. The impressive building to the right, the Palais Eynard, has been put to a variety of uses but is now a part of the University. Just across from that, and almost underneath the ramparts, is the **Reformation Wall** (Mur dés Réformateurs), built in 1917. This will be the main attraction for visitors to the Promenade. Here there are large, and appropriately rather somber, sculpted figures of the leading lights of the Reformation period: Jean Calvin, Théodore de Bèze, John Knox and Guillame Farel. And you'll note Geneva's motto Post Tenebras Lux—After the Darkness, the Light; "Darkness" referring to the times before the Reformation and "Light" to those after, when they believed the Bible was finally understood. A reminder here not to ignore the more aesthetic attributes of this park. Take a few moments to relax and enjoy a drink, maybe even a snack, at the open-air restaurant near the gates where you entered.

The illustrious Old Town of Geneva now beckons from above. To get there take the Rampe de Treille that leads from the Place Neuve. Yes, Rampe does mean "ramp," and it is quite steep too; but the trees on the right side offer considerable shade and the architectural characteristics of the houses to the left provide an interesting diversion. The long, rectangular promenade at the top, embellished with a statue or two, offers an ideal vantage point from which to gain a better perspective of both the park below and the surrounding hills. You may be surprised, also, at just how close the city is to the countryside. In the middle of the promenade one small street leads, through a colonnaded archway, into the Old Town proper, where the two interesting buildings face each other at the first crossroads.

Immediately to the right is the **Town Hall** (Hôtel de Ville) (4) originally constructed in the 15th century, but with substantial additions over the next two centuries. It now houses Geneva's parliament, and boats international connections too. In 1864 the First Geneva Convention on the Red Cross met here. Eight years later the international arbitration between the USA and Great Britain, to resolve their "Alabama" dispute, was held in what is now known as the "Alabama Room." Not to be overlooked, either, is the unusual square ramp of the staircase specifically designed to facilitate access for messengers on horseback. Back outside, and more striking, is the building directly across from the Town Hall. On the open ground floor area, five original cannons—dating from the 17th and 18th centuries—once part of Geneva's artillery, give a resounding clue as to one of its former uses. Though built as a granary in the 15th century, it was converted for use as an arms depot in 1720, and is now known as the **Arsenal** (5). The rooms above serve as the state archives, and are open to the public Monday to Saturday from 9 a.m. to 5 p.m. The three mosaics adorning the walls depict the arrival of Julius Caesar in Geneva, Middle Age fairs at the Bourg-de-Four and the arrival of the Huguenot refugees in the city. If you happen to be in Geneva during the Escalade festivities, make a point to stop by here and buy some vegetable soup, which is sold in commemorative bowls.

Though the Cathedral might seem the next logical stop, I recommend you explore a little of the Old Town first. Walking away from the Town Hall and Arsenal along the cobblestoned Grand Rue, you will come upon a series of very solid five-story buildings that house an eclectic array of bars, pubs, and art, antique and antique book shops. Continue on, turning right into Rue de Pélisserie where, at the end, a plaque on one of the houses honors George Eliot, and announces that the celebrated English author lived there between October 1849 and March 1850. Another right will bring you into Rue Jean Calvin, which is named for this famed theologian and reformer of Geneva who lived from 1509 to 1564, and holds some pleasant surprises. The **Barbier-Mueller Museum** (6) ☎ 312 02 70, Rue Jean Calvin 10, has art exhibits from Africa, Oceania, the islands of South-East Asia and the Americas. It is open daily from 11 a.m. to 5 p.m.

At the end of the street another grand fountain, and an accompanying tiny horse fountain, stand before a shortcut to the Cathedral. Detour for the moment, though, to visit the museum just around the corner. The **Maison Tavel** (7), ☎ 310 29 00, Rue du Puits-Saint-Pieree 6, originally constructed by the Tavel family as their private residence during the 12th century is the oldest private house in Geneva. With the exception of the cellars, however, it was destroyed by the fire of 1334. Subsequently reconstructed and then remodeled in the 17th and 18th centuries, it now houses exhibits from the Middle Ages to the 19th century related to the history of, and evolution of life in, Geneva. Visit Tuesday to Sunday from 10 a.m. to 5 p.m.

Return now to the small horse fountain, and take the shortcut to the ***Cathedral of St. Peter** (Cathédrale Saint-Pierre) (8). This was built between 1160 and 1232 and it is somewhat of an architectural hybrid, having elements of Romanesque, Gothic and Greco-Roman styles. Although of grand proportions it, like most in Switzerland, reflects the effects of the Reformation and is rather austere inside. Enlightened by beautiful stained-glass windows, the main attractions are the amazingly intricate tomb of the Duke of Rohan, leader of the French Protestants who died in 1638, and the cleverly sculptured choir. The tower, with its 157 steps, awaits those with the energy to claim a marvelous **view** of Geneva. Visitors wanting to more fully investigate the art from the Cathedral may visit the Museum of Art and History. The Cathedral opens January, February, November and December from 9 a.m. to midday and 2–5 p.m.; March, April, May and October from 9 a.m. to midday and 2–6 p.m.; and June, July, August and September from 9 a.m. to midday. Mass is held on Sunday at 10 a.m.; during July and August there is a bell concert at 5 p.m. and between June and September there is organ music for an hour at 6 p.m. Do not leave, however, before exploring underneath the Cathedral, where you will find one of the largest European subterranean archaeological sites that is open to the public. The size and array of exhibits is most impressive indeed though, sadly, there are no descriptions in English. The **Archaeological Site of St. Peter's Cathedral,** ☎ 738 56 50, Cour Saint-Pierre, is open Tuesday to Sunday from 10 a.m. to 1 p.m. and 2–6 p.m.

Exit from the archaeological site on the side of the Cathedral and walk up to the Rue Hôtel de Ville, following that down and around to the left, to arrive in the **Place du Bourg-de-Flour** (9). Beginning in the Roman era, carrying through the Middle Age Fairs and even to present times this square has, traditionally, been one of the city's main meeting places. A strange bronze statue of a nymph welcomes you on arrival, and it is a good idea to take a seat at one of the many cafés just to soak up the atmosphere. As a bonus you may get a sighting of the towering waters of the Jet d'Eau fountain, if you happen to look down Rue Verdaine.

Leave via the rue de Chaudronniers, passing the Palace de Justice on the way to rue Charles Galland and your next destination, the **Museum of Art and History** (Musée de Art et Histoire) (10), ☎ 418 26 01. This is everything you would expect in a museum; a grand, very classical, façade, elegant staircases and a marvelous inner patio—and that's just the building itself. Built between 1903 and 1909, this structure was donated by Charles Galland (1806–1901), who was a benefactor of the city. It also happens to be Switzerland's only museum whose exhibits, numbering in excess of 1,000,000, relate to the entire span of western culture from its origins to date.

A right out of the museum, still following Galland, will take you across another bridge and into an area of elegant houses. Your curiosity will soon be aroused by the sight, down one of the turnings to the left, of a genuine **Russian Orthodox Church** (Eglise ortodoxe russe) (11). You shouldn't miss the experience of going inside. It's very small, domed, dark and ornate with brown walls adorned by inlaid crosses, modern stained-glass windows, the aroma of incense and, of course, numerous candles. If you want a memorial they will gladly sell you a CD or tape of Russian Orthodox music. Located at 9, Rue Toepffer, ☎ 346 47 09, this opens every morning, with the exception of Monday, from 9 a.m. to 12:30 p.m., and on Saturday afternoon from 2–8 p.m.

The next two destinations, both museums—but very different in character—are not too far away; but it's a rather bland walk. Go back out to Galland, take a left to Boulevard des Tranchées and then turn left again, following up a slight hill to Route de Malagnou where, just across the road and to the right, the gardens and modern building announce that they are a part of the **Natural History Museum** (Musée de Histoire naturelle) (12), ☎ 418 63 00. One of the more modern of its genre in Europe, it offers a very wide array of exhibits, including many animals preserved by the works of taxidermy, that are innovatively displayed. Visit Tuesday to Sunday from 9:30 a.m. to 5 p.m.

A little behind, and set farther back from the road within pretty grounds, you will find (and what could be more appropriate in Switzerland?) the **Clock and Watch Museum** *(Musée de Horlogerie et Emaillerie)* (13), ☎ 418 64 70 or Fax 418 64 71. Modern minded visitors might, erroneously, assume from its name that this has some connection with E-mail. Expect to see watches, clocks, clock-making tools, and snuff boxes etc., most of which were manufactured in Geneva. Find, also, showcases devoted to the Geneva group of enamel workers and the jewelry class of the School of Decorative Arts. And don't be confused, it has nothing at all to do with E-mails! Open Tuesday to Sunday from 10 a.m. to 5 p.m.

You will by now have no doubt, even if you were not previously so informed, that the massive fountain of water emitted from the **Jet d'Eau** (14) is the symbol of this city. So let's not delay a visit there any longer, though, unfortunately, this entails a fairly long walk through a rather uninspiring part of town. Basically, you go around the back of the Clock Museum and work your way down to the Place des Eaux Vives, and the rue of the same name, before taking any one of several turnings to the left. In this instance it is easier to follow the map than to rely on printed directions. Along the way you might want to stop at Number 17 Rue des Eaux-Vives where, at Traiteur, you will find a tantalizingly tempting array of sandwiches. And they are inexpensive too, just the thing to snack on by the banks of Lac Léman.

Now to the fountain itself. Surprisingly, what is now a picturesque scene familiar to people throughout the world was conceived as a matter of practicality. Towards the end of the last century the turbine house on the Rhône river had excess water on days that industrial demand was light. A quick-thinking engineer, Butticaz by name, designed a way to divert this excess water to a fountain, reaching a height of 30 meters (98 feet), outside of the plant. In 1891 the first solely decorative fountain, reaching a height of 90 meters (295 feet), was created in its present position on the lake. This was raised in several stages, and today it gushes 500 liters (132 gallons) a second—which weighs 7,112 Kilograms (7 tons), through an independent pump, to an elevation of 140 meters (459 feet). But don't expect to see it year round! It is turned on to celebrate the coming of spring, at the beginning of March, and operates, weather permitting, until the first Sunday in October. Beginning on the week of Ascension Thursday in May, until its closing, it is illuminated each night. It is possible, also, to walk out towards the jet along the Jetée des Eaux-Vives. Be mindful, though, of the ever-changing waves of spray. In the summer months this, and the surrounding quays, make for delightful places to sunbathe, or just pass the time of day, while swans, ducks, small boats and lake steamers cavort over the glistening waters.

And, this is the scene that greets you as you pass along the Quai Gustav Ador towards the **English Gardens** *(Jardins anglais)* (15), where the Rhône escapes from Lac Léman. There are several attractions here, but the most spectacular, without doubt, is the **Flower Clock** *(Horloge fleurie)*. This was installed in 1955, to commemorating Geneva's long and illustrious watch-making tradition. With a diameter of 5 meters (16.4 feet), a circumference of 15.7 meters (51.5 feet) and a second hand measuring 2.5 meters (8.2 feet), it took no small technical expertise to get the second hand to travel 27 cen-timeters (10.6 inches) each second. The floral decoration changes as well, with as many as 6,300 plants, of varying varieties, comprising each setting. Look, also, in these very pretty gardens, for a dominating statue of Gustav Ador, (1845–1928), and an inscription will tell you he was president of just about every organization that was going. The nearby Four Season's Foun-tain, featuring Neptune with ladies below and children at the top, is a na-tional monument and commemorates Geneva joining the Swiss Federation in 1815.

The tour, proper, ends at the gardens but, behind them and obviously away from the lake, is one of the most important shopping areas in Geneva, especially along the Rue du Rhône. If this idea entices you, look particularly for the Place du Molard. This is the modern city's answer to the Place du Bourg-de-Four, which is just a few hundred feet away up the hill, and it is lined with outdoor cafés and graced by a fountain and a quaint 16th-century tower that was once an entrance in the old walls.

If you are going back across to the other side of the river, don't take the more obvious Pont du Mont-Blanc. Better, instead, to walk alongside the river and down to the next bridge, the Pont des Bergues where, in the mid-dle, you will find a most unusual little island. The **Ile Rousseau** was created in 1583 as a defensive fortification, and later converted to a park. It is named after one of Geneva's most illustrious citizens, the philosopher/writer Jean-Jaques Rousseau, whose statue you will find on the grounds. These days the park is a haven for ducks, swans and other aquatic feathered friends.

Geneva:

(Genève, Genf)

Tour #2

This walking tour features the Right Bank and the United Nations establishment in Geneva.

GETTING THERE:

PRACTICALITIES:

FOOD AND DRINK:
See pages 165–166 for the above.

SUGGESTED TOUR:
Begin, again, at the **tourist office** (1), but this time, as you come to the bottom of Rue du Mont-Blanc, turn left along the attractive Quai du Mont-Blanc. Among the first things you will notice are the steamers moored on the lake, indicative of the many trips originating from here. Continuing, it is a dead certainty that your attention will soon be drawn to the unusual monument in a little park. The elaborate **Brunswick Monument** (2) is actually the tomb of Charles II, Duke of Brunswick who, on condition that the city interred him in a replica of Verona's Scaligeri Mausoleum, left his fortune to Geneva.

Cross to the lakeside where a long narrow park leads up to the Pâquis Plage, a public swimming area. If you prefer not to walk the next stretch of the tour, just board the **Mini-Train Paquis Express,** ☎ 781 04 04 or Fax 781 13 46, for the journey to the **Botanic Gardens** *(Jardin Botanique)*. Though not really a train, it does indeed look like one and runs from March to October, on a daily basis, between 10 a.m. and dusk.

As it rambles on, the Quai du Mont-Blanc transforms itself to the Quai Wilson by the bathing pool, and all along both are huge luxury hotels, the casino and the imposing Palais Wilson. And soon there begins a whole series of absolutely delightful parks, whose imminent arrival is announced by a graceful bronze of **The Youth and the Horse** (L'Adolescent et le Cheval) (3). These days the parks are continuous and, in fact, have no discernible boundaries. Still, each has its own separate identity and intriguing history, and most include a structure, or structures, of not inconsiderable architectural interest. The history of each park is lengthy and complicated, and very well documented on sign boards along the way. Therefore, it is better, I believe, rather than boringly relate them in their entirety here, to allow readers to explore them in their full context—and to the extent of their interest—during the process of the tour. One interesting note, though, is that two of the properties, the Moynier and Perle du Lac, were purchased by the League of Nations in 1926. But, unable to acquire enough land for their needs, they subsequently deeded these to the city in exchange for a portion of the Barembé estate.

History aside, wandering from one to another of these parks as you stroll along the lakeside footpath is a most delightful experience. A wealth of beautiful buildings compete with statues, fountains and arrays of trees, plants and shrubs, along with the activity on the lake, for your attention. And why not rest your legs, and slake your thirst at the same time, at one of the fine restaurants along the way?

The next stop on the itinerary is the **Botanic Gardens** (Jardin Botanique) (4), open daily April to September from 8 a.m. to 7:30 p.m. and between October and March from 9:30 a.m. to 5 p.m., reached via a tunnel passing beneath the road. Very obviously these have thrived since being moved from the Promenade des Bastions in 1904, and as delightful as the parks are, the gardens are more so. Complementary to the expected plant life, expect to find deer, flamingoes, aviaries, ponds, fountains, statues, a 19th-century mansion—Le Chêne, a special conservatory for the herbarium—La Console, and a variety of green houses including a beautiful domed one. There is even a "scent and touch garden" for the pleasure of visually impaired visitors. It is home, also, to a botanical library and the world famous scientific institute. Quite a combination; this is a quiet place to relax in before moving on to the United Nations complex, and more museums.

Take the exit from the gardens that is on the city side and farthest away from the lake, turn right onto Avenue de la Paix, traverse the railway line and walk up the deceptively steep hill. Soon you will come to the Place des Nations, and the main entrance to the United Nations complex. The main entrance, yes, but not the entrance for ordinary visitors like you and me. That is farther up and around the hill, and along the way one really special treat awaits in the gardens to the right.

This once consisted of a surface area of 25.1 hectares (62 acres), forming part of the Barembé estate, which was the property of Gustav Revilliod, a prominent Genèvese citizen. Extensively traveled, he represented the Swiss Federation at such events as the inauguration of the Suez Canal in

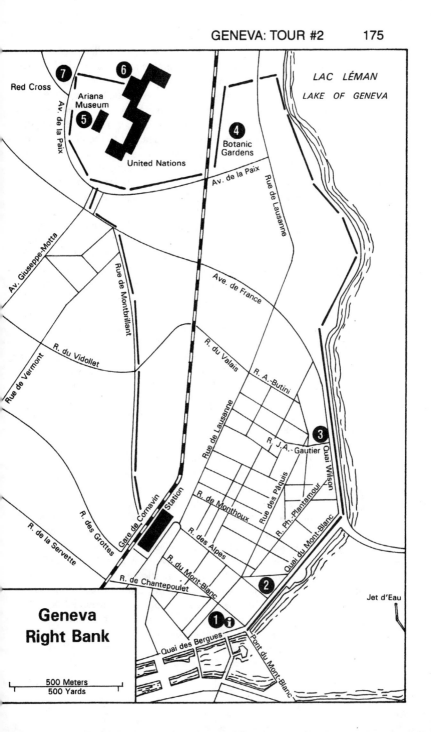

1869. Revilloid also had an inveterate passion for collecting, and he amassed a phenomenal number of objects on his journeys. In 1877 he decided to build an Italian Renaissance-style museum on the grounds to house his treasures, naming it Ariana, after his mother, Arine de la Rive, a member of one of Genève's oldest families. In 1884, he graciously allowed the public admittance to some of its rooms. Upon his death, in 1890, the property, and CHF 1,000,000 for its upkeep, were bequeathed to the city. Fourteen years later, in 1904, the Botanical Gardens were established in the lower part of the grounds, below the railway lines. The remainder of the estate, with the exception of the museum and the immediate land around it, were given to the League of Nations in 1928 in exchange for the two lakeside properties, as described earlier in the tour.

This acquisition enabled that organization to build its headquarters, but at the cost of the Revilloid family home, which was demolished along with various outbuildings and a small zoological gardens. Fortunately, someone had the good sense to preserve the museum itself, and it really is a gem! The classical lines of the domed exterior, attractive in their own right, safeguard an interior that is as beautiful as it is unusual. Its design is deceptive as well; from the outside there is no indication that the main, two-story, hall is oval in shape. Enter now, stepping onto the brown marble floor of the ground level, the perimeter of which is encircled by attractive marble pillars of similar coloring that support the lone upper floor. But, as your attention is drawn upwards, that which immediately surrounds you pales somewhat into insignificance in comparison with the intricate beauty of what rises above. Around the second floor elegant wrought-iron railings connect eighteen marble pillars, each sculpted in a unique, but complementary, helicoidal design. Crowning this majestic display is a ring of stained-glass windows, with one set into the light blue dome above each archway between the columns. Capitalizing on this delightful scene, the authorities have had the insight to create a small café/bar on the higher level where, in agreeable climes, you can sit on the terrace overlooking the U.N. complex.

In 1954 the city opened an International Ceramic Academy in the building. The ***Ariana Museum** *(Musée del'Ariana)* (5), ☎ 734 29 50 or Fax 733 70 11, 10, Avenue de la Paix, is the only museum in Switzerland devoted entirely to the exhibition of ceramics and glass, and boasts a collection of around 18,000 objects. Visit Wednesday to Monday from 10 a.m. to 5 p.m. Just outside the building you will find a majestic Japanese bell, which has an interesting story in its own right. The original, dating from 1657, and the property of a temple in Shinagawa, was lost during the troubled period of Japanese history preceding the fall of the feudal regime around 1867. In 1873, although unaware of its origin, Revilloid rescued the bell from a meltdown and placed it in the museum. In 1930 it was returned home to Japan, and a grateful Shinagawa offered Geneva a consecrated replica that was installed in 1991.

Security, as you might expect, is stringent at Portail Pregny, the entrance to the *United Nations (6), ☎ 907 45 39 or Fax 907 00 32. It is open daily between April to October, from 10 a.m. to midday and 2–4 p.m.; in July and August from 9 a.m. to midday and 2–6 p.m.; and the rest of the year, Monday to Friday from 10 a.m. to midday and 2–4 p.m. It is best to confirm before visiting, however, as these times, and the itineraries, are subject to change in accordance with the demands of the conference program. Expect a request for identification, which will be held by security until you exit. Once approved, you may pass through and walk down to the Visitors Service area located in the main building. Among the highlights of what you will learn during the hour-long guided tour, conducted in any one of your choice of eighteen languages, are the following: The League of Nations was founded by President Woodrow Wilson in 1920. This complex, completed in 1936, has a larger surface area than the Palace of Versailles, located just outside Paris. After the Second World War the League of Nations was succeeded by the United Nations, whose responsibilities are divided between New York—where the political decisions are made, and Genève—where all humanitarian facets are considered. You will also see the conference rooms, previously only visible on television, and learn that, in the old Palais de Nations, materials for its construction and furnishings were donated by different countries. A tapestry from China will most certainly catch your eye, with its optical illusion that a door, no matter what the angle from which it is surveyed, appears always to be facing you. All in all this is a very informative tour, never mind that the guides can be a little too hurried in their delivery. And before leaving you will want to sign the Golden Book for Peace, evidencing your support of the United Nation's never-ending crusade for peace. You may also purchase a personalized "Pass for Peace," available at either the U.N. or the tourist office, whose CHF 25 cost includes the entry fee and guided tour.

Philatelists will enjoy the U.N. also. In 1962 the United Nations Philatelic Museum was opened to house the Charles Mistelli collection. This Genèvese doctor began collecting postage stamps, envelopes etc., relating to the League of Nations, in 1919, and those relating to the United Nations and its specialized agencies in 1951. His collection was purchased using funds raised by the sale of a special stamp issued by the Swiss Post Office and sold on premises provided by the United Nations Organization. The exhibition is now enhanced by audiovisual presentations, a readers' corner with philatelic publications from around the world and various temporary displays. Visit Monday to Friday from 10 a.m. to midday and 2–4 p.m.

Almost directly across from the United Nations is the **International Red Cross and Red Crescent Museum** (Musée de la Croix-Rouge) (7), ☎ 733 26 60, Fax 734 57 23 or www.micr.ch, 17, Avenue de la Paix. This specialized museum, modern in style, utilizes state-of-the-art audiovisual demonstrations to showcase the organizations' activities over its 130-year history. Open Wednesday through Monday from 10 a.m. to 5 p.m.

Time, now, to return to the center of Geneva, though I doubt that even the fittest among you will opt to walk back. And, in any event, the route from here is not so inviting. The preferable alternative is to just walk back down Avenue de la Paix, passing the impressive white walls and metal gates of the Federation of Russia, to the Place des Nations and catch a bus back to the Gare de Cornavin.

Geneva:

(Genève, Genf)

Tour #3

No trip to Geneva is complete without a cruise on its marvelous lake.

GETTING THERE:

PRACTICALITIES:

FOOD AND DRINK:
See pages 165–166 for the above.

SUGGESTED TOUR: LAKE GENEVA (LAC LÉMAN)
Obviously, no chapter about Geneva would be complete without information about trips on Lake Geneva *(Lac Léman)*. In fact, there are any number of options, ranging from simple "taxi" trips that shuttle from one bank
of the city to the other, to a cruise to Montreux located at the other end of
the lake. My favorite, though, operated by the **Compagnie Générale de Navigation Sur Le Lac Léman (CGN)** departs from the Quai du Mont-Blanc and
has as its destination the absolutely charming medieval French village of
Yvoire. The voyage itself is pleasant enough, especially on the weekend
when the lake seems to come alive when the sails of hundreds of yachts flut-
ter in the breeze, and the shores are dotted with sunbathers in the pretty villages on the French side of the lake. Yvoire, though, is something special. A
fortified medieval town, with an interesting castle as well, its narrow lanes
are crowded with wooden and stone buildings that are literally covered with
the brightest, and most colorful, flowers you are ever likely to see. Browse
or shop in delightful craft boutiques, and dine in one of the many, many
restaurants, most of whom specialize in lake perch fillets. Yvoire's charms
have not gone unnoticed, however, and this small village often gets just a
little too crowded for comfort. Even so, it is a charming place that merits a
visit, and you will come away with lovely memories—a priceless souvenir
uniquely your own, and irreplaceable at any cost.

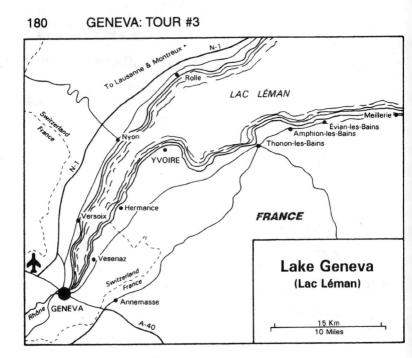

Lausanne

The area in and around Lausanne has an ancient history. A necropolis dating from between 6500 to 4500 BC has been discovered beneath the Roman Ruins at Vidy, and there is evidence that lake dwellers *(lacustrians)* lived in villages built on piles along the lake shore for nearly 3,000 years. Their era came to an end around 800 BC when the Celts arrived to form a new civilization.

In 58 BC the Helvetians attempted to emigrate to Gaul but their defeat by forces of Julius Caesar compelled their return. The Romans then overcame the Helvetians, incorporated their land into the Roman Empire and ruled the area for over four hundred years. The Alemanians invaded, in their turn destructively laying waste to much in their path. Subsequent to their withdrawal in the 5th century the Christian Burgundians settled, peacefully, in the area. A century later the Franks conquered the Burgundians and, around AD 600, Lausanne was designated a cathedral city—thus beginning what would become a nearly 1,000 year line of bishops which would end with the Burgundy Wars of the 16th century.

The late 9th century saw the beginning of the second Burgundy Kingdom, which included Lausanne but which remained distinct from the Frank Kingdom and Holy Roman Empire. That independence, however, lasted only until the death of Rudolf III in 1032, at which time the Burgundy Kingdom was annexed by the Holy Roman Empire, bringing an end to what had been a period of considerable political turmoil. All was not peaceful, though. The substantive power still lay with the bishops, who were also sovereign princes. Problems they encountered with the population were exacerbated by the ongoing struggle for control of Lausanne and the county of Vaud between the House of Savoy and the Bernese.

The 12th and 13th centuries brought good times and expansion. A religious revival occasioned the consecration of the Cathedral on October 20, 1275. And, in the 13th century, the House of Savoy assumed more control over the county of Vaud.

The next centuries were not so kind to Lausanne. With the 14th century came a decline in the city's fortunes and the ravages of the plague. Devastation rained early in the 15th century in the form of the Burgundy Wars which culminated in 1536 with the invasion and conquest by the Bernese forces, who ruled for the next two and a half centuries.

Though the Reformation made inroads in Lausanne, the population was not convinced, an outcome attributable, in part, to a paucity of Protestant clergymen.

The 17th century was another troublesome period as, four times, the plague devastated the city during the early part of the century. Towards the end of the century, the repeal of the Treaty of Nantes gave rise to an exodus of over 1,000 French refugees into Lausanne. This, an increase in population of over 15%, brought its allotment of problems, but, eventually, came to benefit the town. Towards the end of the 18th century Lausanne became fashionable, primarily because of Rousseau, and celebrities and European nobility descended in droves. A young Mozart even honored the city with concerts on two occasions in 1766.

The French Revolution of 1789 brought this peaceful era to an abrupt end. Celebrations by the populace caused consternation in Bern, which sent troops to occupy the town in 1791. One thing led to another and, finally, representations were made to the Directoire in Paris to intervene. After being placed under French protection on December 18, 1797, representatives from the communities in Vaud convened in Lausanne on January 24, 1798, proclaiming a Declaration of Independence. Several days later French troops entered Lausanne to a liberators' welcome.

Though the 19th century was not without problems, the city began to prosper once again. A population explosion ensued—the citizenry quintupled from 10,000 in 1803 to nearly 50,000 just a hundred years later. This trend continued throughout the 20th century, peaking at 137,000 in the 1970s but leveling out, as of this writing, at 125,000, making it the fifth-largest town in Switzerland.

In 1915, Baron Pierre de Coubertin, founder of the modern Olympics, established the first headquarters of the International Olympic Committee (IOC) in Lausanne. And, the very impressive new Olympic museum was opened in 1993. Numerous other international sports federations have also made Lausanne their home, and in 1994 the city was given the official sobriquet Olympic Capital *(Capitale Olympique).*

Lausanne is also home to Switzerland's largest university campus. Its distinguished reputation in the field of medicine dates from the late 18th century, when people came from around the world to receive treatment from various practitioners of that era, most particularly Dr. Auguste Tissot, renowned for his administration of the anti-smallpox vaccination and his expertise in psychology. An array of multinational companies in the service sector—banking, insurance and tourism—have made their headquarters in Lausanne, and it is also celebrated as a center for its culture and sporting activities. These factors combine to give Lausanne a light, cosmopolitan ambiance, and a population of well-educated citizens who are environmentally aware. Fully 30% of the domestic waste is sorted ready for disposal, one of the highest ratios in Switzerland and, in 1995, it won both Swiss and European Solar Energy Awards.

GETTING THERE:

Trains arrive at Lausanne's main station *(Gare CFF)* from almost every other city in Switzerland, and from neighboring countries as well.

By car, Lausanne, located in the center of Lake Léman's northern shore, is easily accessed by *autoroutes* from every other part of Switzerland—with the exception of Graubünden and Ticino.

PRACTICALITIES:

The **Dialing Code** for Lausanne is 21. The **Tourist Office** *(Lausanne Tourisme)*, ☎ 613 73 73, Fax 616 86 47, E-mail information@lausanne-tourisme.ch and www.lausanne-tourisme.ch, is found at 2, Avenue de Rhodanie, Case postale 49, CH-1000 Lausanne. **Tourist information** may be obtained by calling on Monday to Friday between 8 a.m. to 6 p.m. The annex at the railway station opens between April and September daily from 9 a.m. to 8 p.m., and between October and March it opens daily from 9 a.m. to 7 p.m. At times when both of these offices are closed, information about Lausanne can still be obtained from a literature dispenser located at the main office.

The **City of Lausanne Tourist Office** *(Ville de Lausanne Bureau d'information au Public)*, ☎ 315 63 63 or Fax 315 23 04, 2, escaliers du Marché, opens Monday to Friday from 7:45 a.m. to midday and 1:15–5 p.m.

Bucherer Lausanne can be found in an attractive building in the Old Town, at 1, Rue de Bourg, ☎ 312 36 12. It is open Monday to Friday from 9 a.m. to 6:30 p.m. and Saturday from 8:30 a.m. to 5 p.m.

There are two shops in the city that carry an excellent selection of **Swiss Army Knives**. And, not only are they next to each other, they are run by a brother and sister. The **Coutelleries du Petit-Chêne**, ☎ 312 01 86, 2, Petit-Chêne, has the most extensive collection of Swiss Army Knives, as well as numerous pen knives, scissors, kitchen knives, sewing sets with thimbles, corkscrews and an array of collectors' swords. **Heidi's Shop**, ☎ 311 16 89, 22, Petit-Chêne, provides quite a contrast. You will find Swiss Army Knives, of course, but also on offer are clothes, cuckoo clocks, backpacks, mugs, soft toys, dolls, sweatshirts, etc. This store also features a recently introduced line of goods, Vaca Lechera Switzerland, which is comprised of a wide array of products that, as you may have deduced, revolves around the cow motif.

ACCOMMODATION:

The **Lausanne Palace Hotel *******, ☎ 331 31 31 or Fax 323 25 71, 7-9, Grand Chêne, CH-1002 Lausanne, a member of the Leading Hotels of the

World organization, is a palace by name and palatial by nature. Opened in 1915, this hotel, with its beautiful, classical façade, boasts a location with dual merits—it is in the heart of the business and shopping district and offers fantastic views over Lake Léman and the majestic Alps. The interior, completely renovated between 1993 and 1996, features 150 guest rooms and suites, each distinctively decorated with fine fabrics and appointed in a traditional style that combines Old World charm and modern conveniences. Expect air-conditioning, two telephone lines, connections for personal computers and faxes, TV and radio, minibar, private safe, two toilets in each room, and even heated mirrors in the bathrooms that won't steam up! Be sure, too, to visit the Le Tinguely, an avant-garde restaurant/bar created by the highly imaginative Jean Tinguely—about whom more information may be found in the chapter on Basel. Look, also, for the largest wellness center in the Lake Genève region, with an indoor pool and offering specialized beauty treatments. $$$

The **Beau-Rivage Palace** *****, ☎ 613 33 33 or Fax 613 33 34, Ch-1000 Lausanne 6 Ouchy, a member of the Leading Hotels of the World organization, was established in 1861, and epitomizes, in royal manner, the neo-Baroque architectural style so popular in Ouchy during that era. Its name, "lovely lakeside," gives more than a clue to its fantastic location. Each of the 180 rooms, including 15 suites and 30 of deluxe standard, are distinctively decorated and magnificently appointed. Many also have glorious views over the lake to the distant mountains. Three restaurants cater to a variety of tastes. These include the gourmet La Rotonde and the informal Parisian Brasserie-styled Le Café Beau-Rivage. Before and/or after dining you may enjoy a drink at either the Wine bar or Bar Anglais, with an English atmosphere. For recreation, guests enjoy a choice of an indoor/outdoor pool, sauna, steam bath, massage, solarium, fitness equipment, two tennis courts and/or table tennis. The indoor boutique will be of interest to shoppers and, to keep you looking your best, there is a beauty salon and hairdresser on site. $$$

The **Mövenpick Radisson Hotel** ****, ☎ 616 20 41 or Fax 616 15 27, 4, Avenue de Rhodanie, CH-1006 Lausanne, is a modern hotel with an unusual façade, found just across from the Place de la Navigation in the Ouchy, lakeside, area of Lausanne. The 265 impeccably furnished rooms have every modern convenience. Guests may also dine in their choice of three restaurants, enjoy a favorite drink in the on-site bar and/or relax in the fitness and sauna area. If your schedule allows, be sure to inquire about special weekend rates. $$

The **Hôtel City** ***, ☎ 320 21 41 or Fax 320 21 49, 5, Rue Caroline, CH-1003 Lausanne, is in the heart of the Old Town between the Cathedral and the rue de Bourg. They advertise, and justifiably so, that they offer four-star service at three-star prices. The Art-Deco lobby sets the style for the rest of the hotel. Fifty guest rooms, some with kitchenettes, each have a bath/shower, a TV with free 24-hour video, fax and computer connections and a minibar. And, non-smoking rooms are available upon request. **$$**

FOOD AND DRINK:

Restaurant Le Relais (7-9, Grand Chêne) As expected of a restaurant affiliated with the Lausanne Palace Hotel, this is one of the finest places to dine in the city. An intriguingly contemporary classical decor is enhanced by expansive vistas over the lake and Haute-Savoie Alps. Unobtrusive, but exemplary, service ushers in a tantalizing array of imaginatively prepared and beautifully presented dishes. Dine daily from midday to 2 p.m. and 7–10:30 p.m. ☎ 331 31 31. **$$$**

Brasserie Bavaria (10, rue du Petit-Chêne) A typical German-style drinking house, with painted murals and dark wooden ceilings. Look for a wide selection of foreign beers, sandwiches and breadsticks on the bars, and regional specialties such as *Choucroute* and *Rösti.* ☎ 323 39 13. **$**

El Chiringuito Café-Restaurant (38, Saint Laurent) is a Spanish snack bar found, rather improbably, in the middle of a pedestrian shopping area not far from the Old Town. Those who hunger for authentic tapas, and other Spanish dishes will certainly want to find their way here. The ambiance is realistic as well. ☎ 312 73 47. **$**

SUGGESTED TOUR:

This tour begins at the **Flon Métro Station** (1), the location of which may cause some confusion and, also, may pose some difficulty for those visitors not staying in the Old Town. Lausanne, a city with a most unusual topography, is, effectively, set upon three levels: Ouchy is the area down by the lakeside; the Old Town sits on the upper level; and the Central Railway station is nestled between the two. Of course, walking from one level to another is an option, but not a very good one. The roads are steep and the routes meandering. Bus, also, is a possibility. But, for the same reasons that would deter you from walking, it is not the simplest journey. The fastest and most direct mode of transport between Lausanne's three levels is also the simplest—take the Métro. Be aware, however, that the term Métro, as it is applied to this section of track, is somewhat of a misnomer. It is actually a rather steep funicular. So, those staying in a hotel on the lakeside should plan to take the Métro up to the Métro Flon Station to start the tour.

Turn left out of the station, passing the majestic Lausanne Palace Hotel on the way to the **Place St. François** (2), which is dominated by the 13th-century church—with a 15th-century bell tower—of the same name. This once served as the sanctuary of a monastery but has been Protestant since the Reformation. For centuries a social center of Lausanne, this square is encircled by sidewalk cafés, restaurants, shops and the unmistakable central Post Office. Take the Rue de Bourg, a very pleasant pedestrian shopping street which leads up and away, to the left of the church. A left at Rue Caroline will take you past the interesting Hôtel City to the **Pont Bessières** (3), which was opened in 1910 and named in honor of Charles Bessières. As you cross this metal bridge, with posts standing sentinel at each corner, you will have a clear perspective of Lausanne's layout on three hills, the Cité, Bourg and Saint Laurent. Far beneath you will be a street, not a river, and in the background will be the peaceful valley nestled in the shadow of the towering mountains. Beautiful, yes; but, as you scan the horizon, your gaze will most certainly come to rest on the majestic Cathedral, situated across the bridge and to the right. This, your next destination, is reached via the Rue Louis Curtat.

As you approach this fascinating structure, you will be increasingly fascinated by its irregular, and architecturally diverse, façade. An interesting note, also, is that just four of the five towers included in the original plans were ultimately constructed. Outside the Cathedral is a terrace, with a welcome water fountain, that offers yet more imposing views of the surrounding countryside. You will also find a rather aristocratic structure, the former Episcopal Palace *(Ancien-Evêche)*, adorned by a 13th-century fortified tower that was home to the bishops of Lausanne until the early 15th century. Today it houses the **Lausanne Historical Museum** *(Musée Historique de Lausanne)* (4), ☎ 312 13 68, 4, Place de la Cathédrale, where the main exhibit is a 24-square-meter (28.7 square yard) scale model, complete with sound and lighting effects, of the Old Town as it looked in the 17th century. This is open Tuesday to Sunday from 11 a.m. to 6 p.m., with hours extended on Thursday until 8 p.m.

Turn your attention back, now, to the ***Cathedral** *(Cathédrale)* (4) itself. Constructed during the 12th and 13th centuries, this has the distinction of being the largest Gothic building in Switzerland. Present at its consecration, on October 20, 1275, were Pope Gregory X and Rudolf of Hapsburg, upon whom, having sworn an oath of allegiance to the Church, was bestowed the title of Emperor. A major portion of the Cathedral was under renovation when last I visited but, even typically unadorned, it was still impressive. Pay particular attention to the beautifully sculptured portals, the 16th-century carved choir stalls, numerous sepulchers and 105 stained-glass panes, most of which are set in an glorious circular window. Hours are Monday to Friday from 7 a.m. to 5:30 p.m. and Saturday from 8 a.m. to 5:30 p.m. It is also open on Sunday afternoon, from the conclusion of the religious service until 5:30 p.m. Guided tours are available by calling 323 84 34.

Just outside the main doors of the Cathedral, the 160 steps of the *Escaliers du Marché*—a wooden-roofed stairway similar to two seen in Thun, take you down to another, open, set of steps which lead into the Place de la Riponne. This large plaza, adorned by a marvelous fountain from which spout dozens upon dozens of jets of water, is totally dominated by the huge,

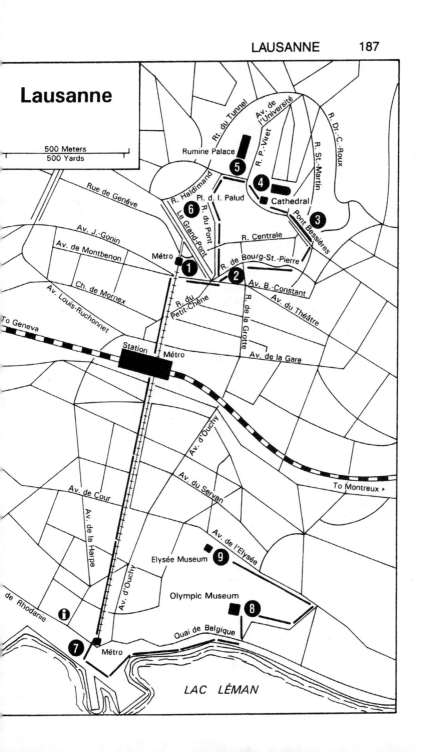

classical, façade of the **Rumine Palace** *(Palais de Rumine)* (5). Named after its donor, this Florentine Renaissance style structure was built in 1906 as the principal building of Lausanne University. Presently, however, as a center of culture, it is home to an eclectic collection of museums. Among these, the **Cantonal Fine Arts Museum** *(Musée cantonal des Beaux-Arts)*, ☎ 312 83 32, with works by French-Swiss artists of the 18th, 19th and 20th centuries will, in all likelihood, be the most popular with readers of this guide. It is open Tuesday and Wednesday from 11 a.m. to 6 p.m., Thursday from 11 a.m. to 8 p.m. and Friday, Saturday and Sunday from 11 a.m. to 5 p.m. The others, and their opening hours and phone numbers, are as follows: the **Cantonal Museum of Archaeology and History** *(Musée cantonal d'Archéologie et d'Histoire)*, ☎ 312 83 32, Thursday to Sunday from 10 a.m. to midday and 2–5 p.m.; the **Cantonal Geological Museum** *(Musée géologique cantonal)*, ☎ 692 44 70, daily from 10 a.m. to midday and 2–5 p.m.; the **Cantonal Zoology Museum** *(Musée cantonal Zoologie)*, ☎ 312 83 36, daily from 10 a.m. to midday and 2–5 p.m., and the **Coin Room** *(Cabinet des Médailles du Canton de Vaud)*, ☎ 323 39 20, Monday from 10 a.m. to midday and Tuesday, Wednesday and Thursday from 10 a.m. to midday and 2–5 p.m.

Continuing on, take Rue Madeleine out of the plaza and down, past neat shops, to what has become one of the traditional meeting places for the people of Lausanne, the **Place de la Palud** (6). This really is quite an interesting square. Upon the 17th-century Town Hall, the preeminent structure, is an ornamental clock—that strikes on the hour between 9 a.m. and 7 p.m.—which has become a Lausanne landmark. That overlooks, but fails to overshadow, the elegant and colorful Fountain of Justice dating from 1726. If you are lucky, or plan your itinerary carefully, your visit will coincide with one of two lively market days.

The next stop on the tour is down by the lakeside. To get there, follow Rue du Pont down the hill, then up the other side to the Place St. François, from where you can follow the Rue du Grand Chêne back to your starting point, the Métro Flon station, where you board the underground funicular. Be sure to grab a window seat, then sit back and enjoy the short ride down to Ouchy.

Upon exiting the station, which is right under the Aulac Hotel, your attention is sure to be drawn towards the imposing, neo-Gothic, castle-like structure to the left. This former defensive structure, dating from 1893, today houses the four-star Château d'Ouchy hotel, which is surrounded by gardens running down to the lake. Immediately behind, or in front if you like, of the hotel is the embarkation point for the lake steamers *(Débarcadere d'Ouchy)*.

Turn your attention, though, to the right, where you will find the **Place de la Navigation** (7), a combination of a series of shallow water ponds and fountains and an open meeting space abutting the small inner harbor. The ponds, it appears, are most popular with the children of Lausanne; their parents bring them here on weekends, strip them to their underwear, and let the romp through the cooling waters. If you are lucky, as I was one early summer weekend, you may find that you have chanced upon a European Beer Festival—and that should be to your taste. Also note, that if you are in need of assistance or further information, the main tourist office is just across the road.

The final two destinations on the tour are on the opposite side of the Château d'Ouchy, a pleasant stroll away. Before pressing on, however, you may be tempted to take to the water for a while. It is my suggestion that, if you are so inclined, you forgo the lake steamers—at least for the moment. At the Port d'Ouchy you can rent either a paddle boat or motorboat.

Lausanne does not come by one of its nicknames, the Garden City, without reason. And nowhere is this more apparent than along the lakeside promenade of Quai d'Ouchy where, in 1901, more than a kilometer (nearly 1,100 yards) of trees and flower beds were planted. In fact, Lausanne has a total of 319.7 hectares (790 acres) in public gardens, of which 101.2 hectares (250 acres) are at the lakeside. There are also 8 kilometers (five miles) of promenades. The city employs no fewer than 270 professional gardeners, who, during the cooler months, raise 650,000 plants under glass for planting in the spring. But strolling along the Quai d'Ouchy you will see far more than just plants and trees. Interspersed between these are a host of fountains and statues of every kind, including one of General Henri Guisan, leader of the Swiss defensive army in World War II. To your left will be an array of expansive buildings some of which, like the Beau-Rivage Palace and the Royal-Savoy, now serve as luxury hotels. To the south, the Alps glisten in the distance. After about 500 meters (547 yards), you will come upon the layered, curving, Olympic Fountain which heralds your arrival at the **Olympic Museum** *(Musée Olympique)* (8), ☎ 621 65 11 or Fax 621 65 12, 1, Quai d'Ouchy. The museum building itself, up and at the back of a pretty garden, can be reached by taking a pathway which winds its way past an ever-increasing number of Olympian sculptures. Alternatively, if you are in need of a rest, take the escalators up, and wander down once you have explored the museum. And a very impressive museum this is! The architectural futurism of this ultra-modern structure, faced with Thasos marble, is complimented by its penchant to technology. Admission and exit, both to the museum and to the individual exhibitions within, is by a computer coded key. Permanent exhibitions spotlight a multitude of familiar athletes, their respective events, and, in some cases, the equipment that played a role in their victories. These, as well as whatever temporary exhibits are on offer, are enhanced by a variety of innovative audiovisual effects. This, truly, is guaranteed to be a winner for children of all ages. Lausanne is the headquarters city of the International Olympic Committee and this museum, opened on June 23, 1993, is the world's greatest center of information on the Olympic Movement. In addition to the Olympic Archives, the Olympic Documentation Center has 150,000 books, 250,000 photos, and film and video totaling 7,000 hours of viewing. Before leaving, visitors will, likely, be attracted to the museum's souvenir shop; but, be forewarned, the prices can hit Olympian heights. It is open from May 1 to September 30, daily, from 10 a.m. to 7 p.m. Between October 1 and April 30 it opens Tuesday to Sunday from 10 a.m. to 6 p.m. Late night opening is on Thursday until 9:30 p.m., and it closes on January 1 and December 25.

Before leaving the area for the stroll back along the Quai d'Ouchy to the Métro station—the end of the tour, some of you may wish to pay a visit to Switzerland's main photography museum. The **Elysée Museum** *(Musée de l'Elysée)* (9), ☎ 617 48 21, 18, Avenue de l'Elysée, is actually located in a picture-perfect 17th-century mansion set in gardens adjacent to the Olympic Museum. It opens Tuesday to Sunday from 10 a.m. to 6 p.m., with hours extended on Thursday to 9 p.m.

Almost to a person, visitors to Switzerland arrive with a heightened expectation of ascending, via cable car, to one of this country's magnificent, and world celebrated, mountain peaks. Many will also anticipate a tranquil voyage by steamboat on one of her many lovely lakes—a trip that is particularly enchanting when taken upon one of the largest lakes in Europe, Lac Léman—or Lake Geneva, if you prefer—whose shores are shared by Switzerland and France. You will find its astounding statistics detailed in the **Montreux and Vevey** chapter of this guide, as well as suggested trips, departing from Geneva, Montreux/Vevey and Lausanne, in the respective chapters. It is only from Lausanne, however, that you can do what you would not expect to be able to do in Switzerland—delve beneath the surface. From his base in Lausanne, Dr. Jacques Piccard owns and operates a three-seat **submarine** which is primarily chartered for research dives by universities and the like. In fact, this little submarine has really been around, having been used in neighboring countries and even the Mediterranean Sea. As unbelievable as it may sound, by special arrangement, Dr. Piccard also conducts tourist excursions on his craft, highlighting—perhaps that should, in this case, be lowlighting—the surreal specter of the lake bottom which, with its small undulating hills, is reminiscent of a lunar landscape. If this idea appeals to you, contact Jacques Piccard, ☎ 799 25 65 or Fax 799 26 25, to arrange a dive. Be prepared, however. To go to such depths, you will have to dig deep into your pocket, a three-quarter-hour trip costs CHF 350. But, what a story to tell your family and friends back home—and they can't call it a "tall one" either.

Évian-les-Bains (France)

Évian is one of those curious places in the world which, although most people haven't been there—and indeed would be hard pressed to say where it actually is, is world famous. Its claim to fame, of course, is derived from its most important export, and there will not be many people, particularly in the health-conscious Western world, who do not instantly recognize the EVIAN trademark—and the words *Eau Minerale Naturelle*.

Located directly across Lake Geneva *(Lac Léman)* from Lausanne, the settlement of Évian-les-Bains began to prosper during the 13th century when a castle was constructed on the site. During the Middle Ages, it gained the attention of the Dukes of Savoy. It was not until the late 18th century, however, that the news of its refreshing natural spring water began to circulate throughout Europe. For over a century, the wealthy and the aristocratic flocked to this peaceful mountain town to take the waters by day and indulge themselves in what became a glittering and elegant social whirl by night. In 1790, the Marquis de Lessert discovered and reported that natural mineral waters from the Cachat garden in Evian were effective in curing urinary ailments. These developments, in turn, invited the curiosity of the kings of Sardinia and other nobility, who also came to partake of the waters and to enjoy Evian's other natural attributes, its peace and beauty.

The first Mineral Water development company and the first Spa Water Establishment were both opened in 1826. In 1869, the Public Limited Company of Les Eaux Minerales d'Évian-les-Bains was founded. That same year, Cachat water was approved by the Academy of Medicine, and won honors at the Universal Exhibition.

Evian has made an ongoing effort to build upon its natural attributes—the beautiful mountains and lovely lake, refreshing water, pure alpine air, a moderate mountain climate and low atmospheric pressure—by constructing extensive spa and sports facilities. Visitors will also enjoy wonderful restaurants, an array of interesting shops, and a variety of cultural activities—not to mention Évian's delightful ambiance. This town has truly dedicated itself to health and fitness, relaxation and tourism. It is an ideal retreat from the hustle and bustle of daily life.

GETTING THERE:

Lake Steamer is the most practical form of transport—unless you want to drive all the way around the lake. It is also the most pleasant.

PRACTICALITIES:

The **Dialing Code** for Evian is (International 011 33) 4 50. The **Tourist Office** *(Office de Tourisme)*, 75 04 26 or Fax 75 61 08, is at Place d'Allinges, B.P. 74502 Évian-les-Bains, France.

ACCOMMODATION:

The hotels in and around Évian offer approximately 1,200 rooms, ranging from five-star to guest houses. In my mind, the Hôtel Royal stands out from the rest for style, comfort and service. If you want to explore other options, contact the Tourist Office by Fax 75 61 08 for specific information.

Domaine du Royal Club Évian—Hôtel Royal ***, ☎ 26 85 00 or Fax 75 38 40, 74500 Évian, France, sits, with the air of a magnificent palace, on a hill just behind Evian surrounded by a 40-acre park. Built in 1907, recently renovated and decorated with frescos and turn-of-the-century masterpieces, it well merits its membership in the Leading Hotels of the World organization. It is, of course, in France and, being so, you should not be surprised to find a total of seven restaurants on-site. Sports enthusiasts will have a field day choosing between free unlimited golf on the hotel's 18-hole Évian Masters course, tennis on six tennis courts, swimming in the indoor—or semi-Olympic outdoor—heated pools, pounding the pavement on the hotel's jogging track, or testing their skill on the archery shoot. And, after all that physical activity (or not) the hotel's spa, The Better Living Institute, offers a number of treatments to pamper and relax you. $$$

FOOD AND DRINK:

The cuisine in Évian is influenced by the lake—from which char, perch fillets, trout and fera make tasty dishes, and the surrounding high country of the Savoyard—where the likes of fondue and raclett are popular. The cheeses of Reblochon, Abondance, Vacherin and Tomme are particularly popular, as are the white wines of Marin, Marignan Crepy and Ripaille. The local cherry orchards produce an excellent kirsch, and Muratore liqueur, made from Alpine plants, is a local specialty.

As this is a town that caters to its guests, restaurants are plentiful and I would be hard pressed to recommend one above the other. The restaurants in the Hôtel Royal are, of course, always a good bet and you will find listed below some information on my favorite among those. Outside of that, your choices are wide ranging and I would suggest letting your preference of regional cuisine be the guide.

Café Royal (the primary restaurant within the Domaine du Royal Club Évian—Hôtel Royal) serves gourmet creations of the highest stan-

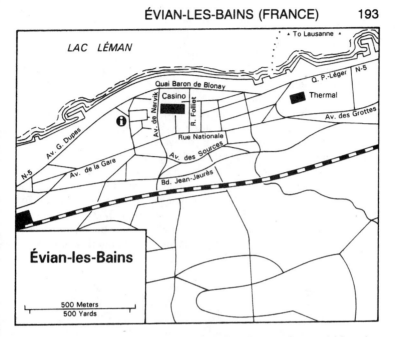

dards and/or the dietetic **La Rotonde** offering what could best be termed as a unique dietetic and gastronomic experience. ☎ 26 85 00. $$$

SUGGESTED TOUR:

Visitors wishing to discover Évian's history, from the Middle Ages to the "Belle Époque" era, should plan a visit to the tourist office. The staff will be pleased to provide you with a brochure, available in several languages, that complements a marked circuit begining at that same office. And, if you happen to be in Évian on a Thursday, between May and September, you may join in a guided tour around town that begins at 10:30 a.m., also from the tourist office, and lasts about one-and-a-half hours.

Many, though, will be content just to wander around this very pretty, flower-filled, town at their leisure, strolling the lakefront promenade, admiring beautiful houses, browsing in the numerous specialty stores in the pedestrian shopping area, and, of course, taking their choice of the bars and restaurants that appear to sprout up from every corner.

One colorful event that is a must-see, if you are visiting between April and October, takes place in the Mouettes harbor square. There you will see the Musical Fountain, where multiple illuminated sprays of dancing waters rise and fall in rhythm to the accompanying music. The actual operating times are available through the tourist office.

Everyone who comes to Évian will be curious to learn more about its famous product; well, products actually. Information on tours of the bottling factory, which may be visited from June to September, is available by calling 26 80 80. Alternatively, make your way to the area directly behind the Belle Époque thermal center. Here you will find a bottling center of a different sort and one that never closes—a fountain springing from the wall where anyone is free to bottle their own water, one bottle at a time. And there is no prize for guessing the label upon the empty plastic bottles the people bring for this purpose. But, if you want some yourself, be prepared for a line; this is both a cheap and popular pastime.

You do not have to travel all the way to Évian to drink the water, it is exported to almost every country in the world. You do, though, have to come to Évian to "partake of the waters," and that is, indeed, a treat to savor. The ***Espace Thermal Évian,** ☎ 75 02 30 or Fax 75 65 99, BP 21, 74502 Évian, located within a park on the lake shore, combines over one hundred years of experience with the most modern of facilities and professionalism to offer a wide range of beauty, fitness and hydrotherapy treatments. Whether you have an hour to spend or are able to stay for the full ten-day package you can come here to, as they say, bathe in the spas and soak up the benefits to your health and fitness. Be advised if traveling with children, however, that access is limited to those over 16 years of age. The Espace Thermal Évian is open daily from 9 a.m. to 12:30 p.m. and 2:30–7:30 p.m.

Montreux and Vevey

While today Montreux is the better known of the two towns, it is Vevey that has the older history—being inhabited, during an earlier period, by lake dwellers *(lacustrians)*. The Romans subsequently established a trading post called Vibiscum at the junction of the road leading from their Helvetian capital of Aventicum (today, Avenches) and the road that connected Lausanne to Martigny, on the way to Italy. Thus, the founding and growth of Vevey was based primarily around trade. Montreux grew differently, however. Unlike many other towns in Switzerland, it was not formed around a church but, rather, was established as a miniature confederation of the small villages physically separated from one another by the area's many vineyards.

The area encompassing Montreux and Vevey was, from early on, primarily under the control of the Counts of Savoy, whose presence was symbolized by the nearby, and now world famous, Château Chillon. The year 1536, however, brought dramatic change. On January 29, over 6,000 Bernese troops blitzed the château, subsequently taking control of the whole of the Vaud and bringing with them the Protestant religion. This had far-reaching consequences—in 1685 the French revoked freedom of religion, and many thousands of French Protestants, known as Huguenots, fled to Switzerland with many of them settling in Vevey. In 1798, after more than two hundred and fifty years of domination by the Bernese, the Vaudois Revolution—which came in the wake of the French Revolution—restored the region's freedom.

In the early decades of the 19th century, artists, writers, musicians, and others of like mind began to discover the unique natural charms of this far eastern section of Lake Geneva *(Lac Léman)*. Beautiful it is, with the peaceful lake and the soaring peaks of the Haute Savoie as a background—but that is expected. After all, this is Switzerland. What would not be expected is the mildness of the weather. The Rochers de Naye—2,042 meters (6,700 feet), immediately behind, protects the slopes and lake shore from the northerly winds, giving rise to a micro climate that ranks as one of the sunniest in Switzerland. Visitors will be amazed at the numerous vineyards and the abundance of palm trees and tropical flowers growing along the 15 kilometers (9.3 miles) distance from Villeneuve to Vevey—truly meriting its name, the "Flowered Path." The springtime is especially delightful when the fields blossom with thousands of fragrant Nascissi. Is it any wonder, then, that the likes of Byron, Jean-Jacques Rousseau, Stravinsky and Charles Chaplin fell in love this place?

Over the years, Montreux and Vevey have established for themselves a worldwide reputation as a center for arts and culture. Today, a variety of events, such as the Golden Rose of Montreux, the Montreux Jazz Festival, the Comedy Film Festival, the Humor Festival, the Classical Musical Festival, and others of international import, follow one after the other throughout the year —drawing visitors from around the globe. And, area leaders have catered to the demands of this discriminating clientele for quality accommodation and dining, developing an infrastructure of hotels and restaurants that is without parallel. Not to be overlooked, either, are the handful of museums in both towns.

A visit to the "Pearl of the Swiss Riviera" is, truly, a pleasure. If it wasn't for the mountains, you might really imagine you were on the shores of the Mediterranean.

GETTING THERE:

Trains arrive at the main stations, *(Gares CFF)*, in both Montreux and Vevey from nearby Lausanne and most other Swiss cities.

By car, Montreux and Vevey, located at the eastern end of Lake Geneva's northern shore, are easily accessed by *autoroutes* from nearby Lausanne and every other part of Switzerland, with the exception of Graubünden and Ticino.

PRACTICALITIES:

The **Dialing Code** for Montreux and Vevey is 21.

The **Montreux Tourist Office** *(Office du Tourisme)*, ☎ 962 84 36, Fax 963 81 13, E-mail tourism@montreux.ch or www.montreux.ch, Pavilion d'information, Place du Débarcardère, is open in the summer, daily, from 9 a.m. to 7 p.m.; and in the winter, daily, from 9 a.m. to midday and 1:30–6 p.m.

The **Vevey Tourist Office** *(Office du Tourisme)*, ☎ 922 20 20 or Fax 922 20 24, Place du Marché, La Grenette, is open between June 15 and September 15, daily, from 8:30 a.m. to 7 p.m.; and the remainder of the year, also daily, from 8:30 a.m. to midday and 1:30–6 p.m.

The best place to buy **Swiss Army Knives** is at **Bazar Suisse**, ☎ 963 32 74 or Fax 963 72 87, Grand Rue 24, Montreux. In addition to the area's largest selection of that popular souvenir, they offer a wonderful variety of music boxes—including collectibles, cuckoo clocks with lovely wood carvings, and a host of other items. And, those traveling with or shopping for children should know that this is a good source for toys, games and even radio-controlled planes or cars.

Lost and Found *(Objets Trouvés)* offices are in the railway stations at both Montreux, ☎ 963 58 13, and Vevey, ☎ 921 29 15.

ACCOMMODATION:
Cully:

The **Auberge Du Raisin**, ☎ 799 21 31 or Fax 799 25 01, Place de L'Hôtel de Ville 1, CH-1096 Cully, is located a short distance away from Vevey, on the way to Lausanne. The less than totally convenient location and the small effort involved in getting there will be quickly forgotten once you are introduced to its charms. The setting is lovely—on the Lavaux shore of Lac Léman and at the foot of the vineyard of the same name. And, the hotel itself is delightful—the owners have filled a wonderful old house with period furniture and paintings by Old Masters. The ten guest rooms are beautifully and classically decorated, and there is also a pleasant, shady terrace. **$$**

Montreux:

The **Le Montreux Palace *******, ☎ 962 12 12, Fax 962 17 17, E-mail in fo@mtx-palace.global.café.ch or www.mtx-palace.globalcafe.ch, Grand-Rue 100, CH-1820 Montreux, built in 1906, is a very grand hotel with a marvelous Belle Époque ambiance and a prestigious position in Montreux. This member of the Leading Hotels of the World organization has played host to numerous special guests from throughout the world, some on a more permanent basis than others—Vladimir Nabokov lived at the hotel from 1961 until his death in 1977. Its 233 rooms and suites are exquisitely appointed and offer all the facilities expected in a hotel of this genre, including air-conditioning and in-room fax, voice mail and computer modem. Among the array of restaurants and bars waiting to serve you are the gourmet Le Veranda restaurant—specializing in French cuisine, Harry's New York Bar, and even an Internet café—very aptly named the Global Bar. It isn't shy in the sports facilities department either—an outdoor pool, tennis court and mini-golf course are on site. The management will be happy to arrange water sports activities, golf, skiing and even hot air ballooning, at your request. The Montreux Casino, a convenient ten minutes away, is also affiliated with this complex. **$$$**

The **Hôtel Eden au Lac *******, ☎ 963 55 51 or Fax 963 18 13, Rue du Théâtre 1, CH-1820 Montreux, has an absolutely wonderful location on Lake Léman, conveniently close to the center of Montreux. Behind a delightful Victorian façade, the interior has been completely renovated while preserving the original style. Each of the 105 rooms are decorated with a Louis XVI style decor and ultra-modern facilities. Look, also, for a fine restaurant. **$$$**

The **Hôtel Victoria Glion ******, ☎ 963 31 31 or Fax 963 13 51, CH-1823 Glion/Montreux, located on the heights behind Montreux and easily reached by public transport, is a delightful Belle-Époque style hotel dating from 1869 and set in large private grounds. Many of the 50 rooms have lake views, and all have a light, airy, decor and many modern amenities. Two specially appointed rooms feature an in-room jacuzzi, a salon, a kitchenette and a large private terrace. The dining rooms provide a delightful atmosphere in which to enjoy sumptuous meals. On the grounds are a pool, a tennis court, a fitness room, a sauna, and a practice golf course. Alternatively, a simple leisurely walk through the gardens is enchanting. $$

The **Hotel Splendid** ***, ☎ 963 64 66 or Fax 963 75 04, Grand-Rue 52, CH-1820 Montreux, is a charming Victorian-style hotel in a privileged position in Montreux. The 23 rooms, many of which feature a private balcony or loggia, have an old-fashioned ambiance, private bath/shower, TV and telephone. Other amenities include a pleasant lounge, a dining room offering fine cuisine, and a private garage. $$

Vevey:

The **Hôtel des Trois Couronnes** *****, ☎ 921 30 05 or Fax 922 72 80, Rue d'Italie 49, CH-1800 Vevey, is a small, luxury hotel by the shores of the lake and close to the center of Vevey. Its 150-year tradition; 63 spacious, traditionally decorated rooms; and stately, marble colonnaded public areas combine to evoke a gracious and refined ambiance. In the summer months, enjoy culinary masterpieces on the charming terrace restaurant. At other times dine in the elegant, colonnaded dining room beneath the soft glow of chandeliers. $$$

The **Hostellerie de Genève** **, ☎ 921 45 77 or Fax 921 30 15, Place du Marché 11, CH-1800 Vevey, is a charming small hotel located in the center of Vevey and just a moment or two's walk from the lake. It offers 11 pleasant rooms, a shady terrace and a restaurant specialing in Italian and classic cuisine. $$

FOOD AND DRINK:

Auberge Du Raisin (Place de L'Hôtel de Ville 1, Cully) Within the small hotel of the same name are two beautiful dining rooms presided over by Adolf Blokbergen. He is renowned for his creative cuisine, especially when working with game and fish, and the desserts are exquisite by any standards. The cellar features wines from Switzerland—including the local St. Saphorin— France, and America. This is a truly special restaurant where you may expect a culinary experience, not just a meal. ☎ 799 21 31. $$$

Le Trianon (Mont-Pèlerin, Vevey) is as elegant and romantic as the hotel with which it is affiliated, Le Mirador, and, from its glass enclosed dining room, offers fantastic views over the Swiss Riviera. A discriminating clientele is allured by exemplary French cuisine and dishes that are as imaginatively prepared as they are beautifully presented. Choose the perfect accompaniment to your meal from a superlative 14,000-bottle wine cellar, featuring French, Swiss, Australian and American vintages. ☎ 925 11 11. $$$

Le Patio (Mont-Pèlerin, Vevey), also located within Le Mirador, offers a more casual dining experience. From late spring until early fall, the menu features delicious international and regional dishes, as well as low-calorie spa specialties. ☎ 925 11 11. $$

Le Palais (Le Hoggar) (Quai du Casino 14, Montreux) is an unusual Oriental restaurant that advertises itself as a "Palace of a Thousand and One Nights." Specialties include Libyan and Iranian cuisine with couscous, of course, and curry. They also offer the "experience" of imported Iranian caviar—at a price, of course. It is closed from the beginning of December to the beginning of January. ☎ 963 12 71. $$

Café-Restaurant et Caveau les Vignerons (Rue Industrielle 30 bis, Montreux) is a quaint bodega-style restaurant on the edge of the Old Town. Look for traditional regional specialties like fondues, raclette and Entrecôte du Vigneron. It is closed on Sunday. ☎ 963 25 70. $

White Horse Pub (Grand Rue 28, Montreux) Quite a realistic interpretation of an English pub with a fantastic location on the main street and just across from the lake. From Monday to Friday, between midday and 2 p.m., the Menu du Jour is good value and well worth consideration. ☎ 963 15 92. $

SUGGESTED TOUR:

Both Montreux and Vevey proper are too small to support formal tours of their own, and the larger area that deserves coverage here is really too diffuse to practically incorporate into a single tour. I will, therefore, simply offer some suggestions of things you may like to see and/or do.

First and undoubtedly foremost, the majority of visitors to Montreux and Vevey will want to see the ***Chillon Castle** *(Château Chillon)*(1), ☎ 963 39 12 or Fax 963 85 81, Veytaux-Montreux. Situated on a little island jutting into the lake, this château is a signature landmark, not only for this portion of the Vaud, but of the country of Switzerland as well. It may be reached in a variety of ways. Depending on your schedule and your preference you may travel by lake steamer, take the walking route—less than an hour from Montreux, or catch a Number 1 bus from Montreux. The site has long been considered of strategic importance by virtue of its position guarding the narrow stretch of land between the lake and the mountains, along which ran the road traversing the Great St. Bernard Pass and continuing on to Italy. It is generally believed that the Romans established an outpost here, although the first documentation of a castle dates from 1150.

First owned by the Bishops of Sion, the castle was built as a base from which to collect taxes on the goods that passed along the road. It was enlarged in the 13th century when it came under the control of the Counts of Savoy. And, it was Peter II of Savoy, the master of Chillon between 1255 to

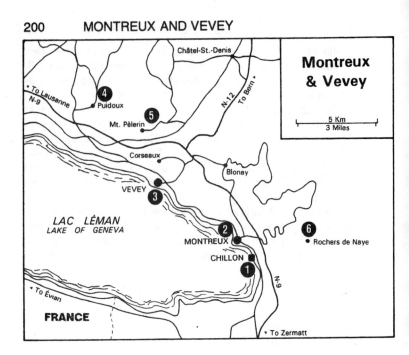

Montreux & Vevey

5 Km
3 Miles

Châtel-St.-Denis

To Lausanne N-9

Puidoux

Mt. Pèlerin

Corseaux

Blonay

VEVEY

LAC LÉMAN
LAKE OF GENEVA

MONTREUX

Rochers de Naye

CHILLON

To Évian

FRANCE

To Zermatt

1268, who was responsible for the size and appearance of the structure as it is seen today.

In 1536 it was captured by the Bernese who used it as, among other things, a depot, armory and residence for their bailiffs. During this period it suffered damage from a violent earthquake that occurred in March of 1584. The castle remained under Bernese control until the Vaudois Revolution of 1798, following which it became the property of the Canton of Vaud.

A century later, in 1897, the renowned restorer and archaeologist, Albert Naef, was appointed as the architect in charge of renovating the château. Seeking to carry out his task as authentically as possible, he consulted numerous archive documents describing much of the work that had been done since the end of the 12th century.

What has evolved today is an irregularly-shaped oval fortress, guarded by numerous towers and graced by three inner courtyards surrounded by a variety of grand rooms overlooking the lake and defensive positions. Really, this is an intriguing place and, as you investigate the carefully reconstructed chambers and listening to the sound of the water lapping at the walls through the open windows, it is almost possible to imagine that you have been transported back through the centuries to the castle's days of glory.

The château has inspired countless writers to put pen to paper—Jean-Jacques Rousseau, Shelley, Victor Hugo and Alexandré Dumas to name a few. The most famous words written about it were authored by Lord Byron in "The Prisoner of Chillon," his poetic recounting of the imprisonment of Bonivard during the 16th century. This Prior of St. Victor's in Geneva was chained for five years to the fifth pillar from the entrance because of his outspokenness in favor of the independence of Geneva. Byron's name is still visible, where he inscribed it, on the third pillar.

As imposing as the façade is, and as beautiful as the surroundings are, the ambiance is somewhat tainted by the twin blights of traffic continually droning on the nearby road and the intermittent passing of trains even closer. Alas, it must have been ever so much more charming in bygone centuries!

The daily opening hours here are complex: during January and February from 10 a.m. to 12:45 p.m. and 1:30–4:45 p.m., during March from 10 a.m. to 12:45 p.m. and 1:30–5:30 p.m., during April, May and June from 9 a.m. to 6:30 p.m., during July and August from 9 a.m. to 7 p.m., during September from 9 a.m. to 6:30 p.m., during October from 10 a.m. to 5:30 p.m. and during November and December from 10 a.m. to 12:45 p.m. and 1:30–4:45 p.m. When planning your schedule you will want to take into account that the cash desk for entrance ceases selling tickets 45 minutes prior to closing time, both at lunch time and in the evening. And, when you purchase your tickets, be sure to pick up a copy of the free brochure which lists and describes the most notable features of the château. If you are in the market for a publication with more detail or, perhaps, a souvenir, I recommend you purchase "The Castle of Chillon VD," issued as part of the "Guides To Swiss Monuments" series.

Now that you have explored the château to your heart's content, it is time for a change of pace as you investigate the contrasting towns of Montreux and Vevey.

You will find Montreux to be vastly more commercialized and splendid than its neighbor. Precocious hotels line the lake front, interspersed with numerous upscale boutiques and shops, many of which are described in a well-presented brochure available from *Montreux VIP Services*, ☎ (89) 212 57 85, Case postale 1419, CH-1820 Montreux. In looking at the brochure and when visiting the shops you will, no doubt, note something surprising. In addition to translations into the expected languages (such as English, Japanese and Arabic), you will find one in Russian. You will also find that stores typically display Russian newspapers, beer, and other goods. This, certainly, is enough to make one think. Having recently been to Russia, I can testify with absolute certainty that 99.9% of the Russian people could never afford a visit to Switzerland. That a city like Montreux would make such efforts to cater to a Russian clientele simply confirms my own personal impressions, and reinforces what is printed on a regular basis—that the Russian Mafia is doing very well indeed.

The topography of the two towns is also quite different. **Montreux** (2) is sandwiched between the mountains and the lake, with the railway line separating the **Old Town** *(Les Planches)* from the new. The former, contained within quite a small area, is worth investigating for its architectural and social style. Some visitors may also be interested in checking out the **Historical Museum of the Swiss Riviera** *(Musée du Vieux Montreux)*, ☎ 963 13 53, Rue de la Gare 40, CH-1820 Montreux. Located within a collection of 17th-century houses, its exhibits chronicle the development of the region from the Paleolithic period through the modern days of tourism. It opens between April 1 and October 31, daily, from 10 a.m. to midday and 2–5 p.m. If this does not interest you, or if you find you have a bit of extra time on your hands, just spend some time wandering along the very pleasant quais that straddle the lakeside.

When you turn your attention to **Vevey** (3), you will find it to be of an entirely different character. Physically it is concentrated within a space that is much narrower and deeper, and the town is somewhat older. The lake front is less commercialized and, at least in this writer's opinion, pleasanter for it. There are a number of museums that may be of interest. Actually, a good and precise guide to the museums of Montreux and Vevey is the *Musées de la Riviera Vaudoise*, available from either city's tourist office.

Among these I would suggest that the dual **Museum of Old Vevey** and **Museum of the Brotherhood of Wine Growers** *(Musée Historique du Vieux Vevey et Musée de la Confrérie des Vignons)*, ☎ 921 07 22, Rue du Château 2, CH-1800 Vevey, is, perhaps, the most entertaining. These are housed within **Le Château** which dates from 1599 and served as a home for bailiffs during the period of Bernese rule. Exhibits, dating from Celtic times, are varied and include memorabilia from the various Vevey Wine festivals, a very famous local celebration which was instituted in the 17th century and continues today.

On the subject of wine, who could resist a ride on the **Wine Train** *(Le Train des Vignes)*? It operates daily year round, traveling to and from **Puidox** (4), with stops at Corseaux and Chexbres along the way. The cost is just CHF 9.60 for a return trip, but you are not obliged to remain on the train for the duration of the journey. You may get on and off wherever you fancy, using the opportunity to explore the vineyards and looking for the welcoming *degústation* sign—which heralds a wine grower's cellar. These are generally open to the public between April 1 and November 30, Thursday through Sunday, and they will be only too pleased to offer you a sample of their products. If all of this makes you just a little hungry, stop at one of the village bistros and sample some of the local cuisine. The distances covered here are not great—only 8 kilometers (5 miles) for the whole length of the trip—so, if you fancy exploring all the way back to Vevey, that is an entirely feasible option.

If you do, eventually, make it to Puidox you will want to check out what is considered a most important and sizable collection—over 2,000 examples—of watches, clocks and antique watchmaking equipment. The opening hours could be a bit more timely, however. From March 15 to September 30 it is open, on Saturday and Sunday only, from 9:30 a.m. to 11:30 a.m. and 1:30–5:30 p.m. During the rest of the year, with the exception of December when it closes, it is open on only the second and last weekends of the month.

Time, now, to get a more elevated perspective of the area and, of the four available options, I prefer the following two:

If you are not staying at the wonderful Le Mirador hotel at **Mount Pèlerin** (5), a trip up on the funicular to the station, 810 meters (2,657 feet), is a must. The panoramic views can be enhanced upon, between Easter and October, by continuing on the shuttle bus to the futuristic *Plein Ciel* tower, where an elevator whisks you to its summit.

The other possibility departs from Montreux and takes you much higher—2,042 meters (6,699 feet)—to the summit of **Les Rochers-de-Naye** (6). From this vantage point the views over the lake are spectacular, and you will also get a much broader perspective of the Alpine region as a whole. In the summer, the **Alpine Garden** at La Rambertia provides another pleasant diversion.

You may be wondering why I have not yet mentioned what is the most dominant feature of the area, **Lake Geneva** *(Lac Léman)* itself. The truth is that the lake is very narrow here and, as the villages on the French side are not nearly so interesting as Évian or Yvoire, detailed in other chapters, I would not recommend that you cross to them. The lake steamers are, however, deserving of some attention. They make an absolutely charming form of transport between Cully, Rivaz, Vevey, Montreux and the Château Chillon.

Also, as this is the point of origin—where the Rhône flows into the lake—this seems an appropriate place to include some interesting statistics. Lake Geneva, the largest freshwater lake in central Europe, holds 89 billion cubic meters (23,511,312,663,600 gallons) of water, which represents 11 years of inflow from the Rhône. It can, therefore, be deduced that it also takes that long—the time it would take to fill it—for the water flowing in to travel the relatively short distance down to Geneva. The surface of the lake covers 582 square kilometers (223 square miles), its length is 72.3 kilometers (44.9 miles), the circumference 167 kilometers (104 miles) and the mean width is 8.1 kilometers (5 miles). The maximum depth is 309.7 meters (1,016 feet), and the maximum temperature never rises above 23 degrees Celsius (73 degrees Fahrenheit).

A Daytrip from Lausanne or Montreux/Vevey

Gruyères

To the majority of people the name Gruyères is synonymous with this area's world-famous product: cheese. And it is that cheese, and perhaps curiosity, which attracts most visitors to Gruyères. Many will have no idea, and will be pleasantly surprised to learn, that there is more to Gruyères than just cheese. Set on an isolated hill that dramatically controls the broad valley and with towering mountains looking down upon it, Gruyères is a charming, fortified, medieval village with an intriguing history and a famous castle as well.

Nineteen counts of the dynasty of Gruyères resided here beginning in the 11th century and ending when the last, Michael I, left the castle in 1554 and died in exile. The cantons of Fribourg and Bern subsequently divided the county between them, and the castle was used as a residence of the bailiff of Fribourg from that time until 1798. In 1848 it passed into private hands and the families of Bovy and Balland, and the many important artists who also lived there from time to time left an unusual heritage of their own. Since 1938 the structure has been maintained by the canton of Fribourg.

A visit to Gruyères, with its population of just 1,500, really is like taking a trip back in time and a walk through the uncluttered village could best be likened to strolling through a living museum. Tourism obviously plays a major part in its sustenance. But, while visitors' needs are certainly catered to—there is even a boutique or two, it is not so obtrusive that it cheeses you off. The restriction of automobiles, too, marvelously enhances the ambiance.

While the town may be difficult to get to, especially via public transport, and even though there are really not many of the type places tourists traditionally seek out, museums etc., it would be quite a shame to exclude Gruyères from your Swiss itinerary—even if you don't like cheese!

GETTING THERE:

By car, a look at a map will verify that Gruyères is directly northeast of Montreux/Vevey, but the topography of this area makes the journey somewhat indirect. Take the N-12 Autoroute north to the Bulle exit and then loop around south to Gruyères. The village itself, however, is car free, so you are obliged to leave you car in the large car park, just below it on the hill.

Trains, or a combination of trains and a bus actually, may be taken from Vevey (easily reached from Lausanne) to Gruyères, though it is a little complicated. The first leg is by bus, which departs from Vevey train station at 8:20, 9:20, or 10:20 a.m. for the 25-minute trip to Châtel-St-Denis train station. From there a train journey of approximately the same duration will take you on to Bulle. A six-minute stopover is scheduled in Bulle, before another train takes six minutes to transport you to Gruyères. But hold on, you are not there yet! Gruyères' train station is not very centrally located, and it's either a long uphill walk, or a short bus ride, to the village itself.

PRACTICALITIES:

The **Dialing Code** for Gruyères is 26. The **Tourist Office** *(Office du Tourisme Gruyères)*, ☎ 921 10 30 or Fax 921 38 50, CH-1663 Gruyères, is open June to September on Monday to Friday from 8 a.m. to midday and 1–5 p.m.; and weekends from 10:30 a.m. to 4:30 p.m. Between October and May it opens on Monday to Friday from 8 a.m. to midday and 1:30–5 p.m.

ACCOMMODATION:

The **Hostellerie St. Georges**, ☎ 921 22 46 or Fax 921 33 13, CH-1663 Gruyères, is a delightful inn, located right in the middle of the village. Expect spacious, comfortable rooms, restaurants, bars and a large covered terrace—all in historic surroundings. $$

FOOD AND DRINK:

The Hostellerie St. Georges, with demi-pension, is the best option here. The **Le Chalet**, ☎ 921 21 54, is a great alternative for fondue or raclette, however. After all, you really must have a cheese dish here!

SUGGESTED TOUR:

Gruyères, itself, at an altitude of 800 meters (2,625 feet), is far too small to support a formal tour. Basically, there is just one street with a castle at the end. Three gates give access to the village, but most will enter from the north through the **Chavonne Gate**. From this vantage point, where the cobblestone street widens somewhat, the castle, framed by the **Dent-de-Broc** mountain, dominates the background. And, without doubt, the castle should be your first destination.

The ***Gruyères Castle** *(Château de Gruyères)*, ☎ 921 21 02 or Fax 921 38 02, CH-1663 Gruyères, is far more, you will quickly learn, than a traditional fortification. This magnificent edifice is the home of the **International Center of Fantastic Art** *(Centre International de L'Art Fantastique)*—an usual combination indeed. Ancient courtyards and rooms mix with an array of traditional art and furniture—including important tapestries and Fantastic Art, serving up a visual cocktail that will delight your senses. The

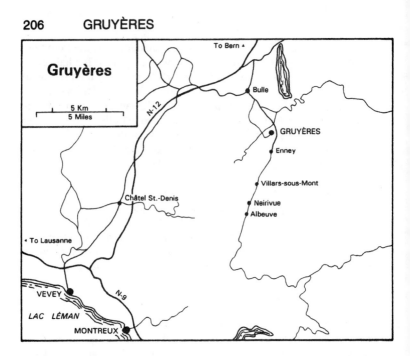

Medieval Garden, too, is a "must see." As you enter request the brochure in English. Though it is brief in its explanations, it is still most helpful. Opening hours are daily between June and September from 9 a.m. to 6 p.m.; March, April, May and October from 9 a.m. to midday and 1–5 p.m.; and during January, February, November and December from 9 a.m. to midday and 1–4:30 p.m.

As for the rest of the village, just wander around and discover its charms at your leisure. Certainly, a cheese fondue, or raclette, for lunch would be most appropriate. Speaking of cheese, you are bound to run across shops trying to sell you some, after all this is Gruyères. But you may want to get it directly from the dairy. Just down the hill from the village, at Pringy-Gruyères, the **Cheese Dairy at Gruyères** has a visitors gallery, open daily from 8 a.m. to 7 p.m., from where you can observe the birth of Gruyères cheese. While this is a commercial dairy, it still adheres to traditions dating back to the 12th century. Of course, the shop on the premises is only too happy to sell you cheese specialties.

Those desiring a view of the area from a different perspective will move on down the valley a few kilometers to **Moléson-sur-Gruyères**, from where a combination of gondola car and cable car will whisk you up to the summit of Moléson at 2,002 meters (6,568 feet). There are panoramic views, of course, and an observatory, ☎ 921 29 96, where you can study the stars through a variety of telescopes. You should not be surprised to know that cheese has a part to play here also, in the form of a 17th-century wooden chalet where cheese is still produced using traditional mountain techniques. This is open every day between mid-May and mid-October from 9:30 a.m. to 6:30 p.m., and fabrication of the cheese takes place from 9–10:30 a.m. and 2–3:30 p.m. For further information ☎ 921 10 44 or 921 23 67.

Les Diablerets

I first ventured upon the village of Les Diablerets in 1962, over thirty-five years ago. It was a bright, sunny day in mid-September—too warm for anything but shorts. Up at the *Glacier des Diablerets*, however, at an altitude of 3,000 meters (9,843 feet), the first heavy snow of the season had fallen. And, I must say that it was curious indeed, having grown up in London where snow is associated only with freezing cold weather, to experience for the first time the contradictory sensations evoked by romping in the snow while wearing summer clothes. Needless to say, that left me, then an impressionable sixteen-year-old, with indelible and very fond memories of Les Diablerets. Consequently, when I received the commission to write this guide, I resolved, with some degree of trepidation as to what had become of this young boy's paradise, to return to Les Diablerets.

These misgivings were not without reason. I had visited other parts of Switzerland several times since my first encounter with this fascinating place and had already been in the country for nearly a month on this particular research trip. During those times, I had become acutely aware of how the passage of time and the coming of technology had changed—not always for the better—many towns and cities. This was reinforced by the growth and changes observed in such nearby places as Gstaad and Montreux, which came contemporaneous with the advance of tourism over the decades.

Happily, I found, on my arrival, that such concerns were totally unfounded. Of course, Les Diablerets has grown some and, inevitably, changed a little—after all it is reliant upon tourists for a living. But it has managed the growth of tourism very well indeed, building upon its original infrastructure, adding new ones and cleverly developing a whole array of outdoor activities for every season—all without impinging upon the ambiance of this charming country village.

Although it has its cultural attractions, most notably the "International Alpine Film Festival" each autumn and the "Snow and Music Festival" between Christmas and Easter, the vast majority of visitors to Les Diablerets come to enjoy themselves outdoors in this outstanding natural wonderland.

What a choice of activities they have! These, at least one of which is unique to Les Diablerets, are described below.

GETTING THERE:

Trains of the *Transports Publics du Chablais* arrive at Les Diablerets from Aigle, via Le Sepey. Aigle is on the line that connects Lausanne, Montreux and Martigny.

By car, Les Diablerets is located on a side road just 12 kilometers (7.5 miles) east of Le Sepey and 17 kilometers (10.6 miles) south of Gstaad.

PRACTICALITIES:

The **Dialing Code** for Les Diablerets is 24. The **Tourist Office** *(Maison du Tourisme)*, ☎ 492 33 58 or Fax 492 23 48, Rue de la Gare, CH-1865 Les Diablerets, is open Monday to Saturday from 8:30 a.m. to 12:30 p.m. and 2–6 p.m.; and Sunday from 9 a.m. to midday and 3–6 p.m.

ACCOMMODATION:

The **Eurotel Victoria ★★★★**, ☎ 492 37 21 or Fax 492 23 71, CH-1865 Les Diablerets, is a large, modern hotel located just outside the center of the village. Its 104 rooms, with a total capacity of 220 beds, are contemporary in style and have all the facilities expected in a four-star hotel. Very pleasant public rooms and fine restaurants are supplemented by an indoor pool and sauna. $$

The **Grand Hôtel ★★★★**, ☎ 492 35 51 or Fax 492 23 91, CH-1865 Les Diablerets, is a traditional-style hotel in the center of the village. The 65 rooms and 4 suites all have a up-to-date decor, a private bath/shower, radio, TV, direct dial telephone and minibar. Look, also, for the Le Café restaurant, an elegant bar, and an indoor swimming pool and sauna. $$

The **Hostellerie Les Sources ★★★**, ☎ 492 21 26 or Fax 492 23 35, CH-1865 Les Diablerets, located just outside the center of the village within spacious private grounds, offers 49 double rooms equipped with shower, toilet, telephone, radio and television. Other amenities are the La Marmotte restaurant, an on-site bar, a lounge with an open fireplace and a leisure room with TV and games. $

The **Auberge de la Poste**, ☎ 492 31 24 or Fax 492 12 68, CH-1865 Les Diablerets, is a typical flower-bedecked Swiss chalet in the very heart of the village. Doubling as a small restaurant—whose specialty is raclette and cheese fondue, it has just seven rooms—with either one, two or three beds. There is a lavatory in each room, with shower and bath available on the floor. But do not plan a visit for November—they are closed. $

FOOD AND DRINK:

It is definitely advisable to take demi-pension at your hotel of choice. But, when you are out and about during the day, the following restaurants deserve your attention:

Les Mezots Restaurant Fromagerie (Les Diablerets), located at an altitude of 1,717 meters (5,633 feet), is a traditional mountain restaurant. What's more, in the summer you can watch the fabrication of the famous mountain cheese *L'Etivaz*—and taste some after, of course. ☎ 492 10 23. $

Lac Retaud Restaurant is, naturally, located overlooking the small lake of the same name, at an altitude of 1,700 meters (5,577 feet). In addition to the expected regional dishes and mushroom specialties, expect to find such mouth-watering desserts as strawberries and cream and meringues. You might want to sample the *Liquor de Maison* and, perhaps, take away some local honey. It is closed between November and the beginning of May. ☎ 492 31 29. $

SUGGESTED TOUR:

Whatever the season, the highlight of a visit to Les Diablerets, as it was when I first went there, is the ***Glacier des Diablerets**, ☎ 492 28 14 or Fax 492 28 27. Actually, there are two starting points for this thirty-minute ascension. One is just outside the village at **Col du Pillon**, 1,546 meters (5,072 feet), ☎ 492 33 77, and the other, a good distance along the road towards Gstaad, at **Reusch**, (4,429 feet), ☎ 755 10 70. From the former, a gondola car glides to **Pierres Pointes**, 2,217 meters (7,274 feet), where it is necessary to change to a cable car for the short trip up to **Cabane des Diablerets**, 2,525 meters (8,284 feet). This is the meeting point for the cable car from Reusch, and another cable car awaits to take you up to the summit at **Scex Rouge** at 2,971 meters (9,747 feet). This, one of the highest vantage points in Switzerland, offers a vast panorama of mountain peaks, including the Matterhorn, 4,478 meters (14,692 feet) and Mont Blanc, 4,807 meters (15,771 feet). It is also a center for skiing, in both winter and summer—when the Swiss Ski Team takes advantage of the network of chair lifts, ski-lifts and cross-country trails for training. The less energetic, in the summer, can take a variety of walks and hikes. Throughout the year, though, most everyone will wish to enjoy a snack, not to say the views, from the panoramic restaurant. There are two other activities up here that are quite different in nature, seasonal, very unusual, and most probably unique to Les Diablerets. The first, in the summer months, will most probably appeal to many more people. Then, you can take a bus ride on the glacier; well, as you might have guessed, it is not actually a bus with wheels. Rather, it's one of those caterpillar like contraptions on tank tracks. And it is certainly no less exciting for that. The other, that can only be experienced at certain times of the year, is certainly a cool experience. But most probably too cool for most. Well, how many people have ever thought of spending a night in an igloo? If the idea intrigues you, and you don't mind spending CHF 140—including breakfast—for the privilege, then contact **Mountain Evasion**, ☎ and fax 492 12

Les Diablerets

5 Km
5 Miles

32, CH-1865 Les Diablerets. Surprisingly, I have only seen this experience offered in one other place in Switzerland, Saas Fee in the Valais.

In fact, **Mountain Evasion** is a name that you will encounter often in Les Diablerets, especially if you are enticed by a range of esoteric outdoor adventures. Some of the company's other summer offerings include: **Canyoning**—a modern sport in Europe, which encompasses a wide range of similar events including aquatic canyoning through waterfalls; the **Big Rap**—claimed to be the first of its kind in Switzerland—which sends you sliding 160 meters (525 feet) down a rope; the **Flying Jump**—a variation of abseiling and the more well known **Hiking**, **Trekking** and **Mountain Biking**. In winter, they offer **Ice Canyoning** where you climb up a wall of ice; **Mountain Bikes** on ice; **Snow Racquets**, an alternative form of skiing and other snow and ice games. If you don't find something among these lists that entices, you may want to check with them on arrival as they are continually adding new selections. It is a shame, though, that they are not as broadminded in their marketing techniques. Unfortunately, as of this writing, all documentation is in French, and one of the guys I met with, who runs the company, speaks only French. As you might imagine, this can cause some degree of difficulty; still, if you have a communications problem, I am sure the tourist office will be only too glad to assist you. The Mountain Evasion experience is closed during November.

Another organization that contributes its inventive genius to the realm of tourists' amusement is the **Centre ParAdventure—Les Diablerets**, ☎ 492 23 82 or Fax 492 26 28, Rue de la Gare, CH-1865 Les Diablerets. They have assembled a wealth of innovative adventures which include: **Paragliding**—for one or two people; **Vols Biplace**—a form of parachute jumping for two people; **Canyoning, Mudbiking**—a ride on a strange contraption, rather like a bicycle but with very wide, fat, tires and the **Snowscoot**—best described as a snowboard in two sections, where the front part is controlled by handlebars. Again, if you experience any communications problems, just consult the tourist office.

In the summertime there over 200 kilometers (124 miles) of hiking paths. One of my favorite excursions is to take the cable car up to **Isenau**, from where a gentle walk of around a half-hour or so will bring you down to **Lac Retaud**. Really, it is not much of a lake, but the restaurant of the same name not only has some delicious dishes, it specializes in local mushrooms, but also serves the **Liquor of the House** *(Liquor de Maison)* which, while not cheap, is guaranteed to refresh. And one too many might give you a desire to take their rowing boat out around the lake—if the price of CHF 4 per quarter-hour doesn't put you off. Another easy walk down deposits you on the main road which, if you decide not wait for the postal bus, leads you back to the village.

Another interesting trip at this time of the year is to take the chair lift to **Les Mazots**, where you will not only find a traditional restaurant but, also, the **Fromagerie**. Here, you can see, and later taste, how the famous mountain cheese *L'Etivaz* is fabricated.

Winter sports lovers will have difficulty deciding what to do first in the Les Diablerets area. Over 120 kilometers (74.6 miles) of ski runs are serviced by an array of transportation, including more than 50 ski-lifts. And, for those wishing to expand their skill, the Swiss Ski-School of Les Diablerets is there to help you out. Look, also, for cross-country skiing, ice-skating, curling, tobogganing and bobsleighing.

The Lötschental

Few things arouse the emotions of a seasoned traveler more than their returning to a favorite place discovered many years ago, and not revisited since. Departing the Lötschental in 1987, I took with me visions of a fantastically beautiful, narrow, attenuated valley *(tal)* surrounded by lofty Alpine peaks. I also carried pleasant memories of the people who, until the railway reached the head of the valley very early this century, lived an isolated lifestyle, and still choose to retain a host of centuries-old traditions.

As I approached the Lötschental nearly ten years later, I must admit that my expectations were tempered by what I had more recently encountered in other parts of Switzerland. During the intervening decade the demands brought by the influx of mass international tourism had a dramatic effect on so many places throughout the country. To the credit of the Swiss people, this transformation has been accomplished while keeping the charm of the cities, towns and villages intact, and without spoiling the natural beauty of the countryside. Inevitably, though, the demands of tourism have taken their toll, however slight. And considering its topography, and small population, I was keenly aware that even subtle influences could have radically altered the unique and delicate ambiance of the Lötschental.

I needn't have been concerned, however; as I entered the valley again it was obvious that not too much had changed. The villages of Ferden, Kippel, Wiler and Blatten—each at a slightly higher elevation than its predecessor—had retained their delightful characters. Following the road through the narrowing valley of these towering snowcapped Alps, I was greeted by the familiar symphony of cascading waterfalls that adorn the mountain sides and, in turn, feed the perpetually roaring Lanza River as it winds its way back down the valley.

As dramatic as the valley is, however, its apex is even more so. The road comes to a dead end at Fafleralp which, at an elevation of 1,795 meters (5,889 feet), is literally surrounded by peaks that rise to majestic pinnacles of between 3,716 to 4,274 meters (12,192 to 14,022 feet). Truly a sight to be savored, in any season. Thankfully, the visible effects of tourism have been limited to a car park and a few very tiny shops. There is, though, a typically charming hotel—well, two actually—well camouflaged by surrounding trees; and it is to these that the Alpine connoisseur should head.

Switzerland boasts a myriad of places whose scenic beauty is renowned throughout the world. Places, though, where the effects of tourism are commensurate with the number of visitors each attracts. And, no matter how much care has been taken, the trappings to accommodate such demands inevitably detract from the inherent natural beauty. So small is Switzerland, and so visible within the international tourist market, that few places which have been blessed with an outstanding natural landscape remain virtually unknown. The Lötschental, certainly, is one of those and, as such, is one place the discerning traveler to Switzerland seeking a combination of breathtaking panoramas and enchanting local customs should make every effort not to miss.

GETTING THERE:

Trains arrive at Goppenstein, at the head of the valley, from all over Switzerland. From there a regular postal bus service continues through the the Lötschental and on to Fafleralp.

By car, the Lötschental can be reached by one of two ways. From the main Valais highway, which connects Brig and Sion, turn off at the Gampel/Steg exit towards Goppenstein, where you enter the valley. Alternatively, from the Bernese Oberland, take the car/rail connection under the Alps to Goppenstein.

PRACTICALITIES:

The **Dialing Code** for the Lötschental is 27. The local **Tourist Office** (*Lötschental Tourismus*), ☎ 939 13 88, Fax 939 19 88 or E-mail Lt@rhone.ch, is located next to the cable car station at Wiler, CH-3918 Wiler. Information is available on the world wide web at, www.loetschen tal.ch but, at the time of writing, this was presented in German only.

Speaking of German, the people of the valley speak a very unusual German dialect, which is difficult for other German-speaking people, let alone foreigners, to understand.

ACCOMMODATION:

Most accommodation in the Lötschental is in the form of hotels and pensions found alongside the lone road through the valley. The following, with the exception of the Kleinhotel-Restaurant Zur Wildi, are listed in order of location beginning at the mouth of the valley, and moving towards its apex.

The **Hotel Lötschberg *****, ☎ 939 13 09 or Fax 939 13 22, is located in Kippel, not very far from Goppenstein and just five minutes from the Lauchernalp cable car lower station. Guests will enjoy comfortable, well furnished and equipped rooms, and traditional lounge and dining rooms. $$

The **Hotel Nest-und Bietschhorn *****, ☎ 939 11 06 or Fax 939 18 22, found between Ried and Blatten, is one of the largest hotels in the valley. Within a traditional-style house, that was completely renovated in 1986, this offers homestyle comforts, a restaurant renowned for its Valais specialties and an in-house sauna. An innovative array of special excursion packages, including snow safaris, ski-packages and cultural weeks, are also available. $$

The **Hotel Edelweiss *****, ☎ 939 13 63 or Fax 939 10 53, located in Blatten, is another fairly large traditional-style hotel with all modern amenities. Its restaurant is famed for its Valais cuisine and selection of fine wines. Of interest to those traveling with children, family rooms are available where guests pay extra for children according to their age. $$

The **Hotels Fafleralp** and **Langgletscher ***, ☎ 939 14 51 or Fax 939 14 53, are located in a delightfully isolated position off the road, at the very end of the valley. Each of the clean, very comfortable guest rooms, as well as the charming public rooms and dining areas, are decorated with wood paneling that adds to the warm ambiance. And there's not even a village to distract from the natural beauty. The Fafleralp is the better of the two. $$

The **Kleinhotel-Restaurant Zur Wildi ***, ☎ 939 19 89 or Fax 939 20 19, in Lauchernalp, is a small, typical mountain hotel and restaurant that is reached via the Lauchernalp cable car. An ideal choice for those interested in summer hikes or winter sports. $

FOOD AND DRINK:

Many of the restaurants in the Lötschental are an integral part of a hotel and for that reason, and the obvious economic advantage, it really does pay to opt for demi-pension (half-board) when staying here. There is one restaurant, however, that merits special mention:

Restaurant Hockenalp (less than a half-hour walk from the Lauchernalp cable car upper station) is run by the owner/cook Thomas Murmann. There are no formal opening hours, nor electricity, but he is there almost all the time between the middle of June and the first snow in the middle of October. His specialty is cheese bread *(Käseschnitte)*, which is washed down with a large glass of white wine *(Hocken-Ballon)*. Reputedly, if you take your own meat he'll cook that as well. ☎ 939 12 45. $

SUGGESTED TOUR:

I must preface this section by stating that suggested tour is a misnomer in so far as the Lötschental is concerned. Expect no museums of note, and no famous houses or monuments. And even in this valley of monumental natural beauty, you will find no one place that particularly overshadows any other. The Lötschental is, simply stated, a place most suited for those who prefer to engage in outdoor activities, in either the summer or winter seasons.

Skiing and/or snowboarding enthusiasts will, most probably, wish to base themselves close to the Lauchernalp cable car, which was opened in

1972, or even in Lauchernalp itself. From there a combination of chair lifts and ski pulls rise to Gandegg, at an elevation of 2,700 meters (8,858 feet). Recent developments have opened up a wide variety of ski runs, for beginners through to experts. Those needing to rent equipment might wish to look up **Lehner Sport**, ☎ 939 15 84, in Lauchernalp. They also offer instruction in skiing, snowboarding and overland skiing, and a variety of ski-adventures, ski-safaris and the always spectacular Heli-skiing—where you are taken to the highest *pistes* by helicopter.

The Lötschental's appeal, though, is not by any means limited to winter sports enthusiasts. During the warmer months the valley offers activities to suit all ages and levels of fitness. Serious hikers will find no end of high mountain trails to explore, either within the valley or venturing as far as Kandersteg—seven hours away over the mountains. For those intent on exploring in this manner the touring map, available at the tourist office, is a necessity. Visitors seeking an easier path will want to take the cable car to **Lauchernalp**, and walk down from there. The most popular place to begin a hike, though, is **Fafleralp**. Starting there, even young children, and all but the most infirmed, can manage the gentle walk leading up to the small, ice cold, lake of **Grundsee** and then on to the foot of the large glacier. Whichever hike you choose, or even if you prefer just to relax and admire the enveloping mountains from a distance, this valley is a place you'll never forget. Be sure, too, to bring plenty of film. The photographs you take home will be an everlasting memory of an unforgettable place.

Your photographs, and your stay, will be enhanced, too, if your visit to the Lötschental coincides with one of the colorful local traditions. The most strange, and sometimes even frightening, of these is the **Tschäggätä**. No written records have been found relating to this custom, which has its roots in a story passed down orally through the generations. The legend has it that just across from Wiler, many centuries ago, there was a settlement—*Schurtendiebe aus dem Giätrich*—which was inhabited by very strange people. Under cover of night these people, dressed in often hideously carved wooden face masks and a fur costume with a large bell tied around the waist, would attack the more prosperous citizens of Wiler. In fact, the University of Basel has excavated ruins confirming that such a settlement did, indeed, exist. Today, a re-enactment of the tradition continues, but one of the strict rules is that only bachelors can participate. After the second of February Maria Candlelight Mass the young men prepare themselves and their expensive costumes for the festivities; the highlight of which is a carnival parade through Wiler on the Saturday before Ash Wednesday.

Another colorful, but far less grotesque, custom is that of the **Herrgotts-grenadiere**—the "Red Soldiers." For many centuries men of the Lötschental worked as mercenaries for foreign armies, and it is recorded that as far back as 1644 six men were killed in the Battle of Lérida, in Catalonia, Spain. They also have fought for the kingdoms of Naples and Versailles, and it is

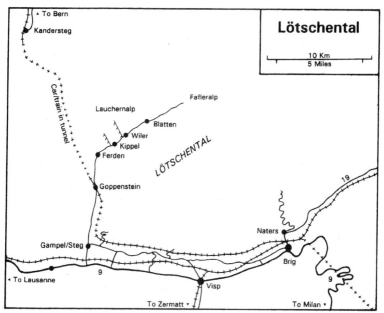

from that era that the red-and-white uniforms originate. Proud of their service with these armies, the soldiers saved their parade uniforms to wear at church services and parades when they returned to the Lötschental. In further remembrance of those times a white silk banner, bearing a red cross and imprinted with the year 1625, is stored in the archives of the church in Kippel. During the celebrations of Corpus Christi, the descendants of these soldiers don scarlet red frocks with golden buttons, white trousers, a white cris-cross holder for swords and bullets and a peaked cap adorned by a tall feather. After the morning church service, with rifles at their shoulders, they parade through the town accompanied by their famous brass band. The attractive Lötschental women, in their own traditional costumes, join in the festivities—making for a resplendent sight indeed.

And if you thought these two customs strange and unusual enough to satiate these people's penchant for the bizarre you'd be wrong. The New Year brings with it the **Festival of the Three Kings** *(Chinigrosslinu)*, during which three young men of military age dress themselves and their steeds in a manner imitating the Three Kings. And not content with "traditional" tradition they are chaperoned by two other men dressed in bright and amusing costumes—basically whatever it is that comes to their minds. This colorful entourage is, in turn, joined by a children's choir, and they go from house to house singing joyous songs until late in the night.

As you might by now imagine, there has to also be a ghostly story in the

Lötschental. It is the tale of Ferden, an old farmer who was killed in mysterious circumstances and whose restless spirit was reputed to chase the animals through the mountains and valleys of the Faldum, Resti and Kummen Alps. After days and nights of relentless pursuit the totally exhausted animals gave up red milk. The inhabitants of the village of Ferden, to which these particular Alps belonged, tried in vain to exorcize the farmer's spirit. Finally, the villagers agreed to donate two day's milk production to the poor folk of the valley. This act of generosity must have appeased the spirit of the farmer Ferden, and he bothered them no more. The custom has been celebrated for centuries since in the community house of Ferden, where the women and children receive a gift of cottage cheese and bread, and drink red wine out of wooden cups.

So there you have the Lötschental; an area of stunning beauty, curious customs and a place still relatively unknown and totally unspoiled by the demands of tourism. This is delightfully charming Switzerland at its best, and an experience not to be missed.

Zermatt Tour #1

Roman coins have been found on the Theodul Pass, indicating that soldiers used this as a means of access to Gaul and Helvetia between 400 and 200 BC. And, it is accepted that the area was populated in the early years of Christendom. Not until 1280, however, does the first documentation mentioning Zermatt, then known as *Protobornum*, originate. A seal of the municipality bears a similar name *Vallis Prato Borni*, the translation of which somehow leads to *zer Matt*, which was first found on a map dated 1495. Although the valley was, traditionally, under the jurisdiction of the Bishop of Sion, those rights were frequently transferred to the most powerful baron of the period. Finally, the people of Zermatt, as was the custom of the day, bought their liberty, paying for it in an ancient Swiss currency, *Mörserpfund.*

Life continued rather uneventfully in Zermatt until the early part of the 19th century, when the first tourists discovered the Matterhorn in 1820. Eighteen years later a surgeon, Dr. Josef Lauber, opened the first inn, the Hotel Cervin, later to be known as the Monte Rosa, which had just three beds. Zermatt, boasting an enviable southern position, yet protected from the wind and with excellent snow conditions, never looked back. These days, the name Zermatt is synonymous with the Matterhorn, and visitors from around the world flock to see the most distinctive, and some say most beautiful, mountain in the Alps. Renowned as both a summer and winter resort, Zermatt is famous, also, for having the longest skiing season in the Alps. And the authorities have acted to preserve the character of the village by banning all traffic. Motor vehicles must be left at Täsch, five kilometers down the valley, with transport to and from there provided by shuttle train or taxi.

In all honesty, though, Zermatt is far from an unspoiled mountain village; quite simply the demands of tourism are too great. As more tourists arrive the infrastructure grows to meet their needs and this, in turn, gives rise to other changes. In fact, the upscale shops, hotels, restaurants and discos, originally appendages to scenery and sport, have now become an attraction in their own right. Daylight hours find the few streets crowded with shoppers, and nightfall brings popular bars and discos very much alive; revelers often being heard in the very early hours of the morning. Zermatt is, therefore, not the quietest of places; but one that combines dramatically beautiful Alpine scenery and unparalleled year-round skiing possibilities with very refined hotels, specialty shops and a lively night life.

GETTING THERE:

By air, international flights arrive at Zürich's Kloten and Geneva's Cointrin airports, with frequent train services connecting from the former in 5 hours, and the latter in 4 hours.

Trains arrive at Zermatt directly from other cities throughout Switzerland, or by changing at Visp and taking a connection from there. Additionally, it is the southern terminus of the world-famous *Glacier Express*.

By car, while Zermatt is "car free," motorists may travel up the valley from Visp, parking at Täsch, 5 kilometers from Zermatt. From there take a shuttle train, or minibus taxis, to Zermatt.

PRACTICALITIES:

The **Dialing Code** for Zermatt is 27. The local **Tourist Office** *(Verkehrsverein)*, ☎ 967 01 81, Fax 967 01 85, E-mail zermatt@wallis.ch or www.zermatt.ch, Bahnhofplatz, CH-3920 Zermatt, is in a central position right outside the railway station. Opening hours, though, are somewhat complicated. During the High Season (mid-December to mid-April) it's open Monday to Friday from mid-December until mid-March from 8:30 a.m. to midday and 1:30–6:30 p.m.; and from mid March to mid-April from 8:30 a.m. to midday and 2–7 p.m. Weekend hours are Saturday from 8:30 a.m. to 5 p.m. and Sunday 9:30 a.m. to midday and 4–5 p.m. All other times of the year it is open Monday to Friday 8:30 a.m. to midday and 1:30–6 p.m.; and Saturday 8:30 a.m. to midday.

Bucherer has just one store in Zermatt, and it is on the Bahnhofstrasse, ☎ 967 53 53, in a typical chalet that blends in perfectly (what else would you expect?) with the regional architecture. The best place to buy **Swiss Army Knives** are the WEGA gift shops, ☎ 967 21 66 or Fax 967 61 60, Bahnhofplatz and other locations in Zermatt. They will engrave the knives free of charge and also have a wide variety of other souvenirs, notably watches, clocks, music boxes, cowbells, books and T-shirts, etc.

Opening hours for shops are: High Season, Monday to Saturday 7:30 a.m. to 7 p.m. (March 1 to April 30, 8 a.m. to 8 p.m.), Sundays and public holidays 8 a.m. to midday and 4–7 p.m. (March 1 to April 30, 4–8 p.m.); Low Season Monday to Saturday 8 a.m. to 12:30 p.m. and 2–6:30 p.m.

The **Lost Property Office**, ☎ 966 22 33 or Fax 966 22 01, in the Haus Irène, c/o aliens office, is open Monday to Friday 8:30 to 11 a.m. and 2–4 p.m.

As Zermatt is car free, all automobiles must be left at Täsch, 5 kilometers (3.1 miles) down the valley. There are a number of indoor garages there, which charge between CHF 7 to 11 per day. There is also a large open car park accommodating 1,800 vehicles at a slightly lower cost of CHF 6 per day. Another alternative is to leave your car at Visp, 33 kilometers (20.5 miles) away, where there is a free car park.

ACCOMMODATION:

The **Grand Hotel Zermatterhof *****, ☎ 966 66 00 or Fax 966 66 99, Bahnhofstrasse, CH-3920 Zermatt, one of only two 5-star hotels in Zermatt, is located within private gardens in a prime position at the end of the main street. In operation since 1879 this very stylish hotel offers conservatively decorated, well equipped rooms, which range in size from twin-bedded to penthouse suites. Dining options include a formal, and informal, restaurant as well as two bars. Guests can also enjoy health facilities with an indoor pool. Transportation to and from the station is provided by horse-drawn carriage, at a cost of CHF 12 per person, or CHF 6 for luggage only. $$$

The **Hotel Monte Rosa ****, ☎ 967 33 33, Fax 967 11 60, E-mail Monterosa.Seiler.Zermatt@spectraweb.ch or www.zermatt.ch/monterosa, CH-3920 Zermatt, is not only a member of The Leading Hotels of the World organization, but is also the most traditional hotel in Zermatt. The 49 rooms and suites all have the most modern facilities and lounges, and one even has a fireplace. Rates include either a copious breakfast buffet, or Swiss breakfast in your own room. And if you opt for half-board that includes a five-course menu, with choices, and if you fancy a selection of dining rooms then you can arrange to eat in any one, or perhaps all, of the other nine Seiler-run hotels in Zermatt. Guests also have use of the indoor pool and fitness and health facilities at the nearby sister hotel, the Mont Cervin. Special attention should be paid to their "Romantic Weekend Package," where besides being treated to the utmost luxury for two nights, the package also includes, weather permitting, a helicopter flight around the Matterhorn. And that's sure to raise your stay in Zermatt to heights otherwise not able to be achieved. $$$

The **Hotel Alpenhof ****, ☎ 967 43 33 or Fax 967 42 32, CH-3920 Zermatt, is centrally located and many of its rooms, often with a contemporary decor, have sitting areas, minibar, balcony and a safe, as well as private bathrooms, phone, TV and radio. Some suites even have their own fireplace. Look, also, for an esteemed restaurant, piano bar, indoor pool and the Vanessa Wellness Center. The latter has an incredible array of therapeutic health experiences that'll refresh and revitalize your mind and body at any time, let alone after a mountain hike. $$$

The **Hotel Alex ****, ☎ 967 17 26 or Fax 967 19 43, CH-3920 Zermatt, found close to the station, has a particularly warm and romantic ambiance, and prides itself on being a carefree vacation destination. No pompousness, or stuffiness, here; but plenty of luxury. Rooms, ranging from small singles to deluxe jacuzzi suites, have a cozy atmosphere, which is also reflected in the public areas. The romantic grotto indoor pool is next to a health club with all kinds of pampered treatments, guaranteed to relax both body and soul. And then there are the bars in the nostalgic dancing area, and the very fine "Alex Grill" restaurant. $$$

The **Hotel Alpenroyal *****, ☎ 967 46 46 or Fax 967 49 36, CH-3920 Zermatt, is a typical mountain-style hotel in an elevated and peaceful location, with excellent views of the Matterhorn. This family-run establishment has comfortable rooms, good food and an indoor pool with sauna and whirlpool. $$

The **Hotel Julen *****, ☎ 966 76 00 or Fax 966 76 76, CH-3920 Zermatt, a member of the Romantik Hotels and Restaurants group, exhibits all of the high standards required by that organization. It is built in the chalet style, and its guests will enjoy comfortable rooms, fine restaurants and glorious views of the Matterhorn. $$

The **Pension Restaurant Burgener ****, ☎ 967 10 20 or Fax 967 55 79, Bahnhofstrasse, CH-3920 Zermatt, is on the main street and in the heart of the village. Clean and simple yet comfortable rooms, and an excellent restaurant ensure a memorable stay. $$

The **Swiss Youth Hostels**, ☎ 967 23 20, Winkelmatten, CH-3920 Zermatt, is simple, basic and clean. Rates of between CHF 18 and CHF 32 per person include breakfast and sheets. $

The **Kulm Hotel Gornergrat *****, ☎ 967 77 66 or Fax 967 67 57, CH-3920 Zermatt, is a unique castle-like building with the distinction of being the highest hotel in the Alps. It sits in splendid Alpine isolation, at an altitude of 3,100 meters (10,286 feet), and can only be reached by the Gornergrat railway, with the last train leaving Zermatt at 6 p.m. Typical mountain decor in the rooms and restaurants, and the most glorious views over huge glaciers to the Matterhorn, and numerous other peaks over 4,000 meters (13,123 feet) in altitude. $$

FOOD AND DRINK:

Many hotels here include demi-pension as part of their rate, and this is to be recommended in Zermatt. You might try the following, though:

> **Restaurant Du Pont** is a neat place which, as the name implies, is right by the bridge next to the church on the main street. The menu, in different languages, is carved into wood and hangs on the wall outside. A varied menu features such delicacies as homemade soups, snails, ham and fried eggs, as well as fondue and raclette which go for CHF 44 for two people. $

SUGGESTED TOUR: KLEIN MATTERHORN AND THE MATTERHORN

Even in the presence of a host of commanding mountain peaks, thirty-six of which ascend to over 4,000 meters (13,123 feet), it is the magnetism of the Matterhorn, and the Matterhorn alone, that draws huge numbers of visitors from all the corners of the world, to Zermatt. So what exactly is the attraction? At 4,478 meters (14,692 feet), it is not the tallest mountain in the area, though the unusually shaped Matterhorn, which stands alone and seems to rise from nowhere, may appear so. It is, in fact, its splendid isolation that creates an optical illusion endowing the mountain with the appearance of a far greater elevation than it actually possesses. Unless you are an expert climber, however, you will need to content yourself with viewing it from a distance, utilizing one of two very contrasting ways to get as close as you possibly can.

Most will be content with the views gained by taking the series of rides which lead up to the Klein Matterhorn, on the **Luftseilbahn**. But remember, children under three years of age are not allowed to go all the way to the top. The first leg from Zermatt, at 1,620 meters (5,315 feet), up to **Furi**, at 1,864 meters (6,115 feet), is by gondola car and covers a considerable distance but elevates you just 250 meters (820 feet). The next leg, by cable car, takes you a further 1,000 meters (3,281 feet) higher, up to **Trockener Steg** at 2,939 meters (9,642 feet). Pause before going any further, as the café sundeck is a wonderful place to partake of refreshments and acquaint yourself with the glorious surroundings. The sheer face of the Matterhorn rises imposingly on one side. To the south stands a veritable wall of mountain peaks, and flowing indeterminably from them are vast glaciers, most notably the Gornergletscher. Time, now, to move on to the final leg of the trip, which will take you steeply upwards for nearly another 1,000 meters (3,281 feet) to the ***Klein Matterhorn** itself. Reaching 3,820 meters, (12,533 feet), this is the highest cable car ride in Europe. The views from this vantage point are, simply stated, unforgettable, and the panorama that unfolds around you takes in about every place from Mont Blanc to Austria, and everything in between. Beware, though, this is about as high as you can go in the Alps, and still keep your feet on the ground, and the air is rarefied indeed. Any sudden, or prolonged, exertion will most surely bring you rapidly to a breathless halt. The curious will want to investigate the strange tunnel which has, at its end, a fine view over Italy, which is also the starting point for the *pistes* of Breuil-Cervinia. This is a great area for summer skiing, and the **Theodul Glacier** and its surroundings offer a natural amphitheater of over 3,626 hectares (8,960 acres) perpetual snow. Between 2,909 and 3,914 meters (9,545 and 12,840 feet) there are 24.1 kilometers (15 miles) of safe, marked, runs including one of 6.4 kilometers (4 miles) with a vertical descent of 1,003 meters (3,290 feet). These are serviced by 9 ski lifts that can accommodate 7,000 people an hour.

The second option for viewing the Matterhorn offers an enviable "bird's eye" view, but requires some nerve. **Air-Zermatt**, ☎ 967 34 87, Heliport CH-3920 Zermatt, offers a twenty-minute helicopter flight around this magic mountain. For those that are even more adventurous, some flights set you down on one of the glaciers! As you might imagine, these flights are not inexpensive, and restricted to a minimum of four people—although Air-Zermatt will help to put together the full complement. This choice is, of course, much more costly than the cable car, but I can personally guarantee it is an experience that will never, ever, be forgotten.

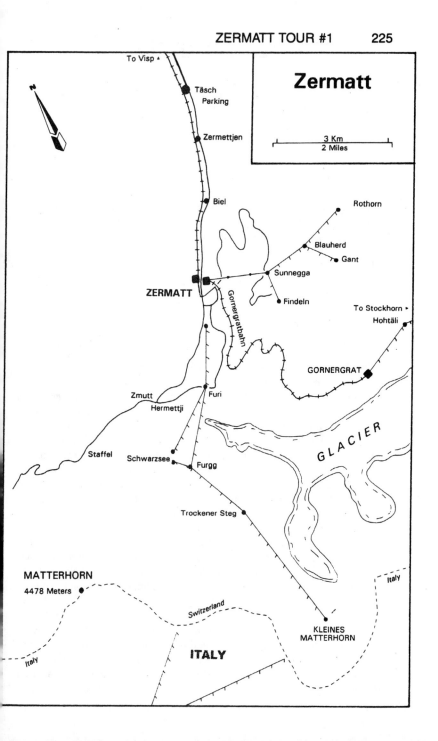

*Zermatt: Tour #2

This tour may be short on words but it is not, by any means, short of surprises. And it offers participants a rare opportunity to experience, at first hand, the eternal ice world of the glaciers.

GETTING THERE:

PRACTICALITIES:

FOOD AND DRINK:
See pages 220–222 for the above.

SUGGESTED TOUR: GORNERGRAT AND STOCKHORN
See map on page 225.

Begin at the second of Zermatt's train stations, **Zermatt Gornergratbahn (GGB)**, which is located directly across from the main station. From here, the modern trains make a 43-minute ascent to Gornergrat at 3,130 meters (10,269 feet), making it Europe's highest totally open-air railway. The initial part of the journey twists and turns through the forested slopes up to the open mountain side. There, in the warmer seasons, you're bound to see numerous marmots scampering around. You'll also quickly realize that the twists and turns offer an ever-changing panorama of glorious Alpine scenery. Upon reaching **Gornergrat**, you will marvel at the unparalleled vista of the massive Monte Rosa, and her sister peaks of this imposing massif, each of which are well over 4,000 meters (13,123 feet). Directly behind you, but in the distance, you will see another range of peaks of equal stature. Amongst these is the Dom, which at 4,545 meters (14,911 feet), is Switzerland's highest. Yet even these magnetic mountains will be unable to distract you from the magnificence of the Matterhorn, splendidly isolated in the distance. Standing on the terrace of the Gornergrat Hotel, a large Swiss flag positioned between you and the Matterhorn, gives the optical illusion that it is flying next to the mountain itself. Besides adding an unexpected element of color to the scene, it offers all the requirements for an excellent photograph.

Ensure, though, that your wonder at these stupendous mountains all around you doesn't preclude you from admiring the glaciers, most notably the **Gornergletscher**. From this vantage point you will be able to clearly define the path along which the massive glacier slowly meanders its way down, as well as its confluence's with other, smaller, glaciers. And what is the source of the amazement and fascination these rivers of ice generate? Perhaps it is their glacial bulk and the knowledge that, however imperceptible it may be to the human eye, they are continually evolving. Perhaps it is the kaleidoscopic array of odd shapes and patterns that nature continually carves into them Perhaps, also, it is the ever-changing colors that play upon their surface; sometimes just a dirty gray on the surface and at others a crystal blue reflection of the sky. Most likely it is a combination of all of these things, enhanced by the natural curiosity raised by their sheer impenetrability. Those wanting to explore this world further will, without doubt, continue by cable car up to **Hohtälligrat** 3,286 meters (10,781 feet) and **Stockhorn** 3,407 meters (11,178 feet), an ice station slap in the middle of the fascinating world of eternal snow and glaciers.

With so many incredible options to explore, time may become a major problem. The last cable car from Stockhorn leaves before 5 p.m., even earlier outside the summer season, and the last train back to Zermatt from Gornergrat departs at 7 p.m. There is a novel solution, however; why not stay overnight at the castle-like Kulm Hotel Gornergrat? After all, how often do you get an opportunity to sleep at an altitude of 3,100 meters (10,171 feet)? What's more, you'll be treated to great Alpine hospitality and a glorious view of the Matterhorn and the surrounding peaks, at sunset and dawn. Just think of all those photo opportunities!

Zermatt: Tour #3

There are any number of other activities to entice visitors to Zermatt that, in themselves, don't constitute a fully fledged tour. The most interesting of these are detailed below.

GETTING THERE:

PRACTICALITIES:

FOOD AND DRINK:
See pages 000–000 for the above.

OTHER SUGGESTED ACTIVITIES:
The trip to **Sunnegga-Blauherd-Rothorn** is a worthwhile adventure, and not just for the views. However, readers should take care not to confuse this with another Rothorn trip, that can be taken from Brienz, in the Bernese Oberland and those at Sörenberg and Lenzerheide/Valbella. Rothorn being the corporate, not the destination, name. This trip starts at the Standseilbahn in Zermatt, just across the river from the Gornergratbahn. The first stage is on the Métro Sunnegga Express which is, in fact, a funicular that ascends, inside the mountain itself, to the plateau of **Sunnegga**, at 2,300 meters (7,546 feet). From there a gondola cable car travels up, and over, to **Blauherd**, 2,627 meters (8,619 feet). The final stage, recently opened in 1996, is by cable car which climbs to **Rothorn**, 3,103 meters (10,180 feet). Besides being the starting point for numerous walks, it also boasts splendid views in its own right.

The Matterhorn is certainly alluring, and those wishing to get as close as possible will want to consider going to **Scwarzsee**. At an altitude of 2,582 meters (8,471 feet), it is not advisable to try the hike up. And why should you? After all, it's much easier to be whisked from Zermatt to Furi by gondola car, and then up to Scwarzsee via the cable car. Here a small lake, and a hotel of the same name, sits right on the foothills of the Matterhorn. A word of caution, though, no matter how tempting it may seem, only the fit, experienced, and well equipped should venture upwards to the **Berghaus**

Belvédère, 3,260 meters (11,877 feet), at least a four-hour return hike. Truly, most will be quite content to take refreshments, and drink in mother nature's wonderful panorama, before beginning their descent back to Zermatt. Of course, the cable car is the easiest way, but this really can be a pleasant hike. The pathway via Hermetjji and Zum-See is the more direct, taking around two hours. Or you may try the path down to Stafelalp and then follow the valley to Zermatt which, most probably, will take about a half-hour longer.

Hiking is, of course, a favorite pastime here, and there are any number of routes to choose from in, and around, Zermatt. These can last for just an hour or so, or even up to a full day. **Mountain biking**, also, is becoming immensely popular, and there are miles of specially laid out, well marked, bike trails. The laws are strict, though, and besides keeping to marked trails— and definitely not wandering off through pastures, footpaths and hiking trails— all bikes must be equipped with certain accessories stipulated by law, including lights and a bell. Further information regarding both hiking and mountain bike trails is available through the tourist office.

In fact the tourist office in Zermatt is rather innovative in putting together its summer and winter information brochures. Considerately multi-lingual, these detail all manner of activity packages, often put together by hotels, that accommodate those wishing to stay a day, week, or somewhere in between. Visitors can choose from such options as Romantic Weekends, Glacier Trekking or even fishing in the mountains. I would strongly suggest that, if you're planning to spend a few days in Zermatt, you request that the tourist office sends you the appropriate brochure in advance of your departure.

Of course, no chapter about Zermatt would be complete without a mention of the **winter sports** facilities and activities. In this wind-protected southern location, Zermatt has three skiing areas that offer excellent snow conditions, and the longest season in the Alps. In fact there are 230 kilometers (143 miles) of ski slopes ranging from the simplest to the most complicated runs. And, to get you around them there are no less than 73 forms of transport, including mountain railway, funicular, aerial cable cars, gondola cars, chair-lifts and ski-lifts. There are also ski walking trails, undertaken at your own risk, cross-country ski runs and curling. The most daring will want to consider **Helicopter Skiing**; so named because a helicopter carries you to starting points which are otherwise virtually inaccessible. The longest of these slopes has an altitude differential of 2,600 meters (8,530 feet). Again, anything involving a helicopter is not inexpensive, but those with both the courage and cash may obtain further information from **Bergführerbüro Zermatt** (Mountain Guide Office) ☎ 966 24 60, CH-3920 Zermatt, between 5 and 7 p.m.

Saas Fee

It is strange that two villages, sitting near the ends of adjacent valleys in the far southern Valais, could be so different in character. The destiny of one was determined by the peculiar silhouette of an adjacent mountain. People around the world have very likely heard of Zermatt, and those that don't know it by name will, most certainly, be aware of it by virtue of that famous mountain—the Matterhorn. How many people, though, have heard of Saas Fee? The answer, unfortunately or, perhaps, fortunately as the case might actually be, is not many. Consequently, far fewer tourists visit Saas Fee than Zermatt, and that works in its favor.

Zermatt definitely caters to mass market international tourism and this brings its share of problems. The town is perpetually crowded. A multitude of shops spar with each other for attention throughout the day and, at night, trendy bars and discos galore spill out their young, and very noisy, clients throughout the night—reminiscent, if you like, of a Spanish Costa.

Saas Fee is different; most obviously by its topography. While its neighbor is hemmed into a fairly narrow and very steep valley, it sits, beautifully indeed, in a natural bowl at an altitude of 1,800 meters (5,906 feet). And, it is very nearly surrounded by no less than 13 mountains that rise to over 4,000 meters (13,123 feet), including the Dom which, at 4,545 meters (14,911 feet), is Switzerland's highest. This charming glacier village, which has preserved many of its customs and traditions, has a population of just under 1,500. As recently as 1850 there were just 236 inhabitants, in part because passage to the village was difficult. The first road to Saas Fee was opened in 1951, but then only on the condition that the village itself remained car-free. Of course, Saas Fee has accumulated its share of shops, but they are manageable in number and, thanks to the layout of the village, they are diffused over a larger area. It also has a variety of bars and restaurants but, very wisely not wanting to spoil nature's peaceful and harmonious setting, no noise or music is allowed on the village streets after 10:30 p.m.

Combine these attributes with the fact that this is an outdoor lovers paradise, in all seasons visitors can hardly fail to be absolutely enchanted with Saas Fee.

GETTING THERE:

Trains go only as far as Brig or Visp, where passengers must disembark and take the bus bound for Saas Fee.

By road: Saas Fee, located at the very end of a dead end valley, is only accessible by one road. Cars, or the postal bus, diverge from the main Valais road at Visp, head due south for a few miles, then take the left fork just past Stalden (the right fork leads to Zermatt) which ascends slowly up to Saas Fee. As Saas Fee is car-free, all vehicles must be parked in the large multi-story car park at the entrance to the village.

PRACTICALITIES:

The **Dialing Code** for Saas Fee is 27. The local **Tourist Office** *(Tourismusorganisation Saas-Fee)*, ☎ 957 14 57, Fax 957 18 60, E-mail to@saas fee.ch or www.saas-fee.ch, CH-3906 Saas Fee, is open Monday to Friday from 8:30 a.m. to midday and 2–6:30 p.m., Saturday from 8 a.m. to midday and 4–6 p.m., and Sunday from 10 a.m. to midday and 4–6 p.m.

ACCOMMODATION:

The **Ferienart Walliserhof ★★★★**, ☎ 958 19 00, Fax 958 19 05, E-mail fe rienart.walliserhof@saasfee or www.Saas-Fee.ch/walhof1.html, CH-3906 Saas Fee, has, behind its chalet-style façade, a warm, stylish and extremely congenial ambiance. Expect innovatively designed and usually wood paneled, beautifully decorated and extremely well-equipped rooms and suites. Dine in your choice of the three restaurants, including the fine Le Gourmet, and afterwards dance to live bands in the bar. And relax, when you feel like it, in the extensive on-site spa and grotto pool. Certainly, a combination that makes for a delightful stay. $$$

The **Beau-Site ★★★★**, ☎ 958 15 60, Fax 958 15 65, E-mail hotel.beau-site@saas-fee.ch or www.romantikhotels.com/rhsaas, CH-3906 Saas Fee, is a charming, family-run hotel that is a member of the Romantik Hotels group. Originally built in 1893, it has been completely renovated in recent years, and careful attention was taken to retain the traditional Valais style. Expect very comfortable well-furnished and appointed guest rooms and suites, and public areas designed to make you feel at home. The restaurants, too, offer you culinary delights. In 1995/96 the hotel opened an extensive spa area, the Beau-Vital. As well as the expected pool guests can partake of the Augusta Raurica—a series of thermal Roman baths; the Aromarium—a steam cabin with plant extracts added to the steam; a Finnish sauna—with temperatures of around 85 degrees Celsius (185 degrees Fahrenheit); a Hay Bath or Cleopatra Bath—in the former your whole body is wrapped in previously moistened Saas mountain hay, and afterwards gently warmed on the soft pack couch, and the latter has an Oriental emulsion of milk and various oils covering your body; and a Hydro Jet Massage. Follow these treatments with a massage, or a session in the Relaxarium—where a 30-minute program is divided into three phases: Withdrawal from everyday routine, Relaxation Phase and, finally, the awakening and revival. $$

The **Hotel Burgener ✳✳✳**, ☎ 957 15 22 or Fax 957 28 88, is a small, 30-room hotel in the heart of the village. You will find a cozy, comfortable, ambiance in the rooms and throughout the hotel. $$

The **Hotel Rendez-Vous ✳✳**, ☎ 957 20 40 or Fax 957 35 34, CH-3906 Saas Fee, a small hotel which offers apartments also, has modern well-appointed rooms each with a balcony and bath. Other features are a restaurant, a bar and a sun terrace. $$

FOOD AND DRINK:

As is true when staying in most villages of this type, it is financially advisable to pay the relatively small amount extra, if it is not already included in the rate, for demi-pension. There is one restaurant, however, that you will certainly want to visit.

> **Drehrestaurant Metro-Alpin**, (at an elevation of 3,500 meters—11,483 feet) is the world's highest revolving restaurant. Making a full 360-degree rotation once every hour, it affords an unparalleled panoramic vista of the surrounding mountain peaks and glaciers.

SUGGESTED TOUR:

When suggesting an itinerary in many Swiss mountain villages, tour is a misnomer. The overriding allure of Saas Fee, regardless of the season, is a magnificent natural setting that facilitates outdoor sports of all kinds. Winter sports enthusiasts, however, can have the best of both worlds, as the glaciers around **Mittelallalin** allow for summer skiing as well. During winter there are over 100 kilometers (62.1 miles) of ski slopes—50% red, 25% blue and 25% black runs, and two 80-meter (262 foot)-long half pipes and funboxes for snowboarders. As a matter of information, snowboarders, or even prospective ones, may be interested in the **Paradise Snowboarding School**, ☎ 957 46 18 or Fax 957 35 18, where, in winter or summer, instructors are ready and waiting to teach you the intricacies of this up-and-coming sport. There are also 20 kilometers (12.4 miles) of winter hiking paths, a 6-kilometer (3.7 miles)-long cross-country ski run and a toboggan run that operates twice weekly under floodlights. Those seeking a slightly less taxing sport may opt for the ice skating rink, or even curling. During summer the runs are reduced to 20 kilometer (12.4 miles) of slopes, for average-to-very-good skiers, but snow boarders can make use of the Swatch Snow Park Allalin. Constructed in 1996 on summer pistes, the glacier has been innovatively carved to create pipes, bumps and jumps, and there is even a permanent BoarderCross course.

Mountain hikers and mountain bikers will be in their element in the summer, also. For those who fall into the latter category, bikes may be rented from **Glacier Sport**, ☎ 957 18 65 or Fax 957 32 71. There are over 280 kilo-

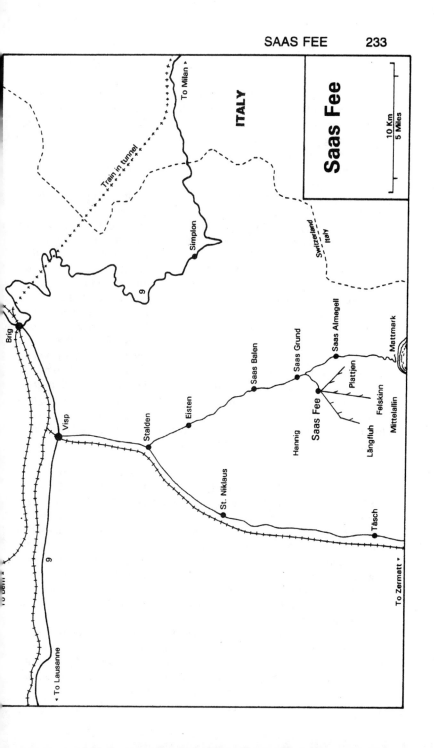

meters (174 miles) of pathways that vary in difficulty, and the tourist office has brochures, panoramic maps and the Saastal hiking map available for visitors. Those wishing to attempt something more adventurous should contact the **Saastal Mountaineering School**, ☎ 957 44 64 which offers, for beginners to experts, a varied program incorporating rock and ice climbing, canyoning, glacier hiking and mountaineering.

Whatever the season, but with certain exceptions when they are closed—typically between seasons, Saas Fee has a particularly impressive mountain transport system. Two large cable cars and three smaller ones, eighteen ski lifts, two chair lifts and a funicular "Metro Alpin" compete for your business. Visitors may choose from a variety of interesting trips to take; though one, winter or summer is an absolute must! Take the cable car from Saas Fee to **Felskinn**, at an altitude of 3,000 meters (9,843 feet), then change onto the **"Metro Alpin"**—the highest funicular in the world—for the 465-meter (1,526 foot) ascent to **Mittelallin**. On arrival, at an altitude of 3,500 meters (11,483 feet), you will find two "highest in the world" places. The *Drehrestaurant*, which seats 220 people and revolves 360 degrees every hour, is a unique place to enjoy a meal and watch as a panoramic feast of Alpine peaks and glaciers slowly reveal themselves to you in all their glory. It is then possible to go down deep into the glacier, and visit the world's highest, and largest—2,500 cubic meters (88,287 cubic feet)—**ice pavilion**. Inside, beneath a ceiling of pure ice that averages a thickness of 10 meters (33 feet) and at a temperature of minus 4–5 centigrade (24.8 to 23 degrees Fahrenheit) in winter and minus 1–2 centigrade (30.2 to 28.4 degrees Fahrenheit) in summer, you will learn much about glaciers—and you can touch as well. Regular visitors will notice, too, the effects of almost imperceptible, but constant, change—the annual movement of both the glacier and ice pavilion is 27-30 centimeters (10.6 to 11.8 inches).

Hikers, as well, have a fine choice of pathways. From Saas Fee, cable cars ascend to your choice of **Plattjen**, 2,570 meters (8,432 feet); **Längfluh**, 2,870 meters (9,416 feet) or **Hannig**, 2,350 meters (7,710 feet). Each of these has a restaurant/bar where you can indulge in a bit of refreshment before beginning the downhill treks back to the village. And, be sure to take along some raw carrots. Along the way you are bound to encounter some of Saas Fee's trademark tame marmots, and these chubby, furry, creatures love nothing better than a carrot snack. Alternatively, take the postal bus up to **Mattmark**, where you will see Europe's largest dam, perhaps continuing on to the Monte Moro Pass, at 2,868 meters (9,409 feet), before returning to Saas Fee the same way.

If you can spare a bit of time in the village, you have options there as well. The **Bielen Recreation Center**, open daily from 10 a.m. to 8 p.m. in season and from 1:30–8 p.m. at other times, offers a 25-meter pool, grotto solariums, a sauna, steam baths and a whirlpool—all ideal for relaxation, or to unwind after a strenuous mountain hike or bike.

Those interested in learning more about the history and culture of Saas Fee will wish to visit the **Saas Museum**. Found within in an early-18th-century home, the main exhibit is the original study of the German writer Carl Zuckmayer, who adopted Saas Fee as his second home. Look, also, for traditional costumes, a sacred art collection, folklore articles, a collection of minerals and an exhibition regarding the history of glaciers.

The tourist office in Saas Fee has been particularly innovative in putting together packages for tourists, one of which may be of interest to many readers of this guide. The **Glacier Igloo Adventure** allows you to spend a night, in the company of a minimum of nine other "friends," in an igloo on the Fee Glacier—which sits at a dizzying an altitude of 3,300 meters (10,827 feet).

Ticino:
Ascona, Locarno
and Lugano

Ticino, making up 7% of Switzerland's land territory, is located across the 46th parallel equidistant from the North Pole and the equator. It has the distinction of being the only one of the country's twenty-six Cantons situated entirely south of the Alps, and its geographical isolation has proved to be a significant factor in its development and history. Fossilized remains from the Triassic period—200 million years ago—found in the fossil beds of Mount San Giorgio indicate that this area was once a part of the sea bed. And, the first evidence of human life dates from the Stone Age.

Ticino's shape can best be described as an upturned triangle, with the base being the Alps and the apex—just fifty kilometers from Milano, Italy—extending into Italian territory. It is that southernmost point of land that has been the source of problems throughout the area's history. Of course, the Romans left behind their typical inheritance but, even following their departure and up until the 14th century, the history of Ticino, and its people *(Ticinesi)*, was inextricably linked with the Italian regions of Lombardy and Piedmont. During this era, Ticino, coveted because of its commercial and strategic prominence, came under the control of either Como or Milan.

In the mid-13th century, during their initial organization and consolidation period, leaders of the Swiss cantons realized that control of the St. Gotthard road was of paramount importance. The Swiss Confederation's "Gotthard policy" was not implemented swiftly or without tragic consequences, however, and it was not until the early 16th century that Ticino passed indisputably into their control. The status quo persevered until the close of the Napoleonic Wars when, in 1803, it became a free and independent Swiss canton.

Even as late as 1860, nearly a third of the population dwelt in the mountain villages, a figure that over the last decades has gradually diminished to 10%. The foremost factor in effecting this redistribution was the completion in 1882 of the St. Gotthard railway tunnel, which finally broke the bonds of isolation, opening routes of travel and lines of communication to other parts of Switzerland and the world. Even today, Ticino has only around 300,000 inhabitants, just over 4% of the country's total, with the bulk of the population centered around the communities of Lugano (99,000), Locarno (42,000), Chiasso (40,000), and the capital city of Bellinzona (37,000). Of the approximately 250 small towns and villages in Ticino, half have populations of less than 500 and 40 have less than 100!

Ticino's claim to international fame arises from its magnificently varied scenery and mild climate which, when compared to other areas of Switzerland, could be termed "warm." The temperature averages 15.5 degrees Celsius (60 degrees Fahrenheit) and the region is blessed with in the vicinity of 2,300 hours of sunshine each year. In the north are untamed mountains and valleys forged by ice and icy-rivers which, in turn, spill into and replenish Lake Maggiore and the other lakes in the region. These natural characteristics endow Ticino with what can best be described as a Mediterranean ambiance—tiny, palm-treed villages cling precariously to steep mountain sides and pretty, oftentimes pastel-colored houses and villas line the balmy lakes. In addition, the area boasts many sites of architectural importance—in large part built by the Ticinesi, who are celebrated for their craftsmanship in such areas, and many places of historical interest. With such attributes to recommend it to tourists, Ticino attracts in excess of 3,000,000 annually.

Although other places will allure—most notably the capital of Bellinzona with its three magnificent castles—most visitors head for Ascona, Locarno or Lugano, all located in the southern sector of Ticino. Ascona and Locarno, from their respective locations on either side of the Maggia River, could be described as twin towns but, in reality, they have little in common. Locarno, by far the larger of the two, has its attractions— particularly in the Old Town. Ascona, with a population of just 5,000, is a magically pretty town, and most visitors would surely choose to stay there.

Its narrow streets and lanes, dominated by the church's towering spire and filled with restaurants, bars and specialty shops, meander down, converging at some point with the long and narrow piazza that separates the lake from the town itself. And, what an eclectic array of hotels, restaurants, bars and shops line this, the main meeting place, of Ascona. Adding to its peaceful charm, the authorities have made a determined effort to restrict the use of cars insofar as possible. You do, however, have to yield to the swans and ducks! It really is quite a place to take your repose, order a cool drink, and admire the tranquil and very appealing panorama—pretty villas; yachts, motor boats and lake steamers sliding gracefully over the water; the unusual Brissago Islands; and, wherever you rest your gaze, tree-lined slopes cascading freely into the lake shore. A scenario definitely conducive to reflection—it is no wonder that the last century saw an influx of philosophers, anarchists and other free thinkers such as Herman Hesse, James Joyce and Carl Gustav Jung drawn to the city. These and others have made the hill overlooking Ascona, Monte Verità, famous in its own right.

These days, a diversity of cultural events that take place throughout the year intensifies Ascona's appeal. These include the Mardi Gras risotto cook-out on the Piazza in February, the New Orleans Music Festival Ascona in June/July and the International Music Weeks of classical music from August through October.

The descriptions of Ascona and Locarno, above, will have provided sufficient information for most visitors. Therefore, no suggested tours are included for those cities. They are, however, used as a base for two of the daytrips found elsewhere in this guide. A suggested tour for Lugano follows, and the daytrip to Milan uses Lugano for its departure point as well.

GETTING THERE:

By air, international flights arrive at Geneva's Cointrin, or Zürich's Kloten, airport. Departing from the former, the train connection to Locarno/Lugano takes you via Zürich—a rather roundabout way but by far the quickest—taking about six hours to Lugano and six and a quarter hours for the leg to Locarno. If you depart from Zürich, the trip takes about three and a quarter hours to either Locarno or Ascona. In both instances, however, be advised that the trip to Locarno involves a change at Bellinzona. Direct flights, from other Swiss cities and certain European ones, arrive at Lugano's Agno airport, the third-busiest in Switzerland.

Trains arrive at Lugano, which is directly on the Zürich-Luzern-Milano line; or Locarno station, following a change at Bellinzona.

By car, when approaching from the north take the St. Gotthard Tunnel, which was opened in 1980 and passes for 17 kilometers (10.6 miles) through the Alps, to the N-2 autoroute which cuts a north/south axis through Ticino until you reach the capital city of Bellinzona. From there, follow the signs to Locarno/Ascona or, alternatively, continue south to Lugano.

When approaching from the west—e.g. Geneva, Lausanne, Montreux and Zermatt, the trip is a bit more complicated. Follow the main Valais road to Brig, traversing the Simplon Pass to Domodossola, Italy. From there the road, rather tricky at times, follows the magnificently beautiful Centovalli valley to Ascona/Locarno. If you wish continue on to Lugano, go via Bellinzona.

From eastern Switzerland, particularly the Upper and Lower Engadine, the route is more than a bit complicated but, in recompense, very interesting. Head south-west from St. Moritz and, just past the lakes, the road drops precipitously at the Malojapass, crossing into Italy shortly before you reach Chiavenna. Continue on around the western side of Lake Como as far as Menaggio, where you may turn inland to Lugano or carry on due north to Locarno/Ascona, via Bellinzona. An alternative route is via the San Bernadino Pass, where you can catch the N-13 highway to Bellinzona, and from there travel on to Ascona/Locarno or Lugano.

PRACTICALITIES:

The **Dialing Code** for Ascona, Locarno and Lugano is 91.

The local **Tourist Office** *(Ente Turistico)* for **Ascona**, ☎ 791 00 90, Fax 792 10 08 or E-mail ascona@etlm.ch, is in the Casa Serodine, CH-6612 Ascona. Open March to October, Monday to Friday, from 9 a.m. to 6:30 p.m., Saturday from 9 a.m. to 6 p.m. and Sunday from 9 a.m. to 2 p.m. November through February hours are Monday to Friday from 9 a.m. to 12:30 p.m. and 2–6 p.m.

The local **Tourist Office** *(Ente Turistico)* for **Locarno**, ☎ 751 03 33, Fax 751 90 70, E-mail locarno@ticino.com or www.tourism-ticino.ch, Largo Zorzi, 1, CH-6601, Locarno is open March to October, Monday to Friday, from 8 a.m. to 7 p.m. and Saturday/Sunday from 9 a.m. to midday and 1–5 p.m. November through February hours are Monday to Friday from 8 a.m. to midday and 2–6 p.m.

The local **Tourist Office** *(Ente Turistico)* for **Lugano**, ☎ 921 46 64, Fax 922 76 53 or E-mail ltoinfo@lto.ch, Riva Albertolli, CH-6901 Lugano is found off the center of town just across from the lake and opens Monday to Friday from 9 a.m. to 6:30 p.m., Saturday from 9 a.m. to 12:30 p.m. and 1:30–5 p.m., Sunday from 9:30 a.m. to 1 p.m., and on holidays from 10 a.m. to 12:30 p.m. and 1:30–6 p.m.

Although politically Swiss, 85% of the people in Ticino are Italian-speaking. This may occasionally cause some difficulty in communicating, but many *Ticinesi* understand English as well.

The shops in this area typically open on Monday to Friday from 8 a.m. to midday and 2–6:30 p.m., although some in Locarno/Lugano extend their hours until 10 p.m. on Thursday, and on Saturday from 8 a.m. to 5 p.m.

ACCOMMODATION:

In Ascona:

The **Castello del Sole Ascona** *****, ☎ 791 02 02, Fax 792 11 18, E-mail castellosole@relaischateaux.fr or www.integra.fr/relaischateaux/castel losole, CH-6612 Ascona, is more than a very fine hotel, it is a self-contained resort complex. The first written documentation of an inn on this site dates from 1756. Subsequently, the spot hosted a villa and popular hostelry before it was transmogrified to 5-star luxury. It is set within an 80,000-square-meter (19.8-acre) park with private grounds extending to the lakeside, and among its amenities are a variety of sports facilities—including a large health club and pool, outdoor courtyards and a number of fine restaurants serving dishes that incorporate vegetables and herbs grown in its gardens as well as an interesting Merlot (red wine) produced and bottled on site. A stay at the Castello del Sole is truly an elegant experience. $$$

The **Albergo Giardino** *****, ☎ 791 01 01, Fax 792 10 94, E-mail giar dino@relaischateaux.fr or www.integra.fr/relaischateaux/giardino, Via Segnale 10, CH-6612 Ascona, sits just across the road from the Castello del Sole, outside of Ascona proper. You will rarely find two 5-star hotels in such close proximity that are so different from, and complementary to, each other. While the grounds of the Albergo are much smaller, they are also prettier. The rectangular courtyard which joins the various buildings is embellished with a large fishpond and adorned with luxurious, verdant, foliage. This is the view from the restaurant's all-weather terrace, making dinner here a romantic experience indeed. Guests enjoy every expected luxury, yet the ambiance is one of friendly informality. The front desk is, literally, a desk, and before dinner on Sunday evening they customarily have a short skit in the lounge. $$$

The **Castello Seeschloss ****,** ☎ 791 01 61 or Fax 791 18 04, Piazza Motta, CH-6612 Ascona, located at the end of the famous Piazza, really is what its name implies—a medieval castle. Recently renovated, it now houses a very modern and comfortable hotel. Of course, expect to pay a little extra for romantic rooms in the tower. $$$

The **Hotel Tamaro ***,** ☎ 791 02 82 or Fax 791 29 28, Piazza G. Motta, CH-6612 Ascona, offers charming and stylish accommodation in traditionally decorated rooms, some with a lake view. The restaurant, also, overlooks the lake and the famous Piazza. $$

In Lugano:

The **Villa Principe Leopoldo *****,** ☎ 985 88 55, Fax 985 88 25, E-mail leopoldo@relaischateaux.fr or www.integra.fr/relaischateaux/leopoldo, 5, via Montalbano, CH-6900, Lugano, is a luxurious hotel situated high above Lugano that affords marvelous views across this pretty, narrow, lake and its steep hillsides. Nothing is spared in their efforts to create an enchanting ambiance in this wonderful 18th-century neo-classical style mansion. An outdoor pool, a sauna, a jacuzzi, and exquisite restaurants complete the package. $$$

The **Grand Hotel Eden *****,** ☎ 993 01 21, Fax 994 28 42 or E-mail eden@fivenet.ch, CH-6900 Lugano-Paradiso, is located in a breathtaking position on the shore of Lake Lugano. Though established in the mid-19th century, it has been regularly renovated to incorporate every modern luxury. Its 113 deluxe rooms and 7 suites (2 to Presidential standard) are each equipped with satellite color TV, mini bar, safe and air conditioning. On site are two exclusive restaurants, an American-style bar, 2 pools—one filled with salt water, a private beach, a sauna, a solarium and a fitness corner. $$$

The **Romantik Hotel Ticino ****,** ☎ 922 77 72 or Fax 923 62 78, Piazza Cioccaro 1, CH-6901 Lugano, is located in the heart of Lugano just a short walk from the lake, the railway station and the shopping and financial districts. It is housed within a charming 400-year-old "Tessin" house that is notable for its flower-bedecked patio and for the beautiful and important art collection on display in the public areas and restaurant. It offers 23 tastefully decorated rooms, each with bath/shower, toilet, radio, direct dial telephone and mini bar. The gourmet restaurant, with its refined ambiance and reputation for excellent cuisine, is an ideal place for those who like a personal touch and a quiet atmosphere. While I have been told by the management that many celebrities have frequented this wonderful establishment over the years, typical of their discretion and consideration of their guests, they will not disclose their identities. $$

The **Hotel International Au Lac ***, ☎ 922 75 41 or Fax 922 75 44, via Nassa 68, CH-6901 Lugano, is the only hotel in the center of Lugano that is on the lake promenade. Behind a classical façade, the decor is traditional in style. Communal amenities include a restaurant, a garden with a pool, a sun terrace, and—quite important in Lugano—a private indoor car park. $$

FOOD AND DRINK:

Special mention must be made here that dining is after the Italian manner. An appetizer *(antipasto)* is followed by a first course *(primo)*—most often pasta, and a second *(secondo)*—usually a meat dish. The meal culminates with cheese, then a dessert, possibly *torta di pane* (a bread cake) or *torte della nonna* (a sugar tart). The choice of wine is wide, but most won't want to leave the area without sampling the famous Ticino Merlot, a claret wine. End, of course, with a *grappa* or *nocino* (a walnut-based liqueur).

As with most places detailed in this guide, it is recommended that demipension be taken at your choice of hotel. Nevertheless, this restaurant is rather interesting, and inexpensive:

Grotto Baldoria, (Ascona) is a most interesting establishment, tucked away in one of the side streets off the Piazza. The menu—well, there isn't one really—is whatever the chef decides he is going to cook that day. The ambiance is pleasing and the fare inexpensive. ☎ 791 32 98. $

SUGGESTED TOUR IN LUGANO:

Lugano is a city of many charms and it is truly a delight to simply to wander through its narrow streets. The main attractions, however, are found along the beautiful lake front. Lake Lugano is not particularly wide at this point, and the steep surrounding hills give the illusion that it is smaller than it actually is.

Beautiful villas are a notable feature of this city, and two of their genre act as bookends to Lugano's lake front. At the southern end, and just a few moments away from the city center, is the **Villa Malpensata** (1). This typically grand 19th-century villa on lovely grounds passed out of private ownership when, in 1893, it was bequeathed to the city. There was a proviso, however. The income from the estate was to be used to found a fine arts museum bearing the name of the donor, Antonio Caccia. Such a museum was opened in 1912 but, just 21 years later, that was relocated to the Villa Ciani—the other in this "pair of bookends," which will be visited later. From that point forward, the Villa Malpensata has been used in a variety of ways

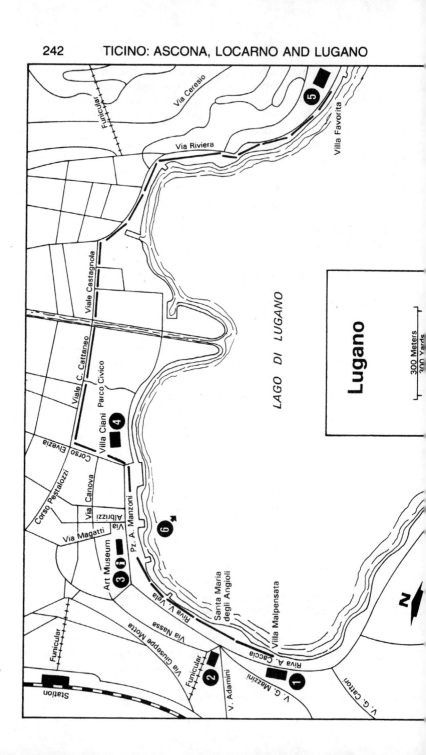

and, presently, houses the **Modern Art Museum** (*Museo d'arte Moderna*), ☎ 994 43 70, Riva. A. Caccia 5. While there is a permanent collection on display, its fame arises from its reputation as a host for major touring exhibitions. It opens Tuesday to Sunday from 10 a.m. to midday and 2 to 6 p.m.

Walking back towards town, it would be entirely possible to overlook the façade of the **Santa Maria degli Angioli** (2). That would be a mistake. Found in the Piazza B. Luini and dating from 1490, this was once a part of a Franciscan monastery that was suppressed in 1848. Most notable here is the wall separating the nave from the chancel, which is entirely overlaid with an immense fresco. Created by Bernardino Luini in 1529, this gloriously depicts the Passion and Crucifixion of Christ.

Continue on now, but this time across the road along the lakeside promenade—which is delightful indeed. Trees, small parks and fountains provide a pleasant distraction to the activities on the lake. I was surprised to find out how active the lake can be—on my last visit a group of youths arrived, stripped to their swim wear, and dove right in! As I learned later, this is apparently quite a normal occurrence. Pressing on, after a few minutes you will come upon the docking points for lake voyages. Remember where they are, as we will investigate these a bit later.

For the moment, though, turn your attention immediately across the road to the imposing façade of the Municipal Building. Next to that, in the Piazza Manzoni, 7, you will find the **Cantonal Art Museum** (*Museo Cantonale d'arte*) (3) ☎ 922 93 56. Housed in a group of buildings dating from the Middle Ages and noteworthy in their own right, this museum boasts a collection of works by Swiss/Italian and Italian artists of the 19th and 20th centuries and hosts a varied program of temporary exhibitions. The headquarters of the Swiss Photography Foundation is also found here and so are regular shows of selected photographs. Visit Tuesday from 2–5 p.m. and Wednesday to Sunday from 10 a.m. to 5 p.m.

Farther around at the termination of the promenade is the Municipal Park that is home to, among other things, the previously mentioned other in the "pair of bookends," the **Villa Ciani** (4). The house and its extensive gardens are named after two brothers, Giacomo and Filippo Ciani. Although their family originated from the Ticino, the brothers were born in Milan. As important figures in liberal politics and very enterprising entrepreneurs, they played a major role in the political and economic of development of Lugano—becoming among its most prominent 19th-century citizens. Between 1840 and 1843, they acquired, expanded and refurbished an existing 17th-century home, fashioning it into the Villa Ciani, as it is known today. The municipality compulsorily purchased the property in 1912 and, initially, used it to house the local history museum. In 1933, it metamorphosed into the **Municipal Fine Arts Museum** (*Museo Civico di Belle Arti*), ☎ 800 72 09, which today exhibits a collection of works by Swiss and other

European artists from the 15th to the 20th centuries. Unfortunately it is problematical whether you will get to see it. Extensive renovations were begun in the late 1980s with a targeted reopening date of 1994. As of this writing, however, work was still ongoing!

There are three other museums of note, all just outside of Lugano. First, let me introduce you to the **Thyssen-Bornemisza Collection** *(Collezione Thyssen-Bornemisza)* (5), ☎ 972 17 41. In 1932, Baron Thyssen-Bornemisza, enchanted with the beauty of the area and, in particular, the magnificent location and design of the Villa Favorita, purchased the home and expanded it to accommodate his large and fabulous collection of fine art, the finest private one in the world. This collection has since been augmented by his son Hans Heinrich who, in addition to an interest in the Old and Modern masters, developed an enthusiasm for 19th- and 20th-century artists. A collection of those works is now on permanent exhibition. In the 1970s and 80s the Villa attracted worldwide attention with a variety of special exhibitions. In 1991, however, many of the major attractions were transferred to the Thyssen-Bornemisza museum in Madrid. The Villa Favorita, located in Castagnola, can be reached by taking a Number 1 bus which winds its way on this pleasant journey from Lugano. If you will be in the area between Good Friday and the end of October, you should factor into your schedule that the hours are curtailed. It is open on Friday, Saturday and Sunday only, from 10 a.m. to 5 p.m.

Farther along the lake in an isolated position near the Italian border is another—very curious—museum. It is accessible only via a lake steamer that departs Lugano Giardno at 1 p.m. The history of this museum revolves around—and this is the curious part—smuggling. Smuggling is an illegal activity that, inevitably, afflicts every border to some degree, and the physical features of this particular coast were certainly conducive to the success of the outlaw. In fact, this was a local way of life that has only recently come to an end. During 1856, in an effort to control the epidemic, the Swiss authorities constructed the first customs house on this site. The present building, which replaced the original in 1904, continued in operation until 1935, at which time the **Swiss Customs Museum** *(Museo Doganale Svizzero)* (6), ☎ 910 48 11, was opened. And, really, this museum has something for people of every age, including, since 1994, an interactive exhibition. The journey to the museum is also pleasant in itself. Between April to October it is open daily from 1:30–5:30 p.m.

When the weather is conducive, usually between March and the end of October/November, numerous other voyages sail on Lake Lugano. Many of these are run by the **Societa Navigazione del Lago di Lugano**, ☎ 971 52 23 or Fax 971 27 93, Viale Castagnola 12, CH-6900 Lugano. They will be pleased to send you a brochure detailing each of their excursions. I suggest two options here that may appeal. The first of these entails taking the lake

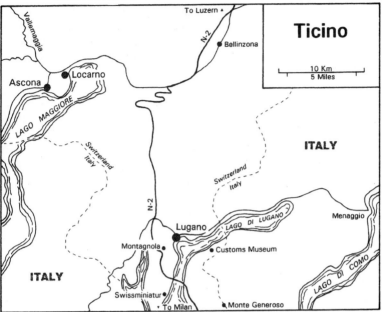

steamer to Capolago and then boarding a funicular to **Monte Generoso** where, at 1,704 meters (5,591 feet), you get a marvelous perspective of the various branches of the lake. As a second option, children of all ages will be utterly fascinated by the **Swissminiatur**, which is reached either by lake steamer or by bus. Here, the entire landscape of Switzerland is replicated in miniature over an area of 11,000 square meters (2.7 acres). Besides being fascinating, this enables you to formulate a mental vision of the country as a whole and to better understand either where you are going or where you have been. Model train lovers will certainly be on track; a model railway has been constructed with a length of 3 kilometers (1.86 miles), and the whole network is centrally controlled. **Swissminiatur**, ☎ 640 10 60, Fax 640 10 69 or E-mail info@swisminiatur.ch, opens from mid-March to the end of October, daily, from 9 a.m. to 6 p.m. During August and September the hours are extended and the complex is illuminated.

Finally, a small but important museum is found within the Casa Carmuzzi complex in Montagnola, approximately ten minutes outside of Lugano. **The Herman Hesse Museum** *(Il Museo Hermann Hesse)* was inaugurated in 1997 in conjunction with the 120th anniversary of this painter, poet, novelist and Nobel Prize winner's birth. One of four museums in the world dedicated to his memory, it contains memorabilia from the last 43 years of his life, during which time he lived in Ticino where he died in 1962.

The museum is open, during the summer months, on Saturday and Sunday only from 10:00 a.m. to 12:30 p.m. and 2:00–6:30 p.m. For more information ☎ 091 993 37 70. Also recently instituted is a walking tour "In the footsteps of Hermann Hesse," which takes visitors through the historic villages of Montagnola, Gentilino and Agra.

Vallemaggia

The Vallemaggia, covering one-fifth of the canton of Ticino, is a wonderland of natural beauty that, surprisingly, remains unknown to many of those visiting Switzerland. It is comprised of a series of valleys whose rivers converge at various points, cascading down to their ultimate and common destination on the Vallemaggia valley floor at Cevio. From here the waters flow into Lake Maggiore, some thirty odd kilometers (18.6 miles) farther south, a geological masterpiece carved out by the glaciers and by the rivers formed by the melting ice in its turn. The mountains to the east, north and west create a virtually impenetrable barrier, yet this area has been inhabited for millennia. By its very nature, though, the valley has constrained upon its residents an isolated lifestyle, a reality clearly evident upon visiting the rural villages and hamlets. Indeed, in combination with its geographical uniqueness, its remoteness is the valley's strongest appeal to visitors.

Those planning on spending a significant amount of time in the Vallemaggia will want to enjoy its natural attributes to the full. The best way to do that is on foot—taking advantage of the nearly 700 kilometers (435 miles) of paths. These meander through magnificent scenery—including more than forty Alpine pools and lakes, and numerous waterfalls. This also will be your best opportunity to investigate, up close and personal, the incredible array of fauna and flora indigenous to the area. Others, with more restrictive schedules, will need to take advantage of the more time-efficient ways to explore this very unusual and majestically pretty valley.

GETTING THERE:

By car, just follow the road from Ascona/Locarno that runs parallel to the Maggio river.

By Postal Bus, Linea 10 operates from Locarno to Bignasco and Cavergno, via Cevio. From Bignasco services run either to San Carlo or Fusio, and from Cevio to the other branches of the valley which end at Cimalmotto and Bosco Gurin.

PRACTICALITIES:

The **Dialing Code** for the Vallemaggia is 91. The local **Tourist Office** *(Ente Turistico di Vallemaggia)*, ☎ 753 18 85, Fax 753 22 12 or E-mail vallemaggia@etlm.ch, CH-6673 Vallemaggia, is open Monday to Friday from 9 a.m. to midday and 2–5 p.m., with additional hours, between June and September, on Saturday from 9 a.m. to midday.

Although one option is to traverse the Vallemaggia by bus—it is possible to ride to one village, hike to another and then take the bus back to Locarno, be forewarned that the buses are not too frequent. Services between Locarno and Bignasco/Cavergno are operated by **Ferrovie Autolinee Regionali Ticinesi**, affectionately known as FART, and to all other destinations by postal bus. If you really wish to see all the "crooks and crannies" of the various valleys it is better to travel by car.

ACCOMMODATION:

The **Albergo Basodino**, ☎ 754 11 01 or Fax 754 21 54, CH-6675 Cevio, is a very pleasant hotel on the main square of this really charming village. Neat and tidy rooms combine with a nice bar, restaurant and terrace to create a delightful ambiance. $

The **Albergo Posta Bignasco**, ☎ 754 11 23 or Fax 754 22 57, CH-6676 Bignasco, is located about half-way up the valley at a fork in the road that leads to Robiei and the higher elevations. This family-run establishment has rustic ambiance and clean, comfortable, rooms. $

The **Albergo Robiei**, ☎ 756 50 20 or Fax 756 50 25, situated at the far end of the valley at an altitude of 2,000 meters (6,562 feet), this is a convenient base for those taking the nearby cable car. You will recognize it by its octagonal shape and, though it is a shade old-fashioned in style, it offers the benefit of an on-site restaurant seating 90. $

The **F. ZIMMER/-WHG**, ☎ 754 21 27, CH-6675 Cevio, in the very quaint village of Cervo, is a tiny place of bed and breakfast genera. Basic, yes; but clean, comfortable and very inexpensive. $

FOOD AND DRINK:

If you decide to stay in the Vallemaggia, I would suggest you opt for demi-pension at any of the above hotels. If not, and you are passing through at mealtime, try out one of the hotel restaurants.

SUGGESTED TOUR:

All tours to the Vallemaggia begin by necessity at Avegno, located at the beginning of the valley just a few kilometers north of Ascona and Locarno. The valley, which runs for 28 kilometers (17 miles) between Avegno and Bignasco—situated at the point where sub-valleys branch off and the roads begin their ascent, differs from its near neighbors in that it has a wide floor accommodating twelve villages, the inhabitants of which account for more than 80% of the entire population.

If you plan on traveling this way on a summer weekend, don't be surprised if the roadsides are lined with cars. This is a very popular place for people to sunbathe and, if they aren't adverse to excruciatingly cold water, swim a little. And, a word of counsel if you are so inclined—you really should exercise caution in these waters. Multi-lingual signs warn of the dangers of the extremely cold water and of sudden surges in the water level. It will look tempting though.

Although **Maggia** is home to the tourist office as well as the remarkable **Madonna delle Grazie** church, I suspect that most visitors will find **Cevio** (1) more attractive. It is the main village of the valley and its square is an absolute delight, especially the beautifully decorated *Pretorio*. Also located here is the **Valmaggia Museum** *(Museo di Valmaggia)*, ☎ 754 13 40, where, housed in two buildings, the Palazzo Franzoni and Casa Respini-Moretti, you will find many exhibits relating to the history and social development of the valley. It is open April through October, Tuesday to Saturday from 10 a.m. to midday and 2–6 p.m., and Sunday from 2–6 p.m.

Cevio is also the ingress to the **Rovana Valley** that itself diverges into two, the **Valle di Bosco** and **Valle di Campo**, both of which run due west and terminate near the Italian border. **Bosco Gurin** (2), nestled in the former at 1,507 meters (4,944 feet), is the highest village in the Ticino and, these days, a favorite skiing destination. It is mainly inhabited by descendants of colonizers from the Valais, who passed over the foreboding mountains to the north. Consequently it is the only village in the canton of Ticino where the official language is Swiss-German. **Campo** (3), in the more southerly Valle di Campo, is notable for the large houses constructed there by returning émigrés. Here, also, the terraces on the mountain sides at Linescio, close to Cevio, stand testimony to the inventiveness of long-deceased farmers.

A short distance from Cevio, the Vallemaggia splits again. To the left is the **Bavona Valley** (4), which is only inhabited during the warmer months of the year and, with the exception of San Carlo, has no electricity. The main points of interest in this rugged, wild valley are the **waterfalls** at Foroglio, the tiny hamlet of Sonlerto and the **cable car** from San Carlo to Robiei. The latter gives you a marvelous perspective of the surrounding mountains, including the Basodino glacier; but, beware, it is only operational from the end of June to the middle of October. Further information can be obtained from the mountain station, ☎ 756 65 53, valley station, ☎ 756 65 46, or from Locarno at ☎ 756 66 66.

The **Lavizzara Valley** branches out, literally, in three directions, but all towards the right. It is populated by approximately six hundred people living in six very distinct villages. Notable among these are Fusio, Mogno, Peccia and one of my favorites, **Brontallo** (5). The latter sits precariously high

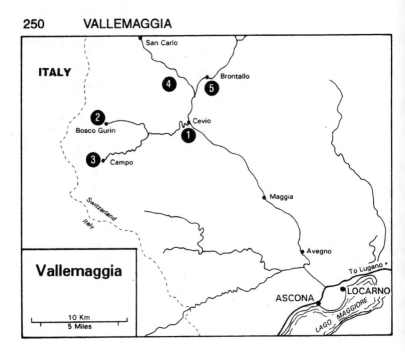

off the main road, where its colorful houses—often constructed of stone—are blessed with a south-facing perspective which gives it a very Mediterranean flavor. Stop for refreshments on the pleasant terrace of the Ristorante La Merla, where you will be refreshed, also, by the marvelous panorama unfolding around you.

Domodossola and Stresa (Italy)

Here's a delightful one-day excursion to nearby Italy by train and boat, passing through spectacular scenery.

GETTING THERE:

By train, from Locarno to Domodossola take the *Treno delle Centovalli*. Be careful, though; this leaves from the lower level platforms of Locarno station, not those by the street. From Domodossola to Stresa take either a *Cisalpino, Regionale* or *InterRegio*. Train buffs, or those just wanting the quickest, most comfortable journey, will opt for the Cisalpino. This is Italy's version of the high-speed train, but with a difference; it tilts as it takes bends in the track.

By boat, returning from Stresa to Ascona.

PRACTICALITIES:

The tourist office in **Domodossola** may be contacted at ☎ 39 324 481308 or Fax 39 324 47974, and in **Stresa** at ☎ 39 323 30150 and Fax 39 323 32561.

This tour is marketed under the name **Lake Maggiore Express**, and information and tickets are available at **Viaggi Fart**, ☎ 751 87 31 or Fax 751 40 77, Piazza Grande 18, CH-6600 Locarno. From the end of March until the end of May there were two departures a day from Locarno, and the connection times in Domodossola and Stresa, effectively left no time to explore the former. After May, and until the end of September, there were three departures a day. This schedule allows the option of spending some time in either, or both, Domodossola and Stresa.

FOOD AND DRINK:

Lunch may be taken at either Domodossola, Stresa or by prior reservation on the boat.

SUGGESTED TOUR:

This is really a most fascinating trip, and one full of surprises. The first leg of the journey is on the ***Centovalli Railway** (1), with the train taking just one and a half hours to wind its way to Domodossola. Centovalli (or *Vigezzo*, on the Italian side) doesn't come by its name, "One Hundred Valleys," without reason. This narrow, precipitous, valley is spectacular indeed. You will be treated to glorious vistas as the train slowly meanders over many bridges along the way, past numerous gorges and crevices, meadows, forests and even vineyards. There are more waterfalls than can be counted, some of which end in glistening, enticing, pure mountain-water pools. As tempting, though, as these are they're most probably inaccessible except to the most ardent of hikers. In fact, a few days before taking this trip, I had made the journey the alternative way, by car. Still spectacular, yes, but not really conducive to seeing the valley at its best; the road is just too difficult in many places. My recommendation, therefore, is to take it easy on yourself and let the train take the strain.

The end of the valley, when it comes, is sudden; and the train takes a very wide loop down the mountain to Domodossola. Incidentally, this is the shortest, and certainly most beautiful, route between Lake Maggiore and the Valais and Bern.

Domodossola (2) is an important junction for routes through the Alps. Besides Ascona and Locarno to the east, the Simplon Pass is just to the northwest and, due south, the road leads to Milan. It is unmistakable that Domodossola has a long, and intriguing, history. Train schedules, however, will not leave you much time for seeing the numerous beautiful palaces, piazzas or museums. Shopping, too, is a problem. The store windows are full of attractively presented goods, and at equally attractive prices when compared to their Swiss counterparts. But, in general, you'll only be able to window shop. The locals here take a long lunch—from 12:30 to 3 p.m., which eats up most of the time you will have available. Saturday, though, is different. Then there is a huge street market, which succeeds in making the jumble of narrow streets and lanes even less navigable than usual. Regardless of these problems a short stop here is certainly worthwhile, if for the cultural differences alone.

On the next leg of the trip, also taken by train, not only will you see a contrast both in the choice of train service, you may be surprised by the striking contrast between Domodossola and Stresa. Indicative of the progress now being made with high-speed trains in Europe, the **Cisalpino** takes only 22 minutes, just half the time of the *Regionale* and even seven minutes faster than the *InterRegio,* to make the journey of less than thirty miles! Upon arrival you will find, in contrast to the somewhat drab, grayness, of Domodossola that **Stresa** (3) is a kaleidoscopic array of color. Beautiful villas, some now serving as hotels, and parks line the shore of **Lago Maggiore** (Lake Maggiore). The town itself is quite obviously affluent and popular with tourists.

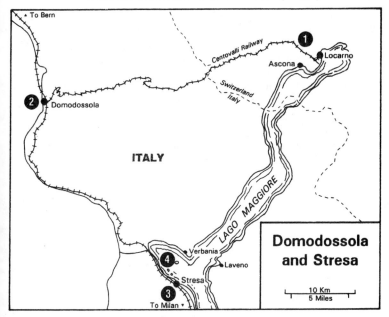

Whatever time you arrive, you will be departing for Ascona at around 4 p.m. on the **Navigazione Laghi Maggiore** steamer. So, at most, you'll have about three and a half hours, and, at least, about one hour in the town. Not much time, for sure; but enough to get a feel of the town, do a little shopping and have a refreshment, or two.

Then, it's time to settle down, choose a comfortable seat with an unobstructed view, and relax for the next two and three quarter hours as the steamer cris-crosses Lago Maggiore bound for Ascona.

And the first, and arguably most impressive, surprise is not long in coming. Sitting out in the lake, not too far from the shore, are islands whose magnificent structures and rare floral beauty indicate they are of some historical interest. The **Isole Borromee** (Borromean Islands) drew to the attention of Count Viraliano Borromeo who, in 1670, began construction of a monumental Baroque palace on **Isola Bella** (4). This he furnished with numerous, and priceless, tapestries, furniture and paintings by the renowned masters. Not content at that, though, he turned his attention to the grounds, directing that the gardens, and ornate terracing, be landscaped with every variety of rare flowers, plants and trees imaginable. This marriage of architectural and botanical grandeur is stunning to the eye, and bears witness, still today, of the splendor of that bygone age. And the surprises continue. The **Isola Madre**, the larger of the islands, is similarly endowed and has become particularly famous for its show of azaleas, rhododendrons and camellias. Also, if you watch carefully, you may catch a glimpse of the white peacocks, parrots and pheasants, which reside here in total freedom.

Over the next two hours your vessel will pass from one enchanting village to another, each with its differing character. That the scenery isn't as starkly dramatic as the neighboring high mountainous regions does not make it any less beautiful. Steep hills slide to the waters edge, forested with a mass of trees interspersed with colorful, uniquely individual, communities and villas. It is for the peaceful, tranquil ambiance, as well as the scenery, that you will long remember Lago Maggiore. Of all the daytrips recommended in the guide this, most probably, is among the most varied; both for the scenery and the character of the towns.

Milan (Italy)

(Milano)

It is generally believed that Milan was founded by the Gallic Insubres, a northern European Celtic tribe, who settled on the banks of the Po in the 7th century BC. The Romans invaded in 222 BC, but it was not until 218 BC that resistance to domination by Rome was finally overcome. Dubbed *Mediolanum*, the city grew and prospered until, several hundred years later—near the beginning of the 4th century AD, it was declared the base of the Western Roman Empire by Diocletian. Soon after, in AD 313, Constantine issued the "Edict of Milan," granting freedom of worship to Christians, and Milan went on, under Bishop (now Saint) Ambrose, to become a very important center for Christianity.

In the 11th century, following a prolonged period of invasions, the city evolved into a commune that was governed by all classes. In 1162, Barbarossa sacked the city, but retaliation was not long in coming. An alliance of Milan and neighboring cities, the Lombard League, reclaimed the city in the late 12th century. An era of great splendor ensued under the Viscontis and their successors, the Sforzas. Among the many treasures bequeathed upon us by that period are the Duomo, the amazing Castello, many splendid churches and, perhaps most well known, Leonardo da Vinci's "Last Supper" which is found in the S. Maria delle Grazie monastery.

Near the beginning of the 16th century, in 1499, a period of foreign control began that would span the coming four centuries. The Spanish ceded control to the Hapsburgs of Austria and, later, Napoleon ruled the city for a relatively short time. Memorable additions to the city during this era are the La Scala Opera House, reputed to have the best acoustics in the world, and the Brera Art Gallery. An architectural achievement of note during this century is the mammoth Central Station *(Stazione Centrale)*, a terminal constructed at the wish of Mussolini. As a quirk of fate, his life terminated in Milan and, once he was dead, he was strung up by a mob in the Piazzale Loreto.

Milan, which for many centuries had been Italy's largest city, lost this distinction to Rome in the years following the Second World War. It remains, however, the financial and industrial center of the nation, and this sophisticated city has earned an international reputation for itself in the area of design and fashion. It is famous, also, for its shops, boutiques, night life and, inevitably, its cuisine—local, national and international.

GETTING THERE:

Trains arrive at Milan's Stazione Centrale F.S. directly from Lugano, with customs and immigration formalities carried out on the train.

By car, Milan is only some 50 kilometers (30 or so miles) from Lugano, but don't even consider it. The twin hassles of parking and crime in the city make it much simpler, and safer, to take the train.

PRACTICALITIES:

The **Dialing Code** for Italy is 39 and for Milan 2. The **Tourist Office** *(Azienda di Promozione Turistica del Milanese)*, ☎ 72524300 or Fax 72524350, Office 1, Via Marconi, 20123, Milano, in the square by the Cathedral, is open Monday to Friday from 8:30 a.m. to 8 p.m., and weekends and holidays from 9 a.m. to 1 p.m. and 2–5 p.m.

Milan is far and away the largest city covered in this guide—and churches, museums and monuments proliferate, making it very difficult to do this city justice in one day. Just what do you decide to see in such a short time? Well, the magnificent Cathedral, the Duomo, must be at the top of everyone's list; closely followed by the convent of Santa Maria delle Grazie, home of Leonardo da Vinci's "Last Supper"; the Brera Art Gallery; the Poldi Pezzoli Museum and the Castello Sforzesco complex. Thereafter, that is if you manage those, it is simply a matter of preference. In reality, though, Milan is one of those cities with treasures so varied, and character so subtle, that it would take years, maybe a lifetime, to begin to partake of all it has to offer. I suspect that many visitors who planned to take a daytrip to Milan will wish they had allocated two or three days instead. Obviously, it depends upon your itinerary, but the most discerning of travelers will want to spend at least one night in Milan.

ACCOMMODATION:

The **Hotel Palace *****, ☎ 6336 or Fax 654485, Piazza della Repubblica, 20, 20124 Milano, subway MM3 Repubblica, is a member of the Leading Hotels of the World organization, and has a fine city center location, between the central station and the Duomo. Each room is individually styled to the highest standards, its restaurants are renowned, and the Campigli American Piano Bar is a popular rendezvous. $$$

The **Hotel Diana Majestic ******, ☎ 29513404 or Fax 201072, Viale Piave, 42, 20129 Milano, subway MM2 Porta Venezia, is found near the Porta Venezia, just a few minutes walk from the Duomo. It is within a turn-of-the-century Art-Nouveau building and surrounded by a lovely private grounds. $$$

The **Hotel Cervo *****, ☎ 29004031 or Fax 6571851, Piazza Princessa Clotilde, 10, 20121 Milano, subway MM2 Garibaldi and MM3 Repubblica, adjacent to the Porta Nuova, is just a couple of blocks from the Piazza della Repubblica and within walking distance of the Duomo. It has been recently restored, and offers pleasant rooms on a series of color coded floors. $$

FOOD AND DRINK:

Be forewarned, Milan is not the cheapest place to eat. It is advisable to check the menu that is, typically, posted outside each restaurant and, to remember when counting your pennies, that your bill will be increased by both a cover charge and a service charge of 10% to 15%. Be aware, also, that you are obligated by local law to retain your receipt upon leaving—failure to do so is punishable by a fine! *Pizzerie* were once inexpensive, but not so these days. These do, however, stay open later than regular restaurants, which ordinarily close at 10:30 p.m.

Ristorante Al Cantinone (Via Agnello, 10), one of the oldest in the city, is housed in a 17th-century palace near to the Duomo and La Scala. Character abounds and specialties include Tuscan and national cuisine. For your refreshment before, or after, your meal, there is an adjoining bar. It is closed Saturday lunch time and Sunday. ☎ 86461338. $$$

Ristorante Bagutta (Via Bagutta, 14), a Milan landmark, is well-nigh a museum its own right. Opened in 1924, it has been one of **the** places to eat in town for decades. A unique ambiance enhances deliciously prepared Tuscan and national dishes. It is closed on Sunday and during Christmas and the New Year. ☎ 76000902. $$$

Boccon di Vino (Via Carducci, 20) would be better classified as a tavern than as a restaurant. Numerous varieties of salami and cheese, and a selection of fine wines are the order of the day. It is closed lunch time and Sunday. ☎ 866040. $$

Collio (Via Nerino, 10), is, aptly, named for an area famous for white wines and hearty food such as shins of pork and goulash. It is closed Sunday evening and Monday. ☎ 86450528. $$

Ciardi (Via San Raffaele, 6) is a typical *pizzerie* in a central location, that serves until the very early hours of the morning. Closed Monday. ☎ 877704. $

SUGGESTED TOUR:

Arriving at Milan's **Central Station** *(Stazione Centrale)* (1), which dates from 1931, is like taking a step back in time. That, at least, was my impression upon returning after an interlude of thirty years. Many of the older stations around western Europe, though extensively modernized, are still operational; at least one, in Paris, has been turned into a museum; and, in the Puerta de Atocha in Madrid, roles have been reversed—the trains now stop outside and the traditional glassed-in concourse has been ingeniously renovated and turned over to the passengers. In Milan, though, tradition reigns; and the only things missing are steam engines. This incredibly vast edifice can be seen in its true splendor—after taking the escalators down—looking back from the Piazza Duca D'Aosta. And if you look around you, as well, you will most probably find yourself an unwitting observer of the less savory face of modern-day Milan, addicts satiating their insatiable cravings—not a particularly appealing introduction to a city with such a glorious history.

Those in a hurry will be tempted to take the MM3, yellow line, from the station to Duomo and the Cathedral; but, really, this would be a mistake. First impressions, though not always correct in retrospect, are an important component to one's assessment of the character of a city—and not many can be made on the Metro. Better, then, to set out down the straight Via Vittor Pisani, following it down to the Piazza Della Repubblica, the dividing line between the old and new cities. Immediately, the almost completely farraginous mix of architectural styles will strike you. A modern, thin, skyscraper competes with, but does not vanquish, the station for honors in grandeur. And, as a whole, the other buildings which inhabit this street are of divergent character each from the other. Planned, I doubt it; not even the worst of town planners could have, even accidentally, arranged this.

Continuing on, take a left at the Piazza and, shortly afterwards, a right along Via Manin, which runs parallel with the **Giardini Pubblici** (2). It may be worth your while to take a quick look around these gardens, where you will find an eclectic array of palaces and villas that now house a number of museums, art galleries and exhibition centers. The corner of the gardens and the Via Manin converge at the Piazza Cavour, and, radiating from that, the Via Alessandro Manzoni will lead you directly into the center of Milan. Along the way you will begin to get a feel for the style of this city and, no doubt, at the same time feel the allure of the eye-catching displays that beckon from store windows.

After a short distance you will come, on the left-hand side, to a museum that could easily be overlooked; but, don't! The **Poldi Pezzoli Museum** *(Museo Poldi Pezzoli)* (3), ☎ 794889, Via Manzoni, 12, was once the home of nobleman, Giacomo Poldi Pezzoli. He bequeathed it to the city in 1871, and it now holds one of the world's most important private collections of 15th- to 18th-century Italian paintings, and an important display of decora-

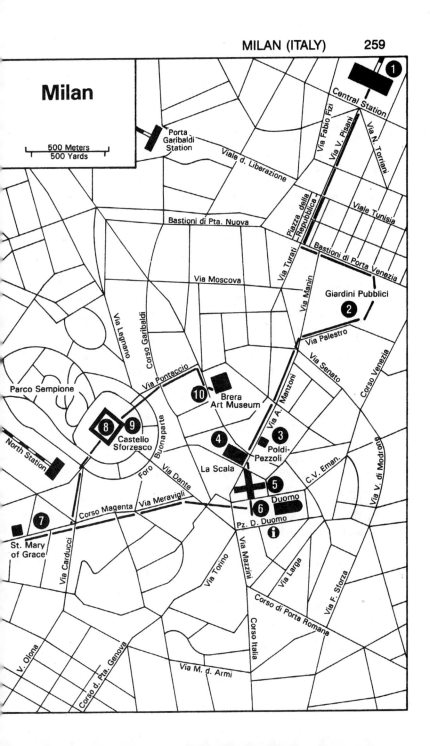

tive arts. Recently, these have been augmented by two additional collections; one of 16th- to 19th-century solar clocks and the other of antique lace. Visit Tuesday to Sunday from 9:30 a.m. to 12:30 p.m. and 2:30–6 p.m. Hours are extended to 7:30 p.m. on Saturday.

Very soon afterwards the Via broadens into another Piazza, this one home to the world famous **La Scala Opera House** (4). In truth, it is not particularly impressive, at least from the exterior and, like many buildings in Milan, it could do with a good cleaning. Those with particular interest may wish to visit the museum, ☎ 8053418, which in addition to detailing the history of the opera house, exhibits a variety of sets and costumes, and offers a memorial to Giuseppe Verdi. The museum is open daily from 9:30 a.m. to 12:30 p.m. and 2–5:30 p.m., but closed on Sunday between October and May. On the opposite side of the Piazza is the 1668 Palazzo Marino, which now functions as the Town Hall of Milan.

Many cities in Europe feature sheltered shopping arcades and markets, and these can range from the most banal to the very beautiful. Barcelona is celebrated for its main street, La Rambla, with its rambling La Boqueria food market, and both Paris and London have architecturally pleasing shopping arcades where the windows are laden with a wide variety of enticing goods. You may not believe it until you see it, but the above pale in comparison to Milan's **Galleria Vittorio Emanuele II** (5), found diagonally across the Piazza from the La Scala. Inaugurated in 1878, this magnificent structure was designed in the shape of a cross, with high ceilings giving it an open airy feel. Besides hosting many of the classy, stylish, stores that have taken up residence in Milan, it is the rendezvous spot of choice. What's more, it will lead you directly out to the Piazza del Duomo, and the façade of Milan's inimitable Cathedral.

While construction on the *Duomo (6) was begun on this, now the signature landmark of Milan, in the late 14th century, it was not completed until the Napoleonic era of the very early 19th century. With a majestic exterior embellished by 135 spires—the planners must have been inspired—and 2,245 statues, this has the distinction of being the largest Gothic structure ever built in Italy. And, if you care to undertake the climb to the roof, it allows wide-ranging views of the city. Inside, of course, there is more than enough to occupy you. In a rather somber ambiance you will find, among other things, immense stained-glass windows, the tomb of Giacomo de Medici—dating from the 1560s, and the famous statue of Bartolomeo. Be sure to investigate the Cathedral Museum also. It is teeming with priceless treasures.

Leonardo da Vinci's famous, if somewhat faded, masterpiece, *The Last Supper, is sure to hold a place of high priority on most everyone's itinerary. However, the opening hours, Tuesday to Sunday 8 a.m. to 1:45 p.m., at the **St. Mary of Grace** (Santa Maria delle Grazie) (7) convent, ☎ 4987588, are sure to cause daytrippers some consternation. The route from Duomo, though, is rather simple. At the opposite end of the Piazza del Duomo take Via Mercanti to the Piazza Cordusio where, in the background, you will see the imposing silhouette of the Castello Sforzesco. Leave to the left, via the Via Meravigli which, after three blocks or so, becomes the Corso Magenta. It is on that street, a little way past the Via Carducci, that you will find the ancient convent, which dates from 1463. Commissioned by the Duke of Milan, Leonardo da Vinci took three years, between 1495 and 1497, to paint his classic concept of "The Last Supper" on the wall of the refectory. Inevitably, the ensuing centuries have taken their toll, though the wall was specially protected in advance from the hostilities brought by World War II. Thankfully, periodic restorations, with the last being in 1995, have ensured that it can still be viewed by the public.

The next stop, the **Castello Sforzesco** (8), is nearby. Simply retrace your steps to the Via Carducci and make a left. The castle is three blocks straight ahead, past the imposing Stazione Ferrovie Nord. Constructed in 1368 and still formidable after more than six centuries, this was originally built for defensive purposes but, later during the Sforzesco dynasty, was transformed into a luxurious palace. Today, it is home to one of the most important museums in the city, the **Sforzesco Castle Art Galleries** *(Civici Musei d'Arte e Pinacoteca del Castello Sforzesco)* (9), ☎ 62083940. Look for an important collection of Lombard paintings and sculptures, decorative arts, tapestries, weapons, musical instruments and even Egyptian art. It is open daily, except Monday, from 9:30 a.m. to 5:30 p.m.

Immediately behind the castle is the **Parco Sempione**. It is within the grounds of this beautiful park that you will find the **Palazzo dell'Arte**—with its architectural exhibition; the **Aquarium** *(Acquario)*; and, at the far end guarding the Piazza Sempione, the **Arch of Peace** *(Arco della Pace)* which was constructed in 1815 to celebrate the ending of the Napoleonic Wars and the ensuing peace in Europe.

Rounding out the "must see" list is the **Brera Art Gallery** *(Pinacoteca di Brera)* (10), ☎ 722631, which is, again, just a few blocks away. It will be easiest to follow the Via Pontaccio, on the opposite side of the castle from where you entered it, then turn right onto the Via Brera. Opened on August 15, 1809, this museum of worldwide significance is actually the National Gallery. Many things could be said extolling its virtues, many more than there are room for here. Suffice for it to say that it exhibits some of the most famous masterpieces of Italian painting dating from the 14th to 20th century. It is open Tuesday to Sunday from 9 a.m. to 5:30 p.m. and on holidays from 9 a.m. to 12:30 p.m.

It is highly unlikely that visitors on a daytrip from Lugano will be able to see even these, the highlights, of Milan. The reality is that most people should consider themselves fortunate if they squeeze in three of them, even rushing from one to another. Besides that, Milan is a city that captivates you, and quickly. To reiterate my earlier counsel, the likelihood is that, having arrived on a daytrip, you will wish that you had allowed for at least two days in this fascinating city.

The Lower Engadine

The Lower Engadine is in the far eastern portion of Switzerland that juts into, and is nearly surrounded by, Austria and Italy. The broad Lower Engadine Valley, a by-product of the frequently torrential Inn river, is flanked to the north by the Silvretta range and to the south by the Lischana mountains. Its geographical peculiarities have constrained this region to be, as it remains to this day, remote from other parts of Switzerland.

Its history stretches far back to the pre-historic era, and recent archaeological digs have yielded evidence of Bronze Age settlements dating from between 1800 to 800 BC. The Rhaetians, however, were the first inhabitants of the valley to leave conclusive proof of their presence here. It was also memorialized that in 15 BC the Romans occupied the whole of Rhaetia, governing it as a province. It is the combination of Rhaetian and Roman influences that bequeathed to the area its distinctive culture and language, Romansch, still much in evidence here today.

The charm of this valley is in its unspoiled villages and beautiful scenery. Unlike many parts of Switzerland—including its neighbor the Upper Engadine, the Lower Engadine has not succumbed to the demands of tourism, nor are its mountains scarred with all manner of cable cars or railways. You will not find any world-famous mountains or celebrated towns here. What you will discover are pure, virgin, Alpine panoramas, and a place where you can explore the glorious beauties of unsullied nature to your heart's content.

Oh, yes; there is one more attraction this area has to offer. And, once you have benefitted from all it has to offer, you may agree that I have, simply, saved the best for last. These days, it is becoming increasingly popular to frequent spas, in one of the many diverse forms that they may take. Most of these, however, are privately owned and, unless you hold a membership, you must pay an excessive fee for the privilege of enjoying their facilities. Not so in Scuol. This small town, of just 1,900 inhabitants, building upon the local phenomenon of healing waters, has revolutionized the traditional concept of spa with its construction of the *Bogn Engiadina Scuol*. Not only is this spa a one-of-its-kind in Switzerland, I have not come across a place of its type in all my travels throughout Europe and North America. Indeed, it offers a multi-faceted experience for both body and mind and, once partaken of, your senses will covet a return visit. Truly, were all the many other charms of the Lower Engadine to fade away, this experience could stand alone as a reason to visit the valley.

GETTING THERE:

Trains arrive at Scuol, the last station in the Lower Engadine Valley, from St. Moritz.

By car, Scuol, 50 kilometers (31 miles) from St. Moritz, is reached by taking Route 27 in a northeasterly direction. It can also be reached from either Davos or Klosters by traversing the Flüelpass to Susch/Süs, and turning left towards Scuol.

PRACTICALITIES:

The **Dialing Code** for the Lower Engadine is 81. The **Ftan Tourist Office** (*Verkehrsverein*), ☎ 864 05 57 or Fax 864 05 37, is located in the heart of the village. It is open Monday to Friday from 9 a.m. to 11 a.m. and 4–6 p.m., and Saturday from 4–5 p.m. The **Guarda tourist office** (*Verkehrsverein*), ☎ 862 23 42 or Fax 862 21 66, is also located in the middle of that village. The **Scuol tourist office** (*Scuol Tourismus*), ☎ 861 22 23, Fax 861 22 23, E-mail scuol@spin.ch and www.scuol.ch, is next to the bus station in the village and opens Monday to Friday from 8 a.m. to 7 p.m., Saturday from 10 a.m. to midday and Sunday from 2–4 p.m.

The majority of visitors, usually before they go and certainly once they arrive, will realize that Switzerland is a multi-lingual nation. German, French and German/French variations predominate in the greater part of the country while Italian is the language of choice in the Ticino area. The Engadine, however, both Lower and Upper, is the home of yet a fourth language, *Romansch,* which is widely spoken throughout the area.

Although Scuol may be reached either by train or by Postal Bus—and Postal Buses do connect with Ftan, Guarda and Tarasp—these latter services may not be as frequent as visitors require. Therefore, unless you have your own transport, it may be best to make your base in Scuol and investigate the area from there.

ACCOMMODATION:
In Ftan:

The **Hôtel Haus Paradies ****, ☎ 861 08 08, Fax 861 08 09, E-mail paradies@relaischateaux.fr or www.integra.fr/relaischateaux/paradies, CH-7551 Ftan, just a short distance outside the village of Ftan, is a marvelous hotel located on a ridge overlooking the valley. It is quiet and peaceful but offers every modern convenience, including a fine fitness center, and a hotel bus that will shuttle you around the valley. $$$

The **Hotel Engiadina ***, ☎ 864 04 34 or Fax 864 86 49, CH-7551 Ftan, is a small hotel typical in style to many found in the Engadine. Each of the 30 rooms, furnished in pieces fashioned from local Cembran pine wood, have private shower/bath, radio, TV and video connection. The owners, Cordula and Richard Grago, do their part to ensure that all guests receive friendly, personalized service. $$

The **Garni Chasa Allegra**, ☎ 864 19 57 or Fax 864 19 75, CH-7551 Ftan, is a tiny, and typical, Alpine pension. Each of the 10 comfortably furnished rooms has a private bath/shower, toilet, telephone and radio. $

In Guarda:

The **Hotel Meisser** ***, ☎ 862 21 32 or Fax 862 24 80, CH-7545 Guarda, built as a farmhouse in 1645, has been run as a hotel by the Meisser family since 1893. Though each room features in-suite bathroom, toilet, telephone and minibar, the "Count's Room" bears special mention. Originally the upper parlor, it has carved into its wooden ceiling the coat of arms of the alliance formed between the Jenatsch and von Planta families in 1720. The imposing dining room, contrived from a hay barn at the turn of the century, boasts wonderful views of the surrounding mountains and valley. It also has a very interesting annex with a curious, but, nevertheless, pleasing, mix of traditional and modern decor. $$

The **Pension Val Tuoi**, ☎ 862 24 70 or Fax 862 24 07, House Number 56, CH-7545 Guarda, is housed within a traditional house in this unusual village. As things go in Switzerland, this is fairly basic but it is still quite comfortable and attractive. $

In Scuol:

The **Romantik Hotel Guardaval** ***, ☎ 864 13 21 or Fax 864 97 67, CH-7550 Scuol, has a comparatively bland façade but do not be deceived. Hiding behind that inconspicuous exterior is a traditionally appointed and courteously serviced interior offering every modern convenience. $$

The **Gasthaus Mayor**, ☎ 864 14 12 or Fax 864 99 83, is a modern, comfortable, guesthouse with more than adequate facilities. It is named after its proprietors. $

In Tarasp:

The **Schlosshotel/Restaurant Chastè** ****, ☎ 864 17 75, Fax 864 99 70, E-mail chaste@relaischateaux.fr or www.integra.fr/relaischateaux/chaste, CH-7553 Tarasp, is found in the center of this delightful village, in the shadow of the imposing castle from where, evidently, it got its name. Throughout the hotel, pine paneling in concert with slightly modern furnishings make for a warm and comfortable ambiance. Rooms, categorized as Standard, Superior, Junior-suite, and grand Panorama-Suite, each have a private bathroom, radio, TV, mini-bar and safe. Guests also enjoy the use of a well equipped, on-site, health club. $$$

FOOD AND DRINK:

As with most places in Switzerland, you will be better able to manage your expenses if you pay the little extra—check to make sure it is not already included—and take demi-pension. The restaurants listed below, however, are worth a mention.

In Ftan:

Hôtel Haus Paradies is a gourmet's delight. Eduard Hitzberger, co-owner with his wife, Waltraud, who also wears the chef's hat, prepares mouthwatering, exquisitely presented dishes which combine classic regional cuisine with a innovative flair. He specializes, also, in delicious Austrian style desserts. ☎ 861 08 08. $$$

Restorant Engiadina is affiliated with the Hotel Engiadina. A menu featuring an array of local fare, including game specialties, is complemented by the typical Alpine decor. The wine list is comprehensive and impressive. ☎ 864 04 34. $$

In Scuol:

Romantik Hotel Guardaval boasts an impressive three-story dining room where you can choose from any number of beautifully prepared and artistically presented dishes. A fine selections of local wines provide the perfect accompaniment. ☎ 864 13 21. $$

In Tarasp:

Schlosshotel/Restaurant Chastè is a *Relais & Chateaux* affiliate offering a culinary experience in addition to fine accommodation. Expect local and International style cuisine prepared and presented with great care and style. ☎ 864 17 75. $$$

SUGGESTED TOUR:

As is the case with most rural Swiss areas, this is not a tour in the traditional sense of the word. It cannot be described as an itinerary, either. Rather, it is a description of the things visitors may like to do and places they may want to see while they are in the Lower Engadine Valley.

Winter sports enthusiasts will want to consider basing themselves around the Scuol/Ftan area. Here, a combination of 15 cable cars, chair and ski-lifts are available to whisk you to a total of 80 kilometers (50 miles) of pistes, including the 12 kilometer (7.5 miles) "Dream Piste"—the longest in the valley, which sit at altitudes of 1,250 to 2,800 meters (4,101 to 9,186 feet). And, you do not need to concern yourself with conditions—snow is guaranteed between December to April.

The **Swiss Ski School**, ☎ 864 17 23 or Fax 864 17 27, in Scuol, employs instructors that will teach you to ski or help you improve your technique. It also offers **private skiing tours**, both within the local region and the larger Alpine region, and **cross-country skiing**, through 60 kilometers (37 miles) of prepared trails in the valley or on the "Motta-Naluns Trail" at an altitude of 2,100 meters (6,890 feet).

A myriad of other winter sports opportunities are available as well. Learn **curling,** or the local version *Eisstockschiessen,* at the **Trü Sports Complex**, ☎ 861 20 06 or Fax 861 20 01, Scuol. And, if you want to add snow-

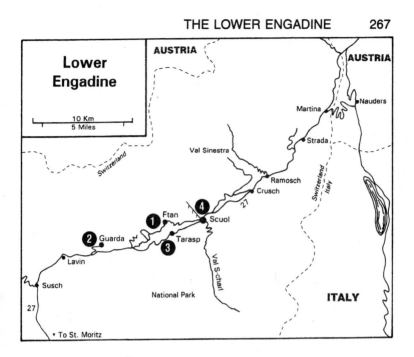

boarding to you repertoire of skills, contact **Snowboard "The School,"** ☎
864 82 20 or Fax 864 18 51, also in Scuol. Those seeking a different sort of
adventure may want to try their luck on the Prui-Ftan **Toboggan track**.
Sledges are available for hire from the top of the Ftan-Prui chair-lift. Visitors
who prefer getting around under their own power will enjoy over 50 kilometers (31 miles) of prepared **winter hiking trails** in the Scuol, Bad Tarasp-
Vulpera area. Can there be a better way of seeing this gorgeous valley when
it is transformed into a winter wonderland? And, to get you from one destination to another the local authorities provide, free of charge, a **Ski Bus**
which connects all parts of Scuol, Sent and Tarasp-Vulpera with the mountain railway terminus.

Not to be outdone, the **summer months** offer a variety of options as well.
Foremost among these must be listed **mountain hiking**, popular no matter
what your level of fitness. In fact, spread throughout the valley are in excess
of 1,000 kilometers (621 miles) of mountain pathways which facilitate access to all areas of this multi-faceted countryside—up and down hill, naturally, but, also, through dales, meadows and pastures and alongside
countless rivers.

One of the more enticing hikes runs from Ftan to Guarda, over a ridge
along the mountain. On the slightly more than two-hour length of the walk,
you will be treated to exhilarating views and an introduction to two villages

with considerable and contrasting charms. In **Ftan** (1), situated an altitude of 1,650 meters (5,413 feet), the population of 450 is dispersed over a fairly wide area and private car use is the accepted norm. **Guarda** (2), which in English translates to "look," is quite different. Here, where cars must be left in a car park below, the village clings as precariously to its traditions as it does to the mountain side. Its attractions are, basically, twofold: breathtaking vistas of the valley below and mountain peaks in the distance; and interesting examples of *Sgraffito*—the name given to the elaborate artwork found on the exterior of houses throughout the Engadine. The sheer number of these enchanting houses found here, and their incredible beauty, have earned for the Guarda the nickname "Museum Village" and, in fact, this has been recognized by the Swiss government as a place of national significance. If the idea of walking back does not appeal to you, take a bus from Guarda down to Guarda Station where you can catch one of the frequent Rhaetian Railway trains to Scuol.

Also of national significance within the valley, and one whose commanding site makes it difficult to ignore, is the **Castle Tarasp** *(Schloss Tarasp)* (3). In years past, many castles were scattered throughout the Inn valley. Today, however, many have disappeared and, of those that remain, most lie in ruins. Fortunately, fate has been kinder to the magnificent and imposing Castle Tarasp. Constructed atop a hill directly in front of the village around the middle of the 11th century, it was, as you may have surmised, originally owned by the Tarasp family. Subsequent centuries brought family feuds, battles and other upheavals which occasioned correspondingly frequent changes in ownership, sometimes leaving the castle unattended and in disrepair. Stability finally came, however, in 1900 and in the person of Dr. K. A. Linger, owner of a Dresden cosmetic and pharmaceutical company. Enchanted by this fairy-tale castle while on a vacation to Tarasp, he purchased it for CHF 20,000. While this was a huge sum, indeed, in those times, it only represented the beginning of the expense necessary to renovate, restore and furnish the castle. Sadly, in the way of such things, Dr. Linger died, in 1916, shortly before the castle was ready for him to move in. And that presented another problem. Although Dr. Linger had bequeathed the castle and its contents to August III, King of Saxony, he declined to take possession in light of the financial burden associated with upkeep of such a structure. Resolution was reached when the castle was offered to, and accepted by, an old friend of Dr. Linger's, the Grand Duke Ernst Ludwig of Hesse and the Rhine, who had at his disposal the necessary financial means to fund what would be costly ongoing expenses. A grandson of Queen Victoria and brother of the last Empress of Russia, the Grand Duke spent as much time as he could manage, during the remainder of his life, at Tarasp. At present, the castle is owned by one of his descendants, Princess Margareta von Hessen. It can be visited, daily, but only by guided tour. As these are offered at odd times, I would suggest calling, Schlossverwaltung Tarasp, ☎ 864 93 68, before visiting to check the schedules.

Nearby, also, are the 168.7 square kilometers of the Swiss National Park. If this will be a part of your itinerary, please take care when you visit to adhere to their rules for the protection of animals, plants and, not least, people.

If you prefer not to investigate on foot, **mountain biking** offers a pleasant and healthy alternative. Be aware that some pathways are restricted to hikers, but the tourist office will be happy to provide you with a special mountain-bike plan that lays out your options. Bikes can be rented, for approximately CHF 35 to 38 a day, from Hanin Conradin Sport, ☎ 864 14 10. Bike Scuol Engiadina, ☎ 864 92 91, also offers day-long or weekend biking excursions.

With fast flowing rivers around, you may be tempted at the prospect of **white water rafting**. If so, you will not be crestfallen if you contact Travel Agency ATR tours, ☎ 864 94 97 or Fax 864 05 95, to arrange a half- or full-day, expertly supervised, excursion.

So, what do you do on a day in the valley when the weather refuses to cooperate? Well, there is one place to which a visit is not dependent on season or weather. It is a place specializing in relaxation, and may prove a welcome respite following a day walking, biking, skiing, etc. By now you may have guessed, it is the *Bogn Engiadana Scuol (4). It is open, year round, with the exception of mid-November through the first week in December when it closes for annual holidays. This is really a comprehensive spa complex, where you can avail yourself of the benefits derived from the **Fun and Health Bath, Finnish Bath Area** and the **Roman/Irish Baths** between 10 a.m. and 10 p.m., or from the **Therapy Center** on Monday from 7:30 a.m. to midday and 2–6 p.m., and Tuesday to Friday from 9 a.m. to midday and 2:30–5:30 p.m. Entrance to the **Fun and Health Bath/Finnish Bath Area**, for a two-and-one-half-hour period, cost CHF 21 in 1997. Entrance to the **Roman/Irish Baths**, which also allows unlimited time access for the day to the **Fun and Health Bath, Finnish Bath Area**, cost CHF 50.

As unimaginative as the approach may seem, I feel that it is best to describe these separately and in turn, as each is a mini-complex within itself. Before continuing in that vein, however, I will dive into a description of the various springs and, briefly, the qualities of their waters.

The waters from the **Luzius Spring**, a high-sulphur spring, are used to treat vegetative, psychosomtic diseases of the gastro-intestinal tract, constipation, hemorrhoids and dysfunction's of bile evacuation. Water from the **Sfondraz Spring** has one of the highest calcium counts in Europe and, although the mineral content is less than that from Luzius, its effects are similar. These waters are also used as treatment for calcium deficiency diseases. The **Bonifazius Spring** gives forth alkaline, sodic, calciferous, chalybeate waters with carbohydrate, which are used to stimulate micturition and guard against infections. The **Lischana Spring** gives forth alkaline sodic waters with sulphates, magnesium and carbohydrate, from among which the magnesium stimulates metabolic reactions and aids in the proper function of muscles and the nervous system. Now back to the three components of the spa itself.

The **Fun and Health Bath** makes up the majority of the public portion of the spa. The centerpiece of this complex is a large, round, indoor pool, equipped with several water fountains, where you will find the water maintained at a relaxing 34 degree Celsius (93.2 degrees Fahrenheit). Arranged around this are several smaller pools. First, there is the ever-popular jacuzzi, at 37 degrees Celsius (98.6 degrees Fahrenheit), where your body enjoys a buoyancy of nearly 90% of its own weight. Next, you will find a Brine pool, at 35 degrees Celsius (95 degrees Fahrenheit), whose waters contain 2% natural salt from the springs of the United Swiss Rhine Salt-Works. Be forewarned, though, before slipping into this pool, that, as brine has the capacity for damaging several minerals and stays on the skin, it is advisable to remove spectacles and/or jewelry and to shower immediately afterwards. There are, then, two contrasting grottoes, and you may use these in the order you wish. The hot grotto is maintained at 37 degrees Celsius (98.6 degrees Fahrenheit). Its cold water mate checks in at a chilly 18 degrees Celsius (64 degrees Fahrenheit). The youths have fun with the latter; it appears to be the custom for the boys to throw their girlfriends into it when they first enter the spa! There is also a vapor bath, where children are allowed as well. The most unusual pool is outside, although it is reached via an interior channel where you pass through weather-protecting strips. Like the large pool, it is circular—although much smaller, and it is sub-divided into three concentric rings. The outer ring is a "Lazy River" with concrete beds built into the walls, and the two inner rings have jacuzzi jets. Remembering that this is in Switzerland, you may be concerned about the snow in winter—no need to worry you here. The water is a warm 34 degrees Celsius (93.2 degrees Fahrenheit), and it is amazingly "cool" to lay there luxuriating in the water while the snow gently falls around you blanketing the nearby mountains—an experience that has to be felt and seen to be believed. If all of this gets too much, there is just one thing left to do. Inside is a solarium with wonderfully comfortable lounge chairs; the perfect place for a little snooze.

The **Finnish Bath Area** is just off the Fun and Health Bath but beware, before passing through the door read the sign posted there. On my first trip, I neglected to do so and was mightily surprised upon entering. The sign reads "Zona Nuda," and that, for everyone, should be easy enough to translate. What it means, in practical terms, is that when you pass through the door—and remember this is a mixed sex area, you must dispense with your swimming costume, depositing it in one of the tiny cubicles provided for that purpose. The only thing that accompanies you further is a towel, although this, generally, is carried over the arm—not wrapped around you. People of other cultures, particularly North Americans, might tend to believe that this can give cause to pruriency. To the Swiss, however, it is as natural as going to a regular swimming pool, and there is absolutely no embarrassment. Those not accustomed to such customs will, no doubt, feel strange, at least at the outset, wandering in and out of steam baths and saunas and bathing in open showers, next to completely naked strangers— of both sexes. But that feeling—actually there is no feeling—soon passes, and the naturalness of it all assumes normalcy. One sauna, outside from the main section, gives out 95 degrees Celsius (203 degrees Fahrenheit) of heat. And, if that leaves you in need of a cooling off, you can follow up with a dive into the open-air cold pool—with a cold water cascade. At just 18 degrees Celsius (64 degrees Fahrenheit), this is an exhilaratingly chilling experience. Along the side of that pool, but back inside, is a glass encased solarium furnished with comfortable lounge chairs and offering complimentary refreshment from a refrigerator filled with bottles of the spa's own natural water. Before you leave this area, make sure you are relaxed from head to toe. Sit for a while with your feet soaking in one of the tepid footbaths. This area is open for mixed bathing on Monday, Wednesday, Friday, Saturday and Sunday from 10 a.m. to 10 p.m. and Tuesday from 10 a.m. to 6 p.m. Ladies only are accommodated on Thursday from 10 a.m. to 10 p.m., gentlemen only on Tuesday from 6 to 10 p.m. and parents with children on Wednesday from 1 to 10 p.m.

The **Roman/Irish Baths** present an absolutely unique experience and, during the two and a half hours it takes to pass through them, the sum total of your senses will be aroused to unanticipated levels of sensuality. These are in an area which is totally separate from the Fun and Health and Finnish bath areas, and admission is by 24-hour advance reservation only, ☎ 861 20 02. This, also is a mixed sex area, and you may choose to visit alone or with a friend of either sex. Access is gained by using a key you will have been given just for that purpose. It fits into a space near the door and, in turn, the automatic doors slide open, giving entrance. At the reception area you will be given, you guessed it, a toga to replace your bathing costume— your clothes having been left in the lockers outside. You will also receive a very important pair of rubber slip-ons—important because these will prevent your slipping on the wet tiled floors. The next stop are the cloakrooms, segregated by sex, where you will deposit your swimming costume. Incidentally, your toga will function as a robe when moving between rooms and, within the rooms, either as a towel or sweat-sheet—depending upon the room. Each toga is numbered, and remember yours. You would not want to wander around with the wrong one! Your second stop will be the Warm-Air (Sauna), where you lie on your toga for 15 minutes at a temperature of 54 degrees Celsius (129.2 degrees Fahrenheit). This is followed, immediately, by 5 minutes in the next sauna, which is 16 degrees Celsius hotter (158 degrees Fahrenheit). Now on to the soap and brush massage—usually performed by a masseuse on the men and by a masseur on the ladies. If the room is occupied when you arrive, have a shower and wait your turn in the round mineral water pool. In addition to its generally relaxing properties, this massage stimulates circulation and peels the skin. Your massage done, have a quick shower and head for the Vapor Baths. It is recommended that you spend 10 minutes in Vapor Bath 1, at 42 degrees Celsius (107.6 degrees Fahrenheit) and a further 10 minutes in Vapor Bath 2, maintained at 6 degrees Celsius warmer (118.4 degrees Fahrenheit). Be sure, though, to hang your toga in front of the bath so that you can readily see the number. You wouldn't want to swan around in someone else's, would you? Shower again and it is time for 15 minutes in the 36 degree Celsius (96.8 degree Fahrenheit) Foaming Bath, followed by 10 minutes in the 34 degree Celsius (93.2 degree Fahrenheit) Mineral-Water Bath. The latter, at the center of the complex, is particularly interesting. It is rather like a small swimming pool, entered via the steps that encircle it, and capped by an intriguing domed roof decorated with rather exotic paintings of mermaids! The penultimate stop—and you will not want to linger long, is the 18 degree Celsius (64.4 degree Fahrenheit) Cold-Water Pool. After showering yet again—by now you should be squeaky clean—and drying off, a ring of the bell brings forth an assistant who will escort you to the Resting Place. There you will lie, wrapped in warm towels upon contoured air-beds, listening to the soft sounds of nature emanating from the ceiling—a luxury which will continue for the next half-hour, or so. The Roman Baths are open for mixed bathing on Tuesday, Thursday, Friday, Saturday and Sunday from 1 to 10 p.m.; for women only Monday 1 to 10 p.m.; and for men only from 1 to 10 p.m.

The **Therapy Center** offers a wide range of treatments, at varying prices, among which the most popular are a **Massage**, either whole or part body; a **Carbonated Water** or **Natural Mud Bath**; an **Underwater Massage** and **Physiotherapy;** or **Inhalation** sessions. Any combination of the above, and a wealth of other options, may be arranged by reservation, ☎ 861 20 04.

A Daytrip from the Lower Engadine
Nauders (Austria)

In 1994, while on another assignment in Switzerland, I was enticed by the idea of venturing into Austria, a country I had never visited. A quick look at the map indicated that, from my base in St. Moritz, Landeck was nearby and easily reached—two essential ingredients for a daytrip. I made a few inquiries to confirm the feasibility of my plan and determined to set out the next morning on my Austrian adventure.

I left St. Moritz early, taking the first train to Scuol—the end of the line in the Lower Engadine. While I was aware that this town had enticements of its own, most particularly a famous spa, I decided to press on, leaving the exploration of its wonders—detailed in the previous chapter—for a future trip. As the Scuol station is a terminal, a change in transportation was necessary, and it wasn't too long before the familiar postal bus arrived to carry me, I thought, to Landeck.

I sat back to enjoy the scenery as the bus made its way down this fairly narrow, attenuated valley, reaching the Austrian border in less than a half hour. Border formalities being simply a formality, the bus soon continued its winding route up the twisting mountain pass. Cresting the summit, a wide panoramic vista unfolded before me, and my first views of the Austrian Tyrol were impressive indeed. In the shadow of the surrounding snow-capped mountains two lovely valleys stretched towards the horizon and, at the point of their divergence one from the other, a quaint village clung to the lower slopes which rose between them. To my surprise that village—not Landeck—was the bus' initial stop; though, in retrospect, I should have realized there would be a stop soon into Austria.

The bus stop in Nauders is, fortunately, directly outside the tourist office, which afforded me the opportunity to get some information in the few minutes I had to make a decision. I learned that, if I continued on to Landeck, I would have only about an hour there before the bus returned to Nauders and, in turn, to Scuol. So, I was in a quandary. I didn't really fancy spending the better part of the day on a bus but, equally, Nauders did not appear to be a town which would hold my attention for the four and half hours which would pass before the bus returned to take me back to Scuol. In fact

I prevaricated—getting on and off the bus—before resolving to spend the time in Nauders. Even after the bus pulled off, I still was unsure that I had made the right decision. What could this small farming village have to offer?

While my initial impression was "not much," curiosity took charge—as it always does in a new place—and I set out to explore. It wasn't long before I came to the conclusion that this tiny village on the Reschen Pass *(Reschenpass)* at 1,380 meters (4,528 feet) had more than its share of virtues.

Wandering around the upper part of the village verified that this was, indeed, an active farming community. Prominently displayed upon many of the barns were medallions, proudly announcing awards received for prized cattle—an indication of present accomplishments. Scattered about the barnyards were a variety of antique wooden farming utensils—evidence of a long agricultural history. And, I couldn't help thinking—just a little covetously—that, stripped and refinished, these would be wonderful conversation pieces in my den! I also came upon a couple of stores and found that prices of goods in Austria are far lower than for comparable items in Switzerland.

What was most surprising, though, was the predominance of hotels; and rather nice ones at that. These had many of the amenities—such as pools, saunas, health clubs and fine restaurants—expected in far larger resorts. In fact, one of the hotels, particularly, caught my attention; and I made a mental note that, whenever I returned to Nauders, it was the place I wanted to stay.

And so I came to realize that Nauders really is a resort village—but with a difference. I could, honestly, have never imagined a place that could successfully combine a working farm village lifestyle with the infrastructure necessary to attract an international clientele. That, though, is exactly what I found in Nauders and, in concert with the breathtaking scenery of the surrounding mountains, these endow a lovely place with its own very unique and personal charms.

For those on a daytrip from Switzerland, who have become accustomed to that country's formal, albeit cordial, ambiance, this part of Austria will prove an interesting contrast. The Austrians have a more easygoing—even laid back—attitude, though I would hasten to say that they are no less professional for that. Also, the mix of tourists who frequent here is somewhat less multinational. In Switzerland, you are likely to find tourists from all corners of the globe; in Nauders, a majority of visitors are German—which makes for a more homogeneous character.

Suffice it to say that, after four and a half hours in Nauders—which passed very quickly, I boarded the bus to Scuol thoroughly beguiled and resolute that, one day, I would return to enjoy this delightful village at my leisure. Obligingly, that opportunity presented itself with the commission to write "Daytrips Switzerland." After my recent two-day visit to Nauders, I can say with assurance that you will thoroughly enjoy a sojourn to this most fascinating of villages.

GETTING THERE:

By car, follow route 27 to the Austrian border. There, turn off the main road and go over the pass to Nauders.

By Postal Bus, you will follow the same route as you would when traveling by car.

PRACTICALITIES:

The **Dialing Code** for Nauders is (011 43) 54 73. The local **Tourist Office** *(Tourismusverband Nauders)*, ☎ 205, Fax 627 or www.tis.co.at/Tirol/nauders and www.nettours.co.at.nauders, A-6543 Nauders am Rescenpass is on the main street in the village. It opens Monday to Friday from 9 a.m. to midday and 1–6 p.m., Saturday from 9 a.m. to midday and 4–6 p.m., and Sunday from 10 a.m. to midday and 4–6 p.m.

ACCOMMODATION:

The **Hotel Almhof Restaurant der Famillie Kröll ******, ☎ 313, 314 or 222 and Fax 644, A-6543 Nauders/Reschenpass, has all the facilities and comforts you expect in a four-star hotel. Well equipped rooms, pleasant public areas, a fine restaurant, an indoor pool and a health club ensure a comfortable stay. The owner, Hans Kröll, ensures a fun stay. This absolutely delightful man, and his family, take great personal pleasure in seeing that all of your needs are taken care of and that you are treated as one of the family. And, as such, you will want not want to neglect a very special member of their family—their pet marmot—who, incidentally, loves a snack of carrots from the salad bar. $$

The **Hotel Tia Monte ******, ☎ 54 73 or fax 82 40-6, A-6543 Nauders, is a fine alternative if the Hotel Almhof has no vacancies. Behind a distinctive blue and white, modern façade, 50 rooms with contemporary decor each feature bath, balcony, telephone, radio, satellite TV and safe. An indoor pool—with sauna, solarium and fitness room, a restaurant, a café, a bank and a boutique complete the package. $$

FOOD AND DRINK:

Without doubt, the best option is to take demi-pension at the Hotel Almhof.

SUGGESTED TOUR:

As you may have suspected, Nauders' small size makes a structured tour superfluous. Those contemplating this trip should be aware that, besides exploring the village—which is an absolute delight, the main tourist activity in Nauders is hiking. Although the tourist office is fairly light on documentation in English, they do offer a two-page guide to "Walks and Hikes Around About Nauders." This will tell you that there are no less than 38 marked— and very well marked they are—hiking trails around the village. It also advises, and this should be heeded, that the trails are classified as either Blue— very easy, suitable for children and older people; Red—moderate; or Black—quite difficult. As, unfortunately, the guide does not include a map, you may consider purchasing the *Wanderkarte Nauders*—also available from the tourist office, so you can see where you are going.

Still, you are left with a decision—which hike to take. Unsure ourselves, my colleague and I turned to the irrepressible Herr Kröll for advice. Not only did he suggest a trail that would give us an unusual perspective of this area bounded by two other countries, but offered, kindly, to give us a ride as far as was possible in his car. On the way up we asked, a bit sheepishly, how difficult the hike was. He assured us, with a grin rather more wry than usual, that it was a simple walk. Simple, maybe, for him. After all, these mountain folk have a sturdy constitution, and legs like mountain goats! For us, though, ***Trail Number 6** up to the Grosser Mutzkopf via the Grüner See, would not be classified as a leisurely stroll. To be fair, though, apart from a few steep stretches, the trek took us mostly through pasture land and could not, either, be classified as mountaineering. And, the views—across a panorama that takes in three countries—are stupendous! You will see, immediately to the south, the Reschenpass, beyond which lies the Reschensee reservoir and the Italian South Tirol (which we will explore at a later time). Farther around, and towards the west, you will have a marvelous view back down the Lower Engadine Valley towards Scuol, in Switzerland.

Of curious interest, on the lower slopes and usually near a wide track, you will certainly have noticed (but probably paid no attention to) huge piles of firewood stacked at random intervals. These have their root in Nauders tradition. One hundred and thirty-two local families have the rights to the wood, but not to the land, on the slopes around Nauders. And, as if that is not complicated enough in itself, those rights are not owned by individuals. Rather, they are tied to a particular property and the fireplaces—up to two— located upon that property. Each designated fireplace owns an entitlement to 8 cubic meters (283 cubic feet) of wood. The piles you see represent that wood. Woodsmen are responsible for cutting the wood, piling it and replenishing the forest. The recipient of the wood must transport it to their residence. When a person moves from their house, the rights do not follow them, but, if a member of an owner's family takes over the house that person inherits the rights to the wood as well.

Your curiosity was, most likely, aroused when looking out over the Reschenpass, and a short excursion into Italy should, definitely, be on everyone's itinerary. You may be surprised, however, to find that that part of Italy, the South Tyrol (*Süd Tirol*), is very Austrian in character. That is because in

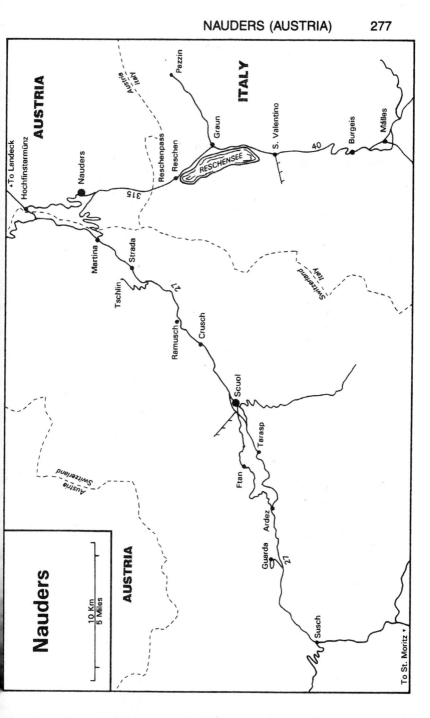

fact it was once a part of Austria, but was handed over to Italy at the end of the First World War.

You will find that the primary attraction in South Tyrol is quite unusual indeed. In the course of the development of an area reservoir, a small village was evacuated. Yet, rising forlornly from the calm waters that have claimed the town is the top portion of the village church spire, a single reminder of the inhabitants and faith of that community. This makes for an eerie scene and one that is consistently photographed—especially on a clear day when, with the snow capped peaks in the background, it makes for a surreal picture indeed. Eerier still, if you are visiting in winter, you can likely visit on foot—by walking on ice, not on water of course.

You will have one obstacle to overcome. Obtaining English-language tourist information here is difficult, to say the least. While there is a very small **tourist office** at **Graun**, halfway along the Reschensee, *(Tourismusverein Vinschgauer Oberland in German or Associazione Turistica Alta Val Venosta in Italian)*, ☎ 0473 634603 or Fax 0473 633140, I.39100 Graun-Curon Venosta (BZ), they do not offer much in English.

It is always tempting, when in a new place and, particularly, in a new country, to push on. You will be curious what treasures the next town holds. That temptation is even greater here, as an enormous wall of mountains beckons from the distance. Realistically, though, distance combined with geographical constraints limit your viable options to venturing only as far as Burgeis. There, the valley abruptly comes to an end, the road winds its way down to a much greater valley, and you suddenly realize those mountain peaks are much farther away than they first appeared. **Burgeis**, or Burgúsio as it is also known, is intriguing, however. It is dominated by a huge Medieval monastery that is certainly worth a visit.

The Upper Engadine: Tour #1

The Upper Engadine is synonymous with St. Moritz, which has gained for itself a worldwide reputation as a glitzy, glamorous destination for the jet set. That city and the three lakes radiating from it are located at an unusually high altitude of over 1,800 meters (nearly 6,000 feet). Consequently, the area is blessed with a climate that bathes it in sunshine for an average of 322 days annually—making it the sunniest spot in Switzerland and one that has been dubbed with the double meaning sobriquet of "Champagne Climate." It also advertises itself as "St. Moritz—Top of the World." In fact, and very unusually if not uniquely so, St. Moritz, in 1986, protected itself as a brandname in no less than twenty-five different countries!

For many, many centuries, the Upper Engadine has been celebrated for its healing mineral springs. So revered were their powers that, in 1519, Pope Leo X promised full absolution to every Christian visiting the spa of St. Moritz. Even so, it grew very little over the centuries, and had a population of merely 200 as late as 1830. That began to change quickly, however, thirty odd years later in 1864, when the first winter visitors arrived. The people of St. Moritz have not looked back since. Winter sports took such a precedence and developed so rapidly that St. Moritz was chosen to host the Winter Olympic Games in both 1928 and 1948.

It is in winter that St. Moritz is seen at its glamorous best. Attracting an affluent, chic and elegant clientele from around the world, it accommodates them stylishly in no less than four five-star hotels and ten four-star hotels. Such panache, and all in a town with a population of only 5,600!

Skiing, of course, is de rigeur, but St. Moritz has developed an eclectic array of other winter activities as well. In some you may participate, with others—such as the Cresta and Bob runs, ski jumping and the Engadine Ski Marathon—you will have to content yourself with being a spectator. Look, also, for curious activities on the frozen lake where, at one time or another, you will find show jumping, polo and real horse races—even over hurdles, the latter being held on three Sundays in February. Golfers will not be disappointed either, Europe's oldest and biggest tournament on snow is played here each January. And, so you won't lose your balls, they are painted red!

In fact, the whole of the Upper Engadine, including the places detailed below, is famous for its comprehensive winter sports facilities. These are so numerous that it is not practical to describe them in full detail in this guide. Complete information is available by contacting the respective tourist offices.

As winter in Switzerland is not really conducive to daytrips, it is assumed that most readers of this guide will visit the country in the warmer months— a time when St. Moritz does not have quite the same sparkle. That's not to say that its not attractive. It is—especially the higher *Dorf* section, where you will find numerous upmarket stores. And, of course, the surrounding mountains and lakes make for a beautiful setting no matter the time of year.

GETTING THERE:

Trains arrive at St. Moritz, often incurring a change at Chur, from all other parts of Switzerland. Most other destinations in the Upper Engadine are reached by postal bus.

By car, the Upper Engadine, in the far southeastern corner of Switzerland, is not that easily reached from other parts of the country. Indeed, from Ticino it is easier to travel through Italy, and arrive in the Upper Engadine via the Maloja Pass.

PRACTICALITIES:

The **Dialing Code** for the Upper Engadine is 81. The **Pontresina Tourist Office** *(Kur und Verkehrsverein),* ☎ 842 64 88 or Fax 842 79 96 is open Monday to Friday from 8:30 a.m. to midday and 2–6 p.m., Saturday from 8:30 a.m. to midday and 4–6 p.m. and Sunday from 4–6 p.m. The **Sils-Maria Tourist Office** *(Büro Verkehrsverein),* ☎ 838 50 50, Fax 838 50 59 or E-mail sils@compunet.ch, is open year round Monday to Friday from 8:30 a.m. to midday and 2–6 p.m.; between July and September and December to April, Saturday from 9 a.m. to midday and 4–6 p.m., and between December and April on Sunday from 5–6 p.m. The **St. Moritz Tourist Office** *(Verkehrsverein),* ☎ 837 33 33, Fax 837 33 77, E-mail kvv@st moritz.ch and www.stmoritz.ch, is open during the high season Monday to Saturday from 9 a.m. to 6 p.m., and at other times of the year Monday to Friday from 9 a.m. to midday and 2–6 p.m. and Saturday from 9 a.m. to midday.

Bucherer St. Moritz is located at Haus Monopol, CH-7500 St. Moritz, ☎ 833 31 03 or Fax 833 83 60. A good place to buy **Swiss Army Knives** is the souvenir shop within the Hotel Schweizerhof.

When you see unusual words on signs and in publications in and around the Upper Engadine, you will be reminded that much of the population speaks *Romansch*, Switzerland's fourth—and very much a minority— language.

Places of interest in The Upper Engadine are quite geographically diffuse and, without your own **transport** you will have to pay particular attention when coordinating your trips with the postal bus schedules.

ACCOMMODATION:
In Bever:
The **Hotel Chesa Salis**, ☎ 852 48 38 or Fax 852 47 06, CH-7502 Bever, located just a short distance from St. Moritz, was built in 1590 as the feudal residence of the von Salis family, nobles of the Grison. A 1992 renovation successfully preserved the inceptive style while incorporating every modern facility. The original features of each of the twenty rooms have been beautifully preserved by expert craftsmen. All have been appointed with classical furnishings, a modern private bath/shower, and a TV. The on-site restaurant serves a surprisingly varied menu. $$

In Pontresina:
The **Hôtel Walther ******, ☎ 842 64 71, Fax 842 79 22, E-mail walther@relauschateaux.fr and WWW.integra.fr/relaischateaux/walther, Hauptstrasse, CH-7504 Pontresina, managed by the owner's family, is located in a magnificent, turreted white building in the center of the village. The public areas have a marvelous Belle Époque ambiance and its 64 rooms and 9 suites are spacious, beautifully decorated and well appointed. The restaurant's cuisine varies according to the season, and the wine cellar offers a collection of fine vintages from Switzerland, France and Italy. It is closed from mid-April to mid-June and from mid-October to mid-December. $$$

In Samedan:
The **Berghotel Panorama Restaurant Muottas Muragl**, ☎ 842 82 32 or Fax 842 82 90, CH-7503 Samedan, which stands, absolutely isolated, at an elevation of 2,456 meters (8,058 feet), is accessed only via the Muottas Muragl Bahn (MMB)—a red funicular. Both the hotel and the restaurant present a traditional mountain ambiance, and offer absolutely spectacular views of St. Moritz alongside the lake at the bottom of the valley, of the towering mountains which stand sentry over other lakes snaking towards the Maloja Pass, and of the immense glaciers of the Tschierva and Morteratsch glistening to the left. $

In Sils-Maria:
The **Hotel Waldhaus ******, ☎ 826 66 66 or Fax 826 59 92, CH-7514 Sils-Maria, which sits dominantly upon the summit of a hill wedged between the lake and the mountains looks more like a castle than a hotel. Opened in 1908 by the great-grandfather of the present owners, Maria and Felix Dietrich, it has played host to such diverse characters as Marc Chagall, Albert Einstein, Richard Strauss, Vivien Leigh, Michael Redgrave, David Bowie, Rod Stewart and numerous prominent politicians. Recently the seven member "Federal Council," the highest level of Swiss government, chose to stay at the Waldhaus. They came to enjoy, as you will too, the reticence and dis-

cretion exemplified by this establishment and a masterful combination of typical mountain ambiance and luxury. The Arvenstube restaurant serves delectable local and regional cuisine and, as an bonus, you will be entertained, prior to and following dinner, by a resident trio. Occasionally, a New Orleans Jazz band performs as well. And, as is expected in a hotel of this genre in Switzerland, there is a health club and indoor pool. $$$

In St. Moritz:

The **Carlton Hotel** *****, ☎ 832 11 41 or Fax 833 27 38, CH-7500 St. Moritz, is situated upon a hill overlooking the town—a convenient five minutes away—the lake and the Engadine mountains. Behind its massive façade you will find a charming combination of tradition and luxury, 105 beautifully decorated rooms, a fine restaurant and an indoor pool. $$$

The **Hotel Steffani** ****, ☎ 832 21 01 or Fax 833 40 97, Sonnenplatz 1, CH-7500 St. Moritz, built in 1869, is in the absolute center of St. Moritz. Its 64 rooms—including 5 suites—are comfortably furnished and well equipped. Among the communal amenities are a selection of restaurants—including a delightful snack bar, an indoor pool, a sauna, a solarium, a hot whirlpool, a fitness room and massage services. If you are visiting in season, be sure to ask about their special ski package weekends which offer very preferential rates. $$$

FOOD AND DRINK:

Demi-pension is the best option here, as all the hotels have very good restaurants. Notwithstanding that, there is one restaurant in the area that really is exceptional. Be forewarned that it not inexpensive; but, if you fancy treating yourself to a real dining experience and not just a meal, try the:

Restaurant Jöhri's Talvo (Via Gunels 15), located in a delightful traditional Grison residence dating from 1658, is the proud recipient of two Michelin stars. Roland and Brigitte Jöhri have created here an ambiance that complements the delectable marriage of the French gastronomic cuisine and local regional traditions that they serve. Each dish—and there may be many—is creatively prepared and served, of course, with an appropriate glass of wine. These are chosen from a well-stocked cellar specializing in fine vintages from Switzerland, France, Italy and Spain. This, however, is not the place to go if you are in a hurry; this is an experience you will want to savor. ☎ 833 44 55. $$$

SUGGESTED TOUR:

From a variety of places in this region, and throughout all of Switzerland, a favorite excursion is taking a cable car to the summit of a mountain where the eternally snow-covered peaks make for fascinating and spectacular high Alpine views. As beautiful as these are, though, they are, by definition, somewhat monochromatic. There is a place in the Upper Engadine, however, where the views are both panoramic and kaleidoscopic. Two other factors recommend this trip as well: the method of transport is unique and it is starting point for a really lovely, and not too strenuous, mountain hike.

First, you must get there, so let's investigate the transport. Between Samedan and Pontresina you will find the **Muottas Muragl Bahn** (MMB) (1), ☎ 842 83 08 or Fax 842 65 71, a rather curious little funicular that raises you up to the Berghotel Muottas Muragl, a hotel and restaurant situated at an elevation of 2,456 meters (8,058 feet). From here, you will enjoy what are among the finest views I have seen in Switzerland. The subtly colorful scene of St. Moritz and the lakes which meander away from it are directly below you. The snow-white vistas of the higher mountains tower in the distance casting a long shadow over icy glaciers which lie in the valley leading to the Bernina Pass to the left. You will agree that it is worthwhile making the journey for this panorama alone. And, if that is the sum total of your plans, lunch at the restaurant is a pleasant diversion. Alternatively, time your visit to coincide with the evening meal, and marvel as the setting sun paints into the palette its glorious dusky hues.

From this base you can also avail yourself of a little mild exercise—a really interesting hike around, and not up, the mountain to **Alp Languard** (2). From start to destination, this will take about two and a half hours and, all along the way, there are enlightening perspectives of the wall of high peaks, the loftiest of which is Bernina—at 4,049 meters (13,284 feet)—across the valley. Among these mountains, too, are massive glaciers with the largest, **Vadret da Morteratsch**, nearly reaching the valley floor. It is, in fact, possible to walk to its lower sections—but more on that later. At **Alp Languard** you will find a small café/bar, a perfect place to rest awhile before making the descent, by chair lift or foot, to Pontresina.

As mentioned above, public transport is certainly available around the Upper Engadine—mostly by postal bus—but, if you are traveling by car, you will be able to leave it in the car park by the funicular. This is no problem. Indeed, it is quite a pleasant walk back there from Pontresina.

It is time, now, to explore the high peaks and there are two quite different ways of doing so. Just a short distance down the valley from Pontresina you will find the **Diavolezza-Bahn** (3). This cable car, with a capacity of 125, will whisk you to the top of Diavolezza, at 2,978 meters (9,770 feet), where there are a couple of restaurants, a souvenir shop and a sun terrace. From here, in the summer months, you can arrange for guided tours, or, alternatively, set out on your own to inspect these awesome glacial formations and the peaks that frame them.

While these incredible sights should whet everyone's appetite for more of the same, there are, unfortunately, no other cable cars on these mountains to take you higher. There is one option, however—take to the air. Call **Heliswiss**, ☎ 852 35 35 or Fax 852 32 72, Flugplatz Samedan, and ask for Martin who will be happy to arrange a ***helicopter ride**. Though there is a

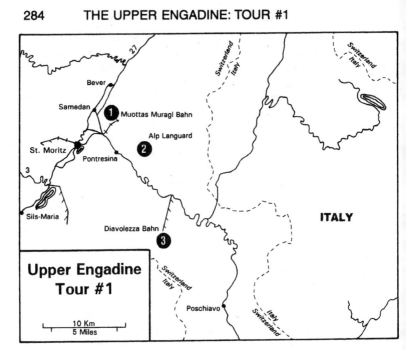

four-person minimum to make a flight, if your number is smaller, Martin will do his best to put together a party. It is not inexpensive either, CHF 100 per person (CHF 150 on a slightly larger 'copter) will buy you a twenty-minute ride. I can testify that this will be the thrill of a lifetime. I can also testify that you will need a strong stomach. Now, picture this: You have just buckled into your seat. You are given earphones and a headset to allow you to communicate over the noise of the chopper. You feel the dual rush of wind and excitement as the craft ascends from Samedan airport and moves slowly in the direction of St. Moritz. After establishing a constant height, the pilot turns the craft down the valley, passing Pontresina, en route to the Morteratsch Glacier. As you turn away from the valley towards the glacier the scene before you will verify what you observed from the opposite mountain when hiking—it really does flow to a place where it can be reached on foot. Indeed, as you are passing over the lower levels, you will likely see people clambering across it. Your pilot now flies you around this side valley, slowly gaining altitude as you go from right to left. You are busily snapping pictures, if you are smart, when you realize that the present trajectory will take you right over the cable car station at Diavolezza. You remind yourself that this is not nearly so hair-raising as it seems. The helicopter is never that far away from where it could land, and you don't really have a perception of being that high above the ground. Just as you have calmed your slightly rattled nerves, you pass over Diavolezza and, all of a sudden, you realize that there is absolutely nothing between you and the valley floor—several thousand feet below (where you imagine your stomach must have also fled to for the moment)! The unnatural angle the helicopter takes as it banks to head back down the valley, however, makes you, once again, acutely aware of your stomach; and you are, most likely, not displeased when your feet touch terra firma. If you are into roller coaster rides, you will feel right at home. But, even for those without a head for heights, like me, it is certainly worth overcoming your fears. Because, although you may be pleased to return to land, you will be absolutely thrilled—and will never forget—being aloft.

The Upper Engadine: Tour #2

Continue your adventures in the Upper Engadine with these tours.

GETTING THERE:

PRACTICALITIES:

ACCOMODATION:

FOOD AND DRINK:
See pages 280–282 for the above.

SUGGESTED TOUR:
As to other attractions in this region, two other cable cars, both within easy reach of Sils-Maria, are worth considering. The higher one, **Luftseilbahn Corvatsch**, ☎ 828 82 42, will take you up to the mountain station at 3,303 meters (10,837 feet) where you may expect to find a lovely panorama of the three lakes below. Narrow, long and enveloped by mountains, these stretch from their origin at St. Moritz to a point just before the dramatic drop of the Maloja Pass down towards Italy. Upon these peaceful waters, regardless of the weather, you will see fishermen, both from the shores and in boats, angling for their supper.

The other option, though, is my favorite. And, it is a very convenient choice for those staying at Sils-Maria—who are just a short walk away from the base station of the **Luftseilbahn Furtschellas**, ☎ 826 54 46. While less dramatic in height—the ascent on this cable car is from 1,797 meters (5,896 feet) to 2,312 meters (7,585 feet), it compensates by being the origination point for a fascinating four-and-a-half-hour hike. The first leg, beginning from **Furtschellas**, takes you up to the summit of **Piz Grialetsch** at 2,694 meters (8,839 feet) then follows on and down a little to the **Lake Sgrischus** *(Lej Sgrischus)* 76 meters (249 feet) lower. The name translates "Grayish Lake" and, although frozen a majority of the year, it is full of trout. Up again now to the **Piz Chüern** ("The Horn"), which is about the same altitude as the Gri-

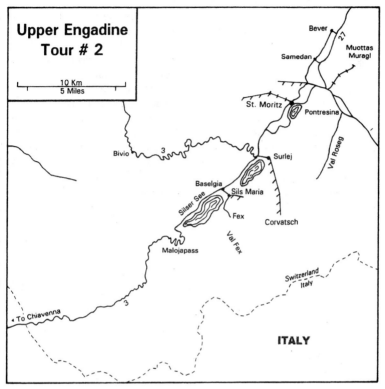

aletsch. From this vantage point you will have a better perspective of the mountains to the south and overviews of the unusual **Fex Valley** *(Val Fex)*— your next destination—which runs laterally to the lakes. This narrow and relatively shallow valley was settled by small farmers from the Bregaglia Valley who practiced then, as they do today, a semi-nomadic form of animal husbandry which entails moving the cattle from one place to another four or five times over the course of a year. It is pretty, too; terminating at a frosty glacier faced mountain. Try, if you can, to spend a few moments in the tiny hamlet of Fex-Cresta. There, in the tiny church, you will find on the chancel arch and apse a marvelous fresco dating from 1511. There is a quaint story that goes with it as well—whitewashed over during the Reformation era, it was only recently rediscovered. The last leg of the hike, back down to Sils-Maria, takes about an hour and, though it is fairly steep, it is not uncomfortably so. Do not be surprised, however, if you have some company in the form of wild deer feeding by the track.

At one time or another everyone, during their stay in the Upper Engadine, will pass through **St. Moritz**. Far and away the largest town in the region, its glamorous international reputation has been described above. It is a bit ironic that during the summer months—its sleepy time—it actually receives a larger number of visitors. It is an excellent place for souvenir shopping but, besides a museum or two, which are only of peripheral interest, the place people will most likely want to visit is the **Health Spa Center,** ☎ 833 30 62 or Fax 833 92 28. No such spa in Switzerland is situated at a higher altitude, and the waters have the strongest iron sources with carbonic acid in Europe. Their value to health has been known for centuries, and were extolled by Theophrastus Paracelsus as far back as 1535. Some may, also, treat themselves to a treatment or two. Among the more unusual of these is the "Peat-baths and pack," a regimen unique to this spa, as the peat used has been formed over a period of a thousand years from alpine plants in the waterlogged bogs and is actually cut in St. Moritz!

Chiavenna and Menaggio (Italy)

Here's a delightful scenic drive, by private car or postal bus, down to Lake Como in nearby Italy.

GETTING THERE:

By car is by far the best option, as it allows you the flexibility to stop along the way when and where you so choose. From St. Moritz, follow Route 3 to Chiavenna, then take 36 south following the signs to Lugano, and turning west on 340D. Menaggio will be at the first main junction.

By Postal Bus, this leaves from the St. Moritz train station, and takes exactly the same route as by car. Obviously, though, it is much slower as it stops along the way.

PRACTICALITIES:

The **Dialing Code** for Menaggio is (011 39) 344. The **Dialing Code** for Promontogno is 81.

ACCOMMODATION:

The **Hotel Bregaglia**, ☎ 822 17 77 or Fax 822 17 89, CH-7606 Promontogno, is in a very dramatic location half way between the Maloja Pass and the Italian border. It has an imposing design as well—two wings radiating out from a central tower. The ducks and geese wandering around the expansive gardens give a clue to the hotel's style. In fact, at first glance, you might think it to be rather run down—but, it is just its mountain style. Don't expect any luxuries, either. You will find no TVs, radios or mini bars here. You will not even find an en-suite bathroom. What it does have is charm— plenty of it, very personal service and fine food. It is closed mid-October to mid-May. $

The **Hotel Bellavista ***, ☎ 32136 or Fax 31793, Via IV Novembre, 21, 22017 Menaggio, Provincia di Como, Italia, certainly lives up to its name. Situated, literally, over the lake, it affords gorgeous views of the distant mountains and the variety of craft gliding over the lake. Its 40 rooms each have a private bath and shower. An on-site restaurant and an open-air pool, also overlooking Lake Como, complete the package. $

FOOD AND DRINK:

The hotels listed above are a good bet, whether you are staying the night there or not.

SUGGESTED TOUR:

This is not, in the truest sense, a tour. Rather, it is an opportunity to experience an eclectic array of both scenery and social customs. The bus departs from the St. Moritz railway station just after 8 a.m. (in 1997), taking about three hours to make the journey that, it must be said, is much more pleasurable if you have your own transport. The first, and very distinct leg, which takes you to Maloja, follows alongside the three lakes that fill the valley. At the close of the final lake, **Silsersee**, you will come upon the absolutely immense Palace Hotel, which turned out not to be a hotel at all, though its present use I cannot vouch for.

Immediately after passing through Maloja, the road begins to drop precipitously, and a series of hair-raising, extremely tight, hairpin bends lead down into the **Bregaglia Valley**. The scenery changes dramatically too. The flat, placid lakes and their wide valley give way to a much wilder, narrower, steep-sided scenario. From here on out you will have a companion, as well—the raging river flowing at ever-increasing speed as it gains tributaries along the way. Soon enough, the valley flattens out, but not for long. After the castle at Stamper it begins to plummet again, as the valley becomes much tighter, leaving barely enough room for the river and the road to pass through the mountains. It may be of interest to some to stay a night or so by here, as the hikes are absolutely amazing. If so, the Hotel Bregaglia is a good bet.

The next point of interest is the border town Castasegna. Clinging precipitously to the mountain side, and with a dull, gray ambiance, it has the usual small tourist shops, bureau de change, bars, etc. Sixteen kilometers (10 miles) farther along, however, is a town that deserves a little more investigation. **Chiavenna** has much character, especially along the main shopping street which still, today, retains a medieval flavor. This is one of those times that having your own car is a great advantage. If you are traveling by postal bus it only allows you a short break here.

Continuing on, you will find that the next stage of the trip, until you reach Lake Como, is not particularly inspiring. But persevere, that will change as the road forks and you cross the bridge to the western side of Lake Como. You will need to exercise extra caution here as the road is very narrow, and particularly hazardous in inclement weather. It is, however, also a delightful stretch dotted by a series of quaint villages and small towns along the

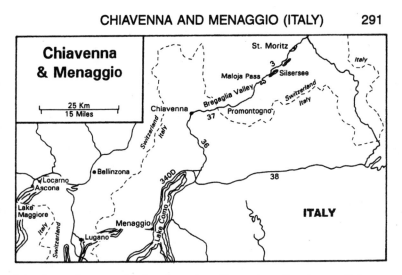

lake shore where pastel colors, imposing villas and small parks are what you can expect to see.

Among these charming villages, none is more winning than **Menaggio**. The lake front is pleasantness personified. Parks with wrought-iron railings, flowers, small marinas and the steady traffic of steamers and hydrofoils which ply their way across Lake Como work in concert with the lovely backdrop of hills and mountains to enchant.

Menaggio itself is large enough to take your interest as you wander around some—maybe purchasing a souvenir or two—and small enough to give you the flavor of Italian informality that contrasts so starkly with the more formal Swiss atmosphere. And who would turn down the chance to sample a delicious, and lengthy, Italian style lunch? As an alternative to the array of trattorias, you may want to give serious consideration to the Hotel Bellavista restaurant. It has the finest view in town.

If you have come by postal bus, it will now be time to catch the afternoon service back. In 1997 this left at 3:40 p.m. Unfortunately, even if you came in your own vehicle, there will not be enough time to take a lake steamer trip. Better, then, to start the journey back, which will give you time to stop off at any place that has caught your fancy.

Index

Special interest attractions are listed under their category headings.

Daytrips

• OTHER EUROPEAN TITLES •

DAYTRIPS SPAIN AND PORTUGAL

By Norman P.T. Renouf. Fifty one-day adventures by rail, bus or car—including many walking tours, as well as side trips to Gibraltar and Morocco. All of the major tourist sites are covered, plus several excursions to little-known, off-the-beaten-path destinations. 368 pages, 18 full-color photos, 28 b&w photos, 51 two-color maps. ISBN: 0-8038-9389-2.

DAYTRIPS IRELAND

By Patricia Tunison Preston. Covers the entire Emerald Isle with 50 one-day self-guided tours both within and from the major tourist areas. 400 pages plus 16 pages of color photos; 58 photos in all, and 55 maps. ISBN: 0-8038-9385-X.

DAYTRIPS LONDON

By Earl Steinbicker. Explores the metropolis on 10 one-day walking tours, then describes 40 daytrips to destinations throughout southern England—all by either rail or car. 5th edition, 336 pages, 57 maps, 94 photos. ISBN: 0-8038-9367-1.

DAYTRIPS FRANCE

By Earl Steinbicker. Describes 45 daytrips—including 5 walking tours of Paris, 23 excursions from the city, 5 in Provence, and 12 along the Riviera. 4th edition, 336 pages, 55 maps, 89 photos. ISBN: 0-8038-9366-3.

DAYTRIPS GERMANY

By Earl Steinbicker. 60 of Germany's most enticing destinations can be savored on daytrips from Munich, Frankfurt, Hamburg, and Berlin. Walking tours of the big cities are included. 5th edition, 352 pages, 67 maps. ISBN: 0-8038-9428-7.

DAYTRIPS HOLLAND, BELGIUM AND LUXEMBOURG

By Earl Steinbicker. Many unusual places are covered on these 40 daytrips, along with all the favorites plus the 3 major cities. 2nd edition, 288 pages, 45 maps, 69 photos. ISBN: 0-8038-9368-X

DAYTRIPS ITALY

By Earl Steinbicker. Features 40 one-day adventures in and around Rome, Florence, Milan, Venice, and Naples. 3rd edition, 304 pages, 45 maps, 69 photos. ISBN: 0-8038-9372-8.

DAYTRIPS ISRAEL

By Earl Steinbicker. 25 one-day adventures by bus or car to the Holy Land's most interesting sites. Includes Jerusalem walking tours. 2nd edition, 206 pages, 40 maps, 40 photos. ISBN: 0-8038-9374-4.

Daytrips

• AMERICAN TITLES •

DAYTRIPS HAWAII

By David Cheever. Thoroughly explores all of the major islands—by car, by bus, on foot, and by bicycle, boat, and air. Includes many off-beat discoveries you won't find elsewhere, plus all the big attractions in detail. 288 pages, 55 maps. ISBN: 0-8038-9401-5.

DAYTRIPS FLORIDA

By Blair Howard. Fifty one-day adventures from bases in Miami, Orlando, St. Petersburg, Jacksonville, and Pensacola. From little-known discoveries to bustling theme parks, from America's oldest city to isolated getaways—this guide covers it all. 320 pages, 47 maps, 28 photos. ISBN: 0-8038-9380-9.

DAYTRIPS NEW ENGLAND

By Earl Steinbicker. Discover the 50 most delightful excursions within a day's drive of Boston or Central New England, from Maine to Connecticut. Includes Boston walking tours. 336 pages, 60 maps, 48 photos. ISBN: 0-8038-9379-5.

DAYTRIPS WASHINGTON, DC

By Earl Steinbicker. Fifty one-day adventures in the Nation's Capital, and to nearby Virginia, Maryland, Delaware, and Pennsylvania. Both walking and driving tours are featured. 352 pages, 60 maps, 48 photos. ISBN: 0-8038-9376-6.

DAYTRIPS NEW YORK

Edited by Earl Steinbicker. 107 easy excursions by car throughout southern New York State, New Jersey, eastern Pennsylvania, Connecticut, and southern Massachusetts. 7th edition, 336 pages, 44 maps, 46 photos. ISBN: 0-8038-9371-X.

• IN PRODUCTION •

DAYTRIPS SAN FRANCISCO & NORTHERN CALIFORNIA

By David Cheever. Fifty enjoyable one-day adventures from the sea to the mountains; from north of the wine country to south of Monterey. Includes 16 self-guided discovery tours of San Francisco itself. 352 pages, 64 maps. ISBN: 0-8038-9441-4

DAYTRIPS PENNSYLVANIA DUTCH COUNTRY & PHILADELPHIA

By Earl Steinbicker. Thoroughly explores the City of Brotherly Love, then goes on to probe southeastern Pennsylvania, southern New Jersey, and Delaware before moving west to Lancaster, the "Dutch" country, and Gettysburg. 320 pages, 54 maps. ISBN: 0-8038-9394-9.

DAYTRIPS THE CAROLINAS AND GEORGIA

By Robert L. Williams. Fifty enjoyable one-day trips by car from convenient bases in North Carolina, South Carolina, and Georgia. There are walking tours of the major cities and historic towns, adventures along the intriguing coastline, forays into the mountains, and much more. 54 maps. ISBN: 0-8038-9434-1.

HASTINGS HOUSE
Book Publishers
9 Mott Avenue., Norwalk CT 06850
Phone (203) 838-4083, FAX (203) 838-4084
Internet: http://upub.com

About the Author:

Although now living in Richmond, Virginia, Norman Renouf was born in London and educated at Charlton Central School, Greenwich. From 1962 to 1989 he was employed by a variety of financial institutions both in the United States and the UK; the last eight of those years being spent in London's insurance industry. Following that he has worked professionally as a freelance travel writer and photographer on what, previously, had been a lifelong hobby.

In the years since, he has traveled frequently and widely in both the USA and Europe. His previous book in this series was "Daytrips Spain and Portugal," with others projected for future release. In addition, he has crisscrossed Europe updating the Berlitz Pocket Guides and, in collaboration with his wife Kathy, has begun a "Romantic Weekends" series of guides to attractive locations in America.